Tell No Lies, Claim No Easy Victories

Tell No Lies, Claim No Easy Victories

Amílcar Cabral

inkani

This edition published October 2022

ISBN 978-1-77637-880-7

© Inkani Books, 2022

Edited by Efemia Chela

Design by Ryan Honeyball

Text set in Source Serif 4 by
Frank Grießhammer for Adobe

Inkani Books
2nd Floor, South Point Corner,
87 De Korte Street
Braamfontein,
Johannesburg,
South Africa,
2001

Inkani Books is the publishing division
of The Tricontinental Pan Africa NPC

inkanibooks.co.za

CONTENTS

A Note on Attribution   1

Abbreviations   3

Foreword   5

Introduction   13

Map of Africa, 1962   18

Map of Guinea-Bissau and Cape Verde   19

Statement to the United Nations Special Committee
on Territories Under Portuguese Administration   21

Brief Analysis of the Social Structure in Guinea   41

Tell No Lies, Claim No Easy Victories ...   57

A Historic Lesson: Pidjiguiti   61

A Situation of Permanent Violence   63

Our Solidarities   65

The Weapon of Theory   69

Determined to Resist   89

Party Principles and Political Practice   103

The Development of the Struggle   189

Analysis of Different Types of Resistance   201

New Year's Message, January 1969   267

The Tactic of Division   271

Portugal is not an Imperialist Country   273

The Danger of Destruction from Within   277

On the African Revolution: Homage to Kwame Nkrumah   281

The Role of Culture in the Struggle for Independence   287

The Relevance of Marxism-Leninism   295

Culture, Colonisation, and National Liberation   297

Fruits of a Struggle   307

The Struggle Has Taken Root   325

New Year's Message, 1973   331

Map of Africa, 1973   343

A NOTE ON ATTRIBUTION

The texts in 'Tell No Lies, Claim No Easy Victories' were first published in English by Penguin, in 1969, in Basil Davidson's *The Liberation of Guiné: Aspects of an African Revolution,* apart from 'The Relevance of Marxism-Leninism' which was first published in 1972 in *Our People Are Our Mountains: Amílcar Cabral on the Guinean Revolution.*

The chapter 'Analysis of Different Types of Resistance' was translated by Jethro Soutar in 2022.

ABBREVIATIONS

CLSTP *Comité de Libertação de São Tomé e Príncipe* (Committee (later, Movement) for the Liberation of São Tomé and Príncipe)

CONCP *Conferéncia das Organizações Nacionalistas das Colónias Portuguesas* (Conference of the Nationalist Organisations of the Portuguese Colonies)

CUF *Companhia União Fabril*

ECM European Common Market

FRAIN *Frente Revolucionária Africana para a Independência Nacional das colonias portuguesas* (African Revolutionary Front for the National Independence of the Portuguese Colonies)

FRELIMO *Frente de Libertação de Moçambique* (Mozambique Liberation Front)

FUL *Front Uni de Libération* (United Liberation Front of Guinea and the Cape Verde Islands)

MING (Movement for National Independence in Guinea)

MLGCV *Mouvement de Liberation de la Guinée Portugaise et des Iles du Cap Vert* (Movement for the Liberation of Guinea and the Cape Verde Islands)

MPLA *Movimento Popular de Libertação de Angola* (Popular Movement for the Liberation of Angola)

NATO North Atlantic Treaty Organisation

OAU Organisation of African Unity

OSPAAAL *Organización de Solidaridad de los Pueblos de Asia, África y América Latina* (Organisation of Solidarity with the People of Asia, Africa and Latin America)

PAIGC or PAI *Partido Africano da Independencia da Guiné e Cabo Verde* (African Party for the Independence of Guiné and Cape Verde)

PDG *Parti Démocratique de Guinée* (Democratic Party of Guinea)

PIDE *Policia Internacional e de Defesa do Estado* (International Police for the Defence of the State)

Foreword

LENIN'S QUESTION

'With the means we have, we can do much more and better.'
Amílcar Cabral (1924–1973),
'Tell No Lies, Claim No Easy Victories', PAIGC Directive 1965.

There is a tendency to make of Lenin's most famous and enduring question a rhetorical device. Lenin's question, 'What is to be done?', is posed only to be left unanswered. Not taken up in the least, as if the question itself signals political and theoretical familiarity not only with Lenin but with Marxism, writ large.

In our moment, where a former taxi driver turned imperial czar threatens the international community, when a former anti-apartheid activist become head of state, Cyril Ramaphosa will not condemn the war crimes committed by Czar Vladimir Putin. In our moment, when Narendra Modi, the leader of one of the founding countries of the Non-Aligned Movement is transforming a historically secular democracy into a Hindu nationalist state, Lenin's question echoes with ever greater intensity. Indeed, what is to be done?

If we are to begin to answer Lenin's question, which is also a plea for history-making action, then those who hold political leadership must confront the situation in which they find themselves honestly. Leaders must be truthful with their people. To do what must be done we must, as Amílcar Cabral urges us, 'tell no lies'.[1] Present the situation as it is. Recognise what requires doing, urgently. Ask of the people that they do their share. Demand of the leadership that they behave always in a responsible and exemplary fashion. Identify with a careful eye the opportunists in the ranks of the oppressed, those who are fluent in the language of resistance but learn this language only to later, at a more convenient moment, turn the situation to their own advantage. Cabral warns us clearly against what he correctly denounces as the 'mentality of petty ambition.'

---

1   Coincidentally Cabral was born on 12 September, the same day on which Steve Biko would be killed 53 years later. Biko was assassinated by the apartheid regime that Cabral never missed an opportunity to condemn, and like many freedom fighters, Cabral himself would be assassinated in 1973.

Sadly, of course, as people in many postcolonial states can attest, the 'mentality of petty ambition' can in the blink of an eye become wholesale state capture, looting of the state's coffers at the expense of the poor. All this occurs in the name of 'the struggle', a struggle long forgotten by elites except when it can be used to manipulate the public, when 'the struggle' can provide a shield against legitimate criticisms of the party's failings. This is to say nothing of failed states, which Cabral did not live to see but anticipated. Cabral knew that the postcolonial state was doomed to fail its people if revolutionary movements turned into national governments that refused to understand their own shortcomings. He feared the failure of the postcolonial state through the abandonment of the revolution or, as he defined it, 'rationalised imperialism' – neo-colonialism, along with the extraction of a nation's wealth, given ideological cover by self-serving native elites.

In this way, perverse as it is to say, we find ourselves grateful that Cabral did not live to see the triumph of petty ambition across the continent. Petty ambition, as exemplified by the multi-million-dollar expropriation of state assets by Isabel dos Santos, daughter of former Angolan president José Eduardo dos Santos, was neither what Cabral nor poet and revolutionary Agostinho Neto intended for the people of Guiné, Cape Verde, and Angola, respectively. Cabral, whose vision of the world was decidedly global, was of course a determined pan-Africanist, always speaking with great feeling about movements on the continent fighting for liberation from colonial rule. Yet he was also deeply dedicated to the cause of Lusophone liberation, locating the PAIGC's work within the context of its battle against the 'criminal Portuguese colonialists'; recognising intimate links between the PAIGC in Guiné and Cape Verde and FRELIMO in Mozambique and the MPLA in Angola.

Cabral operated with the lessons of Moïse Tshombe, the State of Katanga's secession, as well as the brutal fate of Patrice Lumumba often at the forefront of his thinking. As a result, his words try to caution us about what can happen if party discipline shows any sign of slackening. Cabral did everything he could to prevent party members from self-enrichment and spoke repeatedly against it. He reminds us of this in what is surely his favourite phrase: 'Rice is cooked inside the pot and not outside.' All the hard work is crucial to hold the revolutionary movement and the revolutionaries who lead it accountable for all their actions, including their failings. In turn the people are made accountable for supporting the party. He describes this as the kind of work that begins with each and every individual in Guiné and Cape Verde. The work begins within; it is a ceaseless task. To invoke the spirit of Cabral's rice metaphor: the revolution begins right there at home, in the kitchen.

Cabral, in the several addresses that compose *Tell No Lies, Claim No Easy Victories*, is a strong advocate of self-sacrifice and self-discipline of the spartan variety. It is ok to drink, but never to excess, he advised his cadres. Behave with respect towards yourself, the people and your comrades, he urged

PAIGC members. Study, keep mind and body in equally good shape. To win the war against Portuguese colonialism, it is necessary to win every battle, to come out victorious in every skirmish. The first battle in that war is the battle within. Continual self-improvement is the only way. Political work is a permanent task.

LENIN'S QUESTION, ANSWERED

A strain of strict moralism runs through Cabral's speeches. The work of the democratic revolution is to make, if not quite a virtuous person, then certainly a considerate one. A human being who having overcome the oppression inherent to colonialism behaves with a political thoughtfulness in relation to those around them. A mode of behaviour must mark the relations between self and other because that is the surest barometer of the newly liberated society as one of equals. A society in which everyone, regardless of gender, ethnic affiliation, religion, regional origin (Guiné or Cape Verde, it matters not) has the same right of access to the nation's resources. There is to be no distinction in school admissions between boys and girls nor Christian or 'Moslem'. At the end of *Black Skins, White Masks*, Frantz Fanon calls for the coming into being of a 'new man'. Fanon conceptualises a different way of being human, of being in the world, in the relation between the colonial and the imperial worlds.

Fanon's is a concept. A call to the future. However, whatever reservations there are to be had about Cabral's moralistic streak, there can be no denying it is well-rooted in everyday praxis. Cabral's attention to detail, his insisting on codes of revolutionary behaviour, are in fact a manual for how to achieve not only a postcolonial subject, but the citizen of Guiné and Cape Verde who has emerged out of the struggle against Portuguese colonialism. Cabral is explicit. *This* is what you must do, PAIGC cadre. *That* is how you must adjust your thinking on women, PAIGC regional leader. Fanon may have given the anti-colonial world a concept. Cabral provides a specific code of behaviour. He tells PAIGC members exactly what is required to make the future citizen of Guiné and Cape Verde (a union dissolved in 1980, which Cabral worked so hard to prevent) a *different* human being from the man, woman or child denied their fundamental rights by the Portuguese.

The radical new subject of the independent states of Guiné and Cape Verde begins in revolutionary praxis. How the anti-colonial cadre conducts themselves in the struggle is the model for different modes: of being human, of being a citizen, of being an African subject, of being human in the world. Cabral's directions are the how-to for making Fanon's 'new man' in the here and the now. A new humanity must emerge out of the work it takes to successfully execute a revolution; the everyday work is the revolution.

Cabral reminds of us of this with every speech he gives to PAIGC members, every address he delivers overseas. We hear it clearly when he receives an honorary degree from Lincoln University, in Pennsylvania, African-American poet Langston Hughes' alma mater. It is audible when he speaks at the United Nations. Waging the anti-colonial struggle is not enough unless out of it emerges a human being previously unknown in history. Cabral sets the bar high, and in doing so he answers repeatedly Lenin's question. *This*, how we are in the world, it is *this* that must be changed. That, as history shows us, will take some doing. This is no abstraction. It is clearly stated, carefully defined. This is what Cabral demanded of his party members.

It is a call, this Cabralian mode of being in the world, that resounds with a bracing political intensity today. How can we not stipulate what we must do in our moment? We can only ignore Cabral's call of history if we remove ourselves from the ugly realities that confront us. Cabral, as this collection bears testament, always made himself, his Party and his people face squarely their reality, unpleasant or not. Anything else Cabral deemed a 'lie'. Whether or not one is partial to Cabral's moral absolutism, the great advantage of having a moral outlook on the world is that it demands a confrontation with the truth. Such a confrontation requires that we see things as they are rather than how we would want them to be. Would we rather turn our back on Cabral's observations than see what we need to do now? We need to work, to make a world fit for all to live in because our current world is not equal. It is devoid of justice, discriminatory, prejudicial and hostile to the majority of humanity.

CONSTRUCTIVE EMULATION

For Cabral developing a set of revolutionary practices is to work perpetually for the cause of universal good. 'Constructive emulation' was the term he coined to drive home the point of the exemplarity of labour. Political opera-tives, members of the military wing, students abroad enrolled in the PAIGC's Reform School, all had to embody the exemplarity of labour. Older cadres were not only responsible for instructing the party's youth in the ways of struggle but charged with moulding the youth to ensure the legacy of the struggle. Constructive emulation was Cabral's way of demanding that all party members model the kind of behaviour befitting that of a nation-under-construction, a nation-being-born, for the people of Guiné and Cape Verde. Out of exemplary labour, out of revolutionary conduct would emerge the 'flame of patriotism fanned by the fire of your weapons.'

We are more skeptical now, with good reason, about any call to patriotic arms. Our suspicion has a long history. Were we to make our individual lists of the national leaders who first gave us pause about the postcolonial nation, we would find ourselves presented with a great many options such as

Gamal Abdel Nasser, Kwame Nkrumah, Sekou Touré, Eric Williams, Edward Seaga, and Indira Gandhi.[2] We would not lack for options. Taking any path we choose, we would find ourselves by paths direct or circuitous, at our present moment, adding Narendra Modi, Jacob Zuma and Cyril Ramaphosa to our list. Always an incomplete list, one hastens to add. But a list to which we must regularly attend.

Excluding behaviour, another of Cabral's struggles was alimentary, the struggle to secure sufficient food for the people of his country. As much the revolutionary as the agronomist, Cabral called on his people to be careful tenders of the soil. To plant, to reap, to provide food for all. He urged the farmers to practice crop diversification to prevent the depletion of vital minerals in the soil that ensure a greater-yielding crop. Sufficient education was another battle for the PAIGC where concerns of the alimentary arose. Nourishment of the body and nourishment of the mind, from securing the necessary learning materials for teachers and students alike and building schools, to providing enough food and chalk, so learning could take place under optimal conditions. No under-qualified teachers either, the only schools allowed to operate were those that were fully equipped to serve their students.

In the era when he was writing, Guiné had an illiteracy rate of 99 per cent and Cape Verde, at 85 per cent, was only marginally better. Providing proper education was a vital matter for Cabral because he knew how important teachers, doctors, engineers and agriculturally astute farmers would be for the future of his people. Every school, he argued, must be able to ensure the safety of its students, teachers and the surrounding communities from possible colonial attacks. A school that could not protect itself put the lives of many people at risk. In addition, the PAIGC was duty-bound to provide adequate healthcare for every person in every region under PAIGC control, whether they were an injured militant or a sick child. The party took seriously

---

2   In two places in this collection, we see Cabral avoid criticising revolutionary leaders to the fullest extent. One incidence occurs in 'On the African Revolution: Homage to Kwame Nkrumah.' There it can be argued that he is all too quick to lay the blame for Nkrumah's sovereign impulses at the door of historical 'traitors'. I suspect that for Cabral, Nkrumah was too much a revered figure of the anti-colonial movement to bear scrutiny. Ghana, after all, provided the first military training ground for PAIGC operatives. Cabral's lack of historical clarity on Nkrumah is a moment of historical blindness, a failure to hold him to the same standards of revolutionary democracy that he expected of his PAIGC comrades, himself first of all.

Similarly, it is strategically easier to rationalise Cabral's critical lack in relation to his neighbour, Sekou Touré. After all, Touré, the leader of Guinea-Conakry committed a great deal of his national resources to supporting the PAIGC's struggle. Nevertheless, for all his accomplishments regarding equality for women, his dedication to national infrastructure (particularly in basic healthcare access; his commitment to building schools, and so on), Sekou Touré exercised a brutal power over his people.

the importance of training medical staff, both locally and abroad, to carry out these tasks.

Political opportunists and traitors to the PAIGC cause, Cabral had no time for. In order to minimise their impact, to reduce their ability to delay the struggle, Cabral preached vigilance. For the revolution to deliver on its promises, everyone needed to keep safe the project of liberation, to protect it from the enemy. It mattered not if that enemy were a Portuguese colonialist, a recalcitrant tribal chief, or a traitor masquerading as a loyal party member. Everyone was responsible for the success of the revolution. Those who worked against the interest of the majority, would be expelled from the party or dealt with appropriately. The revolution demanded this.

In his dedication to the alimentary, the provision of housing (for the troops and the population), education, security, food, healthcare, Cabral is notable among his revolutionary peers. In his commitment to the alimentary Cabral gives substance to his motto, 'thought and action'. In building well-equipped and adequately staffed schools, by training of qualified medical personnel, in securing the liberated zones, in demanding that farmers learn the science of the soil, Cabral lived out his words 'every practice gives birth to a theory.' As to the order of which comes first, theory or practice? It did not matter to Cabral because the alimentary always preoccupied him. Not simply answering Lenin's question but asking how what needed to be done could be done. From the on-the-ground realities he took his cue.

UNIVERSAL GOOD

The cause of universal good could only be served if, Cabral reminded everyone, women were treated as equals in the struggle. 'We want the emancipation and advancement of our women', he instructed the PAIGC, despite, as he acknowledged time and again, the resistance to gender equality in some quarters. Above all, commit to the struggle. Commit body and soul. Perhaps even take heart in Cabral's call to arms.

There is no single call more stirring than when Cabral offers his definition of 'struggle'. He calls it the 'permanent victory over difficulties.' Not the evasion of difficulty, but such a robust confrontation with it, that difficulty becomes confined to history. Difficulty then is not so much overcome as made redundant.

If we are to seek solutions to the many difficulties that confront our moment – political disorder, nationalist violence fueled by a nostalgia for empire, economic inequalities, intrepid migrations born out of economic inequalities, state capture by elites, corruption, nepotism, and most important of all, the looming threat of planetary destruction – then we are well-advised not to 'claim easy victories'.

The greatest difficulty that confronts us is how to struggle in order to make a world in which all can live. It is doubtful, of course, that we can immediately overcome the array of difficulties that make up our realities. We may not even be able to do so permanently. We are, however, called upon by Cabral's work to set our sights higher. It is not enough, he insisted, to struggle only for liberation. As he insisted to his PAIGC comrades, the struggle is also for the 'progress of our people.'

There is always work to be done. What matters most is not only that we commit ourselves to the work but *how* we undertake to do the work. How can we put our thought into action? How can we make of our thinking an alimentary action? How is our thought revised in light of our action? Most elementary of all might be the need to make our action, like Cabral's insistence on crop diversification, itself sustainable.

Cabral, through no fault of his own, bequeathed to us an incomplete project. What will we do with the legacy he has left us? What actions can we derive from his rooted-in-the-ground thoughts? What new, Cabral-inspired thoughts can we put into action? Cabral offered his work, in all likelihood unwittingly, as a provisional answer to Lenin. Now it is asked of us to begin the work of answering Cabral. Of answering and, in so doing, making ourselves accountable to Cabral.

Grant Farred,
Professor of Africana Studies
and English

Ithaca, United States of America,
July 2022

Introduction

We never encounter a book the same way each time we read it. Every time is different, each word magnified through different lenses. Circumstances, eras, places, and contexts dictate the way we engage with the written work. They dictate the nature of our engagement, which direction it will take this time around, which paths will be followed or left untaken. This is true of the writings of Amílcar Cabral. No matter how often one reads his words, new lines of thought and new directions will always be found. His words lead to strategies for imagining liberation from the past, and radical ways to live in our world today.

Born in Guinea-Bissau in the city of Bafatá in 1924, Amílcar Lopes Cabral was the descendant of Cape Verdean migrants who had settled in the area. Living under the authoritarian colonial rule of the Portuguese in both Cape Verde and Guinea-Bissau during his lifetime came to be crucial for his understanding of the world, especially as it related to the human condition. From 1945 to 1952 he studied and worked as an agronomist in Lisbon. His professional experiences in Portugal and the colonised territories of Angola, Cape Verde and Guinea-Bissau, led him to think about and understand the struggle threefold, through the land, agriculture, and peasants, later conceiving a role for the black working class that lived in the urban centres.

After World War Two (1939–1945) in Lisbon, the political centre of Portuguese colonialism, discontent grew amongst the more politically aware African students who had come from colonised territories to pursue university education. These students made the state-created *Casa dos Estudantes do Império* (House of the Students of the Empire) their base, using it to create the *Centro de Estudos Africanos* (Centre of African Studies).[3] They were intellectually curious, and their political ambitions were nurtured and found expression in clandestine study groups hosted in the private home of the Espírito Santo family from São Tomé and Príncipe. The Santo home became a hub where critical political thought around national independence and liberation began to emerge amongst African students including Amílcar Cabral. By taking seriously these political

---

3   The House of Students of the Empire was a meeting place for African students from Angola, Mozambique, Cape Verde and Guinea-Bissau, who were in Lisbon pursuing higher education. It was funded by the Portuguese government and hosted a cafeteria, sports games and cultural events. Although it was not intended to be a political space, the initiative of the students led to it becoming the breeding ground for independence movements that would later emerge in the students' home countries.

and intellectual rebellions in the metropole, young Africans discovered their generation's mission: to fight for Africa's independence from colonialism. From these beginnings Cabral would go on to lead struggles in Guinea-Bissau and Cape Verde. He became one of the most influential anti-colonial and revolutionary theorists amongst the African liberation leaders of the era, such as Eduardo Mondlane and Samora Machel in Mozambique; Agostinho Neto in Angola, Patrice Lumumba in Congo.

Cabral's poetry from as early as 1943 anticipated the struggle for independence and he wrote of the links between colonial politics and the severe droughts and famines in the Cape Verdean archipelago. His revolutionary fever culminated in his 1946 poem '*Grito de Revolta*' ('Cry of Revolt'):

> Who doesn't remember that cry that sounded like thunder?!
> My cry of revolt echoed
> through the farthest valleys of the Earth,
> crossed the seas and the oceans,
> crossed the Himalayas of the entire the world,
> respected no borders and made my chest vibrate ...
> My cry of revolt made the chest of all men vibrate,
> made fellowship between all men
> and transformed Life ...

The poem explicitly announced the need for liberation of humankind, as well the solidarity and connection between people living in different worlds of oppression. In 1956 this cry turned into action with the creation of the PAIGC (*Partido Africano da Independencia da Guiné e Cabo Verde*) – the African Party for Independence of Guinea-Bissau and Cape Verde.

Founded in Guinea-Bissau but drawing on an extensive diasporic network, the PAIGC emerged out of a long tradition of resistance by Africans in Guinea-Bissau, Cape Verde, and Portugal. From 1903 to 1936, the people of Guinea-Bissau revolted against the *imposto de palhota* (hut tax), a property tax that was imposed on people who owned a house. A similar tactic was used across colonial Africa to force Africans into wage labour for settlers. In Cape Verde, a significant peasant uprising in 1910 known as the Revolt of Ribeirão Manuel saw the population protest deplorable living conditions in the countryside.

The objective of the PAIGC's struggle was very clear: independence and liberation of two colonised territories, Guinea-Bissau and Cape Verde, which were politically and culturally connected by the historical developments of colonialism. To achieve this, the PAIGC sought to overthrow colonial institutions of oppression and exploitation and create a project of national reconstruction to pursue the economic, political, and social liberation of the people. This project would fight against the toxic residues left by colonial structures in the bodies and minds of the people.

The liberation struggle is a social and political phenomenon that I define as an individual and collective process and response where people become conscious. They gain consciousness about their subjugation through racialisation, dehumanisation, oppression and exploitation under the colonial government inside their country and by external forces. They organise themselves to reclaim their political and economic sovereignty and to dismantle and destroy the institutions that overpower their sense of self. They seize the capacity to control the fruits of their labour. The liberation struggle employs – at different times – a range of means to end colonial domination, from armed struggle to labour strikes to educational programmes, and cultural resistance. The liberation struggle against colonialism, if it is to be a total liberation struggle, is not only for the political conquest of territory (so-called 'flag independence'). It is within this framework of struggle that Cabral's well-known statement, 'Tell No Lies, Claim No Easy Victories', as well as this selection of his speeches between 1963 and 1973, are situated.

I first encountered Cabral's intellectual work in my early twenties, while finishing my college degree. Despite his impact on the world I moved in, Cabral's work was (and still is) barely taught in high school or university. Before that, all knowledge of him had come from family conversations, and a few newspaper articles I had seen growing up in Portugal. His work was often difficult to find in print, so I carefully photocopied the two old and fragile volumes of *Unity and Struggle* published by Seara Nova in 1978, that I borrowed from my college library. It is to these precious photocopies, with passages underlined in different colours over the years, and notes made in every margin, that I return as required reading from time to time. Upon every new reading, new knowledge was unveiled which encouraged me to make a deeper study of the education system developed by the PAIGC during the struggle for my doctoral dissertation.

Militant education was a committed, engaged, and conscious anti-colonial educational process focused on an expansive concept of liberation 'rooted and supported by the realities and necessities of the community' and principles of decolonisation. The liberation struggle was first conceived of by the PAIGC as an educational practice which then led to the development of militant education. Through readings, discussions and mobilisation militants were embedded within a larger international struggle. In PAIGC reports from 1978, militant education is described as a 'pedagogical role [that] combined three aspects: political learning, technical training, and the shaping of individual and collective behaviours'. We can trace the roots of this to the very self-education study groups created by African students in 1940s Portugal. Cabral and his comrades reproduced this same practice in the forests of Guinea-Bissau known as the liberated zones, in underground meetings in the Chão de Papel neighbourhood in the city of Bissau, and in Cape Verde during the 1960s and 1970s.

Ideology, revolutionary consciousness, and using national culture as a method of mobilisation, are some of the themes we can use to navigate Cabral's political theory as well as his practice. Here however, I'd like to foreground the practicalities of liberation. On this subject Cabral wrote, 'always bear in mind that people are not fighting for ideas, for things in anyone's head. They are fighting to win material benefits, to live better and in peace, to see their lives go forward, to guarantee the future of their children.' To this end, understanding the conditions under which one is living is crucial. *Tell No Lies, Claim No Easy Victories* starts exactly from this point. With his address to the United Nations in 1962, Cabral exposed the nature of Portuguese colonialism on an international stage, and denounced the situation the people of Guinea and Cape Verde were forced to live in.

In pieces like 'Determined to Resist', he explored the practices that people engaged in to end such a situation. The dock workers' revolt on Bissau's Pidjiguiti docks, is one example that served as a model for future actions. One of the outcomes of the revolt was the attention it brought to the dangers within the resistance movement, such as tactics of division and the absence of ideology. Cabral identified the potential for a great deficiency in the national liberation movement; so he insisted that movements could not aspire to transform material realities while operating in ignorance of their historical realities. It was through the historical lenses of Marxism-Leninism and the Black Radical Tradition that many of Cabral's analyses were made. As he wrote in his famous essay 'The Weapon of Theory', recognising political theories and experiences from other movements is an important source of learning. The success of PAIGC struggle in Guinea-Bissau and Cape Verde, he claimed, could only be achieved 'by detailed knowledge of it, by our own efforts, by our own sacrifices.'

Spread throughout these pages is the thought and process of liberation of Guinea-Bissau and Cape Verde, the dynamics of national liberation integrated into the context of the international struggle. Cabral emphasises the need for solidarity between the international working-class movement and the liberation struggle, by writing, 'I am not going to tell you how to struggle ... but you must find the best means and the best forms of fighting against our common enemy. This is the best form of solidarity.'

Amílcar Cabral was the protagonist of a unique journey, but although his name is the most pronounced one in the PAIGC-led liberation struggle, it is important to understand his intellectual work not as an individual effort but a collective one. This wisdom was gathered in discussions with his comrades of all kinds: soldiers, teachers, children, and peasants, to mention few. It is this combination of thoughts, practices, and experiences that rest in the words presented here which we call today, *O Pensamento the Cabral* (Cabral's Thoughts).

In Guinea-Bissau in the liberated area of Lugadjor, a secret meeting was to be held on 24 September 1973. PAIGC members were invited to attend, and people walked day and night to reach the meeting. Unbeknownst to most of them,

Guinea-Bissau would declare itself to be independent on that day. However, there was one person missing. Amílcar Cabral, assassinated on 12 January earlier that year, could not be present for such an important milestone in the liberation struggle. Less than a year later in Portugal, the Portuguese military overthrew the Estado Novo authoritarian regime on 25 April 1974, a turn of events in which the PAIGC had a crucial impact. This day would come to be known as the Carnation Revolution. When I ask Cabral's comrades and other left allies about the celebration of this date, which is now Freedom Day (*Dia da Liberdade*), and the completeness of the revolution, they say the revolution is incomplete. Their answer, paraphrased, is, '*Não, ... porque faltou Cabral*' ('No, ... because Cabral was missing').

Although Cabral passed on before these two important moments in African liberation history, people continue to repeat the Cape Verdean and Guinean *kriol* (creole) expression '*Cabral ka muri*' ('Cabral is not dead'). This phrase expresses the necessity of continuing to study and understand Cabral. We must keep alive the practice of militant education he explains in the Party Watchwords from 1965. We must 'devote ... seriously to study ... constantly improve their knowledge, their culture, their political training ... Learn from life, learn with our people, learn in books and from the experience of the other. Constantly learn.'

Sónia Vaz Borges,   Grândola, Portugal,
Assistant Professor of History   July 2022
and Africana Studies

MAP OF AFRICA, 1962

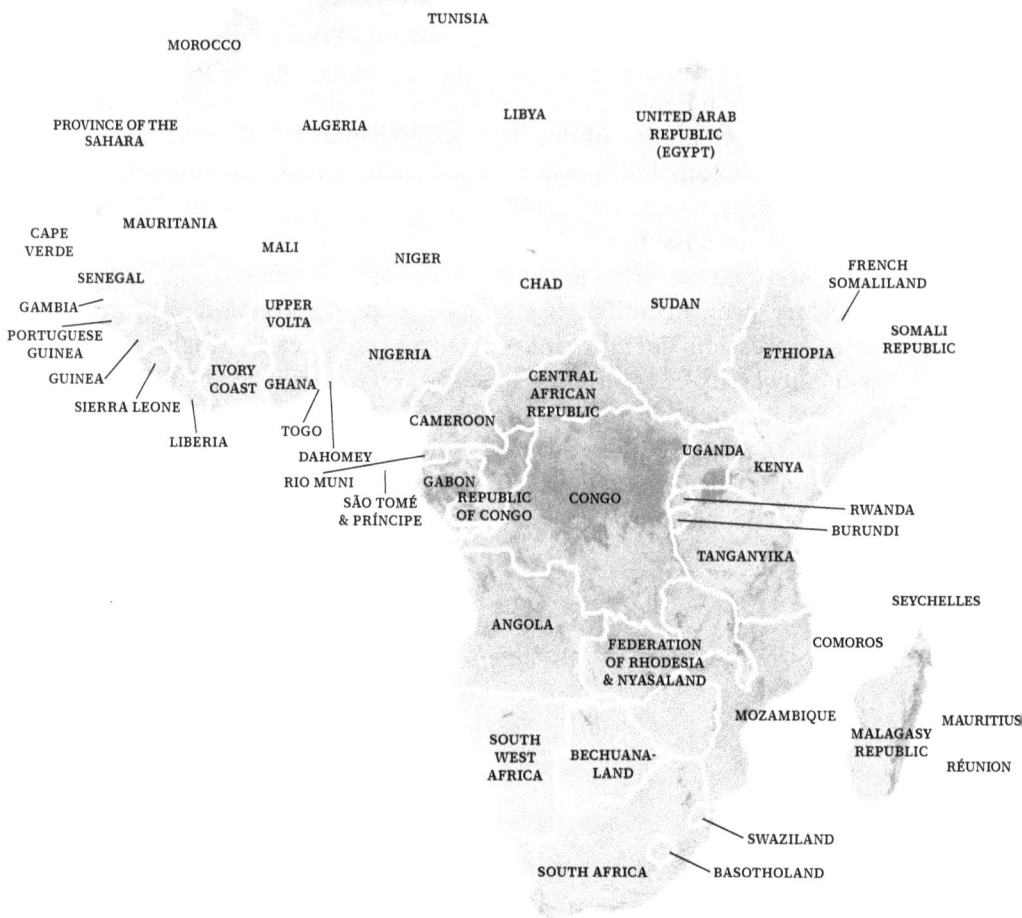

TUNISIA

MOROCCO

PROVINCE OF THE SAHARA

ALGERIA

LIBYA

UNITED ARAB REPUBLIC (EGYPT)

CAPE VERDE

MAURITANIA

MALI

NIGER

CHAD

SUDAN

FRENCH SOMALILAND

SENEGAL

GAMBIA

PORTUGUESE GUINEA

GUINEA

SIERRA LEONE

LIBERIA

UPPER VOLTA

IVORY COAST

GHANA

TOGO

DAHOMEY

RIO MUNI

SÃO TOMÉ & PRÍNCIPE

NIGERIA

CAMEROON

GABON

REPUBLIC OF CONGO

CONGO

CENTRAL AFRICAN REPUBLIC

ETHIOPIA

SOMALI REPUBLIC

UGANDA

KENYA

RWANDA

BURUNDI

TANGANYIKA

SEYCHELLES

ANGOLA

FEDERATION OF RHODESIA & NYASALAND

COMOROS

MOZAMBIQUE

MALAGASY REPUBLIC

MAURITIUS

RÉUNION

SOUTH WEST AFRICA

BECHUANA-LAND

SWAZILAND

SOUTH AFRICA

BASOTHOLAND

Capital Cities

ALGERIA
- Algiers

ANGOLA
- Luanda

BASOTHOLAND
- Maseru

BECHUANALAND
- Mafikeng

BURUNDI
- Usumbura

CAMEROON
- Yaoundé

CAPE VERDE
- Praia

CENTRL AFRICAN REPUBLIC
- Bangui

CHAD
- N'Djamena

COMOROS
- Moroni

DAHOMEY
- Porto-Novo

EQUATORIAL GUINEA
- Malabo

ETHIOPIA
- Addis Ababa

FEDERATION OF RHODESIA & NYASALAND
- Salisbury

GABON
- Libreville

GAMBIA
- Bathurst

GHANA
- Accra

GUINEA
- Conakry

IVORY COAST
- Abidjan

KENYA
- Nairobi

LIBERIA
- Monrovia

LIBYA
- Tripoli

MALAGASY REPUBLIC
- Tananarive

MALI
- Bamako

MAURITANIA
- Nouakchott

MAURITIUS
- Port Louis

MOROCCO
- Rabat

MOZAMBIQUE
- Lourenço Marques

NIGER
- Niamey

NIGERIA
- Lagos

PORTUGUESE GUINEA
- Bissau

REPUBLIC OF CONGO
- Brazzaville

RÉUNION
- Saint-Denis

RIO MUNI
- Bata

RWANDA
- Kigali

SÃO TOMÉ & PRÍNCIPE
- São Tomé

SENEGAL
- Dakar

SEYCHELLES
- Victoria

SIERRA LEONE
- Freetown

SOMALI REPUBLIC
- Mogadishu

SOUTH AFRICA
- Pretoria

SOUTH WEST AFRICA
- Windhoek

SPANISH SAHARA
- El Aaiún

SUDAN
- Khartoum

SWAZILAND
- Mbabane

TANGANYIKA
- Dar es Salaam

CONGO
- Léopoldville

TOGO
- Lomé

TUNISIA
- Tunis

UGANDA
- Kampala

UNITED ARAB REPUBLIC
- Cairo

MAP OF GUINEA-BISSAU AND CAPE VERDE, 1962

Mindelo

Caleijão

Santa Maria

Sal Rei

CAPE VERDE

Tarrafal

São Filipe

Praia

GUINEA-BISSAU

Nova Lamego

Teixeira Pinto

Bissau

Statement to the United Nations Special Committee on Territories Under Portuguese Administration

Extracts from a statement made in Conakry in June 1962.

AFTER THE RESOLUTION ON DECOLONIALISATION – THE 1961 'REFORMS'

An analysis has been made of the position of the people of Guinea as regards to their relations with the metropolitan country, the basic laws governing their lives, the administrative structure and organisation, the political institutions and how they function, the right to vote and its exercise, the organisation and administration of justice, human rights and fundamental freedoms. That analysis presents actual facts culled from legislation in force and day-to-day reality.

The analysis makes clear that the constitutional, political, legal, administrative and judicial status of Guinea, far from that of being a 'province of Portugal' is that of a non-self-governing country, conquered and occupied by force of arms, ruled and administered by a foreign power. The economic, political and social life of the people of Guinea is governed by laws and rules which differ from those applied to the people of Portugal; the people of Guinea have no political rights, they do not help to operate the country's institutions or to draft its laws, which, however, they must obey; they do not elect representatives and cannot invest political and administrative leaders with office or remove them from office; they do not enjoy the most rudimentary human rights or fundamental freedoms. Thus, far from having their own legal identity, the people of Guinea are a colonised and dependent people, whose dignity has been deeply wounded. Neither directly nor indirectly do they decide their present or future fate. Consequently, there can be no doubt that the people of Guinea are being deprived of their right to self-determination, a right proclaimed and established for all peoples in the United Nations Charter.

Nevertheless, those who are not familiar with the actual facts as regards to the present position of the people of Guinea might ask whether the recent

Portuguese 'reforms' of colonial legislation promulgated in 1961 have not significantly changed the constitutional and legal status of Guinea.

As is well known, these 'reforms' of Portuguese colonial legislation were instituted shortly after the United Nations General Assembly, at its fifteenth session, had adopted the resolution on decolonisation (14 December 1960). Before proceeding further, it is worth noting that the hasty promulgation of such 'reforms' after the United Nations adopted that historic and constructive resolution is in itself a striking indictment by Portugal of its own colonial system.

An analysis of the legal texts of these 'reforms' will demonstrate whether they actually did or could change the constitutional and legal status of Guinea to any significant degree. The following legislation was enacted:

a) Decree no. 43,730, which revised articles 489,511 and 516 of the Overseas Administrative Reform Act;
b) Decree no. 43,894, approving the regulation of the occupation and granting of land concessions in the colonies;
c) Decree no. 43,895, establishing provincial settlement boards in the colonies;
d) Decree no. 43,896, organising the cantons in the colonies;
e) Decree no. 43,897, recognising the usages and customs regulating relations in private law in the colonies;
f) Decree no. 43,893, repealing the Native Statute of May 1954.

(Except for the first, all these decrees are dated 6 September 1961.) Thus the matters affected by the enactment of the reforms are: *administrative organisation, land occupation, colonisation, justice* and *political status.*

In actual fact, this legislation made no significant change in those matters, nor was the practice of the Portuguese rulers greatly changed, and from the constitutional and legal standpoint the subjection of the people of Guinea to Portuguese colonialism. For example,

a) although Decree no. 43,730 states in its preamble: 'in accordance with our administrative tradition, both overseas and in the metropolitan country, the commune is the basic administrative unit...', it still leaves local administration in the hands of the Portuguese authorities for it provides that the mairies, the municipal commissions and the local communities shall be presided over by persons appointed by the territorial or provincial governments.
b) Decree no. 43,894 deals with public property and with land concessions granted to settlers, administrative bodies and Catholic missions, and defines measures and establishes organs for the granting of such concessions. All in all, the law opens up to Portuguese settlers in Guinea opportunities for the occupation of land which either never existed before or were very limited.

c) Decree no. 43,895, which explicitly states in its preamble '... We have always regarded these as prerequisites for the desired progress in the overseas provinces, as one of the bases for the permanent establishment of European Portugal in the African territories...', is nothing more than a legal instrument for establishing effective organs and means for stimulating and achieving the long-desired permanent settlement of increased numbers of Europeans in Guinea.

d) Although Decree no. 43,986 lays the basis for the organisation of the *regedorias*, it maintains the old system of replacing traditional chiefs by persons appointed by the colonial authorities.[4]

e) Decree no. 43,897, while it recognises local usages and customs regulating relations to provide law, provides in its article 2 that such recognition shall be limited by the moral principles and basic rules of the Portuguese legal system. The scope of these limitations continues to be defined by article 138 of the political Constitution as 'morality, the dictates of humanity and the *free exercise of Portuguese sovereignty*'.

f) Decree no. 43,893, which repeals the Native Statute, is the only official text in all of the new legislation which should imply a change, however academic, in the colony's constitutional and legal status. But point of fact that is not the case. In the prefatory statement, the reasons for repealing the Statute are candidly stated. It is said that the Statute is being repealed 'because this law was not always understood in a way which did justice to the motives and intentions underlying it...' and because its existence 'provided an opportunity for our enemies to assert that the Portuguese people are subject to two political laws and are consequently divided into two classes with no communication between them...' Thus, the lawmakers' purpose was not to alter the motives and intentions under-lying the Statute, which they do not condemn – despite the fact that the Statute had the effect of placing the African in Guinea in the position of having no identity in law and of being an *indigena*. The purpose of the lawmakers as disclosed in the prefatory statement, was to deprive the enemies of Portuguese colonialism of an effective weapon in the struggle on behalf of the Africans of Guinea – Portuguese law itself. But they did not succeed, for the following reasons.

First, the people of Guinea had no hand in drafting the new law, which is the result of a unilateral act, contrary to their legitimate aspirations. Secondly, Portuguese citizenship, fictitious as it is, is imposed on the African of Guinea without his consent. Although the Statute clearly defined the requirements for citizenship, there was never 'any rush by the natives to secure the identity card

---

4   *Editor's note*: The *regedorias* were part of a controversial Portuguese colonial resettlement project for rural communities.

which would make them citizens', as noted by Teixeira da Mota, a European investigator and official deputy in Guinea. The Africans of Guinea, from the time of the resistance in the colonial wars of conquest to the freedom struggle of today, never fought to acquire Portuguese citizenship. Thirdly, the law repealing the Native Statute was not followed by other legislation which would, in practice, regulate the participation of the people of Guinea in the management of their own affairs. Finally, the daily life of the people of Guinea (their economic, political, social and cultural life), with the exception of a few superficial alterations, particularly in the titles of laws, *has changed not one iota*. For example, although the 'indigenous' identity cards were and still are being hastily replaced by 'provisional' identity cards, the *indigena* tax and its 10 per cent surtax were replaced by the annual personal income tax and the surtax, which not only amount to the same, but are still subject to the legislation governing the old taxes.

Consequently, it is fair to say that far from changing the constitutional status of Guinea, the 1961 'reforms' merely made the situation worse, at least in the following respects:

a) By increasing the number of communes, creating additional local concentration of power and organising the cantons – which are always headed by persons appointed by the Governor – not only was Portuguese rule strengthened, but it was made easier for the colonial authorities to keep an eye on the Africans of Guinea and to carry out repressive measures against individuals and groups.

b) By defining procedures and establishing organs for the application and granting of land concessions to non-indigenous parties, more opportunities were provided for usurping and effectively occupying land which had until then belonged to the African communities.

c) By setting up the Provincial Settlement Boards, contrary to the spirit of the law itself, the way is being opened for European colonisation in Guinea to the detriment of the interests of the overwhelming majority of the people and of all classes of Africans.

Moreover, the 1961 'reforms' are contrary to the spirit of the provisions of resolutions 1542 (XV) and 1514 (XV) of the United Nations General Assembly, because they effect no change in the Portuguese political Constitution which, having been revised in 1961 with the clear intention of evading the obligations arising from the principles of the Charter, continues to state that Guinea is 'an integral part of the Portuguese nation'. Their purpose is to perpetuate the fiction of the 'overseas provinces' and they therefore constitute a flagrant violation of the right of the people of Guinea to self-determination and independence, while at the same time an attempt is made to baffle the vigilance of the forces fighting for freedom, particularly those of the United Nations.

But the Portuguese colonial government has never succeeded and never will succeed in attaining the objectives of the 1961 'reforms'. Despite all subterfuges, they fail to conceal the actual realities of the constitutional and legal status of the people of Guinea. These very 'reforms' show that, now as before, this status continues to be determined by:

a) the Portuguese political Constitution;
b) the Overseas Organic Law;
c) the Administrative and Legal Statute of Guinea.

Moreover, the organs of Portuguese sovereignty – the Head of the Portuguese State, the Portuguese National Assembly, the Portuguese Government and the Portuguese courts – still have the final say in the economic, political and social life of the colony. The National Assembly, the Council and the Portuguese Minister for Overseas Territories still hold special legislative powers with respect to Guinea.

These metropolitan organs enjoy the co-operation of the Portuguese Corporative Chamber, the Conference of Overseas Governors, the Economic Conference of Overseas Portugal and other technical bodies. The Governor and the Government Council, the former exercising executive and legislative powers and the latter acting in an advisory capacity, are still the colony's organs of government. There has been no change either in the system of appointing the Governor or in the composition and the manner of appointment and election of the members of the Government Council.

Today, as yesterday, the Portuguese in Guinea are imbued with the same spirit in which, from the Middle Ages until our times, they practised the slave trade; the spirit in which they engaged in their cruel wars of conquest and occupation, in which they built up and organised, down to the smallest detail, the colonial exploitation of the country's human and natural resources, and which at present motivates the prevalent economic, police and military repression and furnishes the threat of a new colonial war which hangs over the people of Guinea. It is that spirit, which is a historical development of the Middle Ages, which determines and shapes Portugal's colonial legislation and methods.

INTERNAL PEACE AND SECURITY – REPRESSION

The laws and the daily realities of economic, political, social and cultural life to which the people of Guinea are subjected reveal that the people are the target of one of the most violent and best-organised examples of oppression (national, social and cultural) and economic exploitation in the history of colonialism. This system of oppression and economic exploitation was introduced and built up in Guinea by force of arms. Its development and continued implementation could be achieved only by recourse to armed repression (by the army and the police) and by the systematic use of violence in all its forms against any attempt at insurrection made by the people of Guinea.

The 'internal peace and security' imposed by Portuguese colonial domination in Guinea is not, and never has been, anything other than the fruit of a victory achieved by systematic repression, supported by an administrative framework which has engineered down to the most trifling detail its action against the long-standing desire for liberation and the active hatred of the people of Guinea for foreign domination. This situation has been the samefrom the times of the conquest and colonial occupation right up to the active struggle for national liberation which our people is waging today.

In the course of colonial wars lasting over half a century (1870–1936), hardly a year went by, as Teixeira da Mota admits, without some kind of military operation. These operations 'had sometimes to be repeated over and over again against the same populations'. The period from 1936 to 1959, after the administrative machine had been put together and set in motion, was one of silent repression, of secret recourse to violence, of unsung victims, of disorganised, individual reactions, of assaults and crimes of all sorts taking place within the four walls of the administrative buildings. Since 1959, in the face of the great strides of the African peoples along the road to national independence and of the firm resolution of the people of Guinea to free themselves from the Portuguese colonial yoke, there has been a return to open and undisguised repression by the army and police, in the towns as in the countryside, in private homes as in the public services, in the massacre of indigenous populations as in the murder of nationalist prisoners.

A detailed and concrete study of the practical realities of the life of the people of Guinea and the practices of the Portuguese overlords reveals that despite all the precautionary and repressive measures taken by the Portuguese colonialists, they have never actually experienced a real 'era of internal peace and security' in Guinea. One of the most interesting features of the Portuguese colonial laws is that despite all attempts at disguise, they disclose not only the intentions and actions of the Portuguese masters, but also the methods and means they resort to in order to preserve law and order and maintain their presence in peace and security.

Although the structure and organisation of Portuguese colonial domination display both in theory and in practice – down to the most insignificant details – a high degree of efficiency in exploiting the African population, the basic strength of Portuguese colonialism lies not in legal provisions nor in any original features of its political organisation. The basic strength of Portuguese colonialism, whether or not assisted by favourable historical circumstances, lies, and has always lain, in *its moral and physical propensity for repressive practices*, based on an absolute refusal to regard the African as a human being.

The cannon and other firearms of the era of discovery and conquest, the *palmatória*, the whip, the pistol, the modern rifle, the machine gun, the mortar, bombs of all kinds, including napalm bombs, and torture are the instruments of that strength.[5] The navigators and mariners of former days, the mercenaries, the Captains General, the soldiers of the 'pacification', the *sepoys*, the *chefs de posto* (Chiefs of Post), the Administrators, the Governors, the modern colonial troops (army, navy and air force) and the political police are its agents.

This is not the place for a recital of the crimes of Portuguese colonialism, of which world opinion is now well aware. It will suffice to recall that from the time of the slave hunts until the massacres of today, the people of Guinea have been the constant victims of these crimes.

a) More than a million Africans were carried off by the slave traders from the Guinea region.

b) Tens of thousands of Africans in Guinea were killed in the colonial wars of conquest and of occupation.

c) Few adult Africans – the so-called natives – have escaped the *palmatória* or the whip.

d) On 3rd August 1959, 50 African workers who had gone on strike were massacred on the docks at Pijiguiti (Bissao).

e) A number of African nationalists, including Joao Rosa, accountant, Antonio Teixeira, mechanic, and Joao Araujo, farmer, died of the torture to which they were subjected by the political police (PIDE), in whose prisons more than 1,000 African nationalists have been incarcerated since 1957.[6]

f) Over 300 nationalists are still held in the prisons of the PIDE, including: Fernando Fortes, post office employee; Epifânio Amado, assistant pharmacist; Inacio Semêdo, farmer; Quintino Nozolini, official; Mamadu Turé, barman; Bernardo Pereira, clerk; Malan Nanque, farmer; Eduardo Pinto, mechanic; Domingos Furtado, clerk; Renato Furtado, clerk.

g) Recently, hundreds of nationalist Africans have been sent to the concentration camp of the island of Galinhas.

h) Dozens of Africans have been killed in the bush by Portuguese troops, who burn down any villages thought to be rebellious.

i) Hardly a day passes, in town or countryside, without the rattle of machineguns, the thud of mortars or the roar of aircraft engaged in the unceasing hunt for nationalists.

---

5 *Editor's note*: The *palmatória* was a wooden bat with holes in it used for punishment or torture.

6 *Editor's note*: The PIDE (International Police for the Defence of the State) was created for Portugal by António de Oliveira Salazar's regime and extended to African colonies after 1954.

At the present time, as a means of repressing the nationalist forces, attempting to stifle the struggle for national liberation by the people of Guinea, and perpetuating their own domination, the Portuguese colonialists have available:

- Armed forces
  - 4,000 European soldiers
  - 2,500 African soldiers
  - 5 jet aircraft (fighters)
  - 2 bomber aircraft
  - 2 armed avisos (dispatch boats)
  - modern equipment including tanks and napalm bombs
- Security forces comprising 300 African men (including *sepoys*) commanded by European officers and sergeants
- Political police (PIDE)
- 10 European special agents, and about 1,000 European and African intelligence agents, commanded by an inspector
- The European population most of whom act as unpaid intelligence agents for the PIDE
- The government authorities. These supply information and serve the army as well as carrying out civil policy, in addition to engaging in repression on their own account.
- An air base in the Cabo Verde islands, an airfield at Bissao and several airstrips in the interior and in the islands of Guinea are used for purposes of repression by the air force. Since Guinea is eight hours' flying time from Lisbon, the Portuguese colonialists also rely on the possibility of rushing in emergency reinforcements from the home country if necessary.

As the struggle for national liberation takes shape, the number of African soldiers is being progressively decreased and that of European soldiers increased. The African soldiers are recruited by the government authorities and sent under duress to military camps. The European soldiers form part of special overseas contingents, detached to Guinea. The security police are recruited from among the *sepoys* and former soldiers. The intelligence agents of the political police are recruited among Africans who agree to betray their own people in order to protect their own positions or to obtain employment or a means of livelihood. The European agents are exclusively professionals, seasoned men from Portugal. Some of them attended the Nazi schools of repression.

FUTURE PROSPECTS FOR THE COUNTRY

Although living under the threat of another colonial war – whose probable methods and atrocities are tragically and graphically illustrated in the action currently being undertaken by Portuguese colonialist forces against the people of Angola – the people of Guinea are determined to bring about an improvement in the situation of their country. They are resolved to live up to their tradition of resistance to foreign domination by putting a speedy end to Portuguese colonialism and laying down in freedom the groundwork for the progressive development of their African homeland.

The desire to throw off the colonial yoke and rid itself of foreign domination has always been one of the deepest aspirations of the people of Guinea. Wounded in their human dignity, deprived of any legal personality, they have never let slip any opportunity to manifest their non-acceptance of, aversion for and resistance to the 'Portuguese presence' in Guinea. The Africans of Guinea have had recourse to every means at their disposal, from individual opposition to collective action, from refusal to pay taxes to mass emigration, in order to defend their dignity and give proof of their love of freedom and hatred of foreign rule. Suffice to recall that during the last 40 years more than 50,000 Africans have left Guinea in order to settle in neighbouring territories; and also that to this very day, some groups, such as the inhabitants of the island of Canhabaque and of the Oio region (in the interior of the country) have not entirely submitted to Portuguese domination. A glance at the Portuguese colonial laws will show that they have been inspired by anxiety, by the need to remain vigilant and repress the resistance of the African population of Guinea.

The people of Guinea love peace and freedom and wish to put an end to the misery, the suffering, the state of ignorance and the trepidation in which they live. Being aware of their rights in their own country, the people of Guinea aspire to freedom and wish to achieve progress and happiness in peace. But the Portuguese state has always evinced the utmost contempt for the legitimate aspirations of the people of Guinea. Moreover, it has always replied to such demonstrations by resorting to the severest repressive measures.

In addition, the constitutional, legal, political and administrative situation of Guinea – the laws and practices of Portuguese colonialism – have never given the people of that country an opportunity of fulfilling their aspirations, or of making even gradual headway along the path of freedom and progress, 'within the framework of the Portuguese administration'. Thus, there has never been more than one way in which the people of Guinea could attempt to fulfil their aspirations towards liberty and progress, namely, *by a struggle for national liberation*. Despite the particularly difficult conditions confronting them, the people of Guinea, guided by enlightened leaders who at an early stage foresaw the decline and end of the colonial era, roused themselves and in 1953, with courage and enthusiasm, plunged into the struggle for national liberation.

It was the actual internal conditions, the realities of their daily life, which made them decide to undertake the struggle for national liberation and for the speedy and total liquidation of Portuguese colonialism. But the struggles and victories of other African peoples against foreign rule and the progress made by mankind in the realms of freedom, human dignity, social justice and international law have played no small part in influencing and strengthening that decision. That is why the fight of Guinea for national liberation is part and parcel of the struggle of the African peoples for the total abolition of foreign rule in Africa – for the final and irrevocable abolition of the colonial system – which is one of the outstanding features of contemporary history.

Starting in 1953, the Africans of Guinea attempted to organise themselves in order to take up, in an orderly manner and by collective action, the defence of their rights and interests (economic, political, moral and cultural) against the injustice, discrimination and despotism of the Portuguese administration. Although they were concerned with the situation of the so-called 'indigenous' masses with which they had close links (principally in the urban areas), they were forced to confine these attempts at organisation, at least in appearance, to those Africans who at the time were called *assimilados* or *civilizados*.[7] These attempts coincided with the return to Guinea of some Africans who, abroad and for the most part in Europe, had closely followed the evolution of colonial policy and the international situation after the Second World War. In Portugal, they had taken their first steps along the path of 're-Africanisation' and development of national consciousness together with African students from other Portuguese colonies.

All these attempts failed in the face of opposition from the administrative authorities, who went so far as to forbid the establishment of a sports and recreational association for Africans. Sensing that something new was occurring that affected the 'tranquility' of the population, especially in Bissao, the authorities decided to keep close watch on suspect Africans. However, the vanguard of this nationalist movement (composed primarily of Guinean and Cabo Verdean civil servants and business employees) began secretly to mobilise the workers of Bissao into an organisation called the Movement for the National Independence of Guinea (MING).

In 1956, all attempts at lawful action having failed and because of the weakness of the MING, this same group of Africans, together with several craftsmen and manual workers, decided to create a clandestine organisation of the political party type to carry on the struggle for national liberation. Thus was born, in September of that year, the *Partido Africano da Independencia da Guiné e Cabo Verde* (PAIGC), the central organisation of the peoples of those colonies in the struggle for national liberation.

The PAIGC defined its fundamental objectives as follows (article 4 of the Statutes).

---

7   *Editor's note*: This was the term given to African subjects of the Portuguese Empire from the 1910s onward, who had reached a level of 'civilisation', in the eyes of the colonisers. In accordance with Portuguese law, *assimilados* qualified in theory for full rights held by Portuguese citizens.

a) Immediate conquest of national independence in Guinea and the Cabo Verde Islands.
b) Democratisation and emancipation of the African populations of these countries, exploited for centuries by Portuguese colonialism.
c) Achievement of rapid economic progress and true social and cultural advancement for the peoples of Guinea and the Cabo Verde Islands.

To win national independence, the PAIGC set itself the task of mobilising, organising and directing the Guinean and Cabo Verdan masses in the struggle for the total abolition of Portuguese colonial rule (article 5 of the Statutes). Having proclaimed, in its manifesto, its intention to create the means necessary to 'build peace, happiness and progress' in Guinea and the Cabo Verde Islands, the PAIGC defined a minor programme of 'unity and struggle' and drew up a major programme along the following general lines: immediate and total independence; national unification of Guinea and the Cabo Verde Islands; African unification; a democratic and anti-colonialist regime; economic independence, building up the economy and developing production; justice and progress for all; strong national defence with the participation of the people; an independent international policy, in the interests of the nation, Africa, peace and progress of mankind.

With regard to international policy, the PAIGC declared itself for 'peaceful co-operation with all the peoples of the world' and expressed its acceptance of and respect for the principles of the United Nations Charter and those of the Bandung Conference.

Starting in 1958, after overcoming not only the difficulties of building up a clandestine military organisation while exposed to the dangers of Portuguese repression, by then reinforced (since 1957) by the active presence of the political police, but also the resistance to be expected in a society in which political organisations had always been forbidden, the PAIGC undertook to broaden the struggle for liberation both in Guinea and in the Cabo Verde Islands, limiting itself primarily, however, to the working masses and employees in the urban areas. This development was greatly accelerated after 1958, following the national independence of the Republic of Guinea, which opened up new prospects for the historical evolution of the African peoples.

The strikes of July–August 1959, suppressed by the massacre at the Pijiguiti dock, showed that the course followed until then had been a mistaken one. The urban centres proved to be the stronghold of colonialism, and mass demonstrations and representations were found to be not only ineffectual but also an easy target for the repressive and destructive operations of the colonialist forces.

Meeting clandestinely in Bissao in September 1959, the PAIGC adopted the following plan.

a) To reinforce the organisation in the urban areas, but to maintain it clandestinely and avoid all public demonstrations.
b) Urgently to mobilise and organise the rural masses, shown by experience to be the principal force in the struggle for national liberation.
c) To induce Africans of all ethnic groups, of all origins and of all social strata to unite around the Party.
d) To train the greatest possible number of persons, both at home and abroad, for the political leadership, the organisation and the development of the struggle.
e) To strengthen co-operation with the nationalist organisations of other Portuguese colonies, with the African countries, in particular the independent countries, and, further, with the democratic and progressive forces of the world, including those of Portugal. To develop effective action at the international level.
f) To organise or encourage the organisation of nationalist movements abroad, in particular among the émigrés residing in territories neighbouring Guinea and the Cabo Verde Islands, to work for liberation and for the future of their people.
g) To increasingly strengthen and broaden the organisation, to train cadres in increasing numbers and to endeavour to obtain the necessary means for successfully pursuing the struggle. To expect the best, but to be prepared for the worst.
h) To train technical personnel at all levels, and, as far as possible, to study and plan the groundwork for and means of promoting rapid economic progress in Guinea and the Cabo Verde Islands.

In order to ensure the safety of some of its leaders and to develop the struggle abroad, the Party decided to transfer its general secretariat to Conakry. It was able to do so thanks to the fraternal support of the *Parti Démocratique* of the Republic of Guinea.

Although the colonialist forces soon launched the campaign of repression to which the country is still subjected (the first arrests of nationalists by the PIDE took place in April 1960), and although the colonial army and its equipment were greatly strengthened, within a little over two years the PAIGC succeeded in carrying out its plan and thus ensuring the successful continuation of the struggle it is directing. Thus:

a) The Party organisation in the urban areas is today stronger than ever and remains clandestine, in the interests of the struggle, which has just entered a more active phase. This was recently proved most strikingly, at the time of the arrest of the Party's Chairman, Rafael Barbosa, who for 18 months lived in hiding in Bissao. The organisation and discipline of the Party were such that it was able to contain the rebellious masses, and thus avoid the massacres which the colonialist forces expected to perpetrate.[8]

b) The peasant masses are, in the main, mobilised and organised throughout the country. Today, together with the workers and employees of the urban areas, they constitute the principal strength of the Party, to which they have given many of its best leaders.

c) Inside the country, all ethnic groups, all social strata, Africans of all origins, men and women, the young and the old, are solidly united around the Party. This is borne out by the non-existence in the country of any other organisation, by the fact that the people as a whole carry out the Party's instructions, and even by the presence within its leadership of nationalists from all social strata, all beliefs and most of the ethnic groups, men as well as women.

d) Hundreds of cadres (in politics, the trade union movement and the intensification of the struggle), most of them young people, have received their training from the Party and are now in the forefront of the continual mobilisation, organisation and education of the masses of the people, for the achievement of national independence, its consolidation, and the political, economic, social and cultural building up of the country.

e) Co-operation with other nationalist organisations in the Portuguese colonies has been strengthened and organised. After the dissolution of the African Revolutionary Front for the National Independence of the Portuguese Colonies (FRAIN) set up in Tunis in January 1960 by the People's Movement for the Liberation of Angola (MPLA) and the PAIGC, these same organisations, together with those of Mozambique, São Tomé and Goa, created the Conference of Nationalist Organisations of the Portuguese Colonies (CONCP) at Casablanca in April 1961, with general secretariat headquarters at Rabat. The role of the CONCP is fundamentally that of co-ordinating the struggle of the peoples of the Portuguese colonies and ensuring unity, solidarity and co-operation.

At the African and Afro-Asian level, the PAIGC has now developed fruitful relations with the governments and parties of the independent countries and with the nationalist organisations of the countries as yet dependent. As an active member of the Conference of African Peoples and the Council of Solidarity of Afro-Asian Peoples, the PAIGC has participated in all international meetings concerned with the liberation of the colonial peoples. Similarly, it has visited several countries and secured the natural support of African countries (in particular the Republics of Guinea, Ghana, Senegal and Mali, and the Kingdom of Morocco), as well as the active solidarity of Asian countries.

---

8   *Editor's note*: Rafael Barbosa was released by the Portuguese authorities in August 1969, after nearly eight years of imprisonment without trial.

At the international level, after the Secretary-General of the Party had revealed the crimes of Portuguese colonialism to world opinion, something done for the first time by an African from the Portuguese colonies, intensified and persistent action was taken to make known the true situation of the peoples under Portuguese domination and to obtain support and aid for their liberation. Thus, the PAIGC enlisted not only the sympathy but also the active support, political in the main, of peace and freedom-loving peoples and governments, and also of democratic and progressive organisations, in the fight waged by the peoples of Guinea and the Cabo Verde Islands.

At the United Nations, the PAIGC has always expressed the legitimate aspirations of its people to national liberation and independence, and its confidence in the organisation. Clearly emphasising the desire for peace and liberty which motivates its action, the PAIGC sent to the United Nations, among other documents, a memorandum addressed to the sixteenth session of the General Assembly, dated 26 September 1961, in which it proposed specific measures for the peaceful abolition of Portuguese rule.

Moreover, on the principle that the struggle it is directing is neither aimed against the Portuguese people nor contrary to their true interests, the PAIGC has established and developed contacts with Portuguese democratic elements, not only for the purpose of organically strengthening the struggle against Portugal's colonial-fascist regime, but also with a view to preserving the possibility of co-operation between the people of Guinea and the Cabo Verde Islands and the Portuguese people, on the basis of independence and of reciprocity of rights and duties.

f) Following suggestions and proposals made by the PAIGC either from within its home country or locally, the émigrés from Guinea and the Cabo Verde Islands residing in the neighbouring countries have created liberation 'movements'. In the Republic of Guinea, the Movement for the Liberation of Guinea and the Cabo Verde Islands (MLGCV, Conakry), organised with the help of the general secretariat of the PAIGC, groups all émigrés truly interested in the liberation of their people and works in close co-operation with that secretariat.

In July 1961, following an appeal for unity launched by the PAIGC in April 1961, the Conference of Nationalist Organisations of Guinea and the Cabo Verde Islands was held in Dakar. It was presided over by a leader of the Party, and several official bodies were represented. Following a proposal by the PAIGC, the Conference, by means of several resolutions, among them one creating the United Liberation Front of Guinea and the Cabo Verde Islands (FUL) which comprises the Party (the organisation inside the country) and the movements abroad (in the Republics of Guinea and Senegal), assumed the task of co-ordinating joint action in the struggle against Portuguese colonialism (articles I and II of the charter of the FUL).

The 'movements' in Senegal, paralysed by parochialism and by internal and inter-party conflicts and contradictions, were unable to consolidate their organisations (which broke up into a number of sub-groups), and failed to respect the commitments made at the Dakar Conference concerning the creation of the FUL, which they disavowed. These 'movements' have been unable thus far to co-operate usefully in the liberation struggle in which they propose to take part and, in addition, some of them have made difficulties for that struggle, principally by assuming negative attitudes and even attitudes contrary to the interests of the Republic of Senegal itself (we may cite as an example the attacks directed from that country's territory in July 1961, which were halted in time by the Senegalese Government).

At the present time, the PAIGC, which has the support of a large number of the émigrés from Guinea and the Cabo Verde Islands living in Senegal, is sparing no efforts to ensure that, as in the Republic of Guinea, the émigrés who are really interested in the liberation of their people co-operate to the best effect with those carrying on the fight inside the country. In this endeavour has the fraternal sympathy of the Senegalese people and their government.

Continually strengthening and expanding its organisation, the Party now covers all parts of the country. Its membership is constantly growing, particularly among the popular masses who are definitively committed to the struggle. Furthermore, the Party has never spared any effort to secure the ways and means for carrying on the fight to victory in the face of the Portuguese administration's systematic disregard for the aspirations of the people of Guinea. In pursuing those efforts, it has acted on the principle that liberation should be the work of the people themselves, who should rely primarily on their own resources to attain this goal.

Seeking a peaceful solution of its conflict with the Portuguese colonialists, the PAIGC took specific steps to try to persuade the Portuguese government to recognise the right of the people of Guinea and the Cabo Verde Islands to self-determination and national independence and by so doing to enhance the possibilities of co-operation between them and the Portuguese people. These steps which at the same time promoted the interests of international peace and security, included the dispatch of a 'memorandum' and an 'open letter' to the Portuguese government, dated 1 December 1960 and 13 October 1961 respectively. In this way specific proposals were submitted to the Portuguese government for the peaceful elimination of colonial rule in Guinea and the Cabo Verde Islands. But the Portuguese government ignored these efforts, its only response being to reinforce its colonial troops and intensify its repression.

Confronted with the reactionary attitude of that Government and in particular its blatant contempt for the principles of the United Nations Charter and the resolutions adopted by the General Assembly at its fifteenth session, the PAIGC, acting in accordance with the will of the people of Guinea and recognising the urgent need to give practical aid to the people of Angola as a new colonial war of genocide was unleashed against them, proclaimed on 3 August 1961, the anniversary of the massacre of Pijiguiti quay, that the fight for liberation had passed from the purely political phase to the phase of direct action.

In accordance with the specific conditions of that fight and the plans for its development, direct action was limited to sabotage of the bases of colonial exploitation in Guinea. That decision was and continues to be applied in all parts of Guinea, and the action taken has proved to be an effective means of disrupting and disorganising colonialist exploitation.

Interpreting the peaceful attitude of the people of Guinea, the PAIGC still is and always has been desirous of reaching a peaceful solution of the conflict between us and the government of Portugal. Such a solution must not, however, be long in coming, for the people of Guinea, revolted by the crimes and outrages of Portuguese colonialist practice, mobilised, organised and prepared for the task of shaking off the colonial yoke, are willing to make any sacrifice to put an end to foreign rule. What is more, they are now capable of doing so.

If the United Nations itself and all the forces which are really in a position to influence the Portuguese government, with a view to making it respect international legality, prove unable to persuade that government to abandon its reactionary and criminal position, nothing will be able to stop the people of Guinea from resorting to all available means of eliminating once and for all the bases and agents of Portuguese rule. In such an event, the Portuguese government itself would obviously bear sole responsibility for whatever happened in Guinea.

In order to further the important task of consolidating independence and ensuring progress, the PAIGC is organising an extensive programme for the training of cadres (administration, production, health, tourism, etc.) and is putting it into effect as far as circumstances permit. It is eager to avail itself of every possible opportunity to proceed as rapidly as possible with the training of a large body of personnel, particularly at the intermediate level, so that there will be African civil servants ready to go into action immediately following liberation.

These, then, if only in broad outline, are some of the specific aspects of the development of the fight for national liberation being waged by the people of Guinea. As far as the actual conduct of the struggle is concerned, its development, both within the country and abroad, has been determined fundamentally by the activities of the Party, which has its headquarters and the great majority of its active members and leaders inside the country.

Accordingly, it may be stated that national liberation offers the only prospect for Guinea's development. In other words, the necessary and indispensable condition for its development, in terms both of what the Guineans want and of cold fact, is today *national liberation*.

Although it is still in full process of development, the fight for liberation of the people of Guinea has already had certain positive results which, having strengthened it considerably, may be regarded as victories.

For example, it has increased the political awareness of the African masses, who had never before been permitted to exercise those essential functions of man – political thought and action.

It has intensified the feeling of unity of all Africans without distinction and is continuing to do so to an ever greater extent each day. In this connection, two facts are especially noteworthy. Firstly, the fight has erased the differences – many of which are carefully cultivated by the colonialists – between certain ethnic groups in Guinea, which are now united in the pursuit of national liberation and progress. Secondly, it has destroyed an important weapon on which the Portuguese colonialists were relying in their effort to 'resist' the overwhelming desire of the people of Guinea for freedom: the conflict, often superficial and always based on material considerations, between the Cabo Verde minority, deliberately favoured by the colonialists in the matter of public service employment, and the *assimilados* among the native majority. Today, the people of Guinea and the people of Cabo Verde, whether behind prison walls or in hiding in the bush, are increasingly strengthening their unity, sharing a common ideal and acting together for the cause of national liberation and progress.

It has developed and is increasingly strengthening the national consciousness of a free and just fatherland for which all ethnic groups, all religious communities, all men and women are fighting.

Gradually overcoming the complexes engendered by colonial exploitation, it has enabled the 'marginal' human beings who are the product of colonialism to recover their personality as Africans. It has reawakened among the Africans of Guinea in general a feeling of confidence in the future.

It has made the personality of Guinea as an African nation known to the rest of the world, has given its people prestige and has won them the sympathy and friendship of other peoples.

It has influenced and is continuing strongly to influence the development of the fight for liberation in the Cabo Verde Islands, whose people are indissolubly linked with those of Guinea by ties of history and of blood.

It has encouraged the fight for liberation of the peoples of the other Portuguese colonies, has materially assisted the people of Angola in their struggle by making it necessary for the Portuguese colonialists to divert some of their troops from that country, and in general has served the cause of Africa's liberation from foreign rule.

In addition to these results, however, the fight of the people of Guinea has begun to have a significant effect on the actions of the Portuguese colonialists themselves. For example, it has helped to bring about a gradual deterioration in the economy of Portugal as a nation oppressing other nations, for in carrying out its repressive policies Portugal is obliged to spend more and more money and is meeting with increasingly stubborn resistance from those nations.

It has shaken the morale and upset the material life of the families of the colonialists, who have had to send most of the European women and children back to Portugal with the consent of the authorities, because of growing insecurity.

It has obliged the colonial authorities to spend considerable amounts on bribing certain Africans and has caused them to lose confidence in the indigenous troops, in whom they formerly had great trust, and even in some of their own collaborators.

It has obliged the Portuguese state for the first time in history to nominate certain Africans to posts of responsibility, including that of deputy in Guinea.

It has helped to bring about a decline in the income of colonialist commercial and financial enterprises and to aggravate considerably the colony's unfavourable balance of trade during the past three years, thereby worsening Portugal's economic situation.

It has provoked and deepened differences of opinion among Europeans living in Guinea, particularly in the Portuguese army, from whose ranks there have been a considerable number of desertions.

It has obliged the administrative authorities to abandon certain repressive measures, such as those applied in connection with the collection of taxes, and has been one of the causes, together with the United Nations resolution on decolonisation, of the promulgation of the 'reforms' of 1961 and the repeal, if only in theory, of the *Estatuto dos Indígenas*.

ACCESSION TO INDEPENDENCE

The people of Guinea are fighting for their right to self-determination and national independence. They wish to decide their future for themselves, free from any kind of foreign intervention in affairs which are their exclusive concern. They wish to shake off the colonial yoke completely so that they may form a free and sovereign nation in a new and independent Africa.

The people of Guinea know very well that the procedures and methods to be adopted for the prompt restoration of their right to self-determination, for the immediate elimination of Portuguese colonial rule and for the attainment of national independence do not depend on their wishes alone. If that were true, Guinea would already be an independent country and accordingly the situation of its people would not be an international problem.

The people of Guinea consider that the re-establishment of international legality in their country – with respect for the right to self-determination, the elimination of colonialism and the attainment of national independence – depend essentially on the following factors:

a) their own desire and determination to free themselves from the colonial yoke, as manifested in the means and the human and material resources which are available to them for the attainment of this goal;
b) the attitude and conduct (moral, political and legal) of the Portuguese government as a party directly concerned in the matter;
c) international politics, that is, the result of internal and external factors which determine at the international level the specific action (positive or negative) both of governments (considered individually or as members of international assemblies) and of the United Nations itself;
d) the time required for the contradictions inherent in each of the above factors, which are constantly in a state of flux, to be defined, to develop and to straighten themselves out, whether by peaceful or non-peaceful means.

Where the United Nations is concerned, the problem of this people's national independence may be summarised in the following two alternatives: (1) either the United Nations, duly supported by the democratic forces of the world, will succeed in planning and putting into effect practical measures compelling the Portuguese government to respect the Charter and the resolution on decolonialisation, to abide by international legality, to renounce a position which is contrary to civilised interests and to desist from a crime against humanity, or (2) the United Nations, through lack of support, methods and practical measures, or some or all of these factors, will not succeed in persuading the Portuguese government to abandon its stubborn and absurd attitude.

In the former case – which may be called 'effective recognition by the Portuguese government of the respect it owes to the United Nations' – we would have the hypothesis of that government accepting the peaceful elimination of Portuguese colonial domination by negotiation. The attitude of the people of Guinea, as interpreted by its legitimate representatives, would obviously be the one already defined for such a hypothesis. Not only would the prestige of the United Nations be maintained (it would show that the resolution on decolonialisation can indeed be put into effect), but it would also be possible to take into account Portuguese interests in that country, while stubbornly defending the rights of the people of Guinea. Thus, it would still be possible to provide for the possibility of studying and defining the participation and assistance of the United Nations in the practical solution of the problem at issue, through its representatives who are most versed in these matters.

In the second case, the hypothesis that peaceful means can be used to eliminate Portuguese colonialism in Guinea would cease to have any meaning, perhaps even less meaning than in the case of a refusal by the Portuguese government without United Nations intervention. The prestige of the United Nations would be seriously jeopardised, the resolution on decolonialisation would run the risk of being regarded as an academic exercise in international law and the people of Guinea would be obliged to use all means within their power to put an end to the crime perpetrated by the Portuguese government against itself and against mankind.

It is therefore justifiable to conclude that the United Nations' opportunity of contributing to the peaceful solution of the dispute between the people of Guinea and the Portuguese government does not depend on that people, which is seeking national independence and fighting for it, but on the nature and dynamic of the relations, whether peaceful or not, between that international organisation and the Portuguese state. Hence, the measures which will have to be taken to secure the accession of the people of Guinea to national independence will also not depend – at least not immediately – on the people of Guinea, but above all on the United Nations, since that organisation, as the guardian and trustee of international law, is the only body which can compel the Portuguese government to agree to the negotiations in which those measures would be defined.

The people of Guinea, reaffirming their confidence in the United Nations, hope that the organisation will not fail urgently to adopt specific and effective measures to oblige the Portuguese government to respect international law, and thus fulfil the weighty responsibilities incumbent upon it for the final elimination of colonialism in Guinea.

Brief Analysis of the Social Structure in Guinea

Condensed text of a seminar held at the Frantz Fanon Centre in Treviglio, Milan, 1–3 May 1964.

I should like to tell you something about the situation in our country, 'Portuguese' Guinea, beginning with an analysis of the social situation, which has served as the basis for our struggle for national liberation. I shall make a distinction between the rural areas and the towns, or rather the urban centres, not that these are to be considered mutually opposed.

In the rural areas we have found it necessary to distinguish between two distinct groups: on the one hand, the group which we consider semi-feudal, represented by the Fulas, and, on the other hand, the group which we consider, so to speak, without any defined form of state organisation, represented by the Balanta. There are a number of intermediary positions between these two extreme ethnic groups (as regards the social situation). I should like to point out straight away that although in general the semi-feudal groups were Muslim and the groups without any form of state organisations were animist, there was one ethnic group among the animists, the Manjacos, which had forms of social relations which could be considered feudal at the time when the Portuguese came to Guinea.

I should now like to give you a quick idea of the social stratification among the Fulas. We consider that the chiefs, the nobles and the religious figures form one group; after them come the artisans and the Dyulas, who are itinerant traders, and then after that come the peasants properly speaking. I don't want to give a very thorough analysis of the economic situation of each of these groups now, but I would like to say that although certain traditions concerning collective ownership of the land have been preserved, the chiefs and their entourages have retained considerable privileges as regards to ownership of land and the utilisation of other people's labour; this means that the peasants who depend on the chiefs are obliged to work for these chiefs for a certain period of each year.

The artisans, whether blacksmiths (which is the lowest occupation) or leather-workers or whatever, play an extremely important role in the socio-economic life of the Fulas and represent what you might call the embryo of industry. The Dyulas, whom some people consider should be placed above the artisans, do not really have such importance among the Fulas; they are the people who have the potential – which they sometimes realise – of accumulating money.

In general, the peasants have no rights and they are the really exploited group in Fula society.

Apart from the question of ownership and property, there is another element which it is extremely interesting to compare and that is the position of women. Among the Fulas women have no rights; they take part in production but they do not own what they produce. Besides, polygamy is a highly respected institution and women are to a certain extent considered the property of their husbands.

Among the Balanta, which are at the opposite extreme, we find a society without any social stratification: there is just a council of elders in each village or group of villages who decide on the day-to-day problems. For the Balanta, group property and land are considered to belong to the village but each family receives the amount of land needed to ensure subsistence for itself, and the means of production, or rather the instruments of production, are not collective but are owned by families or individuals.

The position of women must also be mentioned when talking about the Balanta. The Balanta still retain certain tendencies towards polygamy, although it is mainly a monogamous society. Among the Balanta, women participate in production but they own what they produce and this gives Balanta women a position which we consider privileged, as they are fairly free. The only point on which they are not free is that children belong to the head of the family and the head of the family, the husband, always claims any children his wife may have. This is obviously to be explained by the actual economy of the group where a family's strength is ultimately represented by the number of hands there are to cultivate the land.

As I have said, there are a number of intermediate positions between these two extremes. In the rural areas I should mention the small African farm owners; this is a numerically small group but all the same it has a certain importance and has proved to be highly active in the national liberation struggle. In the towns (I shall not talk about the presence of Europeans in the rural areas as there are none in Guinea) we must first distinguish between the Europeans and the Africans. The Europeans can easily be classified as they retain in Guinea the social stratification of Portugal (obviously depending on the function they exercise in Guinea). In the first place, there are the high officials and the managers of enterprises who form a stratum with practically no contact with the other European strata. After that there are the middle officials, the small European traders, the people employed in commerce and the members of the liberal professions. After that come the workers, who are mainly skilled workers.

Among the Africans we find the higher officials, the middle officials and the members of the liberal professions forming a group; then come the petty officials, those employed in commerce with a contract, who are to be distinguished from those employed in commerce without a contract, who can be fired at any moment. The small farm owners also fall into this group; by assimilation we call all these members of the African petty bourgeoisie (obviously, if we were to make a more thorough analysis the higher African officials as well as the middle officials and the members of the liberal professions should also be included in the petty bourgeoisie).

Next come the wage-earners (whom we define as those employed in commerce without any contract); among these there are certain important sub-groups such as the dockworkers, the people employed on the boats carrying goods and agricultural produce; there are also the domestic servants, who are mostly men in Guinea; there are the people working in repair shops and small factories and there are also the people who work in shops as porters and suchlike – these all come under the heading of wage-earners. You will notice that we are careful not to call these groups the proletariat or working class.

There is another group of people whom we call the *déclassés*, in which there are two sub-groups to be distinguished: the first sub-group is easy to identify – it is what would be called the lumpenproletariat if there was a real proletariat: it consists of really *déclassé* people, such as beggars, prostitutes and so on. The other group is not really made up of *déclassé* people, but we have not yet found the exact term for it; it is a group to which we have paid a lot of attention and it has proved to be extremely important in the national liberation struggle. It is mostly made up of young people who are connected to petty bourgeois or workers' families, who have recently arrived from the rural areas and generally do not work; they thus have close relations with the rural areas, as well as with the towns (and even with the Europeans). They sometimes live off one kind of work or another, but they generally live at the expense of their families. Here I should just like to point out a difference between Europe and Africa; in Africa there is a tradition which requires that, for example, if I have an uncle living in the town, I can come in and live in his house without working and he will feed me and house me. This creates a certain stratum of people who experience urban life and who can, as we shall see, play a very important role.

That is a very brief analysis of the general situation in Guinea, but you will understand that this analysis has no value unless it is related to the actual struggle. In outline, the methodological approach we have used has been as follows: first, the position of each group must be defined – to what extent and in what way does each group depend on the colonial regime? Next we have to see what position they adopt towards the national liberation struggle. Then we have to study their nationalist capacity and lastly, envisaging the post-independence period, their revolutionary capacity.

Among the Fulas, the first group – the chiefs and their entourages – are tied to colonialism; this is particularly the case with the Fulas as in Guinea the Fulas were already conquerors (the Portuguese allied themselves with the Fulas in order to dominate Guinea at the beginning of the conquest). Thus, the chiefs (and their authority as chiefs) are very closely tied to the Portuguese authorities. The artisans are extremely dependent on the chiefs; they live off what they make for the chiefs who are the only ones that can acquire their products, so there are some artisans who are simply content to follow the chiefs; then there are other people who try to break away and are well-disposed towards opposition to Portuguese colonialism.

The main point about the Dyulas is that their permanent pre-occupation is to protect their own personal interests; at least in Guinea, the Dyulas are not settled in any one place, they are itinerant traders without any real roots anywhere and their fundamental aim is to make bigger and bigger profits. It is precisely the fact that they are almost permanently on the move which provided us with a most valuable element in the struggle. It goes without saying that there are some who have not supported our struggle and there are some who have been used as agents against us by the Portuguese, but there are some whom we have been able to use to mobilise people, at least as far as spreading the initial ideas of the struggle was concerned – all we had to do was give them some reward, as they usually would not do anything without being paid.

Obviously, the group with the greatest interest in the struggle is the peasantry, given the nature of the various different societies in Guinea (feudal, semi-feudal, etc.) and the various degrees of exploitation to which they are subjected; but the question is not simply one of objective interest.

Given the general context of our traditions, or rather the superstructure created by the economic conditions in Guinea, the Fula peasants have a strong tendency to follow their chiefs. Thorough and intensive work was therefore needed to mobilise them. Among the Balanta and the groups without any defined form of state organisation the first point to note is that there are still many remnants of animist traditions even among the Muslims in Guinea; the part of the population which follows Islam is not really Islamic but rather Islamised: they are animists who have adopted some Muslim practices, but are still thoroughly impregnated with animist conceptions. What is more, these groups without any defined organisation put up much more resistance against the Portuguese than the others and they have maintained intact their tradition of resistance to colonial penetration. This is the group that we found most ready to accept the idea of national liberation.

Here I should like to broach one key problem, which is of enormous importance for us, as we are a country of peasants, and that is the problem of whether or not the peasantry represents the main revolutionary force. I shall confine myself to my own country, Guinea, where it must be said at once that the peasantry is not a revolutionary force – which may seem strange, particularly as we have based the whole of our armed liberation struggle on the peasantry. A distinction must be drawn between a physical force and a revolutionary force; physically, the peasantry is a great force in Guinea: it is almost the whole of the population, it controls the nation's wealth, it is the peasantry which produces; but we know from experience what trouble we had convincing the peasantry to fight. This is a problem I shall come back to later; here I should just like to refer to what the previous speaker said about China.

The conditions of the peasantry in China were very different: the peasantry had a history of revolt, but this was not the case in Guinea, and so it was not possible for our party militants and propaganda workers to find the same kind of welcome among the peasantry in Guinea for the idea of national liberation as the idea found in China. All the same, in certain parts of the country and among certain groups we found a very warm welcome, even right at the start. In other groups and in other areas all this had to be won.

Then there are the positions vis-à-vis the struggle of the various groups in the towns to be considered. The Europeans are, in general, hostile to the idea of national liberation; they are the human instruments of the colonial state in our country and they therefore reject a priori any idea of national liberation there. It has to be said that the Europeans most bitterly opposed to the idea of national liberation are the workers, while we have sometimes found considerable sympathy for our struggle among certain members of the European petty bourgeoisie.

As for the Africans, the petty bourgeoisie can be divided into three sub-groups as regards the national liberation struggle. First, there is the petty bourgeoisie which is heavily committed, and compromised by colonialism: this includes most of the higher officials and some members of the liberal professions. Second, there is the group which we perhaps incorrectly call the revolutionary petty bourgeoisie: this is the part of the petty bourgeoisie which is nationalist and which was the source of the idea of the national liberation struggle in Guinea. In between lies the part of the petty bourgeoisie which has never been able to make up its mind between the national liberation struggle and the Portuguese. Next come the wage-earners, which you can compare roughly with the proletariat in European societies, although they are not exactly the same thing: here, too, there is a majority committed to the struggle, but, again, many members of this group were not easy to mobilise – wage-earners who had an extremely petty bourgeois mentality and whose only aim was to defend the little they had already acquired.

Next come the *déclassés*. The really *déclassé* people, the permanent layabouts, the prostitutes and so on have been a great help to the Portuguese police in giving them information; this group has been outrightly against our struggle, perhaps unconsciously so, but nonetheless against our struggle. On the other hand, the particular group I mentioned earlier, for which we have not yet found any precise classification (the group of mainly young people recently arrived from the rural areas with contacts in both the urban and the rural areas) gradually comes to make a comparison between the standard of living of their own families and that of the Portuguese; they begin to understand the sacrifices being borne by the Africans. They have proved extremely dynamic in the struggle. Many of these people joined the struggle right from the beginning and it is among this group that we found many of the cadres whom we have since trained.

The importance of this urban experience lies in the fact that it allows comparison: this is the key stimulant required for the awakening of consciousness. It is interesting to note that Algerian nationalism largely sprang up among the émigré workers in France. As far as Guinea is concerned, the idea of the national liberation struggle was born not abroad but in our own country, in a milieu where people were subjected to close and incessant exploitation. Many people say that it is the peasants who carry the burden of exploitation: this may be true, but so far as the struggle is concerned it must be realised that it is not the degree of suffering and hardship involved as such that matters: even extreme suffering in itself does not necessarily produce the *prise de conscience* required for the national liberation struggle.

In Guinea the peasants are subjected to a kind of exploitation equivalent to slavery. But even if you try and explain to them that they are being exploited and robbed, it is difficult to convince them by means of a technical or economic kind of explanation that they are the most exploited people. Whereas it is easier to convince the workers and the people employed in the towns who earn, say, ten escudos a day for a job in which a European earns between 30 and 50 that they are being subjected to massive exploitation and injustice, because they can see. To take my own case as a member of the petty bourgeois group which launched the struggle in Guinea, I was an agronomist working under a European who everybody knew was one of the biggest idiots in Guinea; I could have taught him his job with my eyes shut but he was the boss: this is something which counts a lot, this is the confrontation which really matters. This is of major importance when considering where the initial idea of the struggle came from.

Another major task was to examine the material interests and the aspirations of each group after the liberation, as well as their revolutionary capacities. As I have already said, we do not consider that the peasantry in Guinea has a revolutionary capacity. First of all, we had to make an analysis of all these groups and of the contradictions between them and within them so as to be able to locate them all vis-à-vis the struggle and the revolution.

The first point is to decide what is the major contradiction at the moment when the struggle begins. For us the main contradiction was that between, on the one hand, the Portuguese and international bourgeoisie which was exploiting our people and on the other hand, the interests of our people. There are also major contradictions within the country itself, i.e. in the internal life of our country. It is our opinion that if we get rid of colonialism in Guinea the main contradiction remaining, the one which will then become the principal contradiction, is that between the ruling classes, the semi-feudal groups, and the members of the groups without any defined form of organisation.

The first thing to note is that the conquest carried out first by the Mandingas and then by the Fulas was a struggle between two opposite poles which was blocked by the very strong structure of the animist groups. There are other contradictions, such as that between the various feudal groups and that between the upper group and the lower. All this is extremely important for the future, and even while the struggle is still going on we must begin to exploit the contradiction between the Fula people and their chiefs, who are very close to the Portuguese. There is a further contradiction, particularly among the animists, between the collective ownership of the land and the private ownership of the means of production in agriculture. I am not trying to stretch alien concepts here, this is an observation that can be made on the spot: the land belongs to the village, but what is produced belongs to whoever produces it – usually the family or the head of the family.

There are other contradictions which we consider secondary: you may be surprised to know that we consider the contradictions between the tribes a secondary one; we could discuss this at length, but we consider that there are many more contradictions between what you might call the economic tribes in the capitalist countries than there are between the ethnic tribes in Guinea. Our struggle for national liberation and the work done by our Party have shown that this contradiction is really not so important; the Portuguese counted on it a lot but as soon as we organised the liberation struggle properly the contradiction between the tribes proved to be a feeble, secondary contradiction.

This does not mean that we do not need to pay attention to this contradiction; we reject both the positions which are to be found in Africa – one which says: there are no tribes, we are all the same, we are all one people in one terrible unity, our party comprises everybody; the other saying: tribes exist, we must base parties on tribes. Our position lies between the two, but at the same time we are fully conscious that this is a problem which must constantly be kept in mind; structural, organisational and other measures must be taken to ensure that this contradiction does not explode and become a more important contradiction.

As for contradictions between the urban and rural areas; I would say that there is no conflict between the towns and the countryside, not least because we are only town dwellers who have just moved from the country; everybody in the towns in Guinea has close relatives in the country and all town dwellers still engage in some peasant activity (growing crops etc.); all the same, there is a potential contradiction between the towns and the countryside which colonialism tries to aggravate.

That, in brief, is the analysis we have made of the situation; this has led us to the following conclusion: we must try to unite everybody in the national liberation struggle against the Portuguese colonialists: this is where our main contradiction lies, but it is also imperative to organise things so that we always have an instrument available which can solve all the other contradictions. This is what convinced us of the absolute necessity of creating a party during the national liberation struggle. There are some people who interpret our Party as a front; perhaps our Party is a front at the moment, but within the framework of the front there is our Party which is directing the front, and there are no other parties in the front. For the circumstances of the struggle we maintain a general aspect, but within the framework of the struggle we know what our Party is, we know where the Party finishes and where the people who just rallied for the liberation struggle begin.

When we had made our analysis, there were still many theoretical and practical problems left in front of us. We had some knowledge of other experiences and we knew that a struggle of the kind we hoped to lead – and win – had to be led by the working class; we looked for the working class in Guinea and did not find it. Other examples showed us that things were begun by some revolutionary intellectuals. What then were we to do? We were just a group of petty bourgeois who were driven by the reality of life in Guinea, by the sufferings we had to endure, and also by the influence events in Africa and elsewhere had on us, in particular the experiences some of us acquired in Portugal and other countries in Europe, to try and do something.

And so this little group began. We first thought of a general movement of national liberation, but this immediately proved unfeasible. We decided to extend our activity to the workers in the towns, and we had some success with this; we launched moves for higher wages, better working conditions and so on. I do not want to go into details here, the only point I want to make is that we obviously did not have a proletariat. We quite clearly lacked revolutionary intellectuals, so we had to start searching, given that we – rightly – did not believe in the revolutionary capacity of the peasantry.

One important group in the towns were the dockworkers; another important group were the people working in the boats carrying merchandise, who mostly live in Bissao itself and travel up and down the rivers. These people proved highly conscious of their position and of their economic importance and they took the initiative of launching strikes without any trade union leadership at all. We therefore decided to concentrate all our work on this group. This gave excellent results and this group soon came to form a kind of nucleus which influenced the attitudes of other wage-earning groups in the towns – workers proper and drivers, who form two other important groups. Moreover, if I may put it this way, we thus found our little proletariat.

We also looked for intellectuals, but there were none, because the Portuguese did not educate people. In any case, what is an intellectual in our country? It could probably be someone who knew the general situation very well, who had some knowledge, not profound theoretical knowledge, but concrete knowledge of the country itself and of its life, as well as of our enemy. We, the people I have talked about, the engineers, doctors, bank clerks and so on, joined together to form a group of *interlocuteurs valables* (valuable informants).

There was also this other group of people in the towns, which we have been unable to classify precisely, which was still closely connected to the rural areas and contained people who spoke almost all the languages that are used in Guinea. They knew all the customs of the rural areas while at the same time possessing a solid knowledge of the European urban centres. They also had a certain degree of self-confidence, they knew how to read and write (which makes a person an intellectual in our country) and so we concentrated our work on these people and immediately started giving them some preparatory training.

We were faced with another difficult problem: we realised that we needed to have people with a mentality which could transcend the context of the national liberation struggle, and so we prepared a number of cadres from the group I have just mentioned, some from the people employed in commerce and other wage-earners, and even some peasants, so that they could acquire what you might call a working-class mentality. You may think this is absurd – in any case it is very difficult; in order for there to be a working-class mentality the material conditions of the working class should exist, a working class should exist. In fact we managed to inculcate these ideas into a large number of people – the kind of ideas, that it, which there would be if there were a working class.

We trained about 1,000 cadres at our party school in Conakry, in fact for about two years this was about all we did outside the country. When these cadres returned to the rural areas they inculcated a certain mentality into the peasants and it is among these cadres that we have chosen the people who are now leading the struggle; we are not a Communist party or a Marxist-Leninist party but the people now leading the peasants in the struggle in Guinea are mostly from the urban milieus and connected with the urban wage-earning group. When I hear that only the peasantry can lead the struggle, am I supposed to think we have made a mistake? All I can say is that at the moment our struggle is going well.

There are all sorts of other generalisations of a political nature, like this generalisation about the peasantry, which keeps on cropping up. There are a number of key words and concepts, there is a certain conditioning in the reasoning of our European friends: for example, when someone thinks, 'revolution', he thinks of the bourgeoisie falling, etc.; when someone thinks 'party', he forgets many things. Yesterday a friend asked me a number of questions about our party and several times I had to say to him, 'but it isn't a European party'; the concept of a party and the creation of parties did not occur spontaneously in Europe, they resulted from a long process of class struggle. When we in Africa think of creating a party now we find ourselves in very different conditions from those in which parties appeared as historic social phenomena in Europe. This has a number of consequences, so when you think 'party', 'single party', etc. you must connect all these things up with the history and conditions of Africa.

A rigorous historical approach is similarly needed when examining another problem related to this – how can the underdeveloped countries evolve towards revolution, towards socialism? There is a preconception held by many people, even on the left, that imperialism made us enter history at the moment when it began its adventure in our countries. This preconception must be denounced:

for somebody on the left, and for Marxists in particular, history obviously means the class struggle. Our opinion is exactly the contrary. We consider that when imperialism arrived in Guinea it made us leave history – our history. We agree that history in our country is the result of class struggle, but we have our own class struggles in our own country; the moment imperialism arrived and colonialism arrived, it made us leave our history and enter another history.

Obviously we agree that the class struggle has continued, but it has continued in a very different way: our whole people is struggling against the ruling class of the imperialist countries, and this gives a completely different aspect to the historical evolution of our country. Somebody has asked which class is the 'agent' of history; here a distinction must be drawn between colonial history and our history as human societies; as a dominated people we only present an ensemble vis-à-vis the oppressor. Each of our peoples or groups of peoples has been subjected to different influences by the colonisers; when there is a developed national consciousness one may ask which social stratum is the agent of history, of colonial history; which is the stratum which will be able to take power into its hands when it emerges from colonial history?

Our answer is that it is all the social strata, if the people who have carried out the national revolution (i.e. the struggle against colonialism) have worked well, since unity of all the social strata is a prerequisite for the success of the national liberation struggle. As we see it, in colonial conditions no one stratum can succeed in the struggle for national liberation on its own, and therefore it is all the strata of society which are the agents of history. This brings us to what should be a void – but in fact it is not. What commands history in colonial conditions is not the class struggle. I do not mean that the class struggle in Guinea stopped completely during the colonial period; it continued, but in a muted way. In the colonial period it is the colonial state which commands history.

Our problem is to see who is capable of taking control of the state apparatus when the colonial power is destroyed. In Guinea the peasants cannot read or write, they have almost no relations with the colonial forces during the colonial period except for paying taxes, which is done indirectly. The working class hardly exists as a defined class, it is just an embryo. There is no *economically viable* bourgeoisie because imperialism prevented it being created. What there is, is a stratum of people in the service of imperialism who have learned how to manipulate the apparatus of the state – the African petty bourgeoisie: this is the only stratum capable of controlling or even utilising the instruments which the colonial state used against our people. So we come to the conclusion that in colonial conditions it is the petty bourgeoisie which is the inheritor of state power (though I wish we could be wrong). The moment national liberation comes and the petty bourgeoisie takes power we enter, or rather return to, history, and thus the internal contradictions break out again.

When this happens, and particularly as things are now, there will be powerful external contradictions conditioning the internal situation, and not just internal contradictions as before. What attitude can the petty bourgeoisie adopt? Obviously people on the left will call for the revolution; the right will call for the 'non-revolution', i.e. a capitalist road or something like that. The petty bourgeoisie can either ally itself with imperialism and the reactionary strata in its own country to try and preserve itself as a petty bourgeoisie or ally itself with the workers and peasants, who must themselves take power or control to make the revolution.

We must be very clear exactly what we are asking the petty bourgeoisie to do. Are we asking it to commit suicide? Because if there is a revolution, then the petty bourgeoisie will have to abandon power to the workers and the peasants and cease to exist *qua* petty bourgeoisie. For a revolution to take place depends on the nature of the party (and its size), the character of the struggle which led up to liberation, whether there was an armed struggle, what the nature of this armed struggle was and how it developed and, of course, on the nature of the state.

Here I would like to say something about the position of our friends on the left; if a petty bourgeoisie comes to power, they obviously demand of it that it carry out a revolution. But the important thing is whether they took the precaution of analysing the position of the petty bourgeoisie during the struggle; did they examine its nature, see how it worked, see what instruments it used and see whether this bourgeoisie committed itself with the left to carrying out a revolution, before the liberation? As you can see, it is the struggle in the underdeveloped countries which endows the petty bourgeoisie with a function; in the capitalist countries the petty bourgeoisie is only a stratum which serves, it does not determine the historical orientation of the country; it merely allies itself with one group or another. So that to hope that the petty bourgeoisie will just carry out a revolution when it comes to power in an underdeveloped country is to hope for a miracle, although it is true that it *could* do this.

This connects with the problem of the true nature of the national liberation struggle. In Guinea, as in other countries, the implantation of imperialism by force and the presence of the colonial system considerably altered the historical conditions and aroused a response – the national liberation struggle – which is generally considered a revolutionary trend; but this is something which I think needs further examination.

I should like to formulate this question: is the national liberation movement something which has simply emerged from within our country, is it a result of the internal contradictions created by the presence of colonialism, or are there external factors which have determined it? And here we have some reservations; in fact I would even go so far as to ask whether, given the advance of socialism in the world, the national liberation movement is not an imperialist initiative. Is the judicial institution which serves as a reference for the right of all peoples to struggle to free themselves a product of the peoples who are trying to liberate themselves? Was it created by the socialist countries who are our historical associates? It is signed by the imperialist countries, it is the imperialist countries who have recognised the right of all peoples to national independence, so I ask myself whether we may not be considering as an initiative of our people what is in fact an initiative of the enemy? Even Portugal, which is using napalm bombs against our people in Guinea, signed the declaration of the right of all peoples to independence. One may well ask oneself why they were so mad as to do something which goes against their own interests – and whether or not it was partly forced on them; the real point is that they signed it.

This is where we think there is something wrong with the simple interpretation of the national liberation movement as a revolutionary trend. The objective of the imperialist countries was to prevent the enlargement of the socialist camp, to liberate the reactionary forces in our countries which were being stifled by colonialism and to enable these forces to ally themselves with the international bourgeoisie. The fundamental objective was to create a bourgeoisie where one did not exist, in order specifically to strengthen the imperialist and the capitalist camp.

This rise of the bourgeoisie in the new countries, far from being at all surprising, should be considered absolutely normal, it is something that has to be faced by all those struggling against imperialism. We are therefore faced with the problem of deciding whether to engage in an out and out struggle against the bourgeoisie right from the start or whether to try and make an alliance with the national bourgeoisie, to try to deepen the absolutely necessary contradiction between the national bourgeoisie and the international bourgeoisie which has promoted the national bourgeoisie to the position it holds.

To return to the question of the nature of the petty bourgeoisie and the role it can play after the liberation, I should like to put a question to you. What would you have thought if Fidel Castro had come to terms with the Americans? Is this possible or not? Is it possible or impossible that the Cuban petty bourgeoisie, which set the Cuban people marching towards revolution, might have come to terms with the Americans? I think this helps to clarify the character of the revolutionary petty bourgeoisie. If I may put it this way, I think one thing that can be said is this: the revolutionary petty bourgeoisie is honest; i.e. in spite of all the hostile conditions, it remains identified with the fundamental interests of the popular masses. To do this it may have to commit [class] suicide, but it will not lose; by sacrificing itself it can reincarnate itself, but in the condition of workers or peasants. In speaking of honesty I am not trying to establish moral criteria for judging the role of the petty bourgeoisie when it is in power; what I mean by honesty, in a political context, is total commitment and total identification with the toiling masses.

Again, the role of the petty bourgeoisie ties up with the possible social and political transformations that can be effected after liberation. We have heard a great deal about the state of national democracy, but although we have made every effort we have thus far been unable to understand what this means; even so, we should like to know what it is all about, as we want to know what we are going to do when we have driven out the Portuguese. Likewise, we have to face the question whether or not socialism can be established immediately after the liberation. This depends on the instruments used to effect the transition to socialism; the essential factor is the nature of the state, bearing in mind that after the liberation there will be people controlling the police, the prisons, the army and so on, and a great deal depends on who they are and what they try to do with these instruments. Thus, we return again to the problem of which class is the agent of history and who are the inheritors of the colonial state in our specific conditions.

I mentioned briefly earlier the question of the attitude of the European left towards the underdeveloped countries, in which there is a good deal of criticism and a good deal of optimism. The criticism reminds me of a story about some lions: there is a group of lions who are shown a picture of a lion lying on the ground and a man holding a gun with his foot on the lion (as everybody knows the lion is proud of being king of the jungle); one of the lions looks at the picture and says, 'If only we lions could paint'. If one of the leaders of one of the new African countries could take time off from the terrible problems in his own country and become a critic of the European left and say all he had to say about the retreat of the revolution in Europe, of a certain apathy in some European countries and of the false hopes which we have all had in certain European groups ...

What really interests us here is neo-colonialism. After the Second World War, imperialism entered on a new phase: on the one hand, it worked out the new policy of aid, i.e. granted independence to the occupied countries plus 'aid' and, on the other hand, concentrated on preferential investment in the European countries; this was, above all, an attempt at rationalising imperialism. Even if it has not yet provoked reactions of a nationalist kind in the European countries, we are convinced that it will soon do so. As we see it, neo-colonialism (which we may call rationalised imperialism) is more of a defeat for the international working class than for the colonised peoples. Neo-colonialism is at work on two fronts – in Europe as well as in the under-developed countries. Its current framework in the under-developed countries is the policy of aid, and one of the essential aims of this policy is to create a false bourgeoisie to put a brake on the revolution and to enlarge the possibilities of the petty bourgeoisie as a neutraliser of the revolution; at the same time it invests capital in France, Italy, Belgium, England and so on. In our opinion the aim of this is to stimulate the growth of a workers' aristocracy, to enlarge the field of action of the petty bourgeoisie so as to block the revolution. In our opinion it is under this aspect that neo-colonialism and the relations between the international working-class movement and our movements must be analysed.

If there have ever been any doubts about the close relations between our struggle and the struggle of the international working-class movement, neo-colonialism has proved that there need not be any. Obviously, I don't think it is possible to forge closer relations between the peasantry in Guinea and the working-class movement in Europe; what we must do first is try and forge closer links between the peasant movement and the wage-earners' movement in our own country. The example of Latin America gives you a good idea of the limits on closer relations; in Latin America you have an old neo-colonial situation and a chance to see clearly the relations between the North American proletariat and the Latin American masses. Other examples could be found nearer home.

There is, however, another aspect I should like to raise and that is that the European left has an intellectual responsibility to study the concrete conditions in our country and help us in this way, as we have very little documentation, very few intellectuals, very little chance to do this kind of work ourselves, and yet it is of key importance: this is a major contribution you can make. Another thing you can do is to support the really revolutionary national liberation movements by all possible means. You must analyse and study these movements and combat in Europe, by all possible means, everything which can be used to further the repression against our peoples. I refer especially to the sale of arms. I should like to say to our Italian friends that we have captured a lot of Italian arms from the Portuguese, not to mention French arms, of course. Moreover, you must unmask courageously all the national liberation movements which are under the thumb of imperialism. People whisper that so-and-so is an American agent, but nobody in the European left has taken a violent and open attitude against these people; it is we ourselves who have to try and denounce these people, who are sometimes even those accepted by the rest of Africa, and this creates a lot of trouble for us.

I think that the left and the international working-class movement should confront those states which claim to be socialist with their responsibilities; this does not of course, mean cutting off all their possibilities of action, but it does mean denouncing all those states which are neo-colonialist.

To end, I should just like to make one last point about solidarity between the international working-class movement and our national liberation struggle. There are two alternatives: either we admit that there really is a struggle against imperialism which interests everybody, or we deny it. If, as would seem from all the evidence, imperialism exists and is trying simultaneously to dominate the working class in all the advanced countries and smother the national liberation movements in all the underdeveloped countries, then there is only one enemy against whom we are fighting. If we are fighting together, then I think the main aspect of our solidarity is extremely simple: it is to fight – I don't think there is any need to discuss this very much. We are struggling in Guinea with guns in our hands, you must struggle in your countries as well – I don't say with guns in your hands, I'm not going to tell you how to struggle, that's your business;

but you must find the best means and the best forms of fighting against our common enemy: this is the best form of solidarity.

There are, of course, other secondary forms of solidarity: publishing material, sending medicine, etc.; I can guarantee you that if tomorrow we make a breakthrough and you are engaged in an armed struggle against imperialism in Europe we will send you some medicine too.

Tell No Lies, Claim No Easy Victories ...

Extracts from a PAIGC directive, 1965.

Always bear in mind that the people are not fighting for ideas, for the things in anyone's head. They are fighting to win material benefits, to live better and in peace, to see their lives go forward, to guarantee the future of their children ...

We should recognise as a matter of conscience that there have been many faults and errors in our action whether political or military: an important number of things we should have done we have not done at the right times, or not done at all.

In various regions – and indeed everywhere in a general sense – political work among the people and among our armed forces has not been done appropriately: responsible workers have not carried or have not been able to carry through the work of mobilisation, formation and political organisation defined by the party leadership.[9] Here and there, even among responsible workers, there has been a marked tendency to let things slide ... and even a certain demobilisation which has not been fought and eliminated ...

On the military plane, many plans and objectives established by the Party leadership have not been achieved. With the means we have, we could do much more and better. Some responsible workers have misunderstood the functions of the army and guerilla forces, have not made good co-ordination between these two and, in certain cases, have allowed themselves to be influenced by preoccupation with the defence of our positions, ignoring the fact that, for us, attack is the best means of defence ...

And with all this as a proof of insufficient political work among our armed forces, there has appeared a certain attitude of 'militarism' which has caused some fighters and even some leaders to forget the fact that we are *armed militants* and not *militarists*. This tendency must be urgently fought and eliminated within the army ...

If ten men go to a rice field and do the day's work of eight, there's no reason to be satisfied. It's the same in battle. Ten men fight like eight; that's not enough ... One can always do more. Some people get used to the war, and once you get used to a thing it's the end: you get a bullet up the spout of your gun and you

---

9   *Editor's note*: The word *responsavel* used in the original Portuguese is translated in this collection as 'responsible worker' or 'supervisor'.

walk around. You hear the motor on the river and you don't use the bazooka that you have, so the Portuguese boats pass unharmed. Let me repeat: one can do more. We have to throw the Portuguese out …

… Create schools and spread education in all liberated areas. Select young people between 14 and 20, those who have at least completed their fourth year, for further training. Oppose without violence all prejudicial customs, the negative aspects of the beliefs and traditions of our people. Oblige every responsible and educated member of our Party to work daily for the improvement of their cultural formation …

Oppose among the young, especially those over 20, the mania for leaving the country so as to study elsewhere, the blind ambition to acquire a degree, the complex of inferiority and the mistaken idea which leads to the belief that those who study or take courses will thereby become privileged in our country tomorrow … But also oppose any ill will towards those who study or wish to study the complex that students will be parasites or future saboteurs of the Party …

In the liberated areas, do everything possible to normalise the political life of the people. Section committees of the Party (*tabanca* [village] committees), zonal committees, regional committees, must be consolidated and function normally. Frequent meetings must be held to explain to the population what is happening in the struggle, what the Party is endeavouring to do at any given moment, and what the criminal intentions of the enemy may be.

In regions still occupied by the enemy, reinforce clandestine work, the mobilisation and organisation of the populations, and the preparation of militants for action and support of our fighters …

Develop political work in our armed forces, whether regular or guerilla, wherever they may be. Hold frequent meetings. Demand serious political work from political commissars. Start political committees, formed by the political commissar and commander of each unit in the regular army.

Oppose tendencies to militarism and make each fighter an exemplary militant of our Party.

Educate ourselves, educate other people, the population in general, to fight fear and ignorance, to eliminate little by little the subjection to nature and natural forces which our economy has not yet mastered. Convince little by little, in particular the militants of the Party, that we shall end by conquering the fear of nature, and that man is the strongest force in nature.

Demand from responsible Party members that they dedicate themselves seriously to study, that they interest themselves in the things and problems of our daily life and struggle in their fundamental and essential aspect, and not simply in their appearance … Learn from life, learn from our people, learn from books, learn from the experience of others. Never stop learning.

Responsible members must take life seriously, conscious of their responsibilities, thoughtful about carrying them out, and with a comradeship based on work and duty done … Nothing of this is incompatible with the joy of living, or with love for life and its amusements, or with confidence in the future and in our work ...

Reinforce political work and propaganda within the enemy's armed forces. Write posters, pamphlets, letters. Draw slogans on the roads. Establish cautious links with enemy personnel who want to contact us. Act audaciously and with great initiative in this way ... Do everything possible to help enemy soldiers to desert. Assure them of security so as to encourage their desertion. Carry out political work among Africans who are still in enemy service, whether civilian or military. Persuade these brothers to change direction so as to serve the Party within enemy ranks or desert with arms and ammunition to our units. We must practice revolutionary democracy in every aspect of our Party life. Every responsible member must have the courage of his responsibilities, exacting from others a proper respect for his work and properly respecting the work of others. Hide nothing from the masses of our people. Tell no lies. Expose lies whenever they are told. Mask no difficulties, mistakes, failures. Claim no easy victories ...

A Historic Lesson: Pidjiguiti

A radio message to the people of Guinea and Cape Verde Islands and members of the PAIGC's armed forces, sent by Amìlcar Cabral, Secretary-General, on 3 August 1965, the 6th anniversary of the massacre of Pidjiguiti. Published in Libertação, *journal of the PAIGC, in the supplement to No. 57, August 1965.*

Exactly six years ago, on 3 August 1959, the Portuguese colonialists committed one of the greatest crimes against our defenceless population. On the wharfs of Pidjiguiti, in the port of Bissau, the agents of the Portuguese colonialists (troops, police, and some armed settlers) shot and killed, in less than a half hour, 50 African workers on strike and wounded more than a hundred...

The massacre of 3 August was, however, more than a crime by the Portuguese colonialists, more than an act of patriotic heroism on the part of our working people. The events of 3 August were a historic lesson for our African people and for the leadership of our party.

In truth, the massacre on the quays of Pidjiguiti showed our people and our national party the true path to pursue in our liberation struggle. With the glorious and useful sacrifice of the workers assassinated in Pidjiguiti, we learned that, faced with the criminal character and lack of scruples of the Portuguese colonialists, we have to mobilise our people, both in Guinea and Cape Verde, unite them around our party, organise them, and prepare them for the struggle. We learned also that our struggle must not be waged in the cities and that, faced with the arms of the Portuguese colonialists, the only form of struggle we can wage is *armed struggle*.

A Situation of Permanent Violence

Excerpt of testimony to the Subcommittee on Foreign Affairs of the US House of Representatives, chaired by Rep. Charles C. Diggs Jr., on 26 February 1970.

We tried during the years of 1950, 1953, 1954, 1955 and 1956 to convince the Portuguese government that it was necessary to change. In that moment, even we didn't think about independence. We hoped in that moment to change, to have civil rights, to be men, not treated like animals in general, because the Portuguese divided us into two groups, the indigenous people and the *assimilado* people.

At that moment, after the adoption of the resolution in the United Nations granting independence for all colonies, the Portuguese changed a little on paper, but not in practice.

We wanted at that moment, when we were beginning to demand our rights, to pass from the situation of second-class Portuguese to Portuguese like Portuguese. We received, as answer, only repression, imprisonment, torture and in 1959 after the creation of our party. When we called a strike in the Port of Bissau, the Portuguese troops killed about 50 workers in 20 minutes and wounded more than 100. This massacre showed us that all was not well, it was not good, it was not intelligent to fight against the Portuguese with empty hands.

We did not want, absolutely not, to resort to violence, but we realised that the colonial Portuguese domination was a situation of permanent violence. Against our aspirations they systematically answered with violence, with crimes, and we decided in that moment to prepare ourselves to fight.

In that moment, as you know, sir, Africa began to become independent. The 'wind of change' was blowing over Africa. The other colonial powers decided to decolonialise. Portugal signed the United Nations Charter and later Portugal voted for the proclamation of the right for independence of all people.

But Portugal never accepted the practical application this international decision. Portugal insisted, the Portuguese government insisted that we were provinces of Portugal.

If in the beginning of our colonial life we were exactly like the Portuguese, we had all the rights the Portuguese had, maybe it would be possible to convince us that we were Portuguese in the Portuguese provinces. But in our country, we never had rights, the minimum rights of man, and in that moment, it was very late to convince us that our country was a Portuguese province.

We saw Africa beginning with independence, in many African states, and we decided to do our best also to get our right to self-determination and independence. That is the reason for seven years of fighting.

We have liberated more than two-thirds of the country. In the liberated areas of our country, facing the Portuguese bombs, we are trying to build a new life. In the liberated areas, for example – I can tell you that all of this has been confirmed by journalists and filmmakers and writers, like some men from Sweden and other countries that have been in our country for one, two, or more months. We have organised the education, the services of education. We have now more than 130 schools. The Portuguese, in all Guinea, in the time of colonialism, had 45 missionary schools, so-called elementary schools, and 11 official schools.

We have now about 15,000 children in the schools. Before, in my country there were only 2,000 school children, but the indigenous people – that is, 99.7 per cent of the population – couldn't go to their official schools, only to the missionary schools.

Now, in our country, we have established in the liberated areas, in spite of the bombing, permanent bombing by Portuguese planes, four hospitals – not very nice hospitals, but what we can do in this stage of our life. We have trained nurses during these years, more than 250 nurses, men and women. We have more than 100 sanitary posts in order not only to assist the wounded or sick fighters, but to assist the population of the liberated regions.

We have organised and developed in the liberated regions, our party, our political organisation, our administration, and in this moment, we can say that our country is like a state of which a part of the national territory is yet occupied by the colonial forces.

Portugal controls only the urban centres and some little parts in the country-side. We control the major part of the countryside, and in the contested regions we are fighting each day in order to complete the liberation of our country.

One can ask how Portugal, an underdeveloped country also, one of the most backward in Europe which has some regions with more than 46 per cent of illiterates – I am referring to official figures – how can Portugal fight all of these colonial wars in my country, in Angola and in Mozambique?

The Portuguese people are progressively realising that colonial wars are not only against the African people, but also against their own interests.

We think that with this war the Portuguese government is losing or making it possible to lose one of the best chances Portugal has in history, because our hopes were and still are, in spite of all the crimes against our people, that we could, in independence, like an African people, develop the best relations with Portugal, even to study and to decide together some problems concerning the development of our country and the progress of our peoples.

Our Solidarities

Excerpt from an interview at the Second Conference of the CONCP, 3–8 October 1965. Translated from French.

In international politics, the CONCP stands for a policy of non-alignment. This is the policy which is most compatible with the interests of our peoples in the present stage of our history. We are certain of it. But for us non-alignment does not mean turning our back on the fundamental problems concerning humanity and justice. For us, non-alignment means not to be drawn into blocs, not to follow the lines drawn by others. We reserve for ourselves the right to make our own decisions, and if by chance our options, or decisions, coincide with those of others, this is not our responsibility.

We support the policy of non-alignment but we also consider ourselves deeply committed to our people and to every just cause in the world. We consider ourselves as part of a broad front of struggle for the good of humanity. You will understand that we fight first of all for our peoples. This is our task in this common struggle. And that has implications in terms of solidarity. We in the CONCP are strongly committed to every just cause. This is why we, from FRELIMO, MPLA, PAIGC, CLSTP, or from any mass movement affiliated to the CONCP, beat our hearts in unison with those of our brothers from Viet Nam who give us a unique example in fighting the most scandalous, the most unjustifiable imperialist aggression of the United States of America against the peaceful Vietnamese people. Our hearts beat also with those of our brothers from the Congo who, in the jungles of such a vast and rich country, seek to resolve their own problems but are faced with imperialist aggression and imperialist manoeuvres via puppets. Thus, we from the CONCP, loudly and strongly proclaim that we are against Tshombe, against all the Tshombes of Africa. Our hearts beat just as strongly with our brothers in Cuba who have also shown how a people, even surrounded by the sea, can victoriously defend its fundamental interests with arms, and decide its own destiny. We are with the Blacks from America, we are with them in the streets of Los Angeles, and when they are denied any possibility of a decent life, we suffer with them.

We are with the refugees, the martyred refugees of Palestine who have been ridiculed, and expelled from their homeland by imperialist manoeuvres. We stand with the Palestinian refugees and we support everything that the children of Palestine do in order to free their country, and we support with all our might all that the Arab and African countries do to aid the Palestinian people to recover its dignity, its independence, and its right to life. We are also with the peoples of South Arabia, of so-called French Somaliland (Somali Coast), of so-called Spanish Guinea, and we side with understanding and sorrow with our brothers from South Africa who confront the most barbaric of racial discriminations.

We are absolutely positive that the development of struggle in the Portuguese colonies and the victory which we are attaining every day against Portuguese colonialism is a significant contribution towards the liquidation of that shameful and vile regime of racial discrimination in South Africa, *apartheid*. We are also sure that peoples such as those of Angola, Mozambique, and we ourselves in Guinea and Cape Verde though distant from South Africa, will one day be able to play a very important role in the final liquidation of the last bastion of colonialism, imperialism and racism in Africa, which is South Africa.

Our solidarity goes to every just cause in the world, but we also derive strength from the solidarity of others. We have concrete help from many people, many friends, many brothers. I would only like to tell you that we, in the CONCP, have a fundamental principle which consists in counting above all on our own efforts, our own sacrifices. But, in the objective framework of Portuguese colonisation, dear friends, we are also aware that our struggle is not solely ours in the present stage of man's history. It is one which comprises all of Africa, all of progressive humanity. This is why we from the CONCP, confronting the peculiar difficulties of our struggle, and in the context of current history, have realised the need for concrete help in what concerns Africa, of concrete help from every progressive force in the world. We accept all help, regardless of where it may come from, but we never ask for help just from anybody. We expect only that aid which each is able to offer to our struggle. This is our *ethic* of help.

We wish to tell you that it is a duty for us to say here clearly and loudly that we do have solid allies in the socialist countries. We all know that the African peoples are our brothers. Our struggle is theirs. Every drop of blood that we shed falls also from the body and heart of these African peoples, our African brothers. But we also know that since the Socialist Revolution and the events following World War II, the world has definitely changed. A socialist camp has emerged in the world.

This has completely changed the balance of forces, and this socialist camp is today quite aware of its international duties, its historic moral duties, not moral ones because the peoples of the socialist countries have never exploited the colonial peoples. They have shown themselves to be conscious of their duty and it is for this reason that it is an honour to tell you here openly that we receive substantial effective aid from these countries, which reinforces that which we receive from our African friends. If there are people who will be unhappy to hear me say this, may they come also to help us in our struggle. But may they be sure that we are proud of our sovereignty.

We will maintain our position: we take help from anyone. And we will take help from the socialist countries because they show today the path which serves man, the path of justice. In this room there are representatives from socialist countries who have come here as friends. I would like to take advantage of this opportunity to tell the representatives of the Soviet Union and of China, those of Yugoslavia and of the German Democratic Republic, who are here as the representatives of the socialist countries, to please convey our gratitude for the concrete aid which their peoples give us in our struggle.

And those who do not like to hear us talk of the aid of socialist countries, what have they been helping us do? They aid Portugal, the fascist and colonialist government of Salazar.[10] It is no longer a secret to anyone that Portugal, the Portuguese government, would not be able to lead a struggle against us if it did not or could not have access to the help from its allies in NATO.

---

10 *Editor's note*: António de Oliveira Salazar was Prime Minister of Portugal from 1932–1968.

The Weapon of Theory

Speech delivered on behalf of the peoples and nationalist organisations of the Portuguese colonies to the First Solidarity Conference of the Peoples of Africa, Asia and Latin America (Havana, Cuba, 3–12 January 1966) in the plenary session on 6 January.

PRESUPPOSITIONS AND OBJECTIVES OF NATIONAL LIBERATION IN RELATION TO SOCIAL STRUCTURE

The peoples and nationalist organisations of Angola, Cape Verde, Guiné, Mozambique and São Tomé and Príncipe sent their delegations to this Conference for two main purposes: first, because we wish to attend and take active part in this epoch-making event in the history of mankind; second, because it was our political and moral duty to bring the Cuban people clear evidence of our fraternal combatant solidarity at this doubly historic moment – the seventh anniversary of the revolution and the first Tricontinental Conference.

Allow me, therefore, on behalf of our struggling peoples and on behalf of the militants of each of our national organisations, to offer warmest congratulations and fraternal greetings to the people of this tropical island on the seventh anniversary of the triumph of their revolution, on the holding of this Conference in their beautiful and hospitable capital and on the successes they have been able to attain on the path to building a new life. This last has the essential aim of achieving in full the aspirations for freedom, peace, progress and social justice felt by all Cubans. I hail in particular the Central Committee of the Cuban Communist Party, the Revolutionary Government and its exemplary leader – Commandant Fidel Castro – to whom I express our wishes for continued success and long life in the service of his country, Cuba, and the progress and happiness of its people, and in the service of mankind.

If any of us, when we reached Cuba, brought any doubt about the deep-rootedness, strength, maturity and vitality of the Cuban Revolution, such doubt was swept away by what we have had the chance to see. Unshakable confidence warms our hearts and encourages us in the hard but glorious struggle against the common enemy.

No power in the world will be able to destroy the Cuban Revolution, which is creating in the countryside and the cities not only a new life but also – what is more important – a new Man, fully conscious of his national, continental and international rights and duties. In all fields of activity, the Cuban people have made significant progress in the past seven years, especially in the last year – Agriculture Year. This progress is demonstrated in material and daily reality and in the Cuban men and women, in their calm confidence as they face a world in effervescence, where contradictions and threats, but hopes and certainties as well, have reached an unprecedented pitch.

From what we have seen and are learning in Cuba, we should like to mention here a particular lesson which we think contains one of the secrets, if not the secret, of what many would not hesitate to call 'the Cuban miracle': the communion, identification, harmony, mutual confidence and loyalty between the mass of the people and their leaders. Anyone who was present at the mass rallies of the past few days and, in particular, heard Commandant Fidel Castro's speech during the seventh anniversary commemoration, we have measured, as we did, in all its grandeur the specific – perhaps decisive – character of this primordial factor in the success of the Cuban Revolution.

The vanguard of the Cuban Revolution has mobilised, organised and politically educated the people, kept them permanently informed about national and international questions which affect their life and made them take active part in answering these questions. The vanguard, which soon understood that the dynamic existence of a strong and united Party was indispensable, has been able not only to interpret correctly the objective conditions and specific demands of the environment, but also to forge the most powerful of weapons for defence, security and guarantee of continuity for the Revolution: *revolutionary consciousness of the mass of the people*. The latter, as we know, is not and never was spontaneous in any part of the world. We believe that this teaches us all a lesson, but especially a lesson for the national liberation movements, and specifically for those who aim that their national revolution should be a Revolution.

Some will not fail to note that certain Cubans, albeit an insignificant minority, have not shared the joys and hopes of the celebrations for the seventh anniversary, because they are against the Revolution. We realise that it is possible that some others will not attend the commemorations of the next anniversary, but we want to state that we regard the policy of 'an open door for the departure of enemies of the Revolution' as a lesson in courage, determination, humanity and confidence in the people, and as a further political and moral victory over the enemy.

To those who, in a friendly way, are concerned about the dangers this departure could represent, we guarantee that we, the peoples of the African countries still partly or wholly dominated by Portuguese colonialism, are ready to send to Cuba as many men and women as may be needed to compensate for the departure of those who, for reasons of class or inadaptability, have interests and attitudes incompatible with the interests of the Cuban people.

Retracing the once sad and tragic path of our forefathers (notably from Guiné and Angola), who were shipped to Cuba as slaves, we would come now as free men, as willing workers and as Cuban patriots, to fulfil a productive role in this new, just and multiracial society, to help defend with our own blood the conquests by the Cuban people. But we would come also as much to strengthen the bonds of history, blood and culture that unite our peoples to the Cuban people, as to enjoy the magical relaxation, the gut rejoicing and the infectious rhythm which make the building of socialism in Cuba a new phenomenon for the world, a unique and for many, unfamiliar event.

We are not going to use this platform to vilify imperialism. There is an African proverb very common in our country – where fire is still an important tool and a treacherous friend – that shows the state of under-development in which colonialism is going to leave us. This proverb goes: 'When your hut is burning, it is no use beating the tom-tom.' In a Tricontinental dimension, this means that we are not going to succeed in eliminating imperialism by shouting or by slinging insults, spoken or written, at it. For us, the worst or best we can say about imperialism, whatever its form, is to take up arms and struggle. That is what we are doing and will go on doing until foreign domination has been totally eliminated from our African countries.

We came here determined to provide this Conference with as detailed information as possible on the specific situation of the national liberation struggle in each of our countries and particularly in those where there is armed struggle. We shall do this before the appropriate committee and through documents, films, photographs, bilateral contacts and the Cuban information media in the course of the Conference.

We ask your indulgence to use this occasion in the way that we think most useful. It is true that we came to this Conference convinced that it provided a rare opportunity for a broad exchange of views between combatants in the same cause, for study and solution of problems central to our common struggle, with the aim not only of strengthening our unity and solidarity, but also of improving the thought and action of each of us in the daily practice of struggle. That is why, as we want to avoid anything which might be a waste of time, we are quite determined not to allow any extraneous factors, or factors not directly connected with the questions which should concern us here, to disturb the chances for success of this Conference. We are justified in saying that this is the position taken by all the other national liberation movements represented at this Conference.

Our agenda includes topics whose importance and acuteness are beyond doubt and in which one concern is predominant: *The Struggle*. We note, however, that one type of struggle we regard as fundamental is not explicitly mentioned in this agenda, although we are sure that it was present in the minds of those who drew it up. We are referring to *the struggle against our own weaknesses*. We admit that other cases may differ from ours. Our experience in the broad framework of the daily struggle we wage has shown us that, whatever difficulties the enemy may create, the aforenamed is the most difficult struggle for the present and the future of our peoples. This struggle is the expression of the internal contradictions in the economic, social and cultural (therefore historical) reality of each of our countries. We are convinced that any national or social revolution which is not founded on adequate knowledge of this reality runs grave risks of poor results or of being doomed to failure.

ABSENCE OF IDEOLOGY

When African people say, in their plain language, that 'no matter how hot the water from the well, it will not cook your rice', they express with staggering simplicity a basic principle not only of physics but also of political science. We know in fact that the unfolding behaviour (development) of a phenomenon-in-motion, whatever its external conditioning, depends mainly on its internal characteristics. We also know that on the political level – however fine and attractive the reality of others may be – we can only truly transform our own reality, on the basis of detailed knowledge of it and our own efforts and sacrifices.

It is worth recalling at this Tricontinental gathering, so rich in experiences and examples, that however great the similarity between our cases and however identical our enemies, unfortunately or fortunately, national liberation and social revolution are not exportable commodities. They are (and increasingly so every day) a local, national, product – more or less influenced by (favourable and unfavourable) external factors, but essentially determined and conditioned by the historical reality of each people. Victory is only achieved by the adequate resolution of the various internal contradictions characterising this reality. The success of the Cuban Revolution, taking place only ninety miles from the biggest imperialist and anti-socialist power of all time, seems to us, in the form and content of its evolution, a practical and conclusive illustration of validity of this stated principle.

We must however recognise that we ourselves and the other liberation movements in general (we are referring here above all to the African experience) have not been able to pay sufficient attention to this significant question of our common struggle.

The ideological deficiency, not to say the total lack of ideology, on the part of the national liberation movements – which is basically explained by ignorance of the historical reality which these movements aspire to transform – constitutes one of the greatest weaknesses, if not the greatest weakness, of our struggle against imperialism. We nevertheless believe that a sufficient number of varied experiences have already been accumulated to enable us to define a general line of thought and action in order to eliminate this deficiency. A full discussion of this matter could therefore be useful, and would enable this Conference to make a valuable contribution towards improving the present and future action of the national liberation movements. This would be a practical way of helping these movements and, in our opinion, no less important than political support and assistance with money, weapons and other material.

It is with the intention of contributing, although modestly, to this discussion, that we present here our view *on presuppositions and objectives of national liberation in relation to social structure*. This view is shaped by our own experience of struggle and by a critical appreciation of the experiences of others. To those who see this view as being theoretical, we would recall that every practice gives birth to a theory. If it is true that a revolution can fail, even though it be nurtured on perfectly conceived theories, nobody has yet successfully practised Revolution without a revolutionary theory.

THE CLASS STRUGGLE

Those who assert – and in our view rightly – that the motive force of history is the class struggle, would certainly agree to re-examining this assertion to make it more precise and give it even wider application, if they had a deeper knowledge of the essential characteristics of some of the colonised peoples (dominated by imperialism). In fact, in the general evolution of mankind and of each of the peoples in the human groups of which it is composed, classes appear neither as a generalised and simultaneous phenomenon throughout all these groups, nor as a finished, perfect, uniform and spontaneous whole.

The formation of classes within one or more human groups is basically the result of progressive development of the productive forces and the way in which the wealth produced by this group – or usurped by other groups – is distributed. This means: the socio-economic phenomenon *class* arises and develops as a function of at least two essential and interdependent variables: the level of productive forces and the system of ownership of the means of production. This development takes place slowly, unevenly and gradually, by generally imperceptible quantitative increases in the essential variables. Once a certain point has been reached in the process of accumulation, it then leads to qualitative changes which are shown by the appearance of class, classes and class conflict.

Factors external to a given dynamic socio-economic whole can have a more or less significant bearing on the process of development of classes, speeding it up, slowing it down or even causing regressions in it. When, for whatever reason, the influence of these factors ceases, the process recovers its independence, and its rhythm is then determined not only by the specific internal characteristics of the whole, but also by the resultants of the temporary action of the external factors. On a strictly internal level, the rhythm of the process may vary, but it remains continuous and progressive. Abrupt advances are only possible as a function of abrupt rises or alterations – mutations – in the level of productive forces or in the system of ownership. These abrupt transformations carried out within the process of development of classes, as a result of mutations in the level of productive forces or in the system of ownership, are, in the convention of economic and political language, called *revolutions*.

Clearly, however, the possibilities for external factors, especially the interaction of human groups, to have a significant bearing on this process was considerably increased by the advance in means of transport and communications. This advance has made one world and mankind, by eliminating the isolation of human groups within one area, of areas within one continent and of continents. The advance, characteristic of a long historical period which began with the invention of the first means of transport, was already more evident with the voyages of the Carthaginians and Greek colonisation, and was accentuated by maritime discoveries, the invention of the steam engine and the discovery of electricity. In our own times with the progressive harnessing of atomic energy, it is possible to promise, if not to sow man across the stars, at least to humanise the universe.

What has been said enables us to pose the following question: does history begin only from the *moment* of the launching of the phenomenon of class and consequently, of class struggle? To reply in the affirmative would be to place outside history the whole period of life of human groups from the discovery of hunting, and later of nomadic and sedentary agriculture, to cattle raising and to the private appropriation of land. It would also be to consider – and this we refuse to accept – that various human groups in Africa, Asia and Latin America were living without history or outside history at the moment when they were subjected to the yoke of imperialism. It would be to consider that the populations of our countries, such as the Balanta of Guiné, the Cuanhama of Angola and the Makonde of Mozambique, are still living today – if we abstract the very slight influence of colonialism to which they have been subjected – outside history, or that they have no history.

Our refusal, based as it is on detailed knowledge of the socio-economic reality of our countries and on analysis of the process of development of the phenomenon of class as we saw earlier, leads us to conclude that if class struggle is the motive force of history, it is so in a specific historical period. This means that *before* the class struggle (and, necessarily, *after* the class struggle, since in this world there is no before without an after) some factor (or several factors) was and will be the motive force of history. We have no hesitation in saying that this factor in the history of each human group is the *mode of production* (the level of productive forces and the system of ownership) characteristic of that group. But, as we have seen, the definition of class and class struggle are themselves the result of the development of productive forces in conjunction with the system of ownership of the means of production. It therefore seems permissible to conclude that the level of productive forces, the essential determinant of the content and form of class struggle, is the true and permanent motive force of history.

If we accept this conclusion, then the doubts in our minds are cleared away. Because if on the one hand we can see that the existence of history before the class struggle is safeguarded, and we thus avoid for some human groups in our countries (and perhaps in our continents) the sad position of being peoples without history, then on the other hand we can see that history has continuity even after the disappearance of class struggle or of classes. And as it was not we who, on scientific bases, postulated the disappearance of classes as a historical inevitability, we can feel content with this conclusion. To a certain extent it re-establishes coherence and at the same time gives to those peoples who, like the people of Cuba, are building socialism the agreeable certainty that they will not cease to have a history when they complete the process of elimination of the phenomenon of class and class struggle within their socio-economic whole. Eternity is not of this world, but man will outlive classes and will continue to produce and to make history, since he can never free himself from the burden of his needs, of hand and brain, which are the basis of the development of productive forces.

ON THE MODE OF PRODUCTION

The foregoing and contemporary reality enable us to state that the history of a human group or of mankind goes through at least three stages. In the first, corresponding to a low level of productive forces – of man's mastery over nature – the mode of production is of rudimentary character; private appropriation of the means of production does not yet exist, there are no classes, nor, consequently, is there class struggle. In the second, when the raising of the level of productive forces leads to private appropriation of the means of production, the mode of production is progressively more compli- cated; conflicts of interest are provoked within the dynamic socio-economic whole, the eruption of the phenomenon of class and hence of class struggle is possible, as the social expression of the contradiction in the economic field between the mode of production and the private appropriation of the means of production. In the third stage, once a given level of productive forces is reached, the elimination of private appropriation as the means of production is made possible and is carried out; the phenomenon of class, and hence of class struggle, is removed and new and unknown forces in the historical process of the socio-economic whole are unleashed.

In politico-economic language, the first stage would correspond to the communal agricultural and cattle raising society, in which the social structure is horizontal, without a State. The second stage would correspond to agrarian societies (feudal or assimilated and agro-industrial bourgeois societies), in which the social structure develops vertically, with a State. The third stage would correspond to socialist and communist societies, in which the economy is mainly, if not exclusively, industrial (since agriculture itself becomes an industry), and in which the State tends progressively to disappear or actually disappears: the social structure returns to developing horizontally, at a higher level of productive forces, social relations and appreciation of human values.

At the level of mankind or of parts of mankind (human groups within one area or of one or more continents), these three stages (or two of them) can be concomitant, as is shown as much by the current reality as by the past. This is the result of the uneven development of human societies, whether caused by internal reasons or by one or more external factors speeding up or slowing down their evolution. On the other hand, in the historical process of a given socio-economic whole, each of the stages mentioned contains, once a certain level of transformation is reached, the seeds of the following stage.

We should also note that, in the present stage of the life of mankind and for a given socio-economic whole, the sequence in time of the three distinct stages is not indispensable. Whatever its present level of productive forces and characteristic social structure, a society can progress rapidly, through defined steps appropriate to the specific local (historical and human) realities, to a higher stage of existence. Such progress depends on the specific possibilities for the development of the society's productive forces and is mainly conditional on the nature of the political power ruling that society, that is on the type of state or, if we like, on the nature of the dominant class or classes within the society.

A more detailed analysis would show that the possibility of such a *leap* in the historical process is basically a result, in the economic field, of the power of the means available nowadays to man for the mastery of nature, and, in the political field, of the new event that has radically changed the face of the world and the march of history – *the creation of socialist states*.

We see, therefore, that our peoples have their own history, whatever the stages of their economic development. When they underwent imperialist domination, the historical process of each of our peoples (or of the human groups of which each is composed) was subjected to the violent action of an external factor. This action – the impact of imperialism in our societies – could not fail to influence the process of development of the productive forces of our countries and the social structures of our peoples, as well as the content and form of our national liberation struggles.

But we also see that, in the historical context in which these struggles develop, our people have the specific possibility of going from their present situation of exploitation and under development to a new stage of their historical process, which can lead them to a higher form of economic, social and cultural existence.

IMPERIALISM

The political report drawn up by the International Preparatory Committee of this Conference, for which we reaffirm our complete support, placed imperialism, clearly and by succinct analysis, in its economic context and historical position. We will not repeat here what has already been said before this assembly. We shall merely say that imperialism may be defined as the worldwide expression of the profit motive and the ever-increasing accumulation of *surplus values* by monopoly financial capital, in two regions of the world: first in Europe and, later, in North America. And if we wish to place the fact of imperialism within the general direction of the evolution of the epoch-making factor that has changed the face of the world – capital and the process of its accumulation – we might say that imperialism is piracy transplanted from the seas to dry land, piracy reorganised, consolidated and adapted with the aim of plundering the natural and human resources of our peoples. But if we can calmly analyse the phenomenon of imperialism, we shall not shock anybody if we have to admit that imperialism, which everything goes to show is really the last stage in the evolution of capitalism, was a historical necessity, a consequence of the development of productive forces and the transformations of the mode of production, in the general context of mankind, considered as a dynamic whole. This is a necessity like those today of the national liberation of peoples, the destruction of capitalism and the advent of socialism.

The important thing for our peoples is to know whether imperialism, in its role as capital in action, has or has not fulfilled in our countries its historical mission: the speeding up of the process of development of the productive forces and transformation in the direction of increasing complexity of the characteristics of the mode of production; sharpening class differentiation with the development of the bourgeoisie and intensification of class struggle; and appreciably raising average standard levels in the economic, social and cultural life of the populations. It is also worth examining the influences or effects of imperialist action on the social structures and historical processes of our peoples.

We shall neither condemn nor excuse imperialism here, but merely say that, whether on the economic level, or on the social and cultural levels, imperialist capital has been a long way from fulfilling in our countries the historical mission carried out by capital in the countries of accumulation. This means that on the one hand, imperialist capital has had in the great majority of the dominated countries the simple function of multiplying surplus values. It can be seen on the other hand that the historical capacity of capital (as the indestructible accelerator of the process of development of the productive forces) is strictly dependent on its freedom, that is to say on the degree of independence with which it is utilised.

We must, however, recognise that in some cases imperialist capital or moribund capitalism has had sufficient interest, strength and time to raise the level of productive forces (as well as building cities) and to allow a minority of the local population a better or even privileged standard of living, thus contributing, by a process which some would call dialectical, to sharpening the contradictions within the societies in question. In other, rarer cases, there has been the possibility of accumulation of capital, giving rise to the development of a local bourgeoisie.

On the question of the effects of imperialist domination on the social structure and the historical process of our peoples, we should first of all examine the general forms of imperialist domination. There are at least two forms:

1. Direct domination – by means of a political power made up of agents foreign to the dominated people (armed forces, police, administrative agents and settlers) which is conventionally called *classical colonialism*.
2. Indirect domination – by means of a political power made up mainly or completely of native agents – which is conventionally called *neo-colonialism*.
    In the first case, the social structure of the dominated people, at whatever stage they are, can suffer the following experiences:
    a) Total destruction, generally accompanied by immediate or gradual elimination of the aboriginal population and consequent replacement by an exotic population.
    b) Partial destruction, generally accompanied by more or less intensive settlement by an exotic population.
    c) Ostensible preservation, brought about by confining the aboriginal society to areas or special reserves generally offering no means of living and accompanied by massive implantation of an exotic population.

The two latter cases, which are those we must consider in the context of the problematic of national liberation, are widely present in Africa. One can say that in either case the main effect produced by the impact of imperialism on the historical process of the dominated people is paralysis, stagnation (even in some cases, regression) in that process. However, this paralysis is not complete. In one sector or another of the socio-economic whole in question, noticeable transformations may occur, caused by the continuing action of some internal (local) factors, or as a result of the action of new factors introduced by the colonial domination, such as the introduction of money and the development of urban conglomerations.

Among these transformations, we should particularly note, in certain cases, the gradual loss of prestige of the native ruling classes or strata, the forced or voluntary exodus of part of the peasant population to the urban centres, with the consequent development of new social strata: salaried workers, employees of the State and in commerce and the liberal professions, and an unstable stratum of workless. In the countryside, there grows up with very varied intensity, and always with ties to the urban milieu, a stratum made up of petty farm-owners. In the case of so-called neo-colonialism, whether the majority of the colonised population is aboriginal or of exotic origin, imperialist action takes the form of creating a local bourgeoisie or pseudo-bourgeoisie, in fee to the ruling class of the dominating country.

The transformations in the social structure are not so marked in the lower strata, above all in the countryside, where the structure largely retains the characteristics of the colonial phase, but the creation of a native pseudo-bourgeoisie, which generally develops out of a petty bourgeoisie of bureaucrats and intermediaries in the trading system (*compradores*), accentuates the differentiation between the social strata. By strengthening the economic activity of native elements, this opens up new perspectives in the social dynamic, notably by the gradual development of an urbanised working class and the introduction of private agricultural property, which slowly gives rise to the appearance of an agricultural proletariat. These more or less noticeable transformations of the social structure, determined by a significant rise in the level of productive forces, have a direct influence on the historical process of the socio-economic whole in question.

While in classical colonialism this process is paralysed, neo-colonialist domination, by allowing the social dynamic to be awakened (conflicts of interest between the native social strata or class struggle) creates the illusion that the historical process is returning to its normal evolution. This illusion is reinforced by the existence of a political power (national State), composed of native elements. It is only an illusion, since in reality the subjection of the native 'ruling' class to the ruling class of the dominating country limits or holds back the full development of the national productive forces. But in the specific conditions of the present-day world economy, this subjection is an inevitability, and thus the native pseudo-bourgeoisie, however strongly nationalist, cannot effectively fulfil the historical function that would fall to this class; it cannot *freely* guide the development of productive forces, in short cannot be a *national bourgeoisie*. For, as we have seen, the productive forces are the motive force of history, and total freedom of the process of their development is an indispensable condition for their full functioning.

We see, therefore, that both in colonialism and in neo-colonialism the essential characteristic of imperialist domination remains the same – denial of the historical process of the dominated people, by means of violent usurpation of the freedom of the process of development of the national productive forces. This observation, which identifies the essence of the two apparent forms of imperialist domination, seems to us to be of primordial importance for the thought and action of national liberation movements, both in the course of the struggle and after the winning of independence.

On the basis of the foregoing, we can state that national liberation is the phenomenon in which a socio-economic whole rejects the denial of its historical process. In other words, the national liberation of a people is the regaining of the historical personality of that people, it is their return to history through the destruction of the imperialist domination to which they were subjected.

Now we have seen that the principal and permanent characteristic of imperialist domination, whatever its form, is the usurpation by violence of the freedom of the process of development of the dominated socio-economic whole. We have also seen that this freedom, and it alone, can guarantee the normal course of the historical process of a people. We can therefore conclude that national liberation exists when, and only when, the national productive forces have been completely freed from all and any kind of foreign domination.

It is often said that national liberation is based on the right of all peoples to decide their destiny freely and that the aim of this liberation is to gain national independence. Although we might agree with this vague and subjective way of expressing a complex reality, we prefer to be objective. For us the basis of national liberation, whatever the formulas adopted in international law, is the inalienable right of every people to have their own history; and the aim of national liberation is to regain this right usurped by imperialism, that is to free the process of development of the national productive forces.

For this reason, in our view any national liberation movement that does not take into consideration this basis and this aim may struggle against imperialism, but will certainly not be struggling for national liberation.

This means that, bearing in mind the essential characteristics of the present-day world economy, as well as experiences already gained in the field of anti-imperialist struggle, the principal aspect of national liberation struggle is the struggle against what is conventionally called neo-colonialism. Furthermore, if we accept that national liberation demands a profound mutation in the process of development of the productive forces, we see that the phenomenon of national liberation necessarily corresponds to a revolution. The important thing is to be aware of the objective and subjective conditions in which this revolution may occur, and to know the types or type of struggle most appropriate for its accomplishment.

We will not repeat here that these conditions are openly favourable in the present stable of the history of mankind. We shall merely recall that unfavourable factors also exist, just as much on the international level as on the internal level of each nation struggling for its liberation.

On the international level, it seems to us that the following factors at least are unfavourable to the national liberation movement: the neo-colonial situation of a great number of states which, having won political independence, are tending to join up with others already in that situation. The progress made by neo-capitalism, notably in Europe, where imperialism is resorting to preferential investments to encourage the development of a privileged proletariat with a consequent lowering of the revolutionary level of the working classes.

The open or concealed neo-colonial situation of some European states which, like Portugal, still have colonies; the policy of so-called 'aid' to underdeveloped countries, practised by imperialism with the aim of creating or reinforcing native pseudo-bourgeoisies necessarily subjected to the international bourgeoisie, and thus obstructing the path to revolution. The claustrophobia and timidity about revolution which leads some recently independent states, whose internal economic and political conditions are favourable to revolution, to accept compromises with the enemy or with their agents. The growing contradictions between anti-imperialist states; and, finally, the threats to world peace, posed by the prospect of atomic war on the part of imperialism. All these factors combine to strengthen the action of imperialism against the national liberation movement.

If the repeated interventions and growing aggressiveness of imperialism against the peoples can be interpreted as a sign of desperation before the extent of the national liberation movement, they are to some extent explained by the weaknesses within the general front of anti-imperialist struggle created by these unfavourable factors.

At the internal level, it seems to us that the most significant weakness or unfavourable factors are inherent in the socio-economic structure and in the trends of its evolution under imperialist pressure. Or, better still, in the little or no attention paid to the characteristics of this structure and these trends by the national liberation movements in drawing up their strategy for struggle.

By saying this we do not wish to minimise the significance of other internal factors which are unfavourable to national liberation, such as economic underdevelopment and the consequent social and cultural backwardness of the mass of the people, tribalism and some other minor contradictions. It should, however, be noted that the existence of tribes is only manifested as a significant contradiction as a function of opportunist attitudes (generally on the part of detribalised individuals or groups) within the national liberation movement. Contradictions between classes, even when the latter are embryonic, are of far greater importance than the contradictions between tribes.

Although the colonial and neo-colonial situations are identical in essence, and the main aspect of the struggle against imperialism might be the neo-colonialist aspect, we feel it is vital to distinguish between these two situations in practice. In fact, the horizontal structure of the native society, whether more or less differentiated, and the absence of a political power composed of national elements in the colonial situation, make possible the creation of a broad front of unity and struggle that is vital for the success of the national liberation movement. But this possibility does not remove the need for a rigorous analysis of the indigenous social structure and the trends of its evolution, and for the adoption in practice of appropriate measures for ensuring a genuine national liberation. While we admit that everyone knows best what to do in his own house, we feel that among these measures it is vital to create a firmly united vanguard, conscious of the true meaning and objective of the national liberation struggle which it must lead.

This necessity is more acute because it is certain that, with rare exceptions, the colonial situation neither allows nor invites the meaningful existence of vanguard classes (an industrial working class and rural proletariat) which could ensure the vigilance of the mass of the people over the evolution of the liberation movement.

On the contrary, the generally embryonic character of the working classes and the economic, social and cultural situation of the major physical force in a national liberation struggle – the peasants – do not allow these two principal forces of that struggle to distinguish on their own genuine national independence from fictitious political independence. Only a revolutionary vanguard, generally an active minority, can have consciousness *ab initio* of this distinction and through the struggle bring it to the awareness of the masses. This explains the fundamentally political nature of the national liberation struggle and to some extent provides the significance of the form of struggle in the final outcome of the phenomenon of national liberation.

In the neo-colonial situation, the more or less accentuated structuring of the native society as a vertical one and the existence of a political power composed of native elements – national state – aggravate the contradictions within that society and make difficult, if not impossible, the creation of as broad a united front as in the colonial case. On the one hand, the material effects (mainly the nationalisation of cadres and the rise in native economic initiative, particularly at the commercial level) and the psychological effects (pride in believing oneself ruled by one's fellow countrymen, exploitation of religious or tribal solidarity between some leaders and a fraction of the mass of the people) serve to demobilise a considerable part of the nationalist forces.

But on the other hand, the necessarily repressive nature of the neo-colonial state against the national liberation forces, the aggravation of class contradictions, the objective continuance of agents and signs of foreign domination (settlers who retain their privileges, armed forces, racial discrimination), the growing impoverishment of the peasantry and the more or less flagrant influence of external factors contribute towards keeping the flame of nationalism alight. They serve gradually to awaken the consciousness of broad popular strata and, precisely on the basis of awareness of neo-colonialist frustration, to reunite the majority of the population around the ideal of national liberation.

In addition, while the native ruling class becomes increasingly 'bourgeois' the development of a class of workers composed of urbanised industrial workers and agricultural proletarians – all exploited by the indirect domination of imperialism – opens renewed prospects for the evolution of national liberation. This class of workers, whatever the degree of development of its political consciousness (beyond a certain minimum that is *consciousness of its needs*), seems to constitute the true popular vanguard of the national liberation struggle in the neo-colonial case.

However, it will not be able completely to carry out its mission in the framework of this struggle (which does not end with the gaining of independence) unless it allies itself firmly with the other exploited strata: the peasants in general (farm labourers, tenants, sharecroppers, petty farm-owners) and the nationalist petty bourgeoisie. The achievement of this alliance demands the mobilisation and organisation of the nationalist forces within the framework (or by the action) of a strong and well-structured political organisation.

Another important distinction to draw between the colonial and neo-colonial situations lies in the prospects for struggle. The colonial case (in which the *nation class* fights the repressive forces of the bourgeoisie of the colonising country) may lead, ostensibly at least, to a nationalist situation (national revolution): the nation gains its independence and theoretically adopts the economic structure it finds most attractive. The neo-colonial case (in which the class of workers and its allies fight simultaneously the imperialist bourgeoisie and the native ruling class) is not resolved by a nationalist solution; it demands the destruction of the capitalist structure implanted in the national soil by imperialism and correctly postulates a socialist solution.

This distinction arises mainly from the different levels of the productive forces in the two cases and the consequent sharpening of the class struggle. It would not be difficult to show that in time this distinction becomes scarcely apparent. It is sufficient to recall that in the present historical circumstances – alienation of imperialism which lays its hands on every possible means to perpetuate its domination over our peoples, and consolidation of socialism over a considerable part of the globe – there are only two possible paths for an independent nation: to return to imperialist domination (neo-colonialism, capitalism, state capitalism) or to take the socialist road. This option, on which depends the compensation for the efforts and sacrifices by the mass of the people during the struggle, is considerably influenced by the form of struggle and the degree of revolutionary consciousness of those who lead it.

THE ROLE OF VIOLENCE

The facts make it unnecessary for us to waste words proving that the essential instrument of imperialist domination is violence. If we accept the principle that *the national liberation struggle is a revolution*, and that it is not over at the moment when the flag is hoisted and the national anthem is played, we shall find that there is and there can be no national liberation without the use of liberating violence, on the part of the nationalist forces, in answer to the criminal violence of the agents of imperialism.

Nobody can doubt that imperialist domination, whatever its local characteristics, implies a state of permanent violence against the nationalist forces. There is no people in the world which, after being subjected to the imperialist yoke (colonialist or neo-colonialist, has gained independence (nominal or effective) without victims. The important thing is to decide what forms of violence have to be used by the national liberation forces, in order not only to answer the violence of imperialism but also to ensure, through the struggle, the final victory of their cause, that is true national independence.

The past and recent experience of various peoples; the present situation of national liberation struggle in the world (especially the cases of Vietnam, Congo and Zimbabwe); as well as the very situation of permanent violence, or at least of contradictions and upheavals, in certain countries which have gained independence by the so-called peaceful way show us not only that compromises with imperialism are counter-productive. But also that the normal road of national liberation, imposed on peoples by imperialist repression, is *armed struggle*.

We do not think we shall shock this assembly by stating that the only effective way of completely and definitively fulfilling the aspirations of peoples for national liberation is by armed struggle. This is the great lesson that the contemporary history of liberation teaches all those who are truly committed to the national liberation of their peoples.

ON THE PETTY BOURGEOISIE

It is obvious that both the effectiveness of this road and the stability of the situation to which it leads after liberation depend not only on the characteristics of organisation of the struggle but also on the political and moral awareness of those who, for historical reasons, are in a position to be the immediate heirs of the colonial or neo-colonial state. For events have shown that the only social stratum capable both of having consciousness in the first place of the reality of imperialist domination and of handling the state apparatus inherited from that domination is the native petty bourgeoisie. If we bear in mind the unpredictable characteristics and complexity of the trends naturally inherent in the economic situation of this social stratum or class, we find that this specific inevitability in our situation is yet another weakness of the national liberation movement.

The colonial situation, which does not admit the development of a native pseudo-bourgeoisie and in which the mass of the people does not generally reach the necessary degree of political consciousness before the launching of the phenomenon of national liberation, offers the petty bourgeoisie the historical opportunity of leading the struggle against foreign domination. By virtue of its objective and subjective position (higher standard of living than that of the masses, more frequent humiliation, higher grade of education and political culture, etc.) it is the stratum that soonest becomes aware of the need to rid itself of foreign domination. This historical responsibility is assumed by the sector of the petty bourgeoisie that, in the colonial context, one might call *revolutionary*, while the other sectors retain the characteristic hesitation of this class or ally themselves to the colonialist so as to defend, albeit illusorily their social position.

The neo-colonial situation, which postulates the elimination of the native pseudo-bourgeoisie so that national liberation is achieved, also offers the petty bourgeoisie the opportunity of playing a prominent – and even decisive – role in the struggle for the elimination of foreign domination. But in this case, by virtue of the relative advances made in the social structure, the function of leading the struggle is shared, to a greater or lesser extent, with the most enlightened sectors of the classes of workers and even with some elements of the national pseudo-bourgeoisie inspired by patriotic sentiment.

The role of the sector of the petty bourgeoisie that takes part in leading the struggle is all the more important as it is clear that, in the neo-colonial situation too, it is the most ready to assume these functions, both because of the economic and cultural limitations of the mass of workers, and because of the complexes and limitations of an ideological nature that characterise the sector of the national pseudo-bourgeoisie which joins the struggle. In this case still, it is important to stress that the mission with which it is entrusted demands from this sector of the petty bourgeoisie a greater revolutionary consciousness, and the capacity for faithfully expressing the aspirations of the masses in each phase of the struggle and for identifying with them more and more.

But, no matter the degree of revolutionary consciousness of the sector of the petty bourgeoisie called on to undertake this historical function, it cannot free itself from an objective reality: the petty bourgeoisie, as a service class (that is not directly involved in the process of production) does not have at its disposal the economic basis to guarantee the taking over of power for it. In fact history shows that whatever the role (often important) played by individuals coming from the petty bourgeoisie in the process of a revolution, this class has never possessed political power. And it never could, since political power (the State) has its foundations in the economic capacity of the ruling class. In the circumstances of colonial and neo-colonial society, this capacity is retained in the hands of two entities: imperialist capital and the native classes of workers.

To maintain the power that national liberation puts in its hands, the petty bourgeoisie has only one road: to give free rein to its natural tendencies to become 'bourgeois' to allow the development of a bourgeoisie of bureaucrats and intermediaries in the trading system, to transform itself into a national pseudo-bourgeoisie, that is to deny the revolution and necessarily subject itself to imperialist capital. Now this corresponds to the neo-colonial situation, that is to say, to the betrayal of the objectives of national liberation.

In order not to betray these objectives, the petty bourgeoisie has only one road: to strengthen its revolutionary consciousness, to repudiate the temptations to become 'bourgeois' and the natural pretensions of its class mentality: to identify with the classes of workers, not to oppose the normal development of the process of revolution. This means that in order to play completely the part that falls to it in the national liberation struggle, the revolutionary petty bourgeoisie must be capable of committing *suicide* as a class, to be restored to life in the condition of a revolutionary worker completely identified with the deepest aspirations of the people to which he belongs.

This alternative – to betray the revolution or to commit suicide as a class – constitutes the dilemma of the petty bourgeoisie in the general framework of the national liberation struggle. The positive solution, in favour of the revolution, depends on what Fidel Castro recently fittingly called *development of revolutionary consciousness*. This dependence necessarily draws our attention to the capacity of the leaders of the national liberation struggle to remain faithful to the principles and the fundamental cause of this struggle. This shows us, to a certain extent, that if national liberation is essentially a political question, the conditions for its development stamp on it certain characteristics that belong to the sphere of morals.

This is the modest contribution which, on behalf of the nationalist organisations of African countries still partly or wholly dominated by Portuguese colonialism, we thought we should bring to the general debate of this assembly. As we are firmly united within our many-nation organisation – CONCP – we are determined to remain faithful to the interests and just aspirations of our peoples, whatever our origins in the societies to which we belong. Vigilance in regard to this fidelity is one of the main objectives of our organisation, in the interest of our peoples, of Africa and of mankind struggling against imperialism.

For this reason, we are already fighting, with weapons in hand, against the Portuguese colonialist forces, in Angola, Guiné and Mozambique, and we are preparing to do the same in Cape Verde and São Tomé and Príncipe. For this reason, we devote the closest attention to political work among our peoples, improving and constantly strengthening our national organisations, in whose leadership all the sectors of our society are represented. For this reason, we remain vigilant against ourselves and, on the basis of specific knowledge of our strengths and weaknesses, we try to reinforce the former and to transform the latter into strengths, for the constant development of our revolutionary consciousness. For this reason, we are in Cuba, attending this Conference.

We shall not shout 'vivas' or here proclaim our solidarity with this or that people in struggle. Our presence is in itself a cry of condemnation of imperialism and a proof of solidarity with all peoples who want to sweep the imperialist yoke from their country, and in particular with the heroic people of Vietnam. But we firmly believe that the best proof we can give of our anti-imperialist stand and our active solidarity with our companions in this common struggle is to return to our countries, to develop the struggle further and to remain faithful to the principles and objectives of national liberation.

Our wish is that every national liberation movement represented here may, with weapons in hand, be able to echo in its own country, in unison with its people, the already legendary cry of the people of Cuba: '*Patria o muerte, Venceremos!*' ('Country or death, we shall triumph!').

Death to the forces of imperialism!
A free, prosperous and joyful country for each of our peoples!
We shall triumph!

Determined to Resist

Amílcar Cabral needs no introduction; his stature as a leader goes beyond the borders of the African continent. He was born in Cape Verde and had the exceptional opportunity of obtaining a college education in Portugal; in addition to studying agronomy, he became a revolutionary militant, the leader of the PAIGC.

As an agronomy engineer, Amílcar covered vast regions of his country and through his work found a way to speak to his people, to mobilise them and prepare them for combat. This is how he created the bases for the first guerrillas, who started to operate in 1931–62 with the aim of unleashing armed struggle against Portuguese colonialism on a national scale in 1963.

Years have passed since then. The first armed groups have become powerful guerrilla units, and two-thirds of the country is under PAIGC control. Amílcar Cabral's name and personality are indissolubly tied to this dynamic victory.

In this interview our readers will see how this African leader outlines, with his characteristic intelligence and precision, the qualities of the revolutionary struggle being waged in Guinea and in Africa, the tactical and strategic problems of this struggle, and present-day international questions.

The PAIGC Secretary-General granted *Tricontinental* this interview in Conakry, the capital of the Democratic Republic of Guinea, upon returning from the Eastern Front.

What is the state of the struggle in the cities of so-called Portuguese Guinea, particularly in the capital, Bissau, and in Cape Verde?

We have had a great deal of experience in the struggle in the cities and the urban centres of our country, where the struggle first began. At first we organised mass demonstrations, strikes, etc. to demand that the Portuguese change their position in regard to the legitimate rights of our people to self-determination and national independence. We found out that in the cities and urban centres the concentration of the Portuguese repressive forces – military, police, etc. – was causing us serious losses. For example, in August 1959, during the Bissau dock workers' and merchant seamen's strike, in just 20 minutes the Portuguese shot to death 50 African workers and wounded more than 100 on the Pidjiguiti docks. At that time our Party decided to hold a secret conference in Bissau, and it was then that we changed direction. That is, we began to mobilise the countryside, and we decided to prepare ourselves actively for armed struggle against the Portuguese colonialist forces.

Later we decided that the Party's underground organisation would continue in the cities. The same leaders are still active in the urban centres, among them the present Party President, who, after 18 months of underground work in Bissau, was arrested by the Portuguese authorities and is still under house arrest. We decided that the popular masses in the cities should not organise any event that would give rise to criminal reprisals on the part of the Portuguese colonialists.

Today, in Bissau, Bafatá, Farim, etc., our country's main urban centres, we have an underground Party organisation, but we still have not gone over to any kind of direct action against the Portuguese colonialists in the cities.

It is necessary to explain that our country is a purely commercial colony and not a colony of settlers; therefore, the Portuguese civilians themselves, the *colonos*, have no great interest in establishing themselves on our lands. A few are government employees, and others are simply businessmen. From the beginning they took a somewhat vacillating, if not indifferent, position on our struggle, and many of them wish to return to Portugal. Therefore, we have no reason to take action, from the standpoint of terrorism, against the Portuguese civilians. For that reason, our urban action should be aimed at the Portuguese military infrastructure and military forces. We are preparing ourselves for this, and we expect that, if the Portuguese fail to recognise our right to self-determination and independence after four years of armed struggle, we will be forced to attack in the cities, also.

And we will do it, since we know that the Portuguese are determined to continue their criminal acts against our peaceful forces in the liberated areas. Thus far, we have not carried out any action in the cities, but we are determined to do so insofar as it constitutes an advance in the struggle as well as reprisals for the savage acts committed by the Portuguese against our population in the liberated areas.

As for Cape Verde, we consider that the fight there is of prime importance for the progress of our struggle not only in Guinea but in all the Portuguese colonies, and we can guarantee that our Party is getting ready to unleash armed, struggle in the Cape Verde Islands. During the past few years many political advances have been made in the Cape Verde Islands. The Party leadership functions properly. We have excellent communication with the Cape Verde Islands, and, as I said before, we are ready to begin armed struggle; the decision depends simply on the Party leadership, which must consider the favourable and unfavourable factors for beginning total armed struggle there.

What is the strategic aim of the armed struggle? Are there any possibilities of negotiating with Portuguese colonialism?

The strategic aim of our armed struggle of national liberation is, obviously, to completely free our country from the Portuguese colonial yoke. It is, after all, the strategic aim of all the national liberation movements, which, forced by circumstances, take up arms to fight against repression and the colonial presence. In our struggle, we set down our principles after having become thoroughly familiar with our country's conditions.

For instance, we decided that we should begin the struggle within the country and that we should never struggle from outside the country, for which reason we never had armed forces outside our own land. And, for the same reason, in 1963 we started the armed struggle in the centre of the country, both in the south and in the north. This means that, contrary to what has been done by the peoples in Africa or other places who are fighting for national independence, we adopted a strategy that we might call centrifugal: we started in the centre and moved towards the periphery of our land. This came as the first big surprise to the Portuguese, who had stationed their troops on the Guinea and Senegal borders on the supposition that we were going to invade our own country.

But we mobilised our people secretly, in the cities and in the countryside. We prepared our own cadres, we armed those few that we could with both traditional and modern weapons, and we initiated our action from the centre of our country.

Today the struggle is spreading to all parts of the country, in Boé and Gabú and in the south; in the north, in São Domingos, in the Farim zone; in the west, near the sea, in the Manjacos region, and we hope to be fighting within a short time on the island of Bissau, as well. Moreover, as you were able to see for yourselves in the southern part of the country and as other newsmen and filmmakers have seen in the north and east, we have liberated a large part of our national territory, which forms part of the framework of our strategy.

As to the possibilities for negotiations, we can say that our struggle seeks a political objective; we are not making war because we are warlike or because we like war. We are not making war to conquer Portugal. We are fighting because we have to in order to win back our human rights, our rights as a nation, as an African people that wants its independence. But the objectives of our war are political: the total liberation of our people of Guinea and Cape Verde and the winning of national independence and sovereignty, both at home and on the international plane.

For this reason, it is of no importance when – today, tomorrow, or whenever – the Portuguese colonialists, forced by our armed forces, by the heroic struggle of our people, recognise that the time has come to sit down to discuss the situation with us; it does not matter when – today, tomorrow, or whenever – we are willing to enter into discussions. Therefore, the possibilities for negotiating, since the United Nations was unable to get Portugal to negotiate, depend fundamentally on the Portuguese themselves. We are also convinced that such possibilities depend on what we ourselves are able to do within the framework of our armed struggle. That is our position in regard to the possibilities of negotiating with the Portuguese, in the sure knowledge that, given what we have done, the sacrifice of our people during this difficult but victorious struggle, given the fact that Africa is marching towards total independence, our position today is this: to negotiate with the Portuguese whenever they want, whenever they are ready, but to negotiate for the total and unconditional independence of our people.

That does not mean that we are not interested, as a politically aware people and in spite of the crimes committed by the Portuguese in our land, in establishing with Portugal itself the most excellent relations of collaboration and co-operation on the basis of equality, on the basis of absolute reciprocity of advantage, but likewise on the basis of the highest regard for our sovereignty.

Could you tell us something about the tactical principles followed by the PAIGC guerrilla army?

At present, to carry out the national liberation armed struggle it is not necessary to invent much along general lines. Already a wealth of experience has been gained in the national liberation armed struggle throughout the world. The Chinese people fought. The Vietnamese people have been fighting for more than 25 years. The Cuban people fought heroically and defeated the reactionaries and the imperialists on their island, which is today a stronghold of progress. Other peoples have struggled and have made known to the world their experience in the struggle.

You know very well that Che Guevara, the great Che Guevara for us, wrote a book, a book on the guerrilla struggle. This book, for example, like other documents on the guerrilla struggle in other countries, including Europe, where there was also guerrilla struggle during the last World War, served us as a basis of general experience for our own struggle.

But nobody is committing the error, in general, of blindly applying the experience of others to his own country. To determine the tactics for the struggle in our country, we had to take into account the geographical, historical, economic, and social conditions of our own land, both in Guinea and Cape Verde.

It was by basing ourselves on the concrete knowledge of the real situation in our country that we set down the tactical and strategic principles of our guerrilla struggle.

We can say that our country is very different from other countries. In the first place, it is quite a small country, about 36,000 km² in Guinea and 4,000 km² in Cape Verde. While Guinea is on the African continent, Cape Verde is in the middle of the sea, like an archipelago. We took all of this into consideration, but, in addition, Guinea is a flat country. It has no mountains, and everyone knows that in general the guerrilla force uses the mountains as a starting point for the armed struggle. We had to convert our people themselves into the mountain needed for the fight in our country, and we had to take full advantage of the jungles and swamps of our country to create difficult conditions for the enemy in his confrontation with the victorious advance of our armed struggle.

As for our other tactics, we follow the fundamental principle of armed struggle, or, if you prefer, colonial war: the enemy, in order to control a given zone, is forced to disperse his forces; he thus becomes weakened, and we can defeat him. In order to be able to defend himself from us he needs to concentrate his forces, and when he concentrates his forces he allows us to occupy the areas that are left empty and work on them politically to prevent the enemy from returning.

This is the dilemma faced by colonialism in our land, just as has been the case in other lands, and it is that dilemma, if it is thoroughly taken advantage of by us, that will surely lead Portuguese colonialism to defeat in our country.

This is sure to happen, because our people are mobilised. They are aware of what they are doing. Also, the liberated regions of the country, where we are developing a new society, are a constant propaganda force for the liberation of other parts of our country.

What are the principal tactical and strategic anti-guerrilla principles used by the Portuguese army?

If we have not had to invent a great deal in the course of our struggle, the Portuguese have invented even less. The only thing that the Portuguese do in our land is follow the tactics and strategies used by the US and other imperialists in their wars against the peoples who wish to free themselves of their domination. The Portuguese first attempted to work politically after having experimented with the art of repression: armed repression, police repression, murder, massacres, etc. All of that has not stopped the struggle. Then they tried to work politically. They exploited tribal contradictions. They even exploited racism on the basis of lighter and darker people. They exploited the question of the civilised and the uncivilised, etc., as well as the privileged position of the traditional chiefs. That did not lead to the desired results. The Portuguese then unleashed a colonial war, and in that colonial war they used the strategy and tactics that are common to all imperialists who fight against the peoples.

Against us, they used the most modern weapons given them by their US, German, Belgian, Italian, French, etc., allies. They used every kind of bomb save the nuclear ones. In particular, they used napalm bombs against us at the beginning of the war. They also used armoured cars. They used B-26, T-6, and P-2V planes and fighter jets – Fiat 82s, Fiat 91s, and Sabres supplied by Canada through Federal Germany, etc. None of it worked. Lately they have been using armed helicopters for combined operations with the Navy and Infantry. We are sure that they will not work, either.

The Portuguese find themselves in the position which you have already been able to observe, since you came to our country in a way that, unfortunately, no Portuguese has done – since you came as journalists. They are closed up in their barracks; once in a while they try to make sallies to carry out criminal actions against our people. They do battle against our forces, and almost every day they bomb our villages and try to burn the crops. They are trying to terrorise our people.

We are determined to resist, and the tactics and strategies of Portuguese colonialism – which are the same as those imperialism uses, for instance, in Vietnam – just as they do not work in Vietnam, will not work in our country, either.

We know that the Portuguese carry out offensive operations using two or even three thousand men, trying to recover the already liberated territories. What can you tell us about this?

Yes, the big dream of the Portuguese has been to recover the already liberated territory. For instance, in 1964 they carried out a big offensive with almost 3,000 men against Como Island. The recovery of Como would have two advantages for the Portuguese: first, a strategic advantage, because it is a firm base for the control of the southern part of the country; secondly, a political advantage, because it would constitute a big propaganda victory for the Portuguese and would serve to demoralise our own populations.

But the Portuguese were defeated on Como, where they lost more than 900 soldiers and much material. They had to withdraw, and Como continues to be free. It is today one of the most developed zones of our liberated regions.

The Portuguese have tried and continue to try to recover ground. We can say that during the last dry season they made various efforts in both the south and the north, but they did not manage to establish themselves in either of these zones.

They come with hundreds of men – never less – and at times with thousands. It is our opinion that, the more men they bring, the easier it is for us to cause them losses and damage. We are prepared to repel any attack by the Portuguese; when they advance with their aviation it is generally harder for us, but our combatants have learned from their own experience how to fight under such conditions.

Therefore, we are convinced that, whatever the number of Portuguese who come, the larger the number, the worse it will be for them; we are determined to inflict upon them ever greater defeats.

You mentioned Che Guevara's book *Guerrilla Warfare*. In this book Guevara divided the guerrilla struggle into three phases. According to this, what phase do you think the struggle in so-called Portuguese Guinea is in?

In general, we have certain reservations about the systematization of phenomena. In reality the phenomena always develop in practice according to the established schemes. We intensely admire the scheme established by Che Guevara essentially on the basis of the struggle of the Cuban people and other experiences, and we are convinced that a profound analysis of that scheme can have a certain application to our struggle. However, we are not completely certain that, in fact, the scheme is absolutely adaptable to our conditions.

Within this framework, we believe that, in the present phase of our struggle, we are already in the stage of mobile warfare. This is why we have been reorganising our forces, creating units more powerful than those of the regular army, and surrounding the Portuguese forces; this is why we have been increasing the mobility of our forces, thus diminishing the importance of the guerrilla positions in order to advance against enemy positions. But today an essential characteristic of our struggle is the systematic attacking of Portuguese fortified camps and fortresses. This in itself indicates that we are in the stage of mobile warfare. And we hope that the time is not far off when, advancing with this mobile warfare, we will at the same time have the conditions for launching a general offensive to end the Portuguese domination in our land.

Can you tell us something about the development of guerrilla communications and propaganda work?

We have many difficulties in our propaganda work. First of all, thus far we do not have a radio station – which could play a role at least as important as or more important than many guns. Our Party is actively working on getting a station so as to be able to speak daily (or, if not every day, at least several times a week) to our forces, to our people, and even to the enemy. Meanwhile, we are convinced that friendly peoples who do have stations – such as the Republic of Guinea, Senegal, Cuba, and others – will also be able to work in this area, because their broadcasts are heard in our country. They will be able to help us with broadcasts in favour of our struggle. To do so we need not issue many reports, because all are familiar with the justice and the raison d'être of our struggle.

Moreover, once in a while we communicate the results of our armed struggle. We cannot put out these communiqués with much frequency because communications are difficult between the different fronts of struggle and the centre that coordinates those communications (we do not as yet have an effective radio system – we are now setting up a system of radio communication) and for that reason our communiqués at times come out after some delay. But that does not mean in the least that the struggle is not progressing in any sector. On the contrary, what happens is that our communiqués in general do not reflect the great intensity of the struggle, the frequency of the combats, and many times the victories we achieve against the enemy.

In relation to communications, our struggle has very special characteristics: we cannot fight riding in jeeps or trucks; we are the first to know that our land does not have good roads, as we ourselves have cut down the few existing bridges, we have destroyed many sections of highways, and our people felled trees to block the highways. In fact, the enemy today can travel on almost no highway in our country. Therefore, we do not have trucks, jeeps, etc., to occupy highways, to travel along the highways that we ourselves mine.

As you saw, we must move on foot within our territory. This makes communications extremely difficult.

As I said, we are working actively to improve our radio communications in such a way as not only to give daily reports on the progress of the struggle on all fronts but also to facilitate the coordination of the struggle on all fronts, to make our armed struggle progress.

Can you tell us something about the difficulties met during the development of the struggle with relation to tribal and linguistic problems, difficulties with feudal chieftains in Guinea-Bissau?

The difficulties of our struggle were mainly those inherent in our situation of an underdeveloped – practically non-developed – people whose history was held back by colonialist and imperialist domination. A people that started with nothing, a people that had to begin the struggle almost naked, a people with a 99 per cent illiteracy rate – you have already seen the effort that we have to make now to teach our people to read and write, to create schools – a people that had only 14 university-trained men – this people was surely going to have difficulties in carrying out its armed struggle.

You know that this was the situation with Africa in general, but it was very pronounced in our country. Our people were not only underfed but also the victims of many diseases because the Portuguese never concerned themselves with decent public health in our land. All this caused difficulties at the beginning of the struggle.

Another difficulty is the following: our own African culture, which corresponds to the economic structure we still have, made certain aspects of the struggle difficult. These are the factors that those who judge the struggle from outside do not take into consideration but that we had to consider because it is one thing to struggle in surroundings where everyone knows what rain, high tide, lightning, storms, typhoons, and tornadoes are, and another to fight where natural phenomena can be interpreted as a product of the will of the spirits.

That is very important for a struggle such as ours. Another difficulty is as follows: our people fought as one, opposing their traditional weapons against colonial domination at the time of the colonial conquest. But today we must wage a modern war. A guerrilla war, but a modern one, with modern tactics. That also creates difficulties for us: it is necessary to create cadres, prepare the combatants properly. Before, we had to prepare them during the struggle itself because we did not have time to build schools. Only today do we have schools for combatants, as you know.

All of this created difficulties for us – that is, in training for the armed struggle. While the Portuguese officers who lead the Portuguese fight have seven years of training in military academies, in addition to the other basic courses they receive, we have to bring to the struggle young people from the cities or the countryside, some of them without any education, who have to gain in the struggle itself the necessary experience to confront the Portuguese officers. Suffice it to say that the Portuguese Government had to change its General Staff in our country five times, and some of the chiefs of staff were even punished. This shows that after all it is not necessary to go to a military academy to fight in one's country to win a people's freedom.

As for tribal questions, our opinion on this is quite different from that of others. We believe that when the colonialists arrived in Africa the tribal structure was already in a state of disintegration due to the evolution of the economy and historical events on the African scene. Today it cannot be said that Africa is tribal. Africa still has remnants of tribalism, in particular as far as the mentality of the people is concerned, but not in the economic structure itself. Moreover, if colonialism, through its action, did anything positive at all, it was precisely to destroy a large part of the existing remnants of tribalism in certain parts of our country.

Therefore, we have had no great difficulties as far as tribalism is concerned. We did have trouble creating in our people a national awareness, and it is the struggle itself that is cementing that national awareness. But all the people in general, from whatever ethnic group, have been easily led to accept the idea that we are a people, a nation, that must struggle to end Portuguese domination, because we do not fall back on clichés or merely harp on the struggle against imperialism and colonialism in theoretical terms, but rather we point out concrete things. It is a struggle for schools, for hospitals, so that children won't suffer. That is our struggle.

Another goal of the struggle is to present ourselves before the world as a worthy people with a personality of our own. This is the motivating force of our people. We also know that the vestiges of tribalism in our land have been eliminated through the armed struggle we are waging. Moreover, we want to stress that in general the African people, both in our land and in the Congo, where terrible things took place from the tribal point of view, are not tribalist. Among the people of Africa, the tendency is to understand one another as much as possible. Only political opportunists are tribalists: individuals who even attended European universities; who frequented the cafés of Brussels, Paris, Lisbon, and other capitals; who are completely removed from the problems of their own people – they may be called tribal, these individuals who at times even look down on their own people but who, out of political ambition, take advantage of attitudes still existing in the minds of our people to try to achieve their opportunist aims, their political goals, to try to quench their thirst for power and political domination.

In regard to our land, we want to add that the armed struggle is not only wiping out the remnants of tribal ideas that might still exist but that it is also profoundly transforming our people.

You must have had the opportunity to see how, in spite of the fact that we still live in poverty, in spite of the fact that we still do not have enough clothing and our diet lacks vitamins, fresh foods, and even meat and other protein foods – all of this a part of the colonial heritage and our state of under-development – a great transformation is going on in many places. And you must have found the new man. The new man who is emerging in our land; the new woman who is emerging in our land. And, if you had the opportunity to speak to the children, you would see that even our school children are already politically and patriotically aware and desire the struggle and the independence of our country. An awareness of mutual understanding, of national unity and unity on the African continent.

We want to emphasise in particular that the women of our country are winning an independence for which so many have fought unsuccessfully. You saw, surely, how there were women in charge of the committees in the *tabankas* (villages) and the zones and even of interregional committees. These women are conscious of their worth and their role within our Party, and I can say that there are women in all levels of our Party.

Could you tell us briefly how the political and military leadership of the struggle is carried out?

The political and military leadership of the struggle is one: the political leadership. In our struggle we have avoided the creation of anything military. We are political people, and our Party, a political organisation, leads the struggle in the civilian, political, administrative, technical, and therefore also military spheres. Our fighters are defined as armed activists. It is the Political Bureau of the Party that directs the armed struggle and the life of both the liberated and unliberated regions where we have our activists. Within the Political Bureau is a War Council composed of members of the former who direct the armed struggle. The War Council is an instrument of the Political Bureau, of the leadership of the armed struggle.

Each front has its command. On the sector level there is a sector command, and each unit of our regular army also has its command. That is the structure of our armed struggle, and it is true that the guerrillas are installed in bases and that each base has a base chief and a political commissar. In relation to organisation proper, a Party congress is generally held every two years, but within the framework of the struggle it is held whenever it is possible. The Party has a Central Committee and a Political Bureau which directly lead the local bodies – that is, the northern and southern interregional committees and the sector and *tabanka* (village) committees. That is our structure.

In the cities and urban centres, the Party organisation remains underground, in general under the leadership of a very small number of individuals.

Since outside aid is so important to the national liberation struggle and particularly to that of Guinea-Bissau, we would like to know which countries are giving aid to your guerrilla struggle.

A basic principle of our struggle is our counting on our own forces, our own sacrifices, our own efforts; but, considering the characteristic under-development of our people, of our land, the economic backwardness of our land, it is very difficult for us to produce weapons. Taking into account these circumstances, taking into account the fact that in our country 99% of the people are illiterate, which makes the immediate existence of cadres difficult; and also taking into account that the enemy, which has no scruples, is aided by its NATO allies, in particular the United States, Federal Germany, and some other countries, and above all by its South African racist allies – taking into account all of this and also the essential characteristic of our times, which is the general struggle of the peoples against imperialism and the existence of a socialist camp, which is the greatest bulwark against imperialism, we accept and request aid from all the peoples that can give it to us. We do not ask for aid in manpower: there are enough of us to fight and defeat colonialism in our country.

We ask for aid in weapons, in articles of prime necessity to supply our liberated regions, in medicines to heal our wounded and cure our sick and to provide medical care to the population of the liberated regions. We ask for any and all aid that any people can offer us. We also ask different countries for aid in preparing our cadres. Our aid ethics are as follows: we never ask for the aid we need. We expect that each will conscientiously give what help he can to our people in our struggle for national liberation. As part of this aid, we point above all to that of Africa. Through the OAU, Africa has granted us some aid. We consider that this aid, thus far, is not sufficient to meet our needs, to provide for the development of our struggle, which is today a real war against an enemy that possesses powerful weapons to use against us and which receives aid from its allies. For example, Federal Germany even sends aviation technicians to train the Portuguese in Bissau, and, in addition, it receives Portuguese wounded for treatment in Germany to prevent the Portuguese people from seeing how many we have wounded in our country.

Our opinion is that aid from Africa is good, but insufficient. Therefore, we hope that the African peoples, the African states through the OAU, can increase their aid, both financial and material.

And on the financial plane we want to point out that today our expenses are enormous. In gasoline alone, we use almost 40,000 litres to supply the fighting fronts. All this involves large expenditures, and thus far we have not received the financial aid necessary to cover the costs of the war, while Portugal, in addition to its state budget, receives fabulous aid in dollars, marks, and pounds from its allies.

We want to add that within the framework of Africa there are some countries that aid us bilaterally. For example, we receive the greatest support from the Republic of Guinea, the greatest facilities for the development of our struggle. Algeria continues to help; the UAR, also. At the beginning of the struggle Morocco helped, and we don't understand why it no longer gives us the help it gave us at that time.

Other African countries have aided us. For example, Tanzania, which aids the people of Mozambique, and the Congo (Brazzaville), which aids the people of Angola, also aid us.

We want to mention the special aid given to us by the peoples of the socialist countries. We believe that this aid is a historic obligation, because we consider that our struggle also constitutes a defence of the socialist countries. And we want to say particularly that the Soviet Union, first of all, and China, Czechoslovakia, Bulgaria, and other socialist countries continue to aid us, which we consider very useful for the development of our armed struggle. We also want to lay special emphasis on the untiring efforts – sacrifices that we deeply appreciate – that the people of Cuba – a small country without great resources, one that is struggling against the blockade by the US and other imperialists – are making to give effective aid to our struggle. For us, this is a constant source of encouragement, and it also contributes to cementing more and more the solidarity between our Party and the Cuban Party, between our people and the Cuban people, a people that we consider African. And it is enough to see the historical, political, and blood ties that unite us to be able to say this. Therefore, we are very happy with the aid that the Cuban people give us, and we are sure that they will continue increasing their aid to our heroic national liberation struggle in spite of all difficulties.

At present there is a very important problem, a burning issue in the Middle East, because of the Israeli aggression against the Arab peoples. What is the PAIGC's position in regard to this conflict?

We have as a basic principle the defence of just causes. We are in favour of justice, human progress, the freedom of the people. On this basis we believe that the creation of Israel, carried out by the imperialist states to maintain their domination in the Middle East, was artificial and aimed at the creation of problems in that very important region of the world. This is our position: the Jewish people who follow the Jewish religion have the right to live and have lived very well in different countries of the world. We lament profoundly what the Nazis did to the Jewish people, that Hitler and his lackeys destroyed almost six million during the last World War. But we also understand that this does not give them the right to occupy a part of the Arab nation. We believe that the people of Palestine have a right to their land. We therefore think that all the measures taken by the Arab peoples, by the Arab nation, to recover the Palestinian Arab homeland are justified.

In this conflict that is endangering world peace we are entirely in favour of and unconditionally support the Arab peoples. We do not wish for war; but we want the Arab peoples to obtain the freedom of the people of Palestine, to free the Arab nation of that element of imperialist disturbance and domination which Israel constitutes.

What is the Party's position on the struggle in Vietnam?

For us, the struggle in Vietnam is our own struggle. We consider that in Vietnam not only the fate of our own people but also that of all the peoples struggling for their national independence and sovereignty is at stake. We are in solidarity with the people of Vietnam, and we immensely admire their heroic struggle against US aggression and against the aggression of the reactionaries of the southern part of Vietnam, who are no more than the puppets of US imperialism.

We offer all our support to the people of Vietnam. Under the present historical circumstances of our people, we can do no more than fight every day with valour and determination against the Portuguese colonialists, who are also the lackeys of international imperialism.

What is your opinion of the revolutionary struggle in Latin America?

Within the framework of our firm position in favour of the peoples, we understand that the peoples of Latin America have suffered enormously. The independence of the peoples of Latin America was a sham. The peoples of Latin America never enjoyed true independence. Governments were created that were completely submissive to imperialism, in particular to US imperialism. We all know that the Monroe Doctrine was the US point of departure for the total domination of Latin America. This means that the peoples of Latin America who had been subjected to the Spanish yoke – or to that of Portugal, in Brazil, for example – passed over to the imperialist yoke in spite of having their governments – that is, a fictitious political independence.

Today the peoples of Latin America – whose development has reached a higher level than that of the African peoples, where class contradictions are more clearly defined, and, therefore, so are the positions of different individuals in regard to true independence – are determined, and they prove it in practice, to use whatever means necessary to fight for their genuine national independence. We could not do less than offer the greatest support to the peoples of Latin America. We follow with a great deal of interest the development of new guerrilla focuses in Latin America. We hope that they will develop further with every passing day and that their leaders will show determination in this struggle.

We believe that each people and each leadership should be free to choose the road of struggle that best suits it, but we also expect each people and each leadership to know how to recognise when the real moment of struggle has arrived, because the enemy always fights with every means at its disposal. There will be disputes over whether or not to carry out armed struggle. Within the framework of the national liberation of the peoples, there is no problem of armed or unarmed struggle. For us, there is always armed struggle. There are two kinds of armed struggle: the armed struggle in which the people fight empty-handed, unarmed, while the imperialists or the colonialists are armed and kill our people; and the armed struggle in which we prove we are not crazy by taking up arms to riposte to the criminal arms of the imperialists.

We believe that the people of Latin America have already grasped this and are showing their clearsightedness by taking up arms to fight with valour against the reactionary and imperialist forces infesting the Latin American continent.

Party Principles and Political Practice

These are some of the main lectures delivered by Cabral in crioulo *(a Guinean language consisting of Portuguese loanwords and other words and syntax drawn from local African languages), during a seminar for PAIGC cadres held from 19–24 November 1969.*

UNITY AND STRUGGLE

Let us go on with our work and talk a little to the comrades about some principles of our Party and of our struggle.

Those comrades who were aware of a document published in 1965 under the title *General Watchwords of our Party* should remember that the final part is a chapter entitled 'Apply Party principles in practice'. Obviously those watchwords dealt with fairly general principles and today we can talk about some additional principles. Everyone knows them well, but sometimes overlook that they are the foundation, the basis, the principle of our struggle. In other words, our struggle is seen in its fundamental political aspect, in its principal aspect which is the political aspect. Obviously for us to define, for example, the strategy and even the tactics we adopt in our armed struggle for liberation, other principles were stated, but these are no more than the application of our general principles to the field of armed struggle.

A first principle of our Party and our struggle, that we all know well, is: 'Unity and struggle'; which is even the motto, if you like, the theme of our Party. Unity and struggle. Obviously to study the basic meaning of this fairly simple principle we must know well what unity is and what struggle is. And we must put or treat the question of unity and the question of struggle in a particular context, that is from the geographical viewpoint and bearing in mind the society – social and economic life, etc. – of the environment in which we want to apply this principle of unity and struggle.

What is unity? We can clearly take unity in a sense which one might call static, at a standstill, as no more than a question of number. For example, if we consider the entirety of bottles in the world, one bottle is a unity. If we consider the entirety of men meeting in this hall, comrade Daniel Barreto is a unity. And so on. Is this the unity that we are interested in considering in our work when we speak of our Party principles? It is and it is not. It is to the extent that we want to transform a varied entirety of persons into a well-defined entirety seeking one path. And it is not because here we must not forget that within this entirety there are diverse elements. Rather the meaning of unity that we see in our principles is the following: whatever might be the existing differences, we must be one, an entirety, to achieve a given aim. This means that in our principle, unity is taken in a dynamic sense, in motion.

Let us consider, for example, a football team, which is made up of various individuals, eleven persons. Each person has his specific work to do when the football team is playing. The persons differ from each other: different temperaments; often different education, some cannot read or write, others are doctors or engineers; different religion, one might be Moslem, another Catholic, etc. They may even act differently on the political plane, one might be of one Party, another of another. One might be for the status quo, in Portugal for example, another might be for the opposition. That is, persons different from each other, each one feeling different from the other, but in the same football team. And if this football team, when it comes to playing, does not succeed in achieving a unity of all its elements, it will not be a football team. Each one can preserve his personality, his ideas, his religion, his personal problems, even a little of his style of play, but they must all obey one thing: they must act together to score goals against any opponent with whom they are playing, that is act around this specific aim of scoring the maximum number of goals against the opponent. They have to form a unity. If they do not do this, there is no football team, there is nothing. That is to show you a clear example of unity.

You see a person coming along, for example, with a basket on her head, and the person usually sells fruit. You do not know what fruits are inside the basket, but say: here she comes with a basket of fruit. There might be mangoes, bananas, papayas, guavas, etc. inside the basket. But in our thinking, she is coming with an entirety which represents a unity, one basket on her head, one basket of fruit. You know that it is a unity, whether from the point of view of number: one basket of fruit; or of objective: sale. It is all one thing, even though there are various things inside: various fruits, mangoes, bananas, papayas, etc. But the fundamental question that she is coming with fruit for sale makes it all into a single thing.

That is to give you an idea of what unity is and to tell you that the basic principle of unity lies in the difference between the items. If the latter were not different, it would not be necessary to make unity; the question of unity would not arise. So what is unity for us? What is the objective around which we must make unity in our land? Obviously we are not a football team, or a basket of fruit. We are a people, or members of a people, who at a certain stage of their history, have taken a certain course on their path, have raised certain matters in their spirit and their life, have guided their action in a certain direction, have put certain questions and have sought answers. It might all have begun with one person alone, or two, or three, or six. At a certain stage this question appeared in our midst – unity. And the Party was so far-sighted, that is, it understood this so well, that in its very theme it adopted as its main principle, as the base of everything, unity and struggle.

Now a question arises: was this unity, which arose as a necessity, because our ideas were different from the political point of view? No, we were not accustomed to dabbling in politics in our land. There was no party. But furthermore, under foreign domination – which is our case and that of other lands – a poorly developed society, like that of Guiné and Cape Verde, where there is no great difference between the positions of persons (although as we have seen there are some differences) cannot easily have very divergent political aims. This means that our question of unity was not in the sense of reuniting various different heads, different persons, from the point of view of political aims, of political programmes. In the first place because in the very structure of our society, in the very reality of our land, the differences are not so great as to provoke such differences in political aims. But in the second place and above all because with foreign domination in our land, with the total ban that always operated throughout our life on forming any party in our land, there were no different parties to have to be united, there were no different political courses which would have to be steered to the same path, to come together to form the unity.

So what was the question of unity in our land? Fundamentally it was simply this: in the first place, as everyone knows, union makes for strength. Right from the moment when there came into the heads of some sons of our soil the idea of eliminating foreign colonialist domination, there arose a question of strength, the strength necessary to be pitted against the strength of the colonialists. So, the more persons who join together, the more united we become, the better we reflect what everyone knows: union makes for strength. If I take one matchstick and want to break it, I can break it quickly. If I take two together, it is no longer quite so easy, and then with three or four, five, six, a given moment will come when I cannot break them at all. This is a simple, natural illustration that union makes for strength (and we must realise that union does not always make for strength, there are certain kinds of union which make for weakness – and this is the wonder of the world: all things have two aspects, one positive and the other negative). Those who had the idea of unity, because union makes for strength, put the question of unity into the spirit and letter of our struggle, because they knew that there was much division in our midst.

In Guiné and in Cape Verde there was division, division in *creole*, meaning contradiction. In our society, for example, any person who gives serious thought to our struggle knows that if we were all Moslems, or all Catholics, or animists believing in the *iran* spirits, it would be simpler. At least no force against the interests of our people could try to divide us on grounds of religion. But let us go on and look at the case of Cape Verde. In Cape Verde, where there are no great difficulties over religion, except for minor points of difference between Protestants and Catholics in their fine city life, there are other questions which divide persons – like, for example, that some families own land, and others do not. If everyone owned land or no one owned land, it would be simpler. The enemy, for example, the force opposing us and from which we want to liberate our land, can bring against us and to their side those who own land, on the notion that we want to take their land from them.

Similarly, in Guiné it can set the notables against us, on the notion that we want to take their authority from them. If there were no notables, it would be simpler; if everybody were notables, it would be easier. This means that the question of unity arises in our land, I say it again, not because of the need to bring together persons of different political thought, but to bring together persons of different economic position, although this difference is not as great as in other lands which have a social situation of different cultures, including religion. We posed the question of unity in our land, in Guiné and in Cape Verde, in the sense of removing the enemy's potential for exploiting the contradictions there might be among our population in order to weaken the strength of ours that we must pit against that of the enemy.

So we see that unity is something we have to achieve in order to be able to do something else. If we are going to wash, for example, either by turning on a tap or washing ourselves in the river, unless we are crazy, we are not going into the water without undressing; we must first take off our clothes. It is an action we carry out, a preparation so that we can take a bath. Better still: if we want to hold a meeting in this hall, with persons seated, we must call them, set up tables, arrange pencils and pens, etc. That is, we have to arrange means to be able to hold a meeting as it should be.

Unity is also a means, not an end. We might have struggled a little for unity, but if we achieve it, that does not mean the struggle is over. There are many persons in this struggle of the colonies against colonialism who up till now are still struggling merely for unity. Because, as they are unable to wage the struggle, they confuse unity with struggle. Unity is a means towards struggle, and as with all means, a little goes a long way. It is not necessary to unite all the population to struggle in a country. Are we sure that all the population are united? No, a certain degree of unity is enough. Once we have reached it, then we can struggle. Because then the ideas in the heads of these persons advance and develop and serve increasingly to achieve the aim we have in view. So you have seen more or less what is the basic idea expressed in this principle of ours – unity.

And what is struggle? Struggle is a normal condition of all living creatures in the world. All are in struggle, all struggle. For example, you are seated on chairs, I am seated on this chair. My body is exerting a force on the floor, through the bench which is above it. But if the floor did not have sufficient force to support me, I would go down below, would break through the floor. If beneath the floor there was no force, I would go on breaking through, and so on. So there is a silent struggle between the force I exert on the floor and the force of the soil which holds me up, which does not let me pass.

But you all know that the Earth is constantly in motion – perhaps some of you do not yet believe that the Earth is rotating. If you set a plate spinning, in rotation, and if you put a coin on it, you will see that the plate throws off the coin. Anyone who uses a sling to knock out crows or sparrows with a stone, as is done in Guiné or Cape Verde, knows that once he has put the stone in the sling and swung it round a few times, it is unnecessary to cast; it is enough to release part of the sling and the stone flies out with enormous force. What is needed is good marksmanship to be able to do what one wants, to know the exact moment when the stone must be released. This means that anything which is spinning, within the space in which it is spinning, develops a force which casts things outwards.

So all of us on Earth, which is spinning, are constantly being repelled by a force which pushes us off the Earth, which is called centrifugal force – which pushes us from the centre outwards. But there is also a further force which attracts persons to earth, and this is the force of gravity. This means that the Earth, like magnetic force, attracts all bodies which are close to it, in accordance with the distance and mass of each body. We remain on Earth and do not go outwards, because the force of gravity is much greater than the centrifugal force which draws us outwards. The question of sending bodies to the moon, etc., the basic question for the scientists is the following: to overcome the force of gravity. By overcoming the force of gravity, they can succeed in leaving the earth. And we know today that for a body to be launched outwards from earth, by overcoming the force of gravity, it has to travel at eleven kilometres per second. If it travels at such speed as will reach eleven kilometres per second, it has overcome the force of gravity. However, any force acting on an object can only exist if there is an opposite force. You have your hand on your face, your hand does not move the face because the face also has resistance. You do not feel it, but it is also pushing. Because the weight of it alone is a form of pushing.

In our specific case, the struggle is the following: the Portuguese colonialists have taken our land, as foreigners and as occupiers, and have exerted a force on our society, on our people. The force has operated so that they should take our destiny into their hands, has operated so that they should halt our history for us to remain tied to the history of Portugal, as if we were a wagon on their train. And they have created a series of conditions, within our land; economic, social, cultural conditions, etc. For this they had to overcome a force.

During almost fifty years they waged a colonial war against our people: war against Manjaco, Pepel, Fula, Mandinga, Beafada, Balanta, Felupe, against nearly all the ethnic groups of our land in Guiné. In Cape Verde, the Portuguese colonialists found the islands deserted. At the period when the great exploitation of African men as slaves in the world appeared, and because of the strategic location of Cape Verde deep in the Atlantic, they decided to turn the archipelago into a storehouse for slaves. Folk taken from Africa, namely from Guiné, were placed in Cape Verde as slaves. But little by little, as the numbers grew and laws in the world were changed, they had to give up the slave trade. They then turned to exerting on these folk a pressure similar to the pressure they exerted in Guiné, that is a colonial force. There was constant resistance to this force. If the colonial force was acting in one direction, there was always our force which acted in the opposite direction. This opposite force took many different forms: passive resistance, lies, doffing one's cap, 'Yes, Sir', to use all possible and imaginable stratagems to fool the Portuguese. As we could not challenge them face to face, we had to fool them, but with our energies wasted beneath this force: misery, suffering, death, disease, calamity, in addition to other consequences of a social nature, such as backwardness in comparison with other peoples in the world. Our struggle today is the following: with the creation of our Party, a new force has arisen which opposes the colonialist force. The question is knowing, in practice, if this united force of our people can overcome the colonialist force: this is what our struggle is about.

Now, taken together, unity and struggle mean that for struggle unity is necessary, but to have unity it is also necessary to struggle. And this means that even among ourselves, we are struggling; perhaps you have not understood this properly. The significance of our struggle is not only in respect of colonialism, it's also in respect of ourselves. Unity and struggle. Unity for us to struggle against the colonialists and struggle for us to achieve our unity, for us to construct our land as it should be.

The rest is the application of this basic principle of ours. Anyone who does not understand it, must understand, because if not he has understood nothing of our struggle. And we must carry out this principle in three fundamental contexts: in Guiné, in Cape Verde, and in Guiné and Cape Verde. Anyone who has studied the Party programme knows that this is the case.

From this talk you will already have understood what the contradiction is that we had and have permanently to overcome so that we can ensure the unity necessary for the struggle in Guiné. From the examples I gave you also, you have understood more or less what the contradictions were and are that we have to overcome in Cape Verde so that we can ensure the unity necessary to carry out the struggle in Cape Verde. You know that the Portuguese badly divided us, and we divided ourselves, as a consequence of the evolution of our life.

Take Guiné, for example. On one side at least there are folk of the city, on the other, folk of the bush. What is there in the city? In the city there are whites and blacks. Among the Africans there are senior staff and middle staff who have the assurance that at the end of the month their pay is certain. They have that notion of buying their own little car, as I for example, have my own car. They have a refrigerator, a fine figure of a wife, children who will certainly go to secondary school and who even, if they study hard, will go to Lisbon. Then there are those petty employees who enjoy Saturdays with their red wine and their piece of cod, who can buy a transistor radio, small possessions. Then there are the dock workers, car repairers, and we can include drivers and others who live a little better. Salaried workers in general. And then there are the folk who have nothing to do, who live by their wits each day, here and there, who do not even know what to do to arrange a lifestyle. Or folk with an easy life, like prostitutes, or beggars, tricksters, thieves, folk who have nothing to do. This is what makes up society in the cities.

But if you consider carefully, you can see that those descendants of Guineans and Cape Verdeans who are well off in life have a single common interest: they all cling to the Portuguese, pretend as hard as they can to be Portuguese, even forbidding their children to speak any other language at home except Portuguese, as you well know. And if we look at another group, their interest is also more or less the same. The Zé Marias, the João Vas, and others as well obviously, who were domestics. There are some of you, for example, who were domestics but who are nationalists, isn't that so? But their interests were more or less the same; they always live in the same sphere, the same social group.

Likewise with the dock workers, boat workers, stevedores, who are already part of another group. You might meet them, to chat, but you know that you will not sit down with them at the table to eat. Just like in the Portuguese group, for example, in the families of the governor, of the director of the bank, of the director of finances, etc., we never see there the wife of a Portuguese labourer or of anyone who is a panelbeater. Only if he should have a very beautiful daughter, whom everyone admires, she might now and then go to a dance with the upper crust. But her mother who cannot read and write does not go. She accompanies her daughter to the door and leaves. You remember such instances in Bissau.

Society in Cape Verde is similar: the same kind of city society. Only in Cape Verde this group of Africans of some means was long since much bigger than in Guiné; both as civil servants and as proprietors, owners of land. Although the land is in the bush, they live in the city. And in the city, the situation is more or less like this: civil servants or staff of some standing, petty officials and employees, workers who can be dismissed at any moment and those who have nothing to do. This is the city society, both in Guiné and in Cape Verde. In Guiné or Cape Verde, the number of whites was always low. In Guiné it never went above 3,000, and in Cape Verde it seems that it never even reached 1,000. I mean civilian whites, leading a normal life as officials, technicians, businessmen, employees, etc.

Obviously for us to achieve unity, we must see this city society in relation to the struggle. For against the Portuguese colonialists, we accept even persons from this group of whites in the struggle on our side, it they so wish. Because among the whites there may be some who are in favour of colonialism and others who are anti-colonialists. If the latter join us, that is fine, it is an additional force against the colonialists. Moreover, you know that we make good use of this. If Comrade Luiz Cabral, for example, succeeded in escaping it was because whites took him out of Bissau, to reach Ensalma and go on to the frontier. Two whites, you all know. One person who had an effect on our Party work in Bissau was a Portuguese woman. Only someone outside the Party would not know this. The first person who taught Osvaldo things about the struggle was she, not I. I did not know Osvaldo.

This means: for the struggle against the colonialist enemy, let all the forces we can bring together come. But not blindly; we must know what is the position of each one in relation to the colonialists. So in the cities we see the following: very few whites took any action against the colonialists. First, because they are the *colonial class*, those most representative of colonialism in our land. Second, because some have no interest in this, as they have their own life, want to go away when they have made their pile, are not looking for trouble. Third, because the whites, the Portuguese who live in our land, do not generally have sufficient political training to take a clear, specific position against any regime, wherever they might be.

And what about us as Africans? Among the groups we might term petty bourgeoisie, those with an assured living, whether descendant from Guineans or Cape Verdeans, there always appear three categories of persons. A minute but powerful group who are in favour of the colonialists, who do not even want to hear about this, about struggle against the Portuguese. Some of these persons went to my house in Pessubé, high ranking, with good positions, eating and drinking well, who went on holidays, etc. They sat down and said: 'Well, we want to talk to you. You, the son of so-and-so, we know you well. You are mixing yourself up in matters, you are spoiling your career as an engineer. We want to give you some advice. We have nothing against the Portuguese, we are all Portuguese.' For such as those there is no cure.

The vast majority of the petty bourgeoisie are undecided, were undecided and certainly are still undecided today, because they think: 'Cabral comes along with his schemes with his followers, and in fact it would be good if we could chase out the Portuguese, but...' Those who must suffer from the Portuguese are these city folk, with the Portuguese constantly on top of them, chivvying them in the cities, that is Mansôa, Bissau, Bissorã, Praia, S. Vicente. Whites who arrive, even if they are worthless, climb and become great figures while they themselves remain stuck as cadets or clerks. If there are competitive appointments, the whites soon go to the fore. Take, for example, Cruz Pinto's father – so many persons who passed ahead of him, but he stayed put like the fathers of others who are here. It is such folk who suffer directly from colonialism every day.

While, for example, the man who lives in the bush, deep in Oio, or in Foréa, may well die without ever having seen a white man. I remember, for example, that when a Portuguese agronomist went with me to visit certain areas in Oio, the children came up to him and rubbed his arm to see why he was white like that. Some even asked him: 'But why are you like this?' They had never seen a white man. While anyone who lives in the city sees whites every day. To resume, this is a group of persons, a large group of petty bourgeoisie, who have their pay packet at the end of the month. Their wish in fact is that the Portuguese would go away, but they are afraid, because they do not know if we can really win. 'Cabral comes along with his followers, with his schemes, but what if we lose? We lose our refrigerator, our pay at the end of the month, our radio, our dream of going to Portugal for holidays.' Those holidays in Portugal are so that they can come back afterwards to boast about them (to brag). All this keeps them undecided, on the fence. But there is a smaller group who from the start rose with the idea of struggling against Portuguese colonialism, and ready to die if necessary. And it is from this group that persons came who adhered to the Party. For if you consider carefully, the majority of those who created the Party, neither paid poll tax, nor received beatings, nor suffered from lack of employment, but on the contrary had a reasonable life. This is the position of our petty bourgeoisie towards the struggle, whether in Guiné or in Cape Verde.

And what about our salaried workers? The majority are sympathetic to the struggle, at least at the beginning. The majority – carpenters, masons, above all sailors, mechanics, even drivers – felt exploitation cruelly and earned miserable wages. And when a man who works as a mason earns ten escudos, and a white man earns eighty, if not 800, the former feels greatly exploited in his living conditions. But in this group also there are some who do not want to struggle, who are sympathetic to colonialism.

And in the group who have nothing to do, who do not have jobs, we have not usually found elements for the struggle. Generally many of them serve as agents of PIDE, while others are moderate.

In the case of Guiné, specifically, it should be noted that there is a group who come between the petty bourgeoisie and the salaried workers, and I do not really know what name to give them. Many lads without steady work, who can read and write, who work here and there, and who often live at the expense of an uncle in the city – and we have much of this in our land – but who are in permanent contact with the colonialist. Footballers, a little dazzled by the Portuguese, but also a little humiliated, because despite being good players they cannot go to the dances at the Bissau International Sports Union... These folk came to the struggle very readily. And they have played an important role in this struggle, because on the one hand they are of the city and on the other they are closely tied to the bush. They had nothing to lose except their football playing or some measly job (tailor, carpenter). But they scarcely even wanted that job because they well knew that it was not worth much in allowing them to live (to strut) alongside the Portuguese. They want to strut alongside the Portuguese, but they want Africa as well. These are folk who have learned in the city how agreeable it is to have fine possessions, but who, because of the humiliation they suffer, feel that the Portuguese are superfluous. And the Party helped them to deepen their consciousness of this situation.

And what about the bush? In the bush it all depends: if it is our Balanta society, there is no difficulty. The Balanta have what is called a horizontal society, meaning that they do not have classes one above the other. The Balanta do not have great chiefs; it was the Portuguese who made chiefs for them. Each family, each compound is autonomous and if there is any difficulty, it is a council of elders which settles it. There is no state, no authority which rules everybody. If there has been in our times, you are young: it was imposed by the Portuguese. There are Mandinga imposed as chiefs of the Balanta, or former African policemen turned into chiefs. The Balanta cannot resist, and they accept, but they are only play-acting towards the chief. Each one rules in his own house and there is understanding among them. They join together to work in the fields, etc., and there is not much talk. And it can even happen in the Balanta group that there are two family compounds close to each other and they do not get on with each other because of a land dispute or some other quarrel from the past. They do not want anything to do with each other. But these are ancient customs whose origin one would need to explain, if we had time.

Old stories, of blood, of marriage, of beliefs, etc. Balanta society is like this: the more land you work, the richer you are, but the wealth is not to be hoarded, it is to be spent, for one individual cannot be much more than another. That is the principle of Balanta society, as of other societies in our land. Whereas the Fula and Manjaco have chiefs, but they were not imposed by the Portuguese; it is part of the evolution of their history. Obviously we must tell you that in Guiné the Fula and Mandinga at least are folk who came from abroad. The majority of Fula and Mandinga in our land were original inhabitants who became Fula and Mandinga.

It is good to know this well so as to understand certain aspects. Because if we compare the lifestyle of Fula in our land with that of the true Fula in other regions of Africa, there is a slight difference; even in the Fula-Djalon there is a difference. In our land many became Fula: former Mandinga became Fula. Even the Mandinga, who came and conquered as far as the Mansôa region 'Mandingised' persons and changed them into Mandinga. The Balanta refused and many people say that the very word 'balanta' means those who refuse. The Balanta is someone who is not convinced, who denies. But they did not refuse so much, because we find the Balanta-Mané, the Mansôaner. There were always some who accepted, and who were gradually growing in number, as they accepted becoming Moslems.

Balanta, Pepel, Mancanha, etc., were all folk from the interior of Africa whom the Mandinga drove towards the sea. The Sussu of the Republic of Guinea, for example, come from Futa-Djalon, from where the Mandinga and the Fula drove them. The Mandinga drove them and later came the Fula who in turn drove the Mandinga. As we have said, the Fula society, for example, or the Manjaco society are societies which have classes from the bottom to the top.

With the Balanta it is not like that: anyone who holds his head very high is not respected any more, already wants to become a white man, etc. For example, if someone has grown a great deal of rice, he must hold a great feast, to use it up. Whereas the Fula and Manjaco have other rules, with some higher than others. This means that the Manjaco and Fula have what are called vertical societies. At the top there is the chief, then follow the religious leaders, the important religious figures, who with the chiefs form a class. Then come others of various professions (cobblers, blacksmiths, goldsmiths) who, in any society, do not have equal rights with those at the top. By tradition, anyone who was a goldsmith was even ashamed of it – all the more if he were a 'griot'[11].

So we have a series of professions in a hierarchy, in a ladder, one below the other. The blacksmith is not the same as the cobbler, the cobbler is not the same as the goldsmith, etc.; each one has his distinct profession. Then come the great mass of folk who till the ground. They till to eat and live, they till the ground for the chiefs, according to custom. This is Fula and Manjaco society, with all the theories this implies such as that a given chief is linked to God. Among the Manjaco, for example, if someone is a tiller, he cannot till the ground without the chief's order, for the chief carries the word of God to him. Everyone is free to believe what he wishes.

But why is the whole cycle created? So that those who are on top can maintain the certainty that those who are below will not rise up against them. But in our land it has sometimes occurred, among the Fula, for example, that those who were below rose up and struggled against those at the top. There have sometimes been major peasants' revolts. We have, for example, the case of Mussa Molo who overthrew the king and took his place. But as soon as he had taken the place, he adopted the same ancient law, because that was what suited him. Everything remained the same, because like that he was well off. And he soon forgot his origin. That, unhappily, is what many folk want.

In this bush society, a great number of Balanta adhered to the struggle, and this is not by accident, nor is it because Balanta are better than others. It is because of their type of society, a horizontal (level) society, but of free men, who want to be free, who do not have oppression at the top, except the oppression of the Portuguese. The Balanta is his own man and the Portuguese is over him, because he knows that the chief there, Mamadu, is in no way his chief, but is a creature of the Portuguese. So he is the more interested in putting an end to this so as to remain totally free. And that is also why, when some Party element makes a mistake with the Balanta, they do not like it and become angered quickly, more quickly than any other group.

Among the Fula and Manjaco it is not like this. The broad mass who suffer in fact are at the bottom, tillers of the soil (peasants). But there are many folk between them and the Portuguese. They are used to suffering, to suffering at

---

11 *Editor's note*: A griot is a West African historian, storyteller, praise singer, poet, musician. They are known to keep oral traditions alive.

the hands of their own folk, from the behaviour of their own folk. Someone who tills the soil has to work for all the chiefs, who are numerous, and for the district officers. We have found the following: once they had really understood, a large proportion of the peasants adhered to the struggle, except one or other group with whom we had not worked well. Among those above them (the professionals), some adhered and others not. But among the self-interested, those who work largely on their own account (artisans) and among the religious leaders and the chiefs, very few adhered to the Party, because they are afraid of losing their privileges in favour of the struggle. In these class societies, there is one group which plays a special role: those who transport merchandise from one point to another, for sale or barter (within or outside the country). They barter merchandise, lend money to the chiefs, etc. They are the Dyulas. It is a very special group in the framework of our society.

These are societies divided into classes: a ruling class, an artisan class, a peasant class. It was essential for us to achieve the greatest possible unity of the forces of the different classes, of the different elements of the society, so as to wage the struggle in our land. It is not necessary to unite everybody, as I have already said, but it is necessary to have a certain degree of unity. But this is looking at society only from the viewpoint of its *social structure*, in the broad sense. For in our society there are various ethnic groups, that is groups with differing culture and customs, who in their own belief came from various groups of differing origin: Fula, Mandinga, Pepel, Balanta, Manjaco, Mancanha, etc., not forgetting descendants in Guiné of Cape Verdeans.

In Cape Verde in the countryside, in the bush, it is complicated. There are landowners (large and small), tenant farmers (usually linked to the large land-owners), and sharecroppers, who till land that does not belong to them and later share with the owner the product of the harvest. Tenants till the land but must pay rent to the owner of the land. And there are some agricultural labourers, but few; they are not enough to form a class. They work on the properties of others. Happily in one respect but unhappily in another, as there was great calamity, the large landowners lost much of their land in the crises in Cape Verde, through drought, but mainly through Portuguese maladministration. They had to mortgage, that is deliver the title to the Bank for the Bank to lend them money, but then they could not pay back and lost their land. The Bank and the Savings Bank are today the largest landowners in our land. There are still some small landowners. The tenants, however, rent land from the Bank or the Savings Bank, or from one or other of the remaining landowners. This means that this group is a group of folk who do not have land. Whereas in Guiné we cannot say to anyone, 'let us struggle to have land', in Cape Verde we can already tell these folk: 'let us struggle because anyone who struggles can have his own plot of land to cultivate'.

This is the basic difference between the bush in Guiné and the bush in Cape Verde. All the latter group will, if we do our work properly, support the struggle. The large landowners certainly will be against the struggle. Of the small landowners, some will be for and some against, for they are comparable to the petty bourgeoisie: some for, others against and others undecided. Some are against because they think that we want to take the land and will abolish private property, and that group is against because it is still hoping. Some are for because they think that we shall take the land and there will be liberty, and they can turn their tiny plot into a large holding. Others are in doubt because they do not know what we want; they might gain something, they might lose, they are still more or less well off under the Portuguese, and they are hesitant.

But there are other contradictions: for example, in Guiné, there are ethnic groups, the so-called tribes, whom we call races in creole. We know how great the contradictions were between them in the past, and sometimes a not-so-distant past. In the thirties in Bissau, in the Bissalanca area, in Chão-dos-Manjacos. And we know that, for example, in Oio in 1954 (I was there myself) there was serious contradiction between Balanta and Oinca. All that because of old ideas, which persist in the heads of persons, but because of specific practical interests; either because they had stolen cattle, or had carried off young women, or were tilling land which did not belong to them, etc. And the Portuguese can and do exploit this to provoke conflicts between our folk. These are some of the contradictions we wanted to explain to you.

In Guiné and in Cape Verde our aim was to eliminate the contradictions in the best way possible, to raise everybody to unite around a common objective: to chase out the Portuguese colonialists.

And what about the context of Guiné and Cape Verde taken together? Is there any contradiction? Each one can think carefully and see. The contradiction there, or the seeming contradiction, was as follows: many colonial civil servants and staff in Guiné, and some district officers in Guiné, are Cape Verdeans. Given that in Cape Verde education was more developed, there is more potential for Cape Verdeans to gain posts than for the Guineans themselves. This might suggest that they (the Cape Verdeans) are taking into their hands the interests of the people of Guiné. They are the ones who are benefiting. But if we look carefully, there are also Guineans in the same situation as Cape Verdeans and there has never been any contradiction between these folk in the cities and our folk in the bush. It is in the city that we find contradiction.

Contradiction between whom? Among Guinean descendants who would like to lead the life that the Cape Verdeans had (as district officers, who are agents of the colonialists) against our people. Whereas in Cape Verde, the people are also exploited just as they are exploited in Guiné. And in some respects more harshly exploited in Cape Verde, with starvation and with the export of men as contract workers for S. Tomé and for Angola, almost like animals. The contradiction which might exist between Guineans and Cape Verdeans is a contradiction in the hunt for jobs, for good positions.

For example, an individual who has primary school certificate or third year of secondary school in Guiné, sees a Cape Verdean come along and take up a district officer's appointment; the latter eats chicken and goat, people doff their cap to him, etc., and the former has not yet risen so high. A certain resentment is born in him. But if we study the question closely, we see that the general tendency of this Guinean petty bourgeoisie is to coexist easily with the Cape Verdean petty bourgeoisie. The general tendency is for them to understand each other, alongside the Portuguese. And we have never seen in the bush, for example, any contradiction between Cape Verdeans and Guineans. Nothing which can at all match the profound contradiction we have seen between certain ethnic groups from Guiné itself. Almost all of you can see this clearly.

So we, PAIGC, have not found such difficulties from the analytical point of view in the objective of our struggle for unity of Guiné and Cape Verde, as we have in the case of unity in Guiné and unity in Cape Verde. If we just take Guiné we see many internal contradictions. In Cape Verde, taking this case on its own, there are many contradictions. But taking them together, the contradictions are lessened. The contradiction is limited to that among the petty bourgeoisie, that is where there are some contradictions. And it is from this petty bourgeoisie that the opportunist groups arise who have fought PAIGC. Groups of opportunists who, in the first movement they launched, were already ministers of this and that, with a sense of careerism, appointments, nothing more.

Obviously for us the question of unity of Guiné and Cape Verde is not raised merely as our caprice. It is not because Cabral is the son of a Cape Verdean, but born in Bafatá, that he has great love for the people of Guiné, but also great love for the people of Cape Verde. It has nothing to do with this, although it is true. I saw folk die of hunger in Cape Verde and I saw folk die from flogging in Guiné (with beatings, kicks, forced labour), you understand? This is the entire reason for my revolt. But the fundamental reason for the struggle for unity of Guiné and Cape Verde stems from the very nature of Guiné and Cape Verde. It is the interests themselves of Guiné and Cape Verde which lead us to this. Anyone who is not ignorant and who gives serious study to these questions, who has a deep knowledge of history, as much in regard to the ethnic groups in our land, in Guiné and Cape Verde, as to colonial history, such a person, if he is really interested in the advance of our people, must be in favour of the unity of Guiné and Cape Verde.

But there is a further point in the potential for practical struggle for our land of Guiné and Cape Verde. Anyone who wants to struggle seriously, as PAIGC has struggled and is struggling, can understand one thing through analysis and through studying the question in depth. It is the following: struggle in Guiné would be impossible, if it were not jointly, united – in PAIGC; struggle in Cape Verde would be impossible, if it were not jointly, united – in PAIGC. Do you know what is the practical proof of this?

For example, there is no movement which said, 'For us, the sons of Guiné alone', and which advanced. Do you know of one? There is no movement in Cape Verde for the sons of Cape Verde alone which advanced; there is none. This shows that our analysis was right and just, above all if we bear in mind the prospects as a viable political and economic entity in Africa, able in fact to achieve a new life. Obviously all those who struggle for African unity understand that we are a unique example of effective struggle for African unity (with Tanzania, which resulted from union of Tanganyika with Zanzibar). But there is no real difficulty in struggling for the unity of Guiné and Cape Verde, because by nature, by history, by geography, by economic tendency, by everything, even blood, Guiné and Cape Verde are one. Only an ignorant man does not know this.

The Portuguese knew this very well. Carreira, with all his abuses as a colonialist in Guiné, knew it well. But they pretend not to know so as to divide us. Their hope was that if Cape Verde took up the struggle, they would mobilise the Guineans to fight the worthless Cape Verdeans who were in Guiné as district officers. If the Guineans took up the struggle, they would mobilise the Cape Verdeans, in Guiné and in Cape Verde, for a hard fight against the sons of Guiné, to prevent them rising, to prevent them being free. Now our Party has given them a great shock, a tripping up. The greatest shock of their life for the Portuguese was this: in the first batch of folk who went to prison there were Guineans and Cape Verdeans together. The Portuguese were stunned. And if you consider carefully, look at this: there are many folk in Bissau who could speak on the radio. Doesn't this strike you as odd? They could speak on the radio, to slang us, etc., they could produce good talks on the Portuguese radio, but no one does this. On the radio there are only Alfa Umaru, Malam Ndjai and I don't know who else, or perhaps some scoundrel who fled from the Republic of Guinea or from Senegal and went to speak in French in Bissau. Have you already seen the point?

How is it that not one of our countrymen, whether from Guiné or from Cape Verde, who went to school and who knows enough to speak on the radio, would do this in our Guiné? There is no one because the Party long ago scored its blow. The Portuguese have lost confidence in these folk once and for all, and these folk too have lost confidence and do not become mixed up with the Portuguese, because they do not know what might happen. But the Portuguese not so long ago, a little after the beginning of armed struggle, were already declaring in Portuguese and even in creole: 'Sons of Guiné and Cape Verde, you are one, under the flag of Portugal'. Did you never hear that? But at the same time they were saying, in Mandinga, that the Cape Verdeans were worthless. To see if they could still maintain a certain division. Today they are slowly giving this up. But from time to time they put an individual up to say: 'I am one hundred per cent Guinean, not the child of a foreigner like some who were born here.' To see if they can maintain a certain idea of division.

Similarly at the start of the struggle, they would say: 'Fula, it is with your help that we are going to win this war, because you are the best sons of Guiné.' When they speak in Manjaco, they say something similar. They say that the Pepel are harming the Fula, that the Fula are harming the Pepel, to divide. But they have now seen that this serves no purpose. In our Party no one is divided, but on the contrary, we are more united every day. Here there is neither Pepel, nor Fula, nor Mandinga, nor sons of the Cape Verdeans, nothing like that. What we have is PAIGC and we are going forward.

The Portuguese are desperate. So it is they themselves, for example, who in their reviews today, like the one called *Ultramar*, have long articles studying the question of Guiné and Cape Verde.[12] They write: 'Guiné and the Cape Verde Islands – their historical and demographic unity'. And do you know who wrote that article? Carreira. Because in fact he does know about many questions of history. And in this article he collected all the documents in the Portuguese archives and studied where the sons of Guiné went when they were sent to Cape Verde. To Santiago? – Balanta, Mandinga, Beafada, etc. To S. Vincente? – went Fula, etc. With reports, on their arrival, etc. At the beginning the Portuguese were opposed to this, but they know that we are the same folk, in Guiné and in Cape Verde.

This means the same from the viewpoint of historical knowledge, of the reality of our life in the past, of understanding of the interests of our people and of Africa, and from the viewpoint of the strategy of struggle. Anyone who takes the struggle seriously knows this. There is no independence for Guiné without the independence of Cape Verde. Nor is there independence for the Republic of Guinea, for Senegal or for Mauritania, if they want to be treated seriously as countries, without Cape Verde being independent. There is none.

Only someone who understands nothing about strategy can think that this part of Africa can be independent with Cape Verde occupied by colonialists. It is impossible. The converse is true. Cape Verde cannot have real independence without the independence of Guiné and without the real independence of Africa. Anyone who places the interests of his people above his personal interests – the serious analysis of questions above any whims or ambitions – can reach only one conclusion. It is the following: the finest thing PAIGC did, that the group who formed PAIGC did, was to establish as the fundamental basis – unity and struggle: unity in Guiné, unity in Cape Verde and unity of Guiné and Cape Verde.

Anyone who has not yet seen this will see it later. But many Africans have already begun to understand. Many of the forces friendly to us have begun to see it, but our enemies as well. The concern of the imperialists today is the following: 'Will Cabral accept or not the independence of Guiné without Cape Verde?' That is their great concern. Will PAIGC accept or not the independence of Guiné without Cape Verde? That is what the imperialists want to know and

---

12 Antonio Carreira, '*A Guiné e as Ilhas de Cabo Verde: A sua unidade historica e populacional*', *Ultramar*, 23, 1968.

they even asked me. I replied to one of them: 'Tell the Portuguese to ask, you are not Portuguese.' For they know very well the significance of our entirety. One day an African leader said to us: 'You are right.' We asked him how and he said: 'I know your folk in Guiné and your folk in Cape Verde. If you should really succeed in doing what you are doing, despite being a mini-state, you will be a powerful country within Africa.' Let us see, we replied.

So let us go forward, strengthened by the certainty that we are right. The creation of PAIGC, on the basis which I have just outlined, has been the greatest achievement of our people towards the conquest of freedom and the building of their progress and happiness in Guiné and Cape Verde.

TO START OUT FROM THE REALITY OF OUR LAND – TO BE REALISTS

The reality

Another question we can proceed to discuss is the following principle of our Party: *we advance towards the struggle secure in the reality of our land (with our feet planted on the ground)*. This means, as we see it, that it is impossible to wage a struggle under our conditions, it is impossible to struggle effectively for the independence of a people, it is impossible to establish effective armed struggle such as we have to establish in our land, unless we really know our reality and unless we really start out from that reality to wage the struggle.

What is our reality?

Our reality, like all other realities, has positive aspects and negative aspects, has strengths and weaknesses.

Wherever our head might be, our feet are planted on the ground in our land of Guiné and Cape Verde, in the specific reality of our land. This is the key factor that can guide the work of our Party.

There are those in the world who take the view that reality depends on the way in which man interprets it. For such, reality – things seen, touched, felt, the world around each human being – are the consequence of what man has in his head. There are others who take the view that reality exists and that man forms part of reality. It is not what he has in his head that defines reality, but reality itself that defines man. Man is part of reality, man is within reality and it is not what he has in his head that defines reality. On the contrary, reality itself under which the man lives is what defines the things man has in his head.

You may ask: what is our position in PAIGC in respect to these two views? Our view is the following: man is part of reality, reality exists independently of man's will. To the extent to which he acquires consciousness of reality, to the extent in which reality influences his consciousness, or creates his consciousness, man can acquire the potential to transform reality, little by little. This is our view, let us say the principle of our Party on relations between man and reality.

A very important aspect of a national liberation struggle is that those who lead the struggle must never confuse what they have in their head with reality. On the contrary, anyone who leads a national liberation struggle must have many things in his head, and more each day (from the starting point of the particular reality of his land, and of the reality of other lands), but he must weigh up and make plans which respect reality and not what he has in his head. This is very important. Failure to respect it has created many difficulties in the peoples' liberation struggle, mainly in Africa.

I may have my own opinion on various matters, on the way to organise the struggle, to organise a Party – an opinion I formed, for example, in Europe, in Asia, or even perhaps in other African countries, from books and documents I have read, or because of someone who influenced me. But I cannot presume to organise a Party, to organise a struggle, in accordance with what I have in my head. It must be in accordance with the specific reality of the land.

We can give many examples. Obviously we cannot presume, for example, to organise our Party on the lines of parties in France or any other country in Europe, or even in Asia, using the same form of Party. We began a little like that but gradually we had to change to adapt to the specific reality of our land. A further example: at the start of our struggle, we were convinced that if we were to mobilise the workers in Bissau, Bolama and Bafatá to go on strike, to demonstrate in the streets, to challenge the administration, the Portuguese would change and would grant us independence. But it is not true. In the first place, the workers in our land do not have the same strength as in other lands. Their strength is not so great from the economic point of view, because the great economic strength in our land lies basically in the countryside.

But it was almost impossible to have strikes in the countryside, given the conditions of our people's political situation, political awareness, and even their immediate interests. It was impossible to ask our people to halt cultivation of those items the colonialists were exploiting. Moreover, the Portuguese, our colonialist enemy, are not like us who show a measure of respect for certain things. The Portuguese responded to strikes and demonstrations by falling upon us to kill everyone, to finish everything off.

So we had to adapt our struggle to different conditions, to our land, and could not do as was done in other lands.

And many other things show clearly that it is essential to bear in mind the *specific reality* of the land in waging the struggle. Even in the question of mobilisation and training, etc., we had to look at the problem one way in Guiné and another way in Cape Verde. Because in the case of Guiné, we can be temporarily in the Republic of Guinea or in Senegal, coming and going. For Cape Verde it is already more difficult, because it lies in the middle of the sea.

We had to devise another procedure to give better security to the struggle, so that there should not be the need for much to-ing and fro-ing. And in the evolution of the struggle, later on, when we shall begin armed struggle in

Cape Verde, it has to be armed struggle waged a little differently from that in Guiné. Because we cannot face the difficulty as, for example, in 1962 in our land. Our comrades were in great danger in the bush – we did not yet have weapons – and we gave orders for all the cadres to leave. And more than two hundred cadres went out to avoid serious calamity. Later we went in again and we advanced with the struggle. In Cape Verde we cannot do this, cannot pull many folk out rapidly.

We have to consider in each specific case the specific reality. Even in Guiné, for example, we made a serious mistake in our analysis before the struggle. We had given a fair amount of attention to the living conditions of the Balanta people, the Fula, the Mandinga, the Pepel ... and their attitude to the struggle. We had given attention to the petty bourgeoisie, salaried workers, shop staff, port workers and their attitude to the struggle, descendants of Cape Verdeans and their attitude to the struggle. We had given attention to all this, but we made a serious mistake. Namely that we did not really take into consideration the position of the traditional chiefs, of the notables (Fula, Manjaco), above all those two. We did not really take them into consideration, because we started out from the following principle: they (their forebears) had earlier struggled against the Portuguese, and were defeated, so they must have the will to struggle once again. It was an error; we were mistaken.

We must consider that we were learning how to wage struggle in step as we were advancing (on the path). The struggle on the coastline of our land is one thing: among the Manjaco it is another; in Oio it has to be different again. There are many differences. Take for example the Mandinga elders, we have to understand the way to deal with them, not the same way as we treat the Balanta elders. But in Gabú we had to wage the struggle in a completely different way. If we compare the struggle in Gabú with the struggle in the South of our land, they are two struggles as if it were a matter of two different lands.

Realism is essential, to consider the specific reality. Even in respect of certain things which are gradually advancing. At the start, the men did not want meetings with women. We did not force the pace, while in some areas women soon came to the meetings without difficulties. We must be aware of reality, not only of the general reality of our land, but also of the particular realities of everything, so as to be able to guide the struggle correctly. It is only the responsible officials or leaders who take this sense of reality into consideration (who do not think that truth is what they have in their head, but that truth is what is outside their head), who can properly guide their work as militants, as responsible officials, in a struggle like ours. Unhappily, we must acknowledge that many comrades have taken on responsibilities in this struggle without considering this factor, although we have always spoken about it.

But reality never exists in isolation. For example, our comrade Manuel Nandingna is a reality, is a real fact. But he cannot exist alone, he alone is nothing; a reality is never isolated from other realities. No matter what reality we consider in the world or in life, however great or small, it always forms part of another reality, is integrated in another reality, is affected by other realities, which in turn have an effect in or on other realities. So our land of Guiné and Cape Verde, and our struggle, form part of a greater reality that is affected by and affects other realities in the world. For example, if we consider the reality of Guiné and the reality of Cape Verde, immediately there is a greater reality, Guiné and Cape Verde. But the latter reality is within the reality of West Africa, with our two closest neighbouring countries. We can look a little wider, with our two neighbouring countries first, then with West Africa, and with the reality of the whole of Africa, and with the reality of the world, although there might be other realities between these.

This means that our own reality is at the centre of a complex reality, but it is the former that most concerns us. For others it would not be the same, it would be at some other focus, and theirs would be the central reality. But even if we think of ours at the centre, our reality is not isolated, is not on its own. In many of the things we have to do, we have first to realise that we are integrated with other realities. This is very important for us not to make mistakes.

Let us imagine the position of a unit of our army at some point. It can never operate as if it were an isolated reality, but has always to operate as integrated in a PAIGC army, integrated in the struggle of the people of Guiné and Cape Verde. If it operates like this, it is operating correctly; if it does not operate like this, it is operating badly. A political commissar in Quinara, for example, or somewhere else, S. João, for example, has always to operate as integrated in Quinara, but not only in Quinara, in the South, in the whole of the South, and not only there, in the whole of Guiné, and not only there, in Guiné and Cape Verde together. We must at all times see the part and the whole. Only in this way can we operate correctly. Unhappily the tendency of many comrades is to treat their reality as the only reality there is, forgetting the rest. To such an extent that we can find, for example, comrades in a given area who know that the comrades in another area do not have any ammunition and the former are not able to mobilise their folk to deliver ammunition. This shows our failure of awareness in seeing our own reality, and how we are integrated in a greater reality, that we ourselves have created but have not yet fully absorbed into our awareness.

Furthermore we must bear in mind the reality of others. Within our land the work of a political commissar may be very good, in Sara let us imagine. But if the political work is not good in Oio, in Biambi, or in the Bafatá area, the work in Sara does not take us very far. A unit of our army, in Canchungo, or the Nhacra area, let us imagine, can be struggling quite well, attacking the Portuguese every day. But if in other areas other units of our army are not struggling quite well, the sacrifice and the victories of Nhacra or Canchungo do not have their due value. But we are faced with still more: if the struggle in Guiné were to go well forward, but the struggle in Cape Verde did not go forward at all, sooner or later we should seriously prejudice the struggle in Guiné. It suffices to mention the following from the strategic point of view: there can be no peace in Guiné if the Portuguese have air bases in Cape Verde: it is impossible. If we were to liberate Guiné totally, for example, the Portuguese could bombard us with air bases installed in Cape Verde. They could procure many more aircraft, and South Africa, which has interests in Cape Verde, could supply them on a grand scale. We have to study the potential for taking the two realities forward simultaneously as a joint reality, a single reality.

But if we in Guiné and Cape Verde were to struggle hard, and the peoples of Angola and Mozambique did not struggle at all, and if perhaps the Portuguese could withdraw all their troops from Angola and Mozambique and send them to our land, I do not know when we would win our independence, as the Portuguese would stay on in all our villages. They would be so numerous that they could occupy all the villages and cultivate the rice. We are seeing, therefore, that the reality of our struggle forms part of the struggle of the Portuguese colonies, whether we like it or not. It is not a question of wishing. It was not I who decided this, nor the Political Bureau of the Party, nor any of you who decided it. Whether we like it or not, it is so.

This is the strength of reality. To sum up: we must be aware of this, must work so that we can follow the path together, as it should be. It is the only explanation of the policy of our Party, the commitment of our Party to CONCP, that is the group of movements in the Portuguese colonies, in their entirety. Because we know what the reality is. We even had a strong influence on the creation of FRELIMO, the Mozambican movement, because it was essential and urgent to struggle in Mozambique.

But we might struggle in all the Portuguese colonies even to the point of winning our independence, and if racism were to continue in South Africa, with the colonialists still ruling, directly or indirectly, in many African lands, we could not have confidence in real independence in Africa. Sooner or later calamity would strike again. So we form part of a specific reality, namely Africa struggling against imperialism, against racism and against colonialism. If we do not bear this in mind, we could make many mistakes.

It is the same thing for our land facing the Republic of Guinea and Senegal, with Cape Verde before them in the middle of the sea, and in turn Cape Verde facing Mauritania, Senegal and Guiné. We constitute a whole whose parts are interdependent. For example, our struggle depends heavily on the Republic of Guinea and on Senegal. From the start we realised how important the Republic of Guinea and Senegal were for us. We guided our whole struggle in the direction of going forward with them, in creating favourable conditions to take advantage of the consequences of this reality. But we must be aware of the following: both the Republic of Guinea and Senegal are aware that our reality is also important for their reality, and on this awareness depends whether they may give more or less aid. For each of them must think: who will rule that land tomorrow?

Is this to our advantage or against our interest? It is all one question. But the Portuguese too have a clear conception of this.

Just a few days ago I went to Mauritania. All the radio stations of the world reported that I had talks with President Ould Daddah, and that I was very cordially received, etc. Immediately the Portuguese unleashed a campaign on their radio station, and South Africa for its part also unleashed a campaign, to the effect that I went to Mauritania to establish a base for an attack on Cape Verde. And they have been saying for a long time that our aim is to damage the Atlantic treaty. So you see how all the realities are related. But all of us, in Africa, form part of one reality – in the world – which has all the difficulties with which you are familiar. Whether we like it or not, we are involved in these difficulties.

Today man walks on the moon, collecting pieces of the moon's soil to bring back to earth. It might seem that this has nothing to do with us, the sons of Guiné and Cape Verde. We still have our feet in the mud to drive the Portuguese from our land. But the moon walk is of great importance for our cause tomorrow, and if we were not in this difficult struggle, we ought to hold a great celebration of the fact that man has reached the moon. This is of great significance for the future of mankind, of our land, of this planet where we live.

The reality of others therefore concerns us; the experiences of others too. If I knew that one of you went out along a given path, was tripped on all sides and bruised and arrived badly hurt, and then I had to go along the same path, I should have to be careful; someone already knows the reality of this path and I know of his experience.

If there were another, better path, I would try to follow it, but if there were not, then I would have to feel my way with all the care possible, crawling on the ground if need be. The experience of others is highly significant for someone undergoing any experience. The reality of others is highly significant for each one's reality. Many folk do not understand this, and grasp their reality with the passion that they are going to invent everything: 'I do not want to do the same as others have done, nothing that others have done.' This is a sign of great ignorance. If we want to do something in reality, we must see who has already done the same, who has done something similar, and who has done something opposite, so that we can learn something from their experience. It is not to copy completely, because every reality has its own questions and its own answers for these questions.

But there are many things which belong to many realities jointly. It is essential that the experience of others benefits us. We must be able to derive from everyone's experience what we can adapt to our conditions, to avoid unnecessary efforts and sacrifices. This is very important. Obviously it is the same thing with our struggle. A good political commissar is working, for example, and another political commissar is by his side, but the latter does not take an interest in the work of the former, does not try to learn from his experience, does not try to understand why the other is working well. He turns his back and goes off alone to do his work. A commander is in an area, other commanders, even of lower rank than his, are in the same area, but the latter are not able to exchange views with the former, not able to ask him how to solve certain difficulties, on the basis of his greater experience, his longer service in the struggle. They do not want to know. These men are destroying the struggle. Obviously in a struggle like ours, it is essential to link reality with the development of the struggle. Yesterday we spoke a fair amount about certain contradictions on the social plane of our land, both in Guiné and in Cape Verde.

For us to develop our struggle we must examine the geographical reality of our land, its historical reality, its ethnic reality, that is of races and cultures, and the cultural, social and economic reality. And all this is incorporated in the greater reality of our land in struggle, which is the political reality, namely: we are under Portuguese colonial domination in Guiné and in Cape Verde.

Geographical reality

You know in broad terms the geographical reality of our land. We are a tiny territory of about 40,000 square kilometres, counting Guiné and Cape Verde, with Guiné nine times the size of Cape Verde – ten islands – on the west coast of Africa, as an enclave between two African countries (the Republic of Guinea and Senegal) and Cape Verde, about 400 miles offshore. Our reality is that we have one part on the mainland and one part insular, or islands, comprising the Bijagós islets and the Cape Verde islands, making in all more than a hundred islands and islets.

Even today many folk have not perhaps taken in the significance this has, but it is highly significant in all aspects of our land – from the defence of our land to the economy, wealth and strength of our land. Our geographical reality is further that Guiné in almost its entirety has no mountain, no high point (there are merely some hills in the environs of Boé, with a maximum height of 300 metres) and that Cape Verde is made up of volcanic and mountainous islands. Even in this aspect we see that the one complements the other. One land has no mountains and the other is all mountains. This is also of great significance not only for the economy but also for the social and cultural life that we find in our people's circumstances.

In Guiné the land is cut by tongues of the sea that we call rivers, but which at the bottom are not rivers. Farim is only a river near Candjambari. Geba is only a river from Bambadinca onwards, and even near Bambadinca the water is sometimes salt. Mansôa is only a river after Mansôa town, towards Sara, near Caroala. Buba is in no sense a river because until we reach dry land there is only salt water. Cumbidja and Tombali are entirely tongues of the sea, except for the upper reach with a little bit of fresh water in the rainy season, particularly the Bedanda river which draws fresh water from the Balana. The only genuine river in our land is the Corubal. This is a highly significant reality for us because if on the one hand we have many ports though which to enter our land in boats, we can on the other hand see the danger which this presents for us. If our land were entirely closed off, with all the twists and turns entailed by this struggle, the Portuguese would already have become desperate because their barracks would be without food. But as they have boats and our militants do not attack the boats sufficiently, they can use the tongues of the sea to take food and equipment to their barracks in the interior.

But from the economic point of view, for example, it is good and useful to have navigable rivers or tongues of the sea. That is from the point of view of the future of our land. For the struggle itself we can see how important it is for us to bear all these things in mind to develop our struggle. At the start of the struggle it was very helpful that there were many rivers in our land, many tongues of the sea, many streams, etc., for we isolated ourselves, could always defend ourselves from the Portuguese, cause them difficulties on swampy ground, make them cross rivers, etc. Today the difficulty is rather more on our side. If Bissau were on the mainland, if there were no island of Bissau, if it were not for the Corubal, if the river Mansôa were not on the other side, we should already have been inside Bissau. We could fire on Bissau every day as we did at Mansôa, for example. But in this respect geography favours the Portuguese, as the river Buba favours the Portuguese who make good use of it for their boats. On the Farim it is the same. You see therefore the significance attached to this simple aspect of geographical reality.

Anyone who has read books about guerrilla warfare will certainly remember the assertion that the major physical feature conducive to guerrilla warfare in a terrain is the mountains. But in Guiné there are no mountains. If we did not attach importance to our own reality, to put it under analysis and draw conclusions on how to operate, we should have said that it is impossible to wage guerrilla warfare in Guiné because there are no mountains. Cape Verde has mountains, this is significant, but what kind of mountains? It is essential to take this into account, and furthermore that mountains alone do not suffice. It is not the mountains which open fire; the people must be mobilised. In Guiné we have, for example, the Bijagós islands. Why is it that we did not start the struggle in the Bijagós islands but began on the other side, on dry land? Because of another reality, the economic reality.

In Cape Verde we face a serious difficulty. If Cape Verde were a single island, like Cyprus, or like Cuba, it would be easier, but there are ten islands. So we have to consider in which of the islands are we going to start armed struggle, if it is going to be effective? The same goes for mobilisation: in which island or islands should we begin mobilising? All this was and is highly relevant. We had the difficulties of communications from where we are to the islands, between the islands, etc. All this is a consequence of the geographical reality of our land.

Economic reality

Another reality we have to consider is economic reality. Our principal economic reality is that we are Portuguese colonies, because when all is said and done the political situation is a consequence of the economic situation.

We, in Guiné and Cape Verde, are a people exploited by Portuguese colonialists, our labour is exploited by Portuguese colonialists. This is what is significant. This is the economic reality.

But are we a developed country? No. We are economically backward, with scarcely any development, in Guiné or Cape Verde. There is no real industry, agriculture is backward, our agriculture belongs to the age of our grandparents. The wealth of our land was drained off, above all man's labour. But the Portuguese did nothing to develop any resource in our land, absolutely nothing. Our ports are worthless, both in Bissau and in S. Vicente. They could have made good ports, but they merely made some mooring quays which are worthless. When we look at Dakar's port, or Conakry's port, which are good ports, or better still those of Abidjan, and of Lagos, in Nigeria, we can see how the French and the British built big ports, where twenty or so ships can moor. And then we see how much time the Portuguese wasted in teasing us, tinkering and playing with us. They did nothing for our land.

So that is our economic reality and, for peace or war, we in Guiné and Cape Verde are an economically backward people, whose principal means of livelihood is agriculture. Tilling the soil for subsistence food, and not always reaching subsistence level, as in Cape Verde, for example. Even in Guiné in some areas, if there is not much rain, there are always shortages at least until the *fundo* is ripe. The Portuguese have been here for so many years and the situation has remained static, economically backward. We have no real industry to speak of, either in Guiné or Cape Verde. In Guiné we have a so-called mini-plant for pressing oil from rice shelling. This is not a factory, it is no more than a great 'pestle'. We have a mini-plant for treating rubber (tappings), and a small fishmeal factory in Bijagós. In Cape Verde, there are three fish-packing stations, where the Portuguese work for as long as they feel like it, fill their pockets with money, close down the factory and go away to relax.

And just to give you some idea of the shamelessness of the Portuguese, I recall, for example, how when I was at secondary school, my mother went to Cape Verde and took a job at the fish-packing station, because she made nothing from sewing. And do you know how much she earned per hour? Fifty cents an hour. If there were a lot of fish, she might work eight hours a day, earning four pesos (escudos). But if fish were scarce (and she had to walk a long way to reach the factory), she would work for one hour and earn 50 cents.

So, a backward economy; this has a strong bearing on the war. You see: we are a people who do not have factories, we cannot capture factories from the Portuguese to start manufacturing something. Today we have vast liberated areas; if there were factories there, it would be useful. Perhaps we could make cloth, perhaps we could make soap on a proper scale, instead of comrade Vasco's tiny soap bars. We could manufacture other things if we had mines. Then there would be many more folk wanting to help us, more than those who now help us. Friends and enemies would try to help us if we had mines in operation, with the promise of a lot of bauxite, a lot of petrol. Many of them would come rushing.

And if the petrol in our land had already begun to be exported, perhaps even Standard Oil would be sympathetic to us against the Portuguese. Perhaps the American government would be sympathetic to us against the Portuguese. Perhaps it would even have the courage to say to the Portuguese: 'Either you stop and give independence to Guiné now, or we shall withdraw all our aid to you, and attack you in the United Nations.' And why? Out of their own interests. But as our land has nothing developed, they think of us as a corridor between the Republics of Guinea and Senegal, a simple passageway.

But as I have said, the backwardness of our economy has a bearing on the war situation, and so does our unfamiliarity with our resources. For example, it would be a lot different if our people already had enough experience in iron casting to manufacture weapons. There are peoples who are struggling and while some fight at the front others are making weapons in the rearguard. We cannot do this; we can only make muskets, but muskets are ineffective. If it is only with muskets that we are going to win the war against the Portuguese, or against any colonialist, our struggle will be very long indeed.

But if we had a developed economy, this would mean that our people would also be culturally stronger in the modern perspective, would have more schools, more secondary schools, and would be able to handle mortars, artillery and even aircraft. The commanders would be more capable of understanding all the questions of strategy and tactics and would all know how to read maps. We see, therefore, the significance of having to struggle in an economically backward country.

Social reality

All of you know what the social reality of our land is, the disastrous consequence of colonialist exploitation. But let us not put all the blame on the colonialists. There is also exploitation of our folk by our own folk. You saw this yesterday when I spoke to you about the social structure of our land. We are in fact exploited by colonialists in our land of Guiné and Cape Verde. In trade in Cape Verde and in Guiné it is always the colonialists who profit most to the last, because in Cape Verde, for example, there is no commercial enterprise which is not tied to an enterprise in Portugal. Likewise in Guiné, the monopoly on all our trade (not ours, their trade) belonged to Gouveia and Ultramarina, tied to the banks, all Portuguese. But we must tell the truth. Many of the Cape

Verdean people suffered because of exploitation by landowners, themselves Cape Verdeans. Similarly, in Guiné, part of the great suffering of our people was at the hands of our own folk. We must not at all forget this, so that we shall know what to do in the future.

This therefore is the specific reality. In Cape Verde our population endure wretchedness. In years of heavy rains there is abundance, one eats well, fills the belly and can even stretch out and relax a little; but for most of the time when there are insufficient rains, there is famine. During the last 50 years more people have died from starvation in Cape Verde than the population today. Others were contracted for S. Tomé and transported like animals in the holds (those who died were thrown into the sea), some were sent to Angola. In Guiné, as you know, the whole range of colonialist exploitation existed: forced labour on the roads, all kinds of outrages, abuses and humiliations.

And Portuguese doctors who studied the situation in Cape Verde said that they came away with one certainty, the certainty in their scientific opinion, that the whole population showed symptoms of malnutrition. If it was not a question of total starvation, it was a case of specific starvation, meaning a lack of certain elements which are essential to the well-being of the human body. This specific starvation also exists in Guiné. In Guiné nearly everyone has malaria; if we were now to make tests on all the comrades present here, we would find that nearly all have intestinal worms. There is widespread leprosy, diseases of all kinds.

Social disaster for our people, which makes us a weak people from the scientific and sanitary point of view. A man who lives almost exclusively on rice cannot have the same resistance as a man who eats rice, meat, milk, eggs etc. It is true that when a foreigner comes to our land and goes marching with our comrades in the bush he lags behind. That is something else. But from the point of view of fitness, we know that a person in our land who is aged thirty has already begun to age. In our land it is unusual to come across old men with a beard and white hair. The average life span in our land of Guiné and Cape Verde is 30 years. Our life expectancy is thirty years; anyone who lives beyond the thirties is lucky.

Now life expectancy in other lands where one eats well, drinks well (I do not mean getting drunk) as one should, is 60 and 67 years and each year grows higher. On any count it is more agreeable. If someone is born with the certainty that he is going to live for seventy years, he has time to make something of it. But what can one do in thirty years? The difference is due to inadequate diet, hygiene and health care and to wretched living conditions. That is the social condition of our land: abuses by the Portuguese, abuses by some sons of our land who misuse others, wretchedness, diseases, famine, and on top of all that a short life span. A difficult situation, very difficult.

From the cultural point of view, it is true that conditions in Cape Verde are a shade better than in Guiné. Given the conditions under which the population developed, the question of being or not being an *indigenous inhabitant* never arose, so in theory any Cape Verdean child can go to school (the official school). It is no less true that overall there are far fewer schools than in Guiné.

There are some things that you do not know and which might mislead you. It is true that in Cape Verde more folk learned to read and write than in Guiné under the colonial system. But the level of illiteracy in Cape Verde, contrary to the boast of any Cape Verdean who thinks he knows it all, is 85 per cent. The Portuguese liked to boast that in Cape Verde there were no illiterates. This is a lie! When I went there for holidays in 1949, I made some tests of those who could read. There were folk who had gained primary school certificates (some four or five years before) in the bush, in Godim or in Santa Catarina, for example, to whom I would give the newspaper to read, but they did not know what they were reading. There are also illiterates who can pick out the letters. There are many such folk in the world, even some doctors. But we must shed many illusions.

In Guiné 99 per cent of the population could not go to school. Schooling was exclusively for the assimilated, the children of the assimilated – you know the whole story, I am not going to tell it again. But it was a disaster that the Portuguese caused in our land, by not allowing our children to advance, to learn, to understand the reality of our life, our land, our society, to understand the reality of Africa and the modern world. This is a great obstacle, an enormous difficulty for the development of our struggle. Only today I told you that the Fula people migrated across Africa, as did the Mandinga people, as it happens, though many of you did not know, nor do many comrades. A Beafada who is called Malam something or other, for example, does not know that in ancient times Malam, Braima and suchlike were not Beafada names. And what happened with the Beafada happens to many folk of our land.

Take for example, Vasco Salvador Correia. Formerly his folk would not be called Vasco, nor Salvador, still less Correia. It means that the Mandinga in dominating the peoples of our land practised assimilation (the Portuguese were not the first to want to *assimilate* in our land) and so those dominated began to adopt Mandinga names. Likewise, the Mandinga of today did not have the same names in that epoch. The ancient names of the Fula were not Mamadu or anything of the sort. All this is borrowed from Arabic. Mamadu means Mohamed, Iussufe means Joseph, Mariama is Mary, semitic names.

The cultural reality of our land in Cape Verde (raising now the question of the colonialists who did not allow us much advance) is the consequence of the fact that the colonialists allowed Cape Verdeans to study, to the extent that they needed to train folk as agents of colonialism, as they had used Indians. Just as the British used Indians in colonisation and the French used Dahomeyans, so the Portuguese too used Cape Verdeans, by teaching a certain proportion. But at a certain stage they closed the path once and for all; no more than a certain number of primary schools, no more than one secondary school; one secondary school which moreover Vieira Machado, the then Minister for 'Overseas', wanted to change into a training centre for fishermen and carpenters, just when I was about to begin secondary school. I waited three months without going to classes at secondary school, because they had closed it. For them what they had done was enough, no more was needed. From then on only training centres for fishermen and carpenters. The population rose and protested, and the secondary school began operating once more.

But now the reality of our own cultural situation in Cape Verde is the following: it is the transfer of African cultural reality to the islands. Then came contact between this African culture with other cultures from outside, from Portugal and elsewhere. Many folk think of Cape Verde as Praia or S. Vincente. But anyone who knows the bush in Cape Verde feels in Cape Verde an African reality as palpable as any other fragment of Africa. The culture of the Cape Verde people is quintessentially African: in beliefs it is identical – in Santiago there is the *polon* which some still regard as a sacred tree. The *polon* is not common because of the many droughts. But those which still exist are sacrosanct. There is moreover *morundade*, sorcery. 'Spirits' which walk at night, flying creatures, who make up an interpretation on life's reality which almost totally matches that in Africa – not to speak of the casting of spells.

Cape Verde was a melting pot of various ethnic groups and there was a fusion of their cultures; but until the 1940s, for example, some distinct groups retained some of their own characteristics. For instance, groups who were settled around Praia in Santiago retained the word *tabanca* for the village and their festivals were of a given kind, while elsewhere, in Achada Santo Antonio, for example, the village was of another type, and different again for the folk of Santa Catarina, Picos, etc.

In Guiné, the culture of our people is the product of many African cultures: each ethnic group has its own culture, but they all share a common base, in their world view and their relations in society. And we know that although there are Moslem populations, at bottom they are also animists, like the Balanta and others. They believe in Allah, but also believe in the *iran* spirit and in sorcerers. They have the Koran but an amulet on their arm and other things. And the success of Islam in our land, as in Africa in general, is that Islam is able to understand this, to tolerate the culture of others, whereas the Catholics want to put a quick finish to all this and have only belief in the Virgin Mary, Our Lady of Fatima and in God and Our Lord Jesus Christ.

This is the cultural reality of our land. But we must consider our culture carefully; it is dictated by our economic condition, by our situation of economic underdevelopment. We must enjoy our African culture, we must cherish it, our dances, our songs, our style of making statues, canoes, our cloths. All this is magnificent, but if we rely only on our cloths to clothe all our folk, we are wrong. We have to be realists. Our land is very beautiful, but if we do not struggle to change our land, we are wrong.

There are many folk who think that being African is being able to sit on the ground and eat with one's hand. Yes, this is certainly African, but all the peoples of the world have gone through the stage of sitting on the ground and eating with one's hand. There are many folk who think that it is only Africans who eat with their hands. No, all the Arabs in North Africa do it. But even before they were Africans, before they came to Africa (they came from the East to Africa), they used to eat with their hands and seated on the ground. We must be aware of our things, we must respect those things of value, which are useful for the future of our land, for the advancement of our people.

No one should think that he is more African than another, even than some white man who defends the interests of Africa, merely because he is today more adept at eating with his hand, rolling rice into a ball and putting it into his mouth. The Portuguese, when they were still Visigoths, or the Swedish, who give us aid today, when they were still Vikings, could also eat with their hands.

If you see a film about the Vikings of olden days, you can see them with great horns on their heads and amulets on their arms, setting off for war. And they would not set off for war without their great horns on the head. No one should think that to be African one must wear horns on one's chest and an amulet round one's waist. Such persons are individuals who have not yet properly understood the relationship between man and nature. The Portuguese did the same, the French did it when they were Franks, Normans, etc. The English did it when they were Anglo-Saxons, voyaging across the sea in canoes, great canoes like those of the Bijagós.

We must have the courage to state this clearly. No one should think that the culture of Africa, what is really African and so must be preserved for all time, for us to be Africans, is our weakness in the face of nature. Any people in the world, of whatever status, has gone through the stage of these weaknesses, or has to go through them. There are folk who have not reached it: they spend their lives climbing trees, eating and sleeping, nothing more yet. And then what myths they still believe! We should not persuade ourselves that to be African is believing that lightning is the fury of the deity (God is feeling angry). We cannot believe that to be African is to think that man has no mastery over the flooding of rivers. Anyone who leads a struggle like ours, who bears responsibility in a struggle like ours, has to understand gradually what concrete reality is.

Our struggle is based on our culture, because culture is the fruit of history and it is a strength. But our culture is filled with weakness in the face of nature. It is essential to know this. And we could point out further, for example, that certain of our dances represent relationships of man to the forest: folk appear clothed in straw, in the shape of birds, and others like great birds, with a huge beak, and folk run in fear. We can do many such dances, but we have to go beyond this, we cannot merely stop there. We can preserve the memory of all these things, to develop our art and our culture which we display to others. But as we have already gone beyond this, we know that it is we who rule in the forest, in the bush, we, human beings, and not any animal or spirit lurking there. This is very important. But this is the cultural reality of our land.

Various comrades who are sitting here have an amulet at their waist, in the belief that this will allow them to escape Portuguese bullets. But not one of you can say to me that not one of the comrades who have already died in our struggle had an amulet at his waist. They all had them! It is just that in our struggle we have to respect this, we have to respect this because we start out from reality. We cannot in the least order the comrades to tear off the amulet, or we would be treating our comrades as the Germans would. Many years ago, the Germans would not go to war without an amulet. Even today there are some who carry an icon of Our Lady of Fatima inside a small book; it is their amulet. The Bible is their amulet and before beginning battles they cross themselves. The Portuguese come along with a great cross on their chest and at the moment of beginning the battle, they kiss it; it is their amulet. And there are still some who believe in our amulets.

This is a question of our cultural level in relation to the specific reality of war. We accept it, but no one should think that the leadership of the struggle believes that if we wear an amulet at the waist we shall not die. We shall not die in the war if we do not wage the war, or if we do not attack from a position of weakness. If we make mistakes, if we are in a position of weakness, we shall die for sure, there is no getting away from it. You can tell me a whole series of tales you have in your head: 'Cabral doesn't know. We have seen occasions when it was the amulet which spared the comrades from death, the bullets were coming and turned back in ricochet.' You can tell me this, but I live in hopes that the children of our children, when they hear of this, will be happy that PAIGC was able to wage the struggle in accordance with the reality of their land. But they will have to say: 'Our fathers fought hard, but they had some funny ideas.' This discussion may be premature, I am talking about the future, but I feel sure that the majority understand what I am saying and that I am right.

The amulet is characteristic of Africa. Even lawyers I know in other African countries go about decked with their amulet at the waist and, when they are going to plead cases at court, put on a big amulet: 'Never know when I might win with this.' Even some comrades from another Portuguese colony, because our struggle was making good progress, sent to ask us if there was some lucky charm which we could send them too.

I merely call the comrades' attention to the fact that they should see this as a strength and as a weakness. It is a strength, because a comrade who puts on his amulet believes in something other than the words of the Party and we cannot overlook that he feels more courageous. It is a weakness because in his trustfulness he could make many mistakes.

There were cases of our comrades dying in the following way. An aircraft arrives, everyone dives for the ground, the aircraft bombards but nothing happens. Suddenly a comrade remembers that he does not have his amulet with him; he stands up, runs to his hut and grabs the amulet; on his return he is machine-gunned and dies with the amulet in his hand. Perhaps some of you know of similar cases. But how many of you can think this: what foolishness this is, how can it be?

The fact of the matter is that our struggle has its strong face and its weak face. Many of us believed that we should not install ourselves in certain bush areas because they belonged to the *iran* spirit. But today, thanks to many *iran* spirits of our land, our folk understood, and even the *iran* understood, that the bush belongs to man and no one is afraid of the bush any more. We are even well established in the Cobiana bush, the more so because that *iran* spirit is a nationalist. It 'said' openly that the Portuguese had to go away, had no right to be in our land.

But you must understand that all this is also an obstacle to the struggle. At one time many comrades who had taken up this life and were solid – my comrades whom I hold in high regard and who had spent a long time with me – if they were told by me: 'Go into the interior, stick tight to the work of mobilising the people', and Secuna Baio or some other soothsayer told them: 'Do not go, I have cast your fortune and see great harm for you if you go into the interior', perhaps they would kill themselves because they were ashamed of facing Cabral, but they would not go. There were comrades who did not make ambushes just because a 'soothsayer' told them they should not make ambushes as one of them was going to die. And the comrades used to be so accustomed to the elders giving them orders, making decisions for them about the war, that later it was the elders who came to complain: 'Cabral, what is happening, the youngsters don't obey us anymore, they go into attack without consulting us?' I answered: 'Elder, look at it this way. If once upon a time the youngsters would not attack without consulting you, I never said anything to them about it. So today I am not saying anything to them. But I never appointed you as commander, they are the commanders. If in the past they consulted you, that is their business. Now they don't want to any more? That's none of my business.' The elder was a little angry, but he is not stupid, he is cunning. When all is said and done, the elders were the intellectuals of our society, of our genuine, real society. They were the ones who saw things clearly, who understood everything (our strengths and our weaknesses) and they soon shifted their ground, adapted themselves to the new situation.

On the cultural plane, our Party has tried to derive the best possible result, the best possible benefit from our cultural reality. It does so by not banning what it is possible not to ban without prejudicing the struggle, or by creating new ideas in the comrades' spirit, new ways of seeing reality. And further by making the best possible use of those who already have a little more education, both to lead the struggle itself and to be sent to study how to train cadres for the future. All this might seem very simple, but it is difficult, it is very complex to find the right answer for this.

Political reality

The political reality of our land is that greater reality that we all know well, it is the fact that we were a Portuguese colony. Our people could rule themselves neither in Guiné nor in Cape Verde. The Portuguese ruled even if they might appoint a black administrator – as only Honorio Barreto had the honour or disgrace of being – and the truth was that the Portuguese ruled in our land, Portuguese colonialism. And it was this greater reality that created the conflict between us and the Portuguese, exploitation of our people, under cover of Portugal's policy. This basically is what generated our struggle.

Our struggle grew so much that we must take advantage of it to transform even geographical reality, to the extent that we can. It would seem improbable, but it is the truth. For when we build dams, bridges, etc., we shall change the geographical landscape of our land, we are going to make a new human geography that we are creating in our land. When we completely transform the islets of Bijagós, when we make Cape Verde into a magnificent centre for world tourism, for example, this will already be a new geographical reality that we are creating. The ships which now pass by far out to sea will begin to stop there. But we must through this struggle transform the economic reality of our land. Let us put an end to exploitation by the Portuguese, but let us put an end to exploitation of our people by our own folk. And we must develop our land, make it progress as much as possible. This is what our struggle means: social reality, cultural reality, everything is going to change. And already a new political reality has arisen in our land and it is the following: we are ruling ourselves.

Obviously our reality has strengths and weaknesses, as I have already shown you. For example, the fact that we do not have great economic development is a serious weakness. But it is also a strength, for if our land had important mines, important factories, etc., the imperialists would have come into the war more quickly and in greater strength. Perhaps we should have had to fight not only against the Portuguese, but against other imperialists as well. As it is, at least we have a quieter life, just bush and desert.

But we cannot let ourselves sleep. Obviously the social reality of our land – where, for example, there are no grand bourgeois, no great capitalists – is helpful for our struggle, because we do not have the difficulty of having to fight those who have super-exploited our folk. But it is also a weakness, because in some lands some local capitalists adhered strongly to the struggle, with all their resources, with all their money, etc., and gave significant help. As in Cuba, in China and in other countries where many local capitalists took the revolution seriously. And some leaders are the sons of great capitalists.

Another advantage is that our land does not have great class differences, very wide differences, and that the better-off classes, who have most resources, are small in number, very few persons. This avoids many difficulties of division on social grounds for us. But in the social reality of our land, and we talked about this yesterday, there is the question of ethnic groups and it is a great weakness. For in this very room there may still be folk capable of thinking: I am Pepel. I am Mancanha and the Mancanha does not fail his companion. I am Mandinga. This is a great weakness of our struggle. And it would be very damaging if in fact we let it go on, if in fact we were not able to eliminate all this on the path of struggle.

I want to call your attention to the factor, which you should consider carefully to see what is happening in Africa, of questions of tribes, the so-called tribalism, wars between ethnic groups, etc. It is not the people who invent all this, the people do not heed it, because the people pursue reality with great realism, defend their own interests. The truth is the following: the era of tribes in Africa has already passed. There was an era in which the tribes struggled against each other because of land, to take land to graze their cattle, etc., to find better soils, or because of their children, their wives, to test their own strength, but this is over and done with.

As soon as our African peoples succeeded in forming States, even States of the military type, as soon as the African peoples succeeded in bringing together folk from different tribes for one task, to serve one class, the tribes had begun to disappear. When the Portuguese and other colonialists came they did away with it once and for all, except that they tried to preserve the superstructure, meaning those who were ruling the tribes, or the groups, so that these would serve as intermediaries to help the colonialists to rule. Our people today, Oinca or Balanta, or some other, may retain ancient memories – 'We and the Mandinga did not get on very well in fact' – but if there were no one to incite them, they would no longer go this way. The same happens with Ibo and Yoruba in Nigeria, or Bakongo and other groups in Congo. It takes someone to incite them, someone who says: 'Let's start something. They've got big ideas, but the Mandinga will show them.'

Some folk even despise their tribes, folk who no longer even want to know about this. They have studied in universities, in Lisbon, or Oxford, or even in the capital city of their own land. Today, because Africa has acceded to independence, they want to rule, they want to be President of the Republic, they want to be Minister, so that they can exploit their own people. So when for some reason this is denied them, they remember their tribe: 'I am Lunda, born of Lunda, descendant of the Lunda king. Lunda people, rise because the Bakongo want to eat us.' But it has nothing to do with Lunda or Bakongo; it is wanting to be president, to have all the diamonds, all the gold, all those fine things in one's hand, to do as one pleases, to live well, to have all the women one wants in Africa or in Europe. It is for the sake of touring Europe, being received as presidents, wearing expensive clothes – a morning coat or even great bubus to pretend that they are Africans.

All lies, they are not Africans at all. They are lackeys or lapdogs of the whites.

What happens in Nigeria also happens among us, at least shows among us, namely some folk want to serve only their own political ambition. It means that we must recognise that only ambition can defend divisiveness, whatever the ground of division might be. The Portuguese, for example, have done much harm to us but we cannot lump all whites together as 'Portuguese'. Only some overly ambitious fellow would be able to say: we cannot accept the help of so and so, in Bissau, who is white or of so and so, in Catio, who is white. How? This is no good. If we want to serve our land, our Party, our people, we must accept everyone's help. But as a friend, as a companion in struggle. Someone who is looking after his own belly, a good job for himself, might think: 'Whether he is clever or stupid, perhaps we could accept him, but to walk over him. Otherwise, it is best for him to clear off, or he might take my place from me.' That is not correct.

This is why we need to know the reality of our land, reality in all aspects, of all kinds, so that we shall be able to guide the struggle, in general and in particular. We have to recognise that in the specific circumstances of reality in our land of Guiné and Cape Verde, much courage is required to answer with confidence this question: 'Can we in fact wage a war like this?' Obviously we can say yes, because we are doing it. But at the start it was difficult. There was the man who asked: 'But how are we going to struggle against the Portuguese, if we do not even have clothing, if we cannot read or write? The Portuguese warfare is made by commanders, majors, etc., trained at university or senior academies; how are we going to struggle against them? We don't have anything. Where are we going to find material for struggle? How can this be?'

We have to do some straight thinking so as to answer yes, we can. We have to place our reality in the reality of the modern world. We can say: we were all divided, each group isolated; but in the reality of the modern world, many folk can bring our people to the understanding that we can be united, Balanta, Pepel, Mandinga, descendants of Cape Verdeans, etc. We can go forward together without panicking. And we have shown that this is really possible. In the reality of the modern world, a new Africa has risen to independence, to progress, and we must count on it. There is a socialist camp which has grown from the October Revolution, which placed the following assertion before everything: self-determination for all peoples, each people must choose their destiny, take it into their own hands. There are moreover international laws established in the United Nations.

We must bear all this in mind, the reality of the whole world, the world wars there were, with all the difficulties they brought, so that we should have the courage to prosecute the struggle in our land. For if we were to limit ourselves to an isolated reality, within our village, it would be impossible to imagine how we should go and struggle against colonialism.

You see therefore the importance of knowing our reality and of knowing also all the realities. It is for us to know where ours is among the others, for us to know our total strength and our total weakness. Only in this way can we see the actual situation. We could struggle, we could wage our own struggle, could make many sacrifices, but it would not be enough to wage the struggle from our own resources. It could not be enough. What was essential was that our Party should be able to take advantage of other favourable conditions in the world and in Africa for us to take our struggle forward. And we did take advantage and we are constantly taking more advantage. So we were able to have weapons, ammunition, clothing, medicines, hospitals, etc., that we could not have in our land. We asked of ourselves the sacrifice and the effort that we could give, but we counted also on the reality of the modern world, on strengths which might come from outside. This is the significance that aid from other countries has for our struggle. Aid for us has only one condition: that it is unconditional. We guarantee that all the aid we receive is put to the service of our Party and our people.

We might say that no liberation movement in the world has made better use of aid given to it than our Party. We all are familiar with the admiration we arouse in all those who see our achievements, outside and inside our land, and who see that we have in fact put everything we received to the service of our struggle, to the service of our people. We have tried to use in the Party's service the skills of all the comrades. If some do not give everything they can, it is because they are unwilling. There is no lack of example, or lack of encouragement. We have tried constantly to raise standards, making direct use of the help we receive in training cadres. So we have the need to use our own experience, our own strength, our own sacrifice and effort to transform our reality. But we need as well to know the experience of others, and to have the help of others and to use this help correctly.

Through the marrying of our strengths with the strengths that might come from outside, we can effectively transform the reality of our land. We have already changed a great deal, because today, in our land, in the greater part of our land, the Portuguese do not rule. In Guiné the Portuguese are squeezed in a colonial war they know is lost. In Cape Verde, where matters are already on the boil, they are harassed to the point of calling on their friends to come to the rescue. The loss of Cape Verde for them means the end of Portuguese domination in Africa. We know therefore that we are able to transform this reality. The mere fact of holding this meeting is further clear evidence of a new reality of our land.

In the land we used to know – in the reality Cruz Pinto left when he went to study in Portugal, or Bobo left when he went to study politics – a meeting of comrades like this one was not possible, whether inside or outside our land. Once upon a time in Bissau, I called the closest friends of my household, and said to them: 'Comrades, you are close friends of my mother, you are my friends too. You come to my house, we eat, we joke, but the time for joking has ended. Let us start a little discussion.' They replied: 'Yes, surely.' We discussed, we arranged a meeting. But only one or two came. The others did not come because they thought that this was madness. If we compare that moment with the moment today, we can see in fact that the creation of PAIGC was the point of departure for creating a new reality in our land of Guiné and Cape Verde. We must go on creating and developing it more and more each day so that we can serve not only and principally the interest of our people, but also the interest of Africa and the progress of mankind.

OUR PARTY AND THE STRUGGLE MUST BE LED BY THE BEST SONS AND DAUGHTERS OF OUR PEOPLE

Our struggle is not mere words but action, and we must really struggle. You will recall that in the early 1960s, many folk persuaded themselves that struggle meant speaking on the radio. Famous victories were scored on the airwaves of Dakar or of Conakry, even against PAIGC, but not against Portuguese colonialism, because the opportunists never did anything against the colonialists. Those were olden days when persons rushed to see who could be the first to speak on the radio. As if that were the struggle.

In our Party we have always considered as basic and correct the following: the struggle is not a debate nor verbiage, whether written or spoken. Struggle is daily action against ourselves and against the enemy, action which changes and grows each day so as to take all the necessary forms to chase the Portuguese colonialists out of our land.

And we must wage this struggle wherever it might be necessary. First, inside our land, because rice is cooked inside the pot and not outside. But we must never forget that a struggle like ours must also be waged outside our frontiers, against our enemies and at the side of our friends, to obtain the necessary means for our struggle and to build the potential for supplying the struggle inside our land.

The fact that PAIGC had established the principle that the struggle must be waged seriously and that everyone, no matter who, must struggle, drove many folk away from the Party. For some persons approached PAIGC, or even managed to join PAIGC, with the idea that they would have to struggle on the radio and that tomorrow they would take up an appointment as Minister. When they discovered that to be in PAIGC's struggle, one had to be inside or outside the country, as the leadership decided, some went away and went so far as to rejoin the Portuguese to have a little enjoyment of the crumbs of colonialism. This is one of the main reasons why the opportunists in Dakar, for example, combat our Party! Some of them would dearly love to join our Party, but they do not have the courage. They know that the Party could tell them: 'Stick tight, let's go inside.' But what they want is to leave Dakar to go straight to Bissau and sit down on a departmental director's chair.

Everyone must struggle – that is another certainty in the context of our Party. And gradually in our Party we have reached the stage when in theory and in practice there is no distinction between the interior and the exterior in our struggle. At the start of the struggle there were some who preened themselves because they were inside the land. They thought that those outside were afraid and did not do much, as they were outside. Anyone who in a struggle like ours hangs on to this idea or other complexes of vanity and fear, because he is inside or is outside, has not understood our struggle.

But anyone who has never left the bush and has withstood seven years of struggle but has failed to understand the significance for the struggle inside the land of the work of those who are working outside the land, has not understood anything either. And someone who is outside, seated in an office or somewhere, and has failed to understand the value of those who are inside the land and who are opening fire, or preparing the political ground and suchlike, and the value of the latter, has also not understood anything. Our Party, without much talk, without great debate, has reached this position: we all know today that there is no interior or exterior, because all are as likely to be inside as outside the land. Obviously we are not going to confuse other people's lands – the Republic of Guinea or Senegal – with our land of Guiné and Cape Verde. Rice is cooked inside the pot, but we know how important firewood and many other things necessary for cooking rice are. Some Party comrades had the idea that by virtue of going into the bush for the struggle, they were kings and could walk over anyone around. They were mistaken.

Now we know that it is not true, it is not like that. The Congress at Cassaca made it known that this was not true. If anyone goes into the bush to command guerrilla warfare and to struggle, but does not strictly follow the Party watchwords, then he should watch out, for we are going to forget the Portuguese a while to go and deal with him first. But some in their work outside pick up bad habits, thinking that they cannot dirty their feet in the mud, that they cannot be bitten by mosquitoes, that they cannot go through what our combatants, our leaders, our responsible workers are going through in our land. They are badly mistaken! They are folk who in fact are not really committed to the struggle. Perhaps we made the mistake in making them leaders of the Party, but sooner or later they will find out that it is not like this.

Our Party has the situation that no one is 'inside' or 'outside', everyone is inside or outside according to the needs of the Party. Leaders of the struggle and the Party must always be abreast of everything happening outside or inside our land which touches the type of work they are doing in the Party. For several years now we have been able to say the following: not one of our leaders, not one of our responsible workers has not carried out missions outside the land, and not one of our leaders has not also worked inside the land.

Obviously there are some militants or responsible workers even who have spent more time outside than inside, and who spend their time pleading to go inside. It is pleasant to hear this, but one must ask if their duties and their training require them to be inside the land or outside. This is the crucial point, because tourism we can leave for later.

There are also folk in the interior who plead to go to Europe. Later on, if they do not manage to go now, if they are not given a mission there, when we have retaken our land, if they work hard, they will fill their pockets with money and can take a trip to Europe and return. But the movement of our workers, whether outside or inside, is determined by the needs of our struggle. This is basic for us. In my case as a leader, I must respond personally to the needs of our struggle in conferences, in meetings with Heads of State or with leaders of other Parties in the world. This represents for me, as for other comrades who work with me, a decisive task in our struggle. But it is a great strength to me to have the certainty that there is no important operation in our war, no important political project of which I am not personally aware, which I do not study. There is no change or real development on the political plane or in the armed struggle which does not go through my hands. The trouble is that we have human limitations. Unhappily I cannot be everywhere at the same time but I have spent as much time as possible at the side of our combatants and militants.

Another principle linked to what I have just mentioned is that we must struggle without rushing, struggle in stages, develop the struggle progressively, without making great leaps.

If you consider carefully, you see that many struggles began by forming a Political Bureau, a General Staff, etc., but we did not begin with this. Many struggles began by forming early on a national liberation army; we did not begin with this. We began our struggle as one plants a seed in the ground, to yield. One plants a seed, a seedling is born, which grows and grows until it produces flowers and fruit: that is the path of our struggle, stage by stage, step by step, progressively without great leaps. Moreover, each stage means at the same time greater demands on our work, on our dedication, on our energy. This is basic; it is like a growing child who at the start is satisfied with a feeding bottle of milk, or mother's breast milk, but when he is aged three complains if he is given a feeding bottle of milk or the breast, because this is no longer enough for him.

The same happens in our struggle, in our Party which co-ordinates our struggle. In step as we grow; as we develop, as the struggle goes on to new stages, it is fundamental that each of us gives more and more and more. More in moral behaviour, in political behaviour, in political awareness, in work each day and each moment, more in the influence that each brings to bear on other comrades to put them on the right course. Unhappily we must admit that this has not been true for everybody, and the opposite even has happened with some comrades. In step as the Party advances, grows, has greater strength, in step as our struggle advances, as our responsibilities grow, these comrades have neglected their work. They have sought comfort, to flee from responsibilities, an easier life, to begin enjoying themselves, thinking that they already have independence in their grasp. This is one of the greatest weaknesses of our Party, one of the biggest factors which has held back the work of our Party. For these comrades, including some leaders, were not able to progress at the same rate as the struggle. Instead of advancing, by studying more, learning more, studying the lessons of each day, they lagged behind, through idleness, softness, even vices. This is happening to various comrades. We have done our best to help them, not to let them follow this course, for our struggle makes constantly greater demands, and the demands are that much greater when the responsibilities of a militant are greater.

These comrades have not matched the greater demands of the struggle. They seek comfort, pretend to be working and are not working at all. In their own conscience, they know it. Other comrades begin to work with enthusiasm, and fervour, making a reasonable contribution, and suddenly it is as if they have been put out by a shower of cold water. Why? Because they were not able to follow the struggle, to understand profoundly the meaning of the work they were doing. This is very damaging; it brings great harm to our struggle. If we are not able to combat this vigourously, if each of you is notable to keep this clearly in mind, particularly you, the youth, who are taking on responsibilities in the Party, if we cannot keep our older comrades firmly on course, we are going to face great difficulties. Neither heroism in the armed struggle, nor the support of our people, nor the skill of the Party leadership, nothing can save us, if we, as men and women, cannot follow the demands of the struggle, to give more, constantly more, in all aspects of our life.

Some comrades, even among those seated in this room, have a tendency to seek comfort in step as their responsibilities grow. It seems that some comrades spend several years waiting for responsibilities in order to make the mistakes which others have made in the position. We must combat this courageously, for the struggle is demanding, and our Party is constantly more demanding. And we must throw out those who do not understand, however much it hurts us. We cannot allow it, while the struggle advances, our people sacrifice themselves in the cause of our struggle, some comrades die and others are wounded or disabled, while we grow old in the struggle, giving our whole life to the struggle with so many folk putting their hope in us, inside and outside our land. We cannot allow some militants or responsible workers to lead a soft life and commit acts which go against our responsibility to ourselves, to our people, to Africa and to the world.

Many folk think that this is Cabral's backyard, that he is the one who has to spot what has gone wrong or who has gone wrong. They are wrong. Each of us has to notice, to stand firm in correction, for if not, nothing can save us, whatever victories we might have won. So our struggle is like the basket which separates clean rice from the husk, like the sieve which sieves pounded flour, to separate the fine flour from the coarse grain and other things. The struggle unites, but it also sorts out persons, the struggle shows who is to be valued and who is worthless. Every comrade must be vigilant about himself, for the struggle is a selective process; the struggle shows us to everyone, and shows who we are. This is one of the great advantages for our people in waging a struggle, above all armed struggle, to liberate themselves.

There was one elder, who by the way is still in the struggle, who said to me three years ago: 'Cabral, I pray every day for Salazar not to die.' 'Why, my elder?' 'So that the struggle continues a while longer, so that Salazar continues obdurate, so that we should continue, so that we should know each other better.' This is a sound truth; today we know each other well, today we know who is worthy and who is not.

We are making an effort for the unworthy to improve, but we know who is worthy and who is not worthy; we even know who may tell a lie. There are some that we do not yet know well. You know me too. You know other leaders of the Party whom we respect highly, for they will be steadfast to the end, and you know this well. There are others of whom some are afraid, because they know that their only merit is the power they wield. Some of you here have seen Party leaders make serious mistakes but you go on obeying them because you are afraid of them. Today we know ourselves well. Some of you have seen responsible workers in the Party treat other persons badly and knew in your conscience that this was not just, but you kept silent, covered it up. But you then were certain that such were not good leaders, were not good responsible workers, as they maltreated, acted against the Party line, and did this with the certainty that the Party leadership collectively would not find out.

Each of you here, who has been close to a responsible worker or a leader, has a clear idea about that man or woman. The struggle has allowed us to know each other very well and this is highly important. Some have been able to improve each day, others have sunk further each day, despite all the help we tried to give, to bring each person on, with head held high in the service of the Party, to serve our people correctly.

Whether we like it or not, the struggle operates a selection. Little by little, some pass through the sieve, others remain, for our firm resolve as long as we are here as leaders of this Party is the following: only those will go forward who really want to struggle, those who in fact understand that the struggle goes in stages. We can advance only those who truly understand that the struggle constantly makes more demands and gives more responsibilities and who are therefore ready to give everything and demand nothing, except respect, dignity, and the opportunity to serve our people correctly.

I should like to remind you, in respect of struggle by stages for example, that many of our comrades thought that the struggle would advance more quickly, that we should soon enter Bissau. It is not like that; it must be by stages and we must be prepared for a long struggle. At the point we have reached, our independence could come tomorrow or the day after or in six months' time, because the Portuguese are driven to desperation in our land and if we stand firm they will be increasingly desperate. But we must have our morale adjusted to a long struggle, we must prepare new militants to carry it on, if need be.

And you, the youth here, must take your responsibilities on your shoulders. You must fully understand the following: if the struggle were to end tomorrow, you should be ready, as youth, to ensure the work of our people, to build the progress our Party wants. But if it were to last ten more years, you, the youth here, have the duty of taking the place of the older men who can no longer carry on, and have the duty of preparing other young men, so that they are trained in time to take up the struggle. The Vietnamese say that they will win the war for certain, because if the Americans are ready to fight for ten years, they are ready to struggle for ten and a half years; if the Americans are ready to fight for 20 years, they are ready to struggle for 20 and a half years. This is the consciousness of a people who know their national rights, that their land is theirs, and whose youth and adults are ready really to serve their people.

It is clear that a struggle like ours, a Party like ours, require secure leadership, united leadership, enlightened leadership, and it is our own reality which shapes awareness. We need to be aware, for to the measure that man is aware of reality, he acquires the strength to change that reality, to transform it into a better reality. In the framework of a struggle like ours, of a Party like ours, the leadership must go to the most aware men and women, whatever their origin, and wherever they come from: that is, to those who have the clearest concept of our reality and of the reality that our Party wants to create. We are not going to look to see where they come from, who they are and who their parents are. We are looking only at the following: do they know who we are, do they know what our land is, do they know what our Party wants to do in our land? Do they really want to do this, under the banner of our Party? So they should come to the fore and lead. Whoever is most aware of this should lead. We might be deceived today, or deceived tomorrow, but the proof of the pudding is in the eating, it is practical experience which shows who is worthy and who is not.

So that is our principle: the best sons and daughters of our land must lead our Party, our people. But does this mean that we have in fact always appointed the best? Some are worthless, but we are still going through an experimental phase. The truth is that we have always given persons the opportunity to improve, we have given all workers in the Party the opportunity to advance, to show their leadership capacity. There are comrades sitting here who three years ago were raw recruits in our military training camps. Today they are members of our Inter-regional Committees or leaders of our armed forces. This shows to what extent our Party has been able to open a broad path for our comrades to progress, for those who are most aware and most worthy to lead.

Our struggle demands enlightened leadership and we have said that the best sons and daughters of our land must lead. It is hard to know soon after they have come in who is the best. Following the principle we talked about at the start – trusting wins trust – and as some reveal their ability, we shall bring them forward. Then we shall see if they are in fact the best or not, if they improve or degenerate.

The truth is that no one can say that in this Party the opportunity to command is not given to everybody. Everybody has this, the way is wide open for everybody. Our hope has always been the following: the more who are able to command the better, for we can choose the best of the best to command. We have done our utmost to improve the training of comrades, to think more about the difficulties, to show more initiative, more enthusiasm, more dedication, to make progress. And we have done our best to be fair, to bring forward those who really deserve it because of their own efforts, and not for their pretty faces or because they can be someone's stooge.

In the Party we have rigorously avoided anything which smacked of some persons being subject to others, or some being stooges of others. From the very start, I said the following: we do not want servants, we do not want stooges, we do not want errand boys. We want men, comrades who know what they are doing, our comrades, who can look us straight in the face, who can engage in debate with due respect on both sides. We want men and women who understand and who hold their heads up. We have struggled firmly against a tendency for leaders and responsible workers to form a retinue of 'laddies', or to treat responsible workers under their orders as if they were their messenger boys. But we have also fought in the morale of comrades the attitude of letting others take their responsibilities.

Obviously there has been some resistance to this. A particular instance was the occasional stubborn, silent resistance to the presence of women among the leadership. Some comrades do their utmost to prevent women taking charge, even when there are women who have more ability to lead than they do. Unhappily some of our women comrades have not been able to maintain the respect and the necessary dignity to protect their position as persons in authority. They were not able to escape certain temptations, or at least to shoulder certain responsibilities without complexes. But the men comrades, some, do not want to understand that liberty for our people means women's liberation as well, sovereignty for our people means that women as well must play a part, and that the strength of our Party is worth more if women join in as well to lead with the men. Many folk say that Cabral has an obsession about giving women leadership positions as well. They say: 'Let him do it, but we shall sabotage it afterwards.' That comes from folk who have not yet understood anything. They can sabotage today, sabotage tomorrow, but one day it will catch up with them.

Another resistance which persisted for a while in the Party was the following: we were the few leaders, and no one else could be a leader. Various comrades of ours, good combatants, able men, were overlooked, held in their tracks, because some of the leadership never gave them the chance to come forward. This is killing the Party, as if one suffocated it. For while we older ones have breathing space, we are getting on, but when our breath is failing, there is no one to take our place. The strength of our Party is only effective if we, the leaders, are able to open the way for the youth to progress, youth like you, other youth who are still behind, in their hundreds, in their thousands, to take over and to bring the best forward to lead.

We in the Party leadership, and I in particular, have done our utmost to back all those who show willingness to work. My greatest joy is to see a comrade, man or woman, carrying out duties conscientiously and willingly without being pushed, as it is so often necessary to push some to do what they have to. This is a great encouragement for us, and gives us the certainty that we can overcome, do what our Party wants. Everyone in the Party knows what friendship, what regard, what respect, what warmth we have for those who can carry out their duty. Everyone we see working with complete enthusiasm is like a part of ourselves, a new part which is a guarantee of the future of our Party and victory for our people. That is why our work is to encourage and to seek to develop in everyone, the youngsters, men and women, the will to stand firm, to understand the Party's aims, and to go forward. This should be the task of every leader, of every responsible worker in our Party.

But some comrades show the following tendency. A political commissar, for example, spots a young lad as a good militant. Instead of taking an interest in him to help him to understand more, to make progress, instead of stimulating him, no, he turns him into a messenger boy. For the latter is wide awake, knowledgeable, quick moving. If you give him something to look after, he looks after it well. So the commissar gives him his kitbag to look after, instead of making him an asset for our land. Or it might be a case of a bright and fairly attractive girl. Instead of helping her, giving her a hand to make progress in becoming a nurse or a teacher, ingoing to study, or become a good militia fighter or something of the sort, no, he makes her his mistress. For the latter is very beautiful and he has the right to take charge of her. We must put an end to this.

We do not want to ban servants, girlfriends, or children, it is not that. What we must do is to stop spoiling the future of our Party. Anyone who wants a servant must wait till the morrow of our independence. Let him work and if he has the means, let him find his servant, if there are folk who want to be servants. He cannot use the authority of the Party, which the Party has put in his hands, to find his servant. Anyone who wants a girlfriend, today or tomorrow, can find her, woo her, marry her, but he must not use the authority of the Party to have all the women he wants. As long as this goes on we are making mistakes and justifying the Portuguese and all the enemies of our people.

We must be aware of this. And you, the youth, as militants or responsible workers in our Party, must be aware of this. Your task is not to have children today, it is to serve the Party, to raise the Party banner high. Your task is to help the men and boys, women and girls of our land to rise in revolt, and not to be running after terylene trousers from Senegal or quick deals here and there. That is not it. If you do that, you will roundly fail in your historic mission which is to be at the age of twenty or so a responsible worker in this Party.

Some of you who have travelled out of our land have seen the respect our Party inspires, the consideration our Party receives, and how much hope our Party has given to other folk in the world, and in Africa. But comrades often forget this, deep in the bush they forget completely their responsibility as leaders. Some have tried to make the utmost use of the authority the Party gave them so as to satisfy their own stomachs, their vices, their convenience. This must stop. And it is you who must stop this at all levels.

This is also why we must be vigilant against opportunists. Opportunists are not only those who are in Senegal trying to make their fringe movements. There are also opportunists among us, who knowing that our leadership requires the best sons and daughters of our land to lead may pretend to be the best. Or they may try their hardest to please their responsible workers, so that the latter will propose them as leaders or as responsible workers. We must be careful of this, we must unmask them and combat them. You must understand that the only good leader, the only good responsible worker is one who face to face can report the mistakes others make. Many comrades in responsible positions at various levels have made the serious mistake of hiding the mistakes of others: 'I shall keep mum. If Cabral finds out, all right, if he does not find out, forbearance.' That is destroying the work and the sacrifice the individual is himself giving, for he is compromising himself and spoiling the other.

We must be careful to unmask all opportunists among us, all the liars, all the cowards, all those who do not respect the Party line. We must have the courage to shoulder our responsibilities; that goes for all of us, young responsible workers or leaders of our Party. We must have the courage to look each other straight in the eye, because our Party can only be led by men and women who do not have to lower their eyes before anyone.

Another important aspect we have to defend in the Party leadership, which is already stated clearly in the published watchwords, is that our Party is led collectively, it is not led by one person. At any level, in political action or in the armed forces, in security or in education, anywhere and at the different levels there is always collective leadership. But the tendency of some comrades is to monopolize leadership just for themselves. They decide everything, they do not consult the views of anyone at their side. This cannot go on, for two heads are always worth more than one, even if one is clever and the other stupid.

On this point you must read carefully the lecture we had on collective leadership (leading in a group). But I remind you that collective leadership (leading in a group) does not mean that everyone must command, and that there is no longer any authority. Some think: 'If we must command, then let's command even if we have no idea how to command, just to give the appearance that everyone commands.' This is a nonsense. Long ago I said that even if it is not necessary to be a doctor to command in our Party, we must not forget that there are some tasks which cannot be done by someone who cannot read or write. Otherwise we are fooling ourselves and we must never fool ourselves. There are some tasks which can or cannot be done according to educational level. We must also remember that the Party has a hierarchy, that is a ladder of persons in command, and this must be respected, really respected, and it has not always been respected as it should be.

In the specific conditions of our national struggle, before the historic needs of our people, our Party must at this moment have clearly defined chiefs so that everyone should know who is who and so that there should be no confusion. Whatever their level of command, in the Political Bureau or whatever, they should aim at this attitude: here is a chief who does not have to remind anyone that he is chief, who mixes with everyone, who does not have the least pretentiousness, and so is the one to be our chief. He is not puffed up by showing to everyone that he is in command, but he never forgets at any moment that he has to be a chief, and he does remind anyone who forgets it.

The leadership of our Party is the strength of our people, and is responsible for everything done by our militants, responsible workers, combatants, etc. Our leadership must be one and united. We cannot allow any division among us. When we speak of the higher leadership of the Party, we are speaking of leadership at any echelon, whether at the Inter-regional Committee or at the Party Zone Committee; no one can turn his back on his companion in struggle. Anyone who does not understand this is a wrecker.

Take, for example, the armed forces leadership. Various instances have occurred when the political commissars did not get on well with the commanders. It is criminal to have these misunderstandings when they have the Portuguese before them to fight. We have had occasion to transfer comrades because they were ambitious and jockeying with other companions in struggle. We can no longer tolerate this. The time has come to reduce the grades of all those who do not get on with each other. There will be no more transfers. They will come down in grade, to become ordinary private soldiers or ordinary militants. We have passed the stage of teaching comrades that we must understand each other. Our enemy is the colonialist Portuguese and not some other enemy.

In this very room there are comrades who worked together and were not able to get on with each other. They should be ashamed. And why? Because they were thinking of their belly, their ambitions, instead of serving the interests of the Party? This is the mentality of petty ambition, of caprice. Instead of devoting their attention to the struggle, to Party work, they look to see who has more, who has less, petty squabbles, shabby intrigues... And at bottom it is a lack of courage, cowardice when all is said and done,

This cannot go on; the time has come to stop this. In the bush or out of the bush, the time has come for each one to bear the weight of his consciousness, to put aside caprices, to take a firm grip on work, so as to make no mistake on the path. And we must remind the comrades from the zones, above all them, of the importance local leadership has for retaining the people's enthusiasm. We cannot tolerate that a comrade should be Political Commissar of any area for one, two or three years and should come to the end without having any authority, so that everyone does what he pleases and takes no notice of his leadership. This is a total failure for a comrade. And we must observe that some local leaderships, which were working very well at the start, only began to do badly and to make mistakes when the leaders began to think of their belly, treating their area as if it were already independent and beginning to think of their own life.

There is a film I never forget because it taught me a great lesson. There was once a young lad who was educated in some priests' college and who believed strongly in miracles. He knew nothing about life, because he had spent his life in the college and left as a man of twenty-one. All the injustices he discovered were one evil; he did not understand that on one side was misery and human suffering and on the other the rich. But he managed to find a dove which wrought miracles. And so, as his thoughts were on the sufferings of others, he resolved to do everything to help others, so that there should be no hunger or cold, so that everyone should have houses in which to live, so that each one should achieve his desires. He did not think about himself but asked the dove to do miracles for others. So the dove appeared to him and perched on his hand.

He said: 'Give houses to the poor' – and the houses appeared, with all their furnishings. 'Give food to the starving' – and food appeared, good food. He would even call persons to ask them what they wanted, and he would grant it. Until the day when he found a girl with whom he fell in love. His beloved would ask him for something and he would grant it. Other folk said that they too had wants, but he had no more time, now he had time only for his beloved. Suddenly the dove took wing and flew away. The miracles ended and everything he had done as a miracle began to disappear; while the dove was still in his hand, the miracles ended. He could no longer do anything for others, because he was thinking only of his girlfriend, of his belly.

There is a great moral in this. So far as we are able to think of our common problem, the problems of our people, of our own folk, putting in their right place our personal problems, and, if necessary, sacrificing our personal interests, we can achieve miracles. That is how all the leaders, responsible workers and militants of our great Party must be – in the service of the liberty and progress of our people.

STRUGGLE OF THE PEOPLE, BY THE PEOPLE, FOR THE PEOPLE

A basic principle for our struggle is that it is the struggle of our people, and that it is our people who must wage it, and its result is for our people.

You have already clearly understood what the people are. The question we now pose is the following: against whom are our people struggling?

Obviously a people's struggle is effectively theirs if the reason for that struggle is based on the aspirations, the dreams, the desire for justice and progress of the people themselves and not on the aspirations, dreams or ambitions of half a dozen persons, or of a group of persons who are in contradiction with the actual interests of their people.

Against whom must our people struggle? We answered this clearly right from the start. We, as colonies of Portugal in Guiné and Cape Verde, are dominated by a foreigner, but it is not all foreigners who dominate us and within Portugal it is not all the Portuguese who dominate us.

The force and oppression which is exerted on us comes from the ruling class in Portugal, from the Portuguese capitalist bourgeoisie, which exploits the people of Portugal as much as it exploits us. And as we know well, the ruling class in Portugal, the colonialist class in Portugal, is tied to world domination by other classes in other countries, who together make up imperialist domination. It is tied to the ensemble of capitalist forces in the world which as well as dominating their own countries have a vital need to dominate other peoples, other countries, both to have raw materials for their industry and to have markets for their manufactures. In short we are dominated by the Portuguese colonialist capitalist class, tied to world imperialism.

Our people are therefore struggling against the Portuguese capitalist colonialist class, and struggling against that means necessarily to struggle against imperialism, because the Portuguese class is a piece, albeit minute and rotting, of imperialism. So we know against whom we are struggling.

But we face the question not only of liberation but also of progress for our people. And on this basis we quickly see that our struggle cannot only be against foreigners, but must also be against their internal enemies. Who? All the social strata of our land, of *classes* of our land, who do not want progress for our people, but merely want progress for themselves, their family, their own. And so we say that our people's struggle is not only against anything that might be contrary to their liberty and independence, but also against anything that might be contrary to their progress and happiness.

The struggle in our land must be made by our people. We cannot for a moment think of liberating our land, of building peace and progress in our land, by bringing in foreigners from outside to come and struggle for us. In Guiné and Cape Verde we are the ones who must struggle, we are the ones who must buckle down to all the means of struggling. And in fact this is what has happened.

It is now quite common to hear this exchange in our Party; someone asks: 'Are you of the people?', and the other replies: 'No, I'm army'. 'Are you of the people?', 'No, I'm militia'. 'Are you of the people?', 'No, I am a responsible worker.' That is how we commonly talk, but all those folk are people. It is enough to see where our combatants, our responsible workers, our leaders come from to understand that they are all people from our land. Naturally enough in the armed struggle in Guiné, the majority are from Guiné itself. Likewise in the struggle in Cape Verde, the majority are from Cape Verde itself. Guiné and Cape Verde are separated by sea and it is not easy to transfer large forces from one point to the other.

But there can be no doubt that it is our people who wage our struggle, through their children as militants, leaders, combatants, militia, etc. The fundamental strength is our people, themselves. Our population, or rather the population linked to the work of our Party, mobilised and organised by our Party, has from the beginning fed our struggle, borne sacrifices for our struggle, and so has been the principal strength of our struggle. It would have been impossible for us to wage the struggle, in the era of clandestineness, were it not that our people kept us alive among them like a fish in water.

The enemy know that it is our own people who share in the struggle, and so they make efforts to separate the part of our people who are Party and the part of our people who are population, to draw from us this principal strength in the liberation struggle, namely the support of the mass of the people. We might say that our struggle has the more potential for victory, the more we can keep on our side the support of the mass of the people in our land. The Portuguese know this too, and so they are making every effort to take this support from us.

Our struggle is for our people, because its objective, its purpose, is to satisfy the aspirations, dreams and desires of our people: to lead a decent and worthy life, as all the peoples in the world want, to have peace in order to build progress in their land, to build happiness for their children. We want everything we win in this struggle to belong to our people and we have to do our utmost to form an organisation such that even if some want to divert the conquests of the struggle to their own advantage, our people will not let them. This is very important.

Our people now do really feel that the struggle is theirs. Not only because it is their children who have the weapons in their hands. Not only because it is their children who study and are trained as cadres, nurses, doctors, engineers, technicians, etc. Not only because it is their children who lead. But also because even in the villages, the militiamen or civilian population take up what principally symbolises our struggle: weapons. It is not by chance, or for any other reason, that our Party leadership has given weapons, and constantly gives more, to our population. It is precisely so that no one should take it into his head that only those who take up arms in the people's army or in the guerrilla force are effectively struggling for results in this struggle. The more weapons there are for our supporters, the more certainty our population and our people will feel that the struggle is really theirs, and the fewer illusions there will be in the heads of our combatants and leaders that the struggle is their exclusive concern.

We are struggling for the progress of our land. We must make all the sacrifices to succeed with progress for our land of Guiné and Cape Verde. We must put an end to all injustices, miseries and suffering. We must guarantee for the children born in our land today and tomorrow a certainty that no barrier or wall should be put in their way. They must go forward, according to their capacities, to give their utmost. They must constantly improve the lot of our people and our land, serving not only our interests but also those of Africa and of all mankind. That is why from the start our Party set out on the best course for this, namely organisation based on mobilising our people, mobilising the population of our land for the struggle against Portuguese colonialism.

Our Party has trained the children of our land to mobilise the people of our land. This work was no laughing matter. Many of you here, young lads who are today responsible workers in the Party, cannot imagine how difficult this work was. Moreover, we have organised within the framework of our Party a large proportion of the population of our land. This was the principal political strength of our struggle, which provided the potential for our struggle to advance as well as it has advanced. We must train our people, we must train ourselves – leaders and militants of our Party, our combatants who are making the sacrifice today – to defend at all costs the conquests our people are making through their struggle.

Today the people born in the bush, who yesterday could express no views on their lives and on their destiny, can express their views, can make decisions. They can decide issues in the Party committees and in the people's courts, where the descendants of our land have shown the ability to try the errors, crimes and other wrongdoings committed by other descendants of our land. This is further clear evidence that this struggle is of our people, by our people and for our people.

But various Party comrades, with high or low responsibilities, and even ordinary combatants have not understood this very well. They have tried to turn the struggle a little to their advantage, after all they are the people, it would seem. The struggle of our people, by our people, but for them. This is one of the most serious mistakes that can be made in a struggle like ours. We cannot in the least allow our armed forces, our militants or our responsible workers to forget for a single instant that the greatest consideration, respect and dedication is owed to the people of our land, to our population, above all in the liberated areas of our land. Anyone who is ready to die from some bullet in this war but is able to show lack of respect for our people, the village folk, the population, will die without knowing why he is dying, or dies under a delusion.

The more we can do in our land to raise the morale of our people, to give them greater courage and greater enthusiasm for the Party, the more it helps the present and future of our people, helps our Party. Anything that is done to destroy the population's confidence in us, to bully the population, to show lack of consideration for them, to steal their goods, to abuse their sons and daughters, is the worst crime that a combatant comrade or a responsible worker could commit. It damages our Party, and damages the future and present of our land.

It is better that we should be few in number but incapable of doing any injury to the population of our land than that we should be numerous but include folk capable of causing harm. For anyone among us who turns the population against our Party, to mistrust the Party, to lose confidence in the Party, is the best ally the Portuguese could have. You know – and what I am saying is not in my imagination – that there are comrades who behaved badly towards our population. Fortunately the situation has become much better because the Party has been vigilant in this matter.

So at each moment of this great struggle we are waging, we must focus on two phases: one, against the colonialist capitalist ruling classes in Portugal and imperialism which want to dominate our land economically and politically; the other, against all the internal forces, whether material or spiritual (meaning ideas from the mind), which might arise against our people's progress on the path of liberty, independence and justice. These demand courageous struggle against imperialist agents. But in addition, permanent and determined struggle against those who, even if they are militants, responsible workers or leaders of the Party, do anything which could prejudice our people's march to total conquest of their dignity, their liberty and their progress.

INDEPENDENCE OF THOUGHT AND ACTION

Another important principle in our Party line is the following: independence in our thought and in our action.

We are struggling for the independence of our land, for the independence of our people. The first condition for this is that our Party and its leadership should be independent in its way of tackling questions and of answering them, and in its action inside or outside our land. This has been our Party line.

All decisions we take in the framework of our Party, about our work inside or outside our land, on the African or the international plane, are taken with absolute independence in our way of thinking and acting. This is one of our sacrosanct principles, which we must defend at all costs.

But we must understand that independence is always relative. In many things we have to decide, for example, we have to gauge them in the light of the interests of our neighbouring countries as well for us to go forward. In many decisions we take on the African or international plane, we are guided by the interests of Angola and Mozambique as well. Some positions we may take, or even some decisions on war material, for example, or our action, are not solely dependent on us but are also dependent on our friends who give us aid. But this does not destroy the truth of the principle.

The PAIGC leadership has always acted on the basis of independence of thought and action. We have been capable, and must constantly be more so in thinking deeply about our problems so as to be able to act correctly, to act strongly so as to be able to think more correctly. Many comrades have not done this in keeping with their responsibilities. Some have limited themselves to acting without thinking, and others have lots of ideas without doing anything in practice. We must be able to bring these two basic elements together: thought and action, and action and thought. This independence in our thought and action is relative. It is relative because in our thought we are also influenced by the thought of others. We are not the first to wage an armed struggle for national liberation, or a revolution. Others have done this, there are other experiences. We did not invent guerrilla warfare – we invented it in our land. But in the framework of this relative independence, we must be aware that no struggle can be waged without an alliance, without allies. In all struggles we must make a choice, that is we have to choose one path or another. We cannot wage a struggle without knowing what path we must follow. So we must first know one thing: who are our allies in Africa and in the world.

We talk a lot about Africa, but we in our Party must remember that before being Africans we are men, human beings, who belong to the whole world. We cannot therefore allow any interest of our people to be restricted or thwarted because of our condition as Africans. We must put the interests of our people higher, in the context of the interests of mankind in general, and then we can put them in the context of the interests of Africa in general.

In Africa our allies are those governments, parties or states, individuals or organisations who really want effective independence for Africa, who really want their people's independence, economic independence so as to hold their history in their hands, for their people to hold the wealth in their hands, so as to advance, so as to build a better life. But our specific and immediate ally is anyone openly opposed to Portuguese colonialism in Africa. You know that there are Africans who are not in the least opposed to Portuguese colonialism. But our closest ally, our real ally is anyone who not merely offers words but also aid against Portuguese colonialism. It is not enough to say 'I am African' for us to say that person is our ally; these are mere phrases. We must ask him frankly: 'Do you in fact want the independence of your people? Do you want to work for them? Do you really want our independence? Are you really opposed to Portuguese colonialism? Do you help us? If the answers are yes, then you are our ally.'

We are also part of the world. Who are our allies in the world? It is not difficult to know today. All our people know. Why? Because we have practical proof. Who gives us aid? They are our allies, those who give us aid. Who gives us aid?

First in the world, the socialist countries. But there are some socialist countries who betrayed their role in providing aid for our struggle, in being our allies, when they put the interests of their states, their concerns, their ideas, above the interests of our struggle. They went so far sometimes as to try in an underhand way to divide us, so as to defend their ideas rather than the interests of our struggle. So even in the socialist environment, one must ask specifically: 'Do you in fact help us? Do you do nothing against us? Are you giving us the aid you can, the aid that you owe as part of the world vanguard? If you are, you are fulfilling your duty as our ally, if not, then you are not in fact our ally.'

There are other men and women in the world who are our allies. In capitalist countries there are persons who are opposed to Portuguese colonialism: they are our allies. We have one criterion to distinguish our friends from the friends of the Portuguese. Anyone who is opposed to Portuguese colonialism is our friend, is our ally. Anyone who supports Portuguese colonialism is our enemy, is the ally of the Portuguese.

But in the world, as part of mankind and of Africa, we have taken a clear stand in the anti-imperialist struggle.

We are not the only ones, there are other peoples. We must be consistent. If we demand solidarity with us from other peoples, we must show solidarity with them as well. We must show solidarity with all the African peoples who struggle for the genuine independence of their land, for the liberty, progress and happiness of their people, and above all with those who struggle against the colonialist-racism of the whites in southern Africa. In pride of place, our comrades in Angola and Mozambique, our companions in struggle. We have to be able to show them the greatest possible solidarity, because their struggle is our own struggle.

We must show solidarity with the Asian people who struggle against imperialism, especially with the peoples of Vietnam, of Laos and of Korea, in their struggle against American imperialism. We must show solidarity with the Latin American peoples in the struggle against imperialism, especially with the people of Cuba who were able to overcome reaction and imperialism in their land, to establish a just system which is encircled and threatened by imperialists. We must show the utmost solidarity with them and with all the Latin American liberation movements.

In North America, we must show solidarity, real solidarity, with the descendants of African slaves who are today part of the North American population and are Americans. We have to give courageous support to their struggle, without pretending that we are going to wage the struggle for them.

Our duty is to wage our struggle in our land. Neither in Africa, nor anywhere else are we going to wage the struggle for others. We are going to struggle in our land. This is difficult enough, let alone struggling for others.

We must be able all the time to show solidarity with the socialist countries. There are many folk who think that it is the duty of the socialists to give everything, but they should receive nothing in return, not even at least a word of thanks. This is wrong. If the German Democratic Republic gives us aid, if the Soviet Union gives us more aid than anyone, if other countries give us aid, this does not fall from the sky. It comes from the labour of their countrymen, the labour of the workers, and the sweat of each one's brow. There nothing falls from the sky except rain and snow and here we have only rain. We have to be aware of this and have the courage to thank them. When something is being done against them, we should close in solidarity with them, stand at their side, because they are our companions in struggle; they help us.

Many comrades went to study in socialist countries and instead of showing solidarity with them, their friends, they live there and come back enraged against them. Because such comrades do not have awareness, but only obsessions, only complexes. Many Africans behave like this, many comrades know what sacrifices are made to help us, but they are not able to develop friendship and dedication towards those who give us aid. That is not the Party's line. Our Party must be appreciative, must show solidarity with those who give us aid. Happily, many comrades have understood this properly and have behaved extremely well in this regard.

In the list of our allies we must put very high the name of the Republic of Guinea, as our first ally, our most cherished brothers, those who have given us most help. Generally speaking, it is the country which helps us most, through all kinds of facilities it gives us. It has also accepted the sacrifice of its own people through the shelling of its villages. We must put high up the name of Senegal, although not as high as that of Guinea, even though we know there have been difficulties for us. Unhappily, Senegal even today is making many difficulties for us. For example, our supporters are not now allowed to go about in Senegal in uniform. Why? This is good for the Portuguese, but it is not good for us. It is a long time since they did not want us to enter Senegal armed, now they do not want us to enter in uniform. Why are they making this trouble? But even so, we must say that Senegal helps us a little. We must be aware that this also has a certain value for our struggle, although, as I say again, there may be many difficulties and we are already beginning to be tired of them.

In connection with Guinea we must put very high the name of the PDG (Democratic Party of Guinea). It is our people's good fortune that Guinea should have a Party like the PDG led by a man like Sékou Touré and by really patriotic folk, really concerned for Africa. Because if on each border of our land we had folk like those who are making such difficulties for us in Senegal, we should be in a bad way. We must be aware of this. There was no shortage of folk in Guinea who also wanted to make difficulties for us, and there are still some today, but the leaders, the Party, always supported the liberation of our people. For a while they watched who was really struggling for this, and when they saw that it was PAIGC they supported us to the hilt.

In the context of the general anti-imperialist struggle, we also have as allies the working class movements in various countries in Europe, or in America, or in Asia – in the capitalist countries of Asia – but above all in Europe and America. They are also our allies as they struggle against imperialism, against the forces which dominate our land. We must be aware of this and develop our ties of friendship and solidarity with these movements.

NOT EVERYONE IS OF THE PARTY

Work of leadership

Let us look at another principle of our Party which is the following: our struggle is based fundamentally on the work of our Party, the PAIGC.

You know what struggle is. You have understood already that struggle is a normal condition of all realities in motion. In everything that moves, that exists, if you like (for everything that exists is in motion), there is always a struggle. There are contrary forces which act on each other. For every force operating in one direction there is another force operating in the opposite direction.

Take a tree, for example. It is an enormous struggle for a tree to grow, live, bear fruit, seed or another tree. First for its root to pierce the soil and find sustenance in the ground. There is an enormous struggle between the root and the resistance of the ground. Moreover a certain capacity is needed, a certain strength to extract from the dampened soil the sustenance which enters the plant's root. When the sustenance has been extracted it must be carried to other parts of the plant. There is always a resistance against a resistance. In addition there is resistance to rain and to storms. And the plant has one great disadvantage: the plant cannot move from its position.

Plants, like animals (and even a piece of wood or iron) contain a struggle within, and there may be thousands of such struggles. But the fundamental struggle is between the capacity for preservation and the destruction which time brings to things. Iron rusts, wood crumbles to dust, the passage of time is written on things, from man to the most trifling thing. All this is expressed in struggle. But the struggle is more visible, evident, when an object exerts a force on another object, when it takes place between two distinct objects.

Our struggle is the consequence of the pressure (or oppression) which the Portuguese colonialists exert on our society. Anyone who acquires a certain awareness, or who was witness to some event, or who has some interest in regard to Portuguese colonialism, faces the following choice: to wage his own struggle or not to wage any struggle. Many folk were struggling in our land, in Guiné and in Cape Verde, and sometimes wrote poems or some other thing as a call to struggle. Closing the windows and doors to one's room and insulting the Portuguese (who cannot hear) is a form of struggling. In Canhabaque a

Bijago woman comes with water to sell. The Portuguese district officer tells her: 'One escudo? No. Five cents', and gives her the five cents. But she pours the water out on the ground – it is a form of struggling. Often subservience (the act of accepting humiliations) is also a form of struggling. But other forms of struggle are revolts.

One case, for example, with which I was familiar and which I never forget, occurred in Angola on the plantations. I used to think that the contract workers were poor devils who never revolted. But they revolted, one by one, and though it was not often possible to sense the revolt, each of them was trying to express revolt. Some would pass themselves off as madmen, would go out with cutlasses and chop down all the young palm trees planted by the colonialists. It is a form of struggling. But when one, two, three or four join together, pool their interests, they can make a revolt. How many silent revolts, which perhaps no one saw, were there in Guiné, how many revolts were there in Cape Verde, at S. Vincente, S. Antao, Santiago; a struggle against Portuguese colonialism.

But for a struggle really to go forward, it must be organised and it can only really be organised by a vanguard leadership. Starting out from scratch, as we did, to wage the struggle to liberate a people can be compared with the struggle man has waged over distance, for example. In olden days one of man's biggest difficulties was the following: man was dominated by distance, by the rivers, by the seas. He wanted to travel but it was difficult, he did not have the means for this.

One day, perhaps, a man sitting on a riverbank saw a tree trunk floating by and for the first time came the idea that perhaps man could go on the tree trunk along the river. If this happened, this was the moment when the first boat appeared, as the legend recounts. But for man to conquer distance, to cross rivers and seas and even to travel through the air, to overcome and to control distance, he had to develop the means. The means were small and weak at the beginning. Little by little they were developed. He used all possible means, water currents, winds, sea currents, and then he began to use forms of energy he had himself discovered: steam power, electrical power and today atomic energy. You see how man's struggle over distance was extraordinary. So much so that man who at quite an advanced stage took years to go round the world can now circle the globe by satellite in eighty minutes, or even less if he wants. In Jules Verne's book the journey took eighty days, and he was a visionary for the future, he foretold the future.

Party

For the struggle against colonialism means are also required. In the first place one must create an instrument of struggle. Our Party is that instrument. You might say that the Party is a base instrument, the mother instrument. Or if we like, the principal means which creates other means linked to it. It is the root and the trunk which produce other branches for the development of our struggle.

The first question we can pose is the following: why have we formed a Party, and others formed movements? Movements, fronts, etc., were formed... but if you consider carefully, we are the only ones who formed a Party, an organisation with the title of Party. It might have had other titles, but we are a Party, although there had never been a Party in our land before. This is not by chance, it is not because we like the title Party. It has a clear meaning for today and tomorrow. It is because we take the view that a Party is a much more defined, much clearer organisation. A Party represents all those who share a given idea, a given aim, on a given path. A movement is something very vague. Perhaps today our Party is still really a movement, but our task must be to transform it increasingly into a Party. And we gave it the title of Party right from the start because everyone understood that we had very clear ideas on the path we were following, on what we wanted, in the service of our people in Guiné and Cape Verde, in the service of Africa and mankind, in so far as we could make some contribution.

We called it Party, because we understood that to lead a people to liberation and progress, the fundamental need was a vanguard, folk who show in fact that they are the best and can prove it in practice. During the liberation struggle, many folk try deception but little by little they must show their position clearly as belonging to that vanguard, the entirety of those who are the best sons of our people in Guiné and Cape Verde.

We know that our Party was formed clandestinely. I am not going to tell you the whole history; it is recorded in many books. You can read it if our comrades in the Ideological Commission do their work properly. But it was formed clandestinely. At the start it was truly a Party, with very few followers, a minuscule Party, but the supporters were of like mind and trusted profoundly in the line we drew, like anyone who has had in his life the opportunity to follow this path. Little by little it grew and grew until it was transformed into a broad national liberation movement. Not a movement in name, but in the hard fact of struggle, as an entirety of folk in movement against Portuguese colonialism.

Objective

But we are, as I say again, a Party. Our case can be explained in this way. Those of us who struggle in Guiné and Cape Verde against Portuguese colonialism are all in the national liberation movement; everyone is for the 'Party'. But admission in fact to the Party is only open to someone who genuinely has a single idea, thinks only towards one target, and who has to have a given kind of behaviour in his private life and his social life. What idea, what target, what behaviour?

Our Party comprises only those who in fact want the Party programme. We are PAIGC – Guiné and Cape Verde. There is no racism, there is no tribalism;

we are not struggling merely so that we may have a flag, an anthem and ministers – we may not even have ministers in our land. We are not going to install ourselves in the Governor's palace, that is not our objective, to take over the palace to place Cabral and others there. We are struggling to liberate our people not only from colonialism but also from any kind of exploitation.

We want no one to exploit our people anymore, neither whites nor blacks, because it is not only whites who practise exploitation, there are blacks who are more ready to exploit than the whites. We want our people to rise and to advance. If we want our people to rise, it is not only the men, because the women too are our people. The members of our Party and those who must rule in our land are those who have understood that a woman has the right to advance, to be taught, to go to school like any other human being, to do any work of which she is capable. They are those who have really understood that so long as a man has three or four wives he will never be a true man and that no people can advance while men have four wives.

They are those who have really understood that a female child is not to be sold, and that the mother likewise cannot be sold, that there are no slave women. They are those who have understood that children are the only beings to whom we must accord privileges, that they are the flowers of our life and it is for them that we make all the sacrifices so that they should live happily. They are those who carry out well the tasks allocated by the Party in the service of our people.

I do not command because I am an engineer or a doctor, but because I really work, and no one who has completed his studies is higher than those who have not. No position is higher than another. Only someone who works more, who produces more is higher. Anyone who has understood our Party programme correctly, whether he is from Guiné or Cape Verde, can be admitted to our Party. But he should be ready at any moment to give his life in the cause for which we are struggling.

But while some are admitted to the Party, others perhaps may leave, without much ado, but they will leave. Why? Because they fail to do some of these things, or because they show that they do not understand them or do not want to understand. For example, there are still some in our Party who do not agree with this unity of Guiné and Cape Verde, but who are waiting to see. Some from Cape Verde and others from Guiné who do not agree much, but who are still hesitant, wanting to see what will emerge. They are mistaken. Perhaps they will form another Party, but ours they will leave, they will leave for sure.

Members

I will state the question of our task clearly to you. There should only be honest and serious persons in the Party. Anyone who is dishonest should leave, as should all those who take advantage of the Party to serve their personal interests. Today they may deceive us, but tomorrow they will leave for sure. Anyone who lies should leave, as should anyone who is only chasing his own idea, to have terylene trousers and pretty shirts, to abuse our girls, or anyone who goes about misusing the people of our land.

All those who fail to respect the people of our land, hiding this in front of the leadership, but behind their backs in their own area treating the people as if they were colonialist district officers or administrators, should leave. All those who have the idea that they are struggling and making sacrifices in this struggle so that they can misuse their authority like district officers, should leave. The time has come for frank speaking about this. There are some comrades who are making great sacrifices but with the idea that tomorrow they will reap the benefit with a fine motorcar, servants, several wives, etc. They are making a mistake. They are not of our Party and they are going to find this out for sure.

Our Party is open to the best sons of our land. Today we are all for the 'Party', but little by little the nucleus who are the Party is being defined. Anyone who is in fact of the Party is in or will join that nucleus; anyone who is not of the Party will leave. We can only genuinely achieve what we want in our land if we form a group of men and women who are strong, able not to cheat their comrades and not to lie, able to look their comrades straight in the eye, and able to accept that the youth will be the masters tomorrow in our land of Guiné and Cape Verde.

We must, therefore, do our duty as well as possible, to provide all the potential for progress. Anyone who has ambitions for chieftaincy in our Party will sooner or later leave. Anyone who has not learned to respect his companion in struggle as a human being, man or woman, correctly will sooner or later leave. Anyone who thinks that tomorrow our policy will be at the bidding of one or other foreign nation will leave, because we are not going to stand this. We are struggling for independence.

So as you can see it is going to be increasingly difficult to be a member of our Party. And this vanguard we are creating, this instrument we have forged to build the independence of our land, as a man builds a house, must be constantly more honed, more sharpened, more perfect, and *our people must constantly embellish it*.

It is essential for all comrades to study the Party programme, above all the younger ones, to understand it properly and prepare themselves to be of the Party in fact. And more still to make an early commitment to the Party, because we are going to demand increasingly of each responsible worker a total commitment to the Party. Not commitment to his own idea, not commitment to Amílcar Cabral, or to João, or N'Bana or Bacar, or to any other person who is his chief. Commitment to the Party, to the ideas of the Party, to the Party's ideas which are its lifeblood. He has to show evidence that he has absorbed the Party's ideas, the ideas which the Party has put forward as obligatory for everyone. Anyone who does not do this is in error. Furthermore, later on before anyone can be a Party member, he will have first to be a candidate for the Party. He will have to show evidence that he deserves in fact to be admitted to our Party, and then he will be admitted. It has to be like this, because we want to serve the people of our land effectively. We cannot afford mistakes.

It is easy to bundle everyone into a Party. As soon as a child is born his name is put down for the Party. But what use is this? What is the Party then? In a football club one must pay a subscription, go to the field to applaud and cheer. Are we going to allow everyone into the Party, children, men, women? No. In a liberation struggle it is all right, and necessary: everyone, let us march onward. But in the midst of all this we shall constantly know better who is in fact of the Party. We must be able to come into a room like this and say: that one yes, that one is of the Party, and that one and the other, but that one over there is not yet of the Party.

It must be like this. This is the only way we can serve our people. If we mix everyone up, we will go wrong. The test of a true element of the Party is the wish for constant improvement, for anyone who stays put, dies. Many comrades have not yet understood this, some comrades take advantage of the Party. For them, being in the Party, being a Party leader, means leading a good life, reaping benefits. They want to take their advantages quickly because they do not believe in the Party, do not believe in the future. They want the benefits now and quickly: fine clothes, money in their pocket, the abuse of power, turning comrades into their servants, and other malpractices. This is candidacy for expulsion from the Party and there are many who, if they do not leave today, will leave tomorrow, however much work they have done, however much help they have given. Either they will break with the Party, or they will be expelled.

But the best way is for them to correct themselves, correct themselves quickly, put themselves on the correct line. We have made every effort to set the comrades on the line so that they will not have to leave the Party tomorrow.

Some have already been lost by the wayside because it was impossible for them to correct themselves. As our situation is vulnerable, if someone does not mend his ways, he will turn against us, will turn traitor. We have to fight this at every step, with all the care necessary, so that we give each person the best possible chance to be of the Party, but we cannot allow them to cheat us, to pretend to be of the Party, when they are not of the Party at all,

Any comrade who has in his head the idea that his 'tribe' is the one which should rule in our land, should watch out because there will be war against him. But there are still comrades in the Party who are unable entirely to kill this idea of 'tribe' that they have in their head. Because they are ambitious, merely because they are ambitious they want to be the highest authority in everything. Folk like that are not of the Party. In our Party someone rules if he is worthy of it; more authority is given to someone who has given practical proof that he knows how to use authority and we have only one objective: to serve the people.

Today our Party means all those in our land who are ready to put an end to Portuguese colonialism and ready to follow the Party's watchwords and to respect and carry out the orders of our Party leadership. They are of the Party. But tomorrow the Party will mean only those who have exemplary moral conduct, as men and women worthy of our land. It will mean those who work and have work, for there can be no place for idlers in our Party. It will mean those who dedicate themselves body and soul to the programme of our Party in our land, ready to fight any enemy. What programme of our Party? The one you know but which you will know better all the time. These will form our Party tomorrow and, among them, the effective leaders of the Party are those who will be able to transform the Party constantly into a better organisation which is still at the service of our people.

But what are the people?

Many comrades say: oh my people! Many comrades who make mistakes or are in a muddle over Party matters quickly begin to talk about the people. This will soon come to an end but we must understand clearly what the people means.

The definition *of people* depends on the historical moment which the land is experiencing.

Population means everyone, but the people have to be seen in the light of their own history. It must be clearly defined who are the people at every moment of the life of a population. In Guiné and Cape Verde today the people of Guiné or the people of Cape Verde mean for us those who want to chase the Portuguese colonialists out of our land. They are the people, the rest are not of our land even if they were born there. They are not the people of our land; they are the population, but not the people. This is what defines the people today. The people of our land are all those born in the land, in Guiné or Cape Verde, who want what corresponds to the fundamental necessity of the history of our land. It is the following: to put an end to foreign domination in our land. Those who are ready to work hard for this, to stand firm, are those in our Party. The majority of our people, therefore, are of our Party. The leadership of our Party most represents the people. No one should think that merely because he was born in Pico da Antonio or in the heart of Oio, he is more representative of the people than the leadership of our Party. The genuine and true cornerstone of the people of our land is the leadership of our Party, which defends the interests of our people and was able to create the whole of this movement for the defence of our people's interests.

I shall try to throw more light on this question. All those of the population of our land who at this moment want the Portuguese colonialists to leave our land, so that we should gain our freedom and independence, are our people. But among them are some who take a real grip on work, who struggle with weapons in their hands, in the political work or in education or in some other branch and under the leadership of our Party: they form our Party. If you like, the vanguard of our people is our Party and the principal element of our people at this time is the leadership of our Party. So those who have love of our people, have love of the leadership of our Party: anyone who has not yet understood this, has not understood anything.

This is true of this phase, this moment. But in a while, when we have gained our independence, anyone who then wants our land to be independent, for example, but does not want women to be liberated, but wants to go on exploiting women in our land, though he is of the people today, he will not be so tomorrow. If we want all children in our land to be respected and someone among us does not want this, he will be part of the population, he will not be part of the people.

Our objective is to ensure progress and happiness for our people, but we cannot achieve this against our people. If some persons in our land do not want this, we face an alternative. Either they are not the people and then we can do anything against them, even imprison them. Or they are numerous and represent the people, and at that point we give up. We can do nothing more because one cannot ensure happiness and progress for anyone against his will.

We have to understand clearly, therefore, that in each phase of a nation's history, of a land, of a population, of a society, the people are defined in terms of the main stream of the history of that society, in terms of the highest interests of the majority of that society.

The term democracy was coined in Greece, in Athens (from demo + cracy = people's rule). But who coined it? In Athens there were nobles, gentlemen (landowners) and then slaves, who worked for all the others. Democracy for them was only for those on top; they were the people, the others were slaves. Even today it is the same in many places. Anyone who has strength in his hand, power, makes a democracy for himself. We in our land want power to be in the hands of the majority. But we want power to be in the hands of our people.

Anyone who follows the correct path, wants increasingly greater progress and happiness in our land, progress not only for Fula, not only for Mandinga, not only for descendants of Cape Verdeans, not only for Balanta but progress for all in Guiné and Cape Verde – such a person is part of our people.

Parties and movements

If I go on talking about the instrument our people forged to develop the action of some of their sons and daughters for the struggle for liberation and progress in our land, I want to stress the fact that right from the start of our work we always had the feeling and certainty that it was not necessary to create several movements to liberate our land. On the contrary, it was essential to make a great effort to have a single organisation for struggle which would take action in Guiné and in Cape Verde. This was the line we drew on the basis of analysing our specific situation, our reality, and the line we defended strongly during several years, although at some moments we found it necessary to retreat to be certain if we were right or not.

Yesterday we talked about contradictions in our society. We saw that in social terms properly speaking, that is strata of society, or classes, if you like, the contradictions are not very great, above all in Guiné. They are a little more pronounced in Cape Verde, where there were some folk with land, with property, and some owners of businesses and small industries. But I drew your attention to the fact that this was insignificant, did not constitute a class properly speaking, from the quantitative point of view, that is in number. But we noted clearly that because of the influence of the past, and as a result of division the enemy caused among us, there were contradictions between ethnic groups, between what we call 'tribes' in Guiné. Obviously in Cape Verde the main contradiction is between the landless peasants and those who have secure means of livelihood, including landowners.

The greatest nonsense that could have occurred in our land would have been to create parties or movements in Guiné on the basis of ethnic groups. This would have been an excellent means for the enemy not only to divide us further during the struggle but also to ensure his victory; the destruction of our independence after the struggle, as you have seen in some African countries. In Cape Verde it would have been absurd to think of creating one Party of those who own something and one Party of those who own nothing to struggle against Portuguese colonialism.

In anti-colonial struggle, it is fundamental, important and decisive to bring together all those who want independence, who want to struggle against colonialism. Precisely for this reason, when some tiny groups of nationalists arose in Bissau in 1959 who were not controlled by us, our comrades, particularly Comrades Aristides Pereira, Fortes, Luiz and others, did their utmost to bring those tiny groups into our Party to avoid dispersing our strength.

You all know that the Party was founded in 1956 and the time I am talking of was 1959. Later on some persons from our land began to talk about a front, even the Party went so far as to talk about a front. Some of you might ask why we did not form a front in our land. Precisely because a front means a union of various organisations. We did not know of any other organisation in our land. When our Party began making contacts outside the country, from 1960 onwards, it was discovered that there were folk outside, whether from Guiné or Cape Verde, who had created the so-called movements outside the land. Our Party had to make a concession. It had to make a step backward from its idea of having only a Party and not a front to see if it could bring in those folk, to struggle for the independence of Guiné and Cape Verde. It was for this reason that we formed a so-called Front with the Liberation Movement for Guiné and Cape Verde which was in Conakry but had been formed by comrades of ours who had become linked to PAIGC, and with the Liberation Movement for Guiné and Cape Verde which was in Ziguinchor.

Later on, I could tell you the history of what was going on in Conakry, but the essence is that because of the great fuss, the difficulties raised by our brothers from Guiné and Cape Verde in Senegal, we decided to launch an appeal for unity of all the Liberation Movements for Guiné and Cape Verde. We organised a conference in Dakar with the then Liberation Movement for Guiné and Cape Verde, which was based in Dakar and which included Guineans and Cape Verdeans. There were certain people there known to you but it is not worth giving them undue importance by quoting their names here. This conference was also attended by the Ziguinchor movement and the Liberation Movement for Guiné and Cape Verde which was based in Conakry and by PAIGC, represented by some of its members. All this was basically a concession on our part, a tactic, to see what those folk really wanted, what their intentions were, just how far they were committed to real struggle and if they in fact wanted to struggle or were merely interested in finding positions. In practice we organised the entire conference. We took well prepared documents, and they, who had been entrusted with preparing the conference, had not even drawn up the programme yet. The conference was held in fact with the help of the Senegalese authorities, with the help of Comrade Marcelino dos Santos, representing the CONCP, and of other bodies.

The point of view of our Party was vigourously defended by its representatives, and supported by the Guiné and Cape Verde liberation movements from Conakry and Ziguinchor. Obviously the objective of those from Dakar was not to create unity, but to put an end to PAIGC. This was their idea and when they saw that it was impossible they accepted all the resolutions proposed in conference. But soon afterwards they began sabotage. Obviously they were later unmasked as folk who did not want unity, and who did not want unity because they did not want to struggle. They made a pretence of talking about unity, but all they wanted was a foothold from which to manoeuvre to gain jobs and to liquidate our Party.

So you see that the Party, although it had established as its vital principle a single organisation, a single banner and no confusion in the establishment of this liberation movement, was able to make concessions. It was able to retreat to give to everyone the chance to demonstrate if they did or did not want really to struggle for our independence. When the Party came to the conclusion that after all those folk were only telling lies, only sought dishonesty and only went looking for jobs, were only trying to create confusion, and so were serving the Portuguese colonialists, the Party made the following resolution: we no longer want unity with anyone; anyone who wants unity with PAIGC should come inside the land to make unity with PAIGC. This was the position we took and we resisted all the pressures brought to bear on us, because we were certain that we were on the certain and sure path.

Rejection of opportunism

Another point we should like to make clear about our Party, our organisation, is the following: right from the start (we have already spoken to you about this among our principles) *we rejected opportunism*. We could have tried to bring into our Party, for example, certain highly influential men in Guiné, invite them into the Party so that we could use their influence, such as some personalities in Bissau, or some chiefs – I recall that several chiefs were Party members – but we never told them that they could come and rule.

There were chiefs in Manjaco territory, or Mancanha territory, who went to call others to come under the Party banner. There were chiefs in the Mansôa area and other areas who were arrested for support of the Party banner, but we never said to them that as they were chiefs of our population, they were also chiefs of the Party. We rejected this once and for all, because we did not want to deceive anyone. In a new organisation, founded to liberate our land, the leaders are and will be those who are equipped for this task, and not because they were chiefs yesterday. It has been shown and is still being shown in various regions of Africa that it mortgages the future, stores up difficulties for tomorrow, to practise the opportunism of putting traditional chiefs into the leadership of a national liberation organisation.

REVOLUTIONARY DEMOCRACY

In the context of the principle of *revolutionary democracy*, to which we have already referred several times, each responsible worker must bear his responsibility bravely, must demand respect from others for his activities and must show respect for the activities of others.

However we must not hide anything from our people, we must not deceive our people. Deceiving our people is to build a foundation for calamity for our Party. We must combat this in some comrades vigourously. We cannot allow the population to come to the frontier to fetch merchandise for the people's stores, for example, and once they have arrived find themselves obliged to load up with war material. Doing this is behaving worse than the colonialists, it is abusing our authority, abusing the good faith and good will of our people. It is preferable to say frankly to elements of the population that they should prepare themselves to go and fetch war material, because the war is for our land, and that if they do not want to go, they will be arrested and taken by force. If necessary they can be arrested, but they must know where they are going. This is better than lying, cheating and looking small in the people's eyes, for they, however wretched and suffering, are like any people, and they know the difference between the truth and a lie, justice and injustice, good and evil, and they are wise enough to lose respect for anyone who has lied to them.

We must put an end to lying, we must be able not to deceive anyone about the difficulties of struggle, about the mistakes we make, the defeats we may suffer, and we cannot believe that victory is easy. Nor can we believe in evasions like 'It seems that' or 'I thought that'. This is one of the great defects of some comrades. 'Comrade, how did this happen?' – 'It seems that...' This is no use for those who are making a revolution, who seek the progress and happiness of their people through a liberation struggle. We must be aware of this.

There are comrades who are not able to make a clear report on what is happening in the area where they are. Happily there are others who are capable. I am focusing on the negative aspects, but you all know that there are many positive aspects. That is exactly why we are seated here and it would be disastrous for us if there were only negative aspects. But my duty is to point out what is not going well, so that we can improve and go forward. We trust appearances, our imagination; we have a tendency to trust our imagination.

Revolutionary democracy demands that we combat all opportunism, as I have already told you, and that we combat as well, the attitude comrades have of being too hasty in forgiving mistakes. I am a responsible worker, you make a mistake, and I forgive you with the following intention: that now you know you are in my hands. This is not acceptable. No one has a right to forgive mistakes without first discussing the mistakes in front of everyone. Because the Party is ours, for all of us, not for each of us but for all of us. We find it too easy to excuse comrades. We find excuses very quickly, and we must fight this. The time has come to stop finding excuses. There is work to be done; it should be done and done well without excuses.

We can find all kinds of excuses. There are responsible workers whose work consists in finding excuses for their group for doing nothing, in trying to explain to the Party leadership why nothing has been done – difficulties in the terrain, poor conditions, the enemy advance, there is heavy bombardment, etc. They do this instead of making an effort and working to overcome all the difficulties. Struggle is the following: permanent victory over difficulties. If there were no difficulties, it would not be a struggle, it would be a cakewalk, a picnic.

We must combat the whole tendency to friendships and comradeships which do not serve the Party, but to scratch one another's backs, which are not in the interest of the Party and our people. We know that this goes on in our Party. There are comrades who fall to pieces when their companion in struggle is changed, they can no longer live without their companion in struggle. We must combat this forcefully in our own mind and in the mind of others. There is no 'matiness' here unless it is to serve the Party, to serve the people in our land. There is no 'matiness', camaraderie or friendship, for us to sit drinking cane spirit or palm wine, or to hide from other comrades what someone does with the young girls of our land, or to hide mistakes in connection with the armed struggle, for example, or for us to remain silent when a responsible worker does not fight as he should. This is a betrayal of our Party and our people, and serves the Portuguese; it is friendship on the side of the Portuguese. We have it among us, and we must combat it forcefully and bravely. You all know that it exists and unhappily some of you are guilty of it.

Our criterion for friendship, 'matiness' or camaraderie, should be the following: you are worthy, respect the watchwords of the Party correctly, you are my comrade, you are my friend. If you do not do this, you had better go and join the opportunists or join the lackeys of the Portuguese. But our passion for friendship is so strong that comrades of ours who know that someone is an agent of the Portuguese are able to spend their time in his house, to frequent his house, to eat in his house, to drink in his house. Tell me if this is right. But comrades say: 'I have known that person for a long time', or 'He is a relative of my mother'. This shows a lack of political awareness, or even a lack of awareness of the sacrifices that our people are making for the struggle. But even Party leaders do this. Happily, it looks as if it is coming to an end.

Then we have this example: everyone knows that a given comrade has made a serious mistake in the Party, inside or outside the land, and was sent for. We are waiting for him. He arrives and all the comrades stand up with hugs, kisses and so on as if he were the best comrade in the world. What is this lack of awareness? What is this lack of sense of responsibility? If someone is unworthy, we must show him that he is unworthy. There is no friendship, there is no consideration for him. He must be cast aside.

The time has come for us to be friends with those who are worthy, but those who are worthless cannot be our comrades, our friends. Anyone who betrays the Party, who tries to divide us, who makes plans to sabotage the Party, who serves the enemy, who consorts with the enemies of our Party can no longer sit with us, cannot eat with us from the same bowl, cannot drink from the same glass or mug, cannot sleep in the same bed. Either we are able to distinguish the worthy from the unworthy or it is not worth our while going on with our struggle as we are doing, because sooner or later we shall drown in a sea of great confusion of our own making.

Irreplaceables

We must avoid the obsession of some comrades that everything is spoiled, everything is over if they should leave the posting where they are. Nobody is indispensable in this struggle; we are all needed but nobody is indispensable. If someone has to go and goes away and then the struggle is paralysed, it is because the struggle was worthless. The only pride we have today, that I myself have, is the certainty that, after the work we have already done, if I were to go away, to be stopped, to die or disappear, there are those here in the Party who can carry on the Party's task. If this were not so, then what a disaster; we would have achieved nothing. For a man who has an achievement that only he can carry on has not yet done anything. An achievement is worthwhile to the extent that it is an achievement of many, and if there are many who can take it up and carry it on, even if one pair of hands is taken away.

But there are comrades who have obsessions that if they should leave their place, everything will be ruined. This is an obsession that we must combat, that we must put a stop to. This is without mentioning cases of other comrades who think, when they are transferred, that they are going to die, because they have already established all the conditions for working in one spot and are called upon to go to another. What blindness! As if our land were just their little corner! This shows a lack of awareness of the real reason, the aim and the characteristics of our struggle.

We must be able to stand by the truth, to tell the truth before everyone, without fear, even if the truth entails some difficulties. We must speak the exact truth face to face.

Militants must not be afraid of any responsible worker in the framework of our Party. Anyone who is afraid has not yet understood or is a coward by nature. Our Party has given everyone the same strength not to be afraid of anyone. We have said that we are struggling to put an end to fear among our people in Guiné and Cape Verde. We must not be afraid of anyone. The lowliest militant must not be afraid of anyone, not of the Secretary-general, nor of anyone. He must show correct respect, for this is a matter of self-respect.

Responsible workers should not fear the militants. There are responsible workers of whom militants and combatants are afraid. The former are barbarian chiefs of olden days, they are not leaders or responsible workers of PAIGC. But they sometimes fear the militants. If they hear militants chatting they want to know what it is about, because they fear that the militants are going to make difficulties for them with the Party leadership. We must put an end to this.

Revolutionary democracy demands in effect that responsible workers and leaders should live among the people, before the people, behind the people. They must work for the Party in the certainty that they are working for the people in our land. And we must struggle so that at all costs the people feel that it is they who have the power in our land in their hands. Up till now they have not felt this very much. In the liberated areas some comrades have usurped this power of our people. We must deliver it into the hands of our people. We are still at war and it is still a little difficult. But in step as we advance we have to deliver power to our people so that they have the certainty that power is in fact theirs.

No one in the Party should be afraid of losing power. Many countries have come to ruin because the rulers were afraid of losing the lead. We must not be afraid of anything. We must tell the truth frankly to our people, to our militants, to our comrades. If they are not happy and they can, they will chase us out, throw us out. But none of us must be afraid of anything, we must riot hide the truth to preserve our position. This would be a betrayal of the interest of our people, our land and all those who put their trust in us.

We must not deceive the people with fine words, with false promises. We must tell them frankly the difficulties. At a meeting in Boé, for example, the population told me: 'Send us this, that. We want this, that, etc. in the shop.' I answered the population; 'No. We cannot do this and that. What we are sending is already a great sacrifice. If you are not satisfied, do what you will, even leave the Party, but we are not sending. You must remember that you are not the only ones with needs. Other persons in our land also have needs.' I took this opportunity of being with our supporters to teach them, to make them aware, not to tell them lies, or deceive them with false promises. They all understood.

As I have said, we must constantly go forward to put power into the hands of our people, to make a profound change in the life of our people, even to put all the means for defence into the hands of our people, so that it is our people who defend our revolution. This is what revolutionary democracy will be in fact tomorrow in our land. Anyone who rules his people but fears the people is in a bad way. We must never fear the people.

In the framework of revolutionary democracy, as I have already said, we must bring to the fore the best sons and daughters of our land. The worst and the worthless must be left behind. Our task is to prepare our hoe, our plough, our hammer, with which we are going to construct the future of our people in freedom, progress and happiness. Let us constantly improve our Party, for the better our Party is, the more certainty we have of achieving what we want for our people. For this reason we must, as we have already said, act so that our Party belongs more each day to those who are able to make it constantly better.

FIDELITY TO PARTY PRINCIPLES

Another principle of our Party that we adopt as a rule in life is: *being faithful to principles.*

Many have principles but when the moment comes to apply them they forget themselves, they are not faithful to principles. We must be faithful to our principles, we must apply them every day, we must not compromise our principles, whether on the internal plane, in our internal life, or on the external plane, in our relations in the external field.

Our leaders and responsible workers have the courage to struggle constantly against all temptation to practise opportunism, to take the easiest path. The path of struggle is never an easy path, but there are many among us who have a tendency for the easy way out. The consequence is that at every step they forget our Party principles; the consequence is that they lie at every step. And when one begins to lie, one lies so much that one ends by being caught out.

We must respect our principles. We have established our strategy, that is the broad line of our struggle, in accordance with our principles, and on this score we make no concessions, we do not retreat for anyone; we do not accept this. But on minor matters, on matters which do not affect our principles, we have to know how to make concessions. We have to be able to give way. We have to be able to use the tactics needed on the political and the military level, above all on the political level.

The skill of a leadership, of a leader, lies in knowing where he may give way and where he must not give way. This means that faced with a given problem we must ask the following question: what is essential and what is secondary? Is it in fact an essential problem or a secondary problem? Is it a problem just for today or for always, permanent or temporary? We must distinguish the essential from the secondary. We must know how to make concessions, to give way, to give Party liaison deeper roots, to open the way for the Party to advance.

In relations with militants, with combatants, we can make certain concessions, we can give way on certain points, but without giving way on our principles. In the armed forces, for example, we cannot make any concession on discipline, but we can give way a little to comrades on matters which do not spoil our work, which do not prejudice our principles as the fundamental rules for our work.

There, put very briefly, are some of the fundamental principles on which our Party work is based. We have based ourselves on them and continue to base ourselves on them: today, in the struggle against Portuguese colonialism; tomorrow in the struggle against misery, suffering and disaster in our land, against all injustices, for the progress and happiness of our people in Guiné and Cape Verde.

FOR THE IMPROVEMENT OF OUR POLITICAL WORK

Let us say something about what we should do at this moment to hasten the victory of our people on the various resistance fronts.

What should we do?

We must improve our political work. We must better organise our armed forces and make them operate more and more intensively. We must strengthen and increasingly consolidate our liberated areas. We should give better guidance to our supporters in all fields of activity, and guide correctly our students and our cadres under training. We should operate with increasing efficiency, with more awareness and for better results on the external plane, in our relations with Africa and with the world in general.

We must constantly improve our thinking and behaviour to give better service to our great Party in the service of our people in Guiné and Cape Verde.

One can never say too strongly that the political work is a fundamental task of our struggle, so fundamental that, as I told you a while ago, every shot fired is also a political act. It is fundamental that in our Party the leaders in the armed struggle are political leaders. Comrade Nino is at this moment deploying his efforts to carry out a plan which I drew up point by point after discussion with all concerned to develop a new kind of operational action in our struggle. He is commander-in-chief of this operation and he is a member of the Political Bureau of our Party. Any leader of our armed struggle, like Tchutchu or Bobo, who are sitting here, or Lucio or Nandingna, or others here, are also Party leaders, in its political leadership, and some of them have already been members of Party Committees at various stages, heads of Party Committees or ordinary members of a Regional Committee.

We feel therefore that we do not draw a distinction between politics and other tasks, for to give health treatment, education, to supply cloth and other goods to raise living standards is also political. To fire shots, to work at the international level is also political. But given that our life is complex with various functions to fulfill, there are persons who have the specific task of devoting themselves to political work. Under the guidance of the higher leadership of the Party, in the various echelons of Party leadership our political commissars have duties of political work, at inter-regional or zone level, aided by political brigades. But Party Committees and village committees must also carry out political work. The latter are also basically political bodies.

Political work by our political commissars, like that of all those who work in politics, aided by all the other responsible workers of the Party at any level, is a decisive task for our struggle. We can defeat the Portuguese at Buba or at Bula, we can enter and take Bissau, but if our population has not been well trained politically, is not fully wedded to the struggle, we shall lose the war, not win it. So it is fundamental that our political commissars should clearly understand this, understand the significance of their work, but also that all the inter-regional and zone Committees should understand the significance of their work, for the latter are the political instruments of the Party working at grassroots level. Whether they be a member of the security service, a political commissar, a responsible worker for health, for education, for supply, they are the political force in operation each day to improve our work.

Clearly the victories of our armed forces must strengthen the political work. Some of our comrades are, for example, trying to win over the Fula population in the areas between Quirafo and Bangacia, but when the latter hear that the Portuguese have pulled out of Madina Xaquili it is easier to make them believe in us. So we see how the two aspects always link up to help the political work.

What is essential is that we, as members of the Inter-regional or Zone Committee, should be capable and devoted to our Party. We must identify totally with the interests of our Party. The first condition for improving our political work is to improve our political workers. It is fundamental that our political commissars, our workers responsible for the militia, security, health, education, should be profoundly conscious of their task. They should most cherish our Party, have most love for our people and are most determined to put into practice the watchwords of the Party. They must be persons who can raise high the name of the Party, the leadership of the Party, and who must have confidence in the Party leadership. They must be such as reflect their conscious willingness to die for our Party by working from morning to night every day for our Party, dedicating their lives, which is much easier than dying.

They must be vigilant, whether or not in the security services, vigilant against any attempt to destroy our Party, to betray our Party. They must be such as to keep as friends only the friends of our Party, and to be implacable enemies of all our Party's enemies. They must be those who will not tolerate any act against the interests of our Party. When they have to speak about Party questions in front of the people, in front of the leaders, in all circumstances they will shout loudest, will raise highest the banner of our Party, the name of our Party. They must draw the masses behind them. They must be behind the masses, among the masses, in front of the masses, to mobilise them and always the first to set the example of our Party's banner. We cannot yet say that we have only had the best Party militants in our committees. Some are by no means the best, others are even afraid really to speak up about the Party.

From now on, you must all work to the end that we can put at the head of our Party Committees those who really are of the Party. If we look into their hearts, we shall find only the banner of the Party. If we look into their heads, we shall find only the ideas of the Party. If we give them the floor, they will shout loud, really loud, the name of the Party, to encourage everyone to struggle for our Party. And night and day, at any hour when work is needed, they buckle down to the work of our Party. This is the first condition for us to improve our political work; to improve the work of our cadres we must improve our cadres who are tied exclusively and directly to the civil and political work of the Party.

We must improve the work among our people, we must hold meetings with our people as much as possible. The zone political commissars must be in permanent contact with the villages within their zone, holding village meetings, discussing people's difficulties, trying to find out what is going on so as to help solve difficulties. The security should be with them also doing this work. And health and education representatives, controlling, helping and solving difficulties. That is how it should be. We must be permanently mobilising, organising our people, helping our village committees to hold their meetings to discuss their difficulties, helping our people to govern themselves, to solve their own difficulties. Only in this way can we match up to the demands of our struggle today. And this work has to be carried out with vigilance in regard to all enemy actions, whether it is enemy infiltration among us – security has to watch out for this – enemy propaganda on their radio or by any other means; we have to neutralise it immediately. We have to explain to our masses, to our population, their difficulties, the deceptions the Portuguese want to plant in their mind. Political work has to be a permanent task among our people. We all know well what we must do.

We have constantly to improve political work among the armed forces as well. All our cadres tied to political work, including our armed forces commanders and political commissars, must work to raise the political level of our armed forces. There cannot be any separation between the political commissar in the zone or the inter-region and the armed forces. No. The political commissar for the inter-region, the security member for the inter-region, the People's Militia in the inter-region or zone, are all part of the armed forces, as our orders that they should all carry weapons show. They are armed forces detached on political duty. Those in the armed forces are detached on duty in the armed struggle.

We must not have any separation; they must always be in harmony, living hand in hand, working together politically. And the zone political commissars must from time to time hold meetings with the armed forces in that zone, in liaison with the armed forces political commissar. They must talk about relations with the population and discuss questions about the population, and about the armed forces. They must discuss whether they are operating well or badly, to praise those who are operating well, to agree on ways of reinforcing aid to the population and ways for the population to aid the armed forces, to co-ordinate their work between the armed forces and the population, and to make it a single body.

It is no use the political commissar and the committee being one thing, and the command political commissar being another, or each working on his own and turning his back on the other. It should not be like this. We must admit frankly that in our armed forces today some political commissars are not political commissars at all. They have never known how to hold a political meeting, never hold political meetings with Party comrades who are in the armed forces. Generally speaking in other countries, the armed forces have some Party members and some non-Party. We accept all the comrades in the armed forces into the Party, and we must work with them, explain to them. There are comrades who die on the battlefronts without knowing what the Party is. Why? Because sometimes our political commissars do not know what the Party is. We must put an end to this. There are some who understand, sometimes even without being taught they understand. There are some who really do political work, but a large proportion do no political work among the armed forces.

Sometimes the commander himself does not allow the political commissar to do anything, because he as commander controls everything. He forgets that he himself is the first political commissar. He is a political commissar and commander, the other is a political commissar. They must work together, do the political work together. The more politicised our armed forces are, the greater certainty we have of security in our land a victory in our struggle. We have also clear watchwords about political work in our armed forces, and I do not need to go over it all again here. I will merely remind you of some fundamental aspects.

We must be constantly more selective about our leaders, our responsible workers, our militants. As I have told you, up till now to belong to our Party it has been enough to want to chase the Portuguese, the Portuguese colonialists, out of our land and to support the PAIGC. There was even an oath to PAIGC. We had this for quite a while, but then we dropped it. At the start when it was difficult, when one joined the Party one had to take an oath and anyone who believed in *kola* nut, had to eat *kola*. We stopped this as the struggle grew very much and there were a lot of people to eat *kola*. I can even remember how comrade Tiago, who supervised the taking of oaths to the Party, began to suffer a little as he ate too much *kola*. We soon stopped this, but at bottom, in the conscience of each one when he joins PAIGC, he takes an oath even if he does not speak, even if he does not sign any document. But very soon it will be necessary to give specific evidence to become a militant of our Party. Today it is not yet required. Tomorrow to become a de facto militant of our Party it will be necessary to give specific evidence that one satisfies certain requirements. One must thoroughly know the Party programme, one must know what the Party seeks, so that it is a conscious act, that one does not come to join and then not know why after all. And we must constantly be stricter about our responsible workers and our leaders; the example must come from the top.

Authority must be based on real work, on the accomplishment of duty and on conduct or behaviour which is an example to everyone. We must constantly demand more from our responsible workers. Some fairly reasonable responsible workers were trained through the difficult struggle we have had, but we must admit that we did not have time or opportunity to deal more strictly with some other responsible workers. I am not going to repeat here all the praises that are due to some responsible workers in our Party, political commissars, members of security, armed forces chiefs, who have worked bravely enough, skilfully enough, albeit making the occasional mistake. Likewise, I am not going to repeat the mistakes that our responsible workers have made (I have already given this in my talk). Our criticism of this is still valid. We stated it in that document we called 'On Reorganisation of the Armed Forces'. Our comrades must read it, because it is all written out there frankly and openly, even explaining why the majority of our responsible workers who make the most mistakes are those who came from the towns.

In this seminar today I call your attention to everything we have already criticized in other talks. I call your attention to the fact that the time has come for us to put a stop to mistakes by responsible workers. The time has come for us to put a stop to responsible workers who receive the Party watchwords and put them aside; they keep them so that they are not lost but they do not read them. The time has come for us to put a stop to responsible workers or leaders who never present a report on the situation of their work.

The time has come for us to put a stop to responsible workers at any level, even Party leaders, who prefer feasting to a serious life of work and study.

The time has come for us to put a stop to responsible workers and leaders who have more than one wife and who in the struggle have provided more children than work.

The time has come for us to put a stop to responsible workers and leaders who are unable to study to increase their knowledge, even in the depths of the bush, so that they should be more responsible workers, more really leaders. The time has come for us to put a stop to responsible workers or leaders who when they are asked something about their work, tell lies. The time has come for us to put a stop to responsible workers and leaders who are able to do harm to others to prevent their advance, for fear that the latter will take their place. The time has come for us to put a stop to responsible workers and leaders who when they are transferred to another spot, think that they are going to die, because they have lost their corner, because where they were they had already built up their chieftaincy.

The time has come for us to put a stop to responsible workers or leaders who are unable to get on with their comrades in a Front or in an Inter-regional Committee. The time has come for us to put a stop to responsible workers or leaders who do not want our women to advance as well to become responsible workers or leaders. The time has come for us to put a stop to responsible workers and leaders who can show disrespect to leaders or responsible workers who are over them. The time has come for us to put a stop to responsible workers and leaders who fail to show in their every act love for our Party, respect for the leadership of our Party, bearing in mind that the most important thing in their life is the Party's work. But it is all of us who must put a stop to this. The time has come for us to put a complete stop to being afraid of responsible workers or leaders of the Party. There is no need to be afraid of authority. And anyone who abuses his authority is committing a more serious crime than those of the Portuguese colonialists.

The time has come too for us to raise really high the names of those militants, responsible workers and leaders who were able to accomplish the Party's task, setting an example for others, showing the right path that we must follow in our work. Every responsible worker, every leader must always keep well in mind that we are an organisation and so we must be organised. Some comrades prefer things disorganised so that they can escape control. Some of our comrades think that when we send someone to see what they are doing he is going to spy. The time has come for us to establish an entire control service so that each person, if he is a leader or a responsible worker, should clearly understand that control and inspection are to serve him, to help him to take a better course. The time has come for us to regard as genuine Party Committees those who can in fact meet periodically, as the Party orders, study difficulties, as the Party orders, make reports, as the Party orders.

Anyone who cannot do this is not a leader, nor a responsible worker of the Party, nor any part of a committee. It is an imposture: he deceives himself and is deceiving us. The time has come for us to insist that our village committees really meet periodically to discuss their difficulties, to give satisfaction to and also receive satisfaction from the leaders in zone or Inter-regional committees, to keep in touch and to take the pulse, to know what is really happening in our land, to solve difficulties before they become worse. In this context, we must do everything to bring on the young comrades who have shown the capacity to become responsible workers capable of leadership.

And in the context of this necessity, there is a great necessity incumbent on us today to strengthen our security service. We can work hard, die in struggle, tire ourselves out, worry, age, sicken, etc., but if we allow the 'termite' to gnaw our timbers from within, one day we shall lean on the timbers and they will fall because they are rotten inside. The 'termite' may as well be agents of the Portuguese among us as ourselves, any one of us.

A responsible worker or leader who gets drunk, for example, is more dangerous for us than an agent of the Portuguese. The former not only fails in his duty and sets a bad example, but he is also killing himself with the bottle. Now it is just what the Portuguese want that he should die, that he should not work well. A responsible worker or Party leader whose concern wherever he is, is to find the prettiest girls to woo is acting worse than an agent of the Portuguese. First, he is cutting off our possibility of giving dignity and status to the women of our land. Second, he is setting a bad example for everyone, for other responsible workers and for militants and combatants and is moreover demobilising our people.

Third, he is ruining himself as a leader or a responsible worker. A good Party worker, a good leader, who fulfils his duty correctly and is aware of our struggle, must be able to choose his company carefully to set a good example. It is normal that a man needs a woman and that a woman needs a man, that we have company. In the present circumstances of our land, anyone who governs can in general have as many women as he wants. That is still the Africa of today. Look at ministers in Africa in general: how many women do they have? But they are not making progress in their land. We have to cut this out completely in our land. Each one of our responsible workers or leaders has to set an example, a good example, which everyone will follow, so as to have the authority to rebuke others when the occasion arises for rebuke.

But we must see all this in the context of our security, we must be vigilant in this regard. Security does not merely mean catching agents of the Portuguese, preventing our people from going to sell rice to the Portuguese. Selling rice is a delicate question, for example. If we were working well, had things under control, we could even send our supporters to go and sell rice to the Portuguese, with the aim of collecting information, carrying out espionage and even to obtain certain things we have not yet been able to have. Unhappily, we believe that it is a bit difficult in our circumstances. But security also means the following: 'I am on your side, you are a leader, you behave wrongly. I tell you so frankly: I complain about you.'

It is not forbidden to drink, for example. Anyone may drink – unless he be a Moslem – but in moderation. But moderation is the hard part, because everyone has his appetite. We must avoid drinking to excess. A security agent must always be ready to act openly against this, whether it be a commander, a Party leader, even the Secretary-general, with all the respect he has for them. If one of them is drunk, arrest him. This is what security means. 'Stop, for you are wrecking our work' – that is real security. Not the security when in order to please the responsible worker you find him drink and even go on the spree with him. This is not security. This is to be an accomplice in the destruction of our struggle.

But we must also strengthen security in our struggle in regard to the enemy. The enemy is very active. We must strengthen our security on the basis of our security services, to which we must give more serious development. The Party has trained many cadres in the security branch. Unhappily, some have not shown that they have really learned this work, because they have displayed much lack of initiative.

We must base our security on the work of our people's militia, which is an instrument for security in our liberated areas. We have made some effort to organise our people's militia, some responsible workers have made efforts either individually or in the framework of our people's militia committees in liaison with the Inter-regional Committee. But we have to do much more. We have to organise the people's militia, but not on the lines of the bi-group, as some have had a tendency to do, going so far as to organise people's militia bases.[13] No. The people's militia must be among the people in the villages or among the people in the bush. The best sons of our land who are in the villages and have not yet joined the army are the ones who must form our people's militia – good militants, who have proved themselves, the youth, according to our definition, between the ages of 15 and 30. They will fulfill a specific role, which is to strengthen our security and self-defence as much against the robbers sent by the enemy as against invasions on the part of the enemy. The vanguard of our village population in the liberated areas must form our people's militia in liaison with the Inter-regional Committee and the Party political commissar. We must form groups of people's militia in the villages within each area, and we can also form groups of people's militia between various villages. The people's militia are folk who work at home, in the fields, etc., but when they are needed, they should muster immediately, when they are needed for a job, they should come. We must train our people's militia in the arts of warfare, in vigilance, to carry out patrols, etc.

We must put into effect the watchword of the Party, which has already been stated, to arm our people's militia. It has already begun but it is not yet

---

13 *Editor's note*: A bigroup was the usual tactical unit of the PAIGC army – a 'double group' of 30–50 men.

completed. Some weapons have rusted, others are at the frontier waiting to be delivered to the people's militia. Other weapons arrived in the people's militia areas and were not distributed as they should be; quite recently the Portuguese came and captured them in the Fifioli area in sector 2 of the Eastern Front. There are weapons for the people's militia such as *Ricos*, which we provide for the people's militia, and carbines of various types for the people's militia, which we still have not distributed as we should. We must strengthen our armed and civil defence, setting to work elements of the population with weapons in their hands. We gave the watchword to arm the population. We ourselves began to arm the population in the Quitafine area: we ourselves carried out the first distribution of weapons. But this work has not been carried on as it should. So we should make an effort to do better, for this is improving our political work.

Another important task for us is to strengthen our organisation, our liaison with the urban centres where the enemy still is, to improve the clandestine organisation of the Party in the urban centres. But anyone who is in the bush as a political commissar, in an Inter-regional Committee, in a Zone Committee, must in his area maintain close liaison with our comrades and our brothers within the towns who really want to struggle for our Party. We must be able to send agents into the towns to prepare supporters, to work with our supporters. Unhappily, it is rare that any responsible worker of the Party has done this to any serious extent. It has been forgotten that our land is also its towns – Bissau, Bafatá, Bambadinca, Mansôa, Bissorã, Catio, etc. It is true that there are some, in security and in political affairs, who have developed their work effectively. But what we have done so far is not enough, we must do much more.

We must strengthen the clandestine organisation of our Party within the urban centres; this is mainly a task for our security, but also for all our workers in the political field. Where there is nobody in an urban centre, we must send one or two there, in disguise, so that they can organise it as it should be. This is fundamental. It is no use our training dozens and dozens of cadres for the security services, who are taught clandestine work, espionage, clandestine organisation, handling of explosives, counter-espionage, reconnaissance, etc., for them then to reach our land, sit down and do nothing. So-and-so is not in security because he can catch someone who is going to sell rice to the Portuguese. That is not enough. The time has come for us to put these cadres from security to work right in the urban centres, to establish new organisations, and to strengthen our Party's presence in these places. This is fundamental.

To improve our work, we must strengthen and constantly consolidate our liberated areas. Our struggle has made great strides, rapid strides, and perhaps even at the beginning too rapid strides. In a short space of time we found ourselves faced with the great responsibility of having liberated areas. This is very good, because the liberated areas are the base, the rearguard for the advance of our armed forces in the struggle. Moreover, they allow us to acquire experience in governing our people. But it also creates much toil. We have to lead the people; we have to meet the wishes of the population. We have to improve the population's living conditions and organise their life better. We have to work much harder. But there is not the slightest doubt that we have made a little headway, to the point that the Portuguese recognise that in the majority of the liberated areas it would be impossible now for our people to return to accepting colonialist domination.

Some good work has been done but we must do still more and better work. We must put a stop completely to the drain of our folk from liberated areas. We must persuade our folk to return to liberated areas in our land, among those who went to the cities and among those who went outside our land. We must do still more to consolidate Party organisation in the liberated areas. We must further develop our educational work, although we have reduced the number of schools to give a better return. We must work well in our hospitals, in our health centres, few though they are, to show that they are useful. Our people's stores should function correctly. Our militants who work in the people's stores should not pilfer. This is very important. We must do everything to give the people in the liberated areas the opportunity to control our people's stores.

The first condition for construction in our liberated areas is the one we have already mentioned: improving our political work. This requires that Party leaders, in the zone or Inter-regional Committee, live in fact among the population, with the population. Unhappily, the tendency is to set up central bases. The Inter-regional Committee has its base, the Zone Committee is in its base, while the population are in their compounds or their villages and the leader is far away, creating a chasm between him and the population he leads. A long time ago we issued the watchword: leaders of the Zone and Inter-regional Committees must be with the people. There are to be no special compounds, special bases. If he is in the zone, his base must be every compound of the people, every village of the people. One day he is in one, the next day in another, always on the move, because as leader of the zone he must never be stuck in one spot. This not only increases the return on his work, makes him carry out his duty better, but also increases his own security.

In the zone, the political commissars, security, the education heads, health heads, supply heads, must never be still, must always be in liaison with the people, following all the difficulties of the people, trying to solve their problems with the people. In the inter-region, the political commissar, security, the responsible worker for education, for health, for supply, for the militia must always be on the move through the zones and even, if they can be, also in the compounds and the villages, always living with the population. At every place they reach, they should meet with the local Zone Committees, giving instructions, taking the pulse to find out the situation, holding meetings with the population, explaining and helping to solve the difficulties which the Zone Committees cannot solve, in close liaison with the zone leaders and through them, and directly as well with the mass of our people in the liberated areas.

This is how we must work hard to lead and to increase the consolidation of our liberated areas.

But our armed forces commanders, principal commanders or army corps commanders, must also be in liaison with the combatants everywhere, not shut up at their commands while the forces are in operation. In the north and the south they shut themselves up at their commands and are not in touch with their forces. We must have forces everywhere. If there are bigroups at the Buba junction, the commander must go there to see them. If they are near Nhala, he must go there to see them. Or at Gangenia, or Madina de Baixo, or in the Jabada area, infiltrated between the Portuguese, or in the surroundings of Gantongo, at Sambuia, N'Goré, or at any other base in the north, in the Mansaba area, or in the Maqué area. A commander or a political commissar must always be with the armed forces, always on the move, finding a place or several places to hold meetings with other responsible workers, but always on the move.

In addition, as our commandants, our principal responsible workers in the armed forces are usually political leaders as well, they have the duty of meeting the Inter-regional Committee to discuss difficulties. They must co-ordinate the work of Zone Committees, and even co-ordinate work with the population, to help political commissars, security, etc., in their work. This is the best method of consolidating our position in the liberated areas, in our struggle as a whole.

We must accept that the place of Party leaders is among the population, not settled at any base. The place of armed forces leaders is among the combatants and not settled at any command. He may have a command, or a really safe position, where there are, for example, a radio, one or two trustworthy persons, a guard, where he can go from time to time but he must be always on the move, even for his own security. There were responsible workers in our armed forces who were killed because they spent too long sitting in the bases.

To consolidate our liberated areas we have to work more closely with our population, to raise production. We must be able to make our people cultivate more land, grow more rice, even prepare our people for new crops. For sooner or later we must begin to grow groundnuts in our liberated areas for sale abroad, and other crops still. We must promote as a Party watchword in the liberated areas: diversification. This means varying the agricultural crops so that our people can eat better, so that our combatants too can eat better. In liberated areas where there are combatants we must make the combatants work as well, as we have already said.

We have to develop our agriculture step by step, patiently. We have to develop our craftwork, help our population make cloth, mats and baskets, pots and pitchers. Above all we should encourage them to make works of art, sculptures. This could be of great value for our Party and demonstrate our skills outside. We must work hard to bring constant improvement to our system of supply to the liberated areas of essential items. One essential item, for example, is soap; our people have to wash their clothes, their bodies, etc. We have already begun to manufacture soap in our liberated areas, but up till now we have not been able to manufacture soap well, although this is easy and we have plenty of palm oil. Our responsible workers in production who were given this task have had some results, but they fell far short of the results they could have reached. There are other items we could manufacture in our liberated areas. We must make an effort to help our people obtain iron to make agricultural implements, tools for the fields, and materials for our smiths to work with.

Our people's stores must be able to distribute properly the goods our Party supplies, must be able to store and distribute properly the goods bought from the people in exchange for essential items, like cloth and other things. So far, we have had some success but our people's stores are still not functioning well. Obviously, there is the big difficulty that sometimes we have nothing to send them, but I am talking of when there is something. The Party in its external work is making greater efforts to achieve a continual rise in the quantity of merchandise. Happily, we have good prospects for this year. If our struggle is well maintained, if we manage to pin the enemy on the ground as we should, so that they can do nothing against us, we should give our people many essential goods this year. But to do this we must distribute properly, at set times, without any funny tricks, without trying to deceive the people. On the other hand we must strictly collect from the people the things they must deliver; rice, *kola*, coconut, wax, animal hides, etc. And our responsible workers in production must store these correctly, preserve them correctly, to be used or sold as appropriate.

We have to have control over production. We cannot tolerate lack of control. We cannot compromise. As happened, for example, when we put one comrade in control of our administration and the comrades did not appreciate this. They were angry with him because he would not let them sell cows belonging to the Party. So then began a series of intrigues against the comrade. There were manoeuvres so that even the combatants would be annoyed on the grounds that he was not letting anyone eat beef. But this was not the motive; the motive was to make them turn against him so that he would be dismissed, because he was the one. who prevented certain responsible workers from selling the cows. We must put a stop to this. We must accept control and inspection. It is not a question of distrust, it is a question of security.

We have constantly to improve our education, our boarding schools, our pilot school. This too is consolidating our liberated areas; although our pilot school is abroad, it forms part of our liberated areas because it takes the best students from our schools in the liberated areas, and is integrated in our educational system for the liberated areas. It is abroad because there we have better conditions to do the work we want to do in the school at this phase of our struggle. Improving our education means increasing the number of schools. But increasing the number of our schools is not enough to improve our education, and may even harm it sometimes. If we make the number of schools too high, then we shall not have enough materials to give to the students and we shall not have good teachers to make the students learn effectively.

It is preferable to have a set number of schools, even a few, guaranteeing a good education for the students at all necessary levels. Then little by little, as the Party has the resources, we can increase the number of schools, above all when we have the human resources, meaning good teachers. For it is not worth anything to have teachers to teach nothing, just to waste time. We have to make our schools fulfill the duty the Party has laid down for them – education and work. Work to maintain the school correctly, work for agricultural production to feed the students and our combatants, for physical exercise for our students, and so that no one thinks that going to school means no more tilling the soil. One of the disasters of modern Africa is the following: anyone who has a primary school certificate no longer wants to take the plough or the hoe to till the soil. In our land even if we take our people as far as the final year of secondary school we will have to take the plough or hoe today and tractors tomorrow to till our soil as we should.

It is fairly important to have boarding schools in our liberated areas, but before we establish boarding schools we have to see if we can really maintain them, if there is sufficient security for the students not to run the risk of being killed in the boarding school, if we have sufficient means to provide food for the boarding school. We cannot found a boarding school with the idea that the Party is going to send food from abroad. The Party can make an effort to send clothes, shoes, shorts and sports clothes in general for the boarding school, books, exercise books, pencils, chalk, ink, pens, etc., but the boarding school must at least supply its own food. This is our instruction: a boarding school which cannot supply its own food should close. The circumstances of our struggle in our land do not allow us to try to send food for boarding schools from outside our land. This is impossible. The boarding school must be sustained either by our people inside our land who give food for their children or by the boarding school itself which cultivates rice and other crops to supply its own food, to store and eat properly.

Our pilot school, which is one of the essential elements in our educational system, is opening the way to train cadres to serve tomorrow, the future of our struggle. The cadres may be military or political, electricians or industrial workers in any branch, doctors or engineers, nurses or radio operators or any speciality (no one should think that going to the pilot school means becoming a doctor or engineer, for he would be mistaken). The pilot school must be constantly more exacting in regard to the students it takes. We must send to the pilot school the best pupils from our land, who receive the highest assessments, within certain age limits. We cannot admit to the pilot school over-age students who have other work to do. But in the Pilot School we must be constantly more exacting. Last year, for example, we only allowed into the Pilot School those who had been graded at least 'fair'. This year we shall only allow in those who have been graded 'good', because the pilot school is for the elite of our students, meaning the best of all our students.

Why? Because our land has many young people, boys and girls, who want to go to the pilot school to learn. We cannot allow that there should be boys and girls in the pilot school who do not learn anything, who fail some years, having to repeat them, and so taking the place from others in our land who have willingness and ability. We cannot allow this. We have made and must make only one exception, which is as follows: we demand from girls a little less than from boys for admission to the pilot school, above all on the question of age and on the question of academic level. Boys must have a primary school certificate. But for girls, mainly because when a girl reaches primary school leaving she is regarded as trained and her father usually looks for some way of marrying her off, we have to do what we can if she is intelligent to take her and put her in the Pilot School quickly. So we admit girls with third-year primary education and even if they are fifteen or sixteen years old we must take them. We want the emancipation and advancement of our women. The best advancement, one of the principal means of advancement, is to teach them to read and write well. This is the reason why we discriminate between boys and girls on the question of admission to the Pilot School.

We must constantly improve health care in our liberated areas. In the north and the south of our land, comrades have for some time worked hard to advance our health services and have made fairly good progress and have established sound foundations for our health services. Hospitals and health centres have been built as far as possible, and health brigades have been formed. In addition to care for our combatants, which is the main objective of our health care as we are at war, we began to provide care for our population. This came as a great surprise to many of our comrades, who were saying that our people did not want doctors. They did not want 'white man's amulet', they only wanted 'native amulet', only wanted 'healers' or *marabouts*.[14] Our people showed that this was false, our people accepted the doctors, took an interest in the doctors and the nurses. They showed such interest, friendship and regard for the doctors that our people began to give their children the names of the doctors, the names of the foreign doctors who had come to help us.

This was a real eye-opener for those of our comrades who were thinking that our people wanted to remain backward instead of progressing. No. Our people want to advance like all and any people in the world. This does not

14 *Editor's note*: Meaning 'Muslim holy man or mystic'.

mean that there are not folk in our land who want their own 'healers', and who when they are given medical treatment in one place go off to find their traditional treatment in another. Even some responsible workers in the Party, who have a big hospital at Boke where they can be treated by good nurses and doctors sometimes say to me: 'Cabral, I want to go for a traditional remedy'.[15] We are still in this situation: let us put up with it.

But the truth is that more and more our people are coming to understand that the doctors and nurses have a great importance for their lives and have saved the lives of many of our children, even when they were not combatants. But we have to improve our work in health, we have to make our men and women nurses work more, we have to set an example, whether in the hospital at Boke, or in the hospitals in the interior, everywhere. Our nurses and doctors must work harder than the foreign doctors who help us. We must improve the distribution of medication, we have to be sparing of medication and must show tenderness to our sick and our wounded. This must be supervised, controlled by our Zone Committees, by our Inter-regional Committees. We must exercise permanent control over the work of the health services and the education services.

For the genuine improvement of our liberated areas, we must from now on be able to establish a principle and practice which stimulate our people very much. It is the following: let us see who is able to work best, in friendship, in esteem and in collaboration. This means we must establish among us what is called constructive emulation, meaning competition but for well-being, not for our stomach, for us to serve our Party, our People. You and I work in some branch of activity which we share. I help you, you help me, but each of us is trying to do the most he can. And we must give high praise to the one who does more, but without jealousy, without jockeying, without elbowing the other. Our political commissars, for example, must say the following: 'Comrades, whoever among the population of this area, this locality, produces the most rice this year will receive a prize or a medal from the Party.

In addition, the Party is going to invite him to go abroad to learn about other lands.' That is just an example. The same goes for whoever produces most potatoes, the same goes for the most manioc. This is what is called constructive emulation. But in the framework of our work day by day, we should always be thinking like this: What the devil, if João or Bakar are working hard, why shouldn't I work hard as well? I am going to make an effort to do even more than Bakar, more than João. But then Bakar sees me and sees that I am advancing and so he decides to do even more. I am content that he has advanced, for our work has improved, but I shall go on doing still more.

In the field of our armed struggle, we should spur on our combatants; push them into doing better all the time. The leadership of our Party must make an

---

15 *Editor's note*: The hospital at Boke was in the Republic of Guinea, next to Guinea-Bissau.

assessment of the action of our commanders, the political commissars, and give them high praise as the best exponents of our work. They are to the fore in the emulation that we are establishing as a practice. We must therefore institute constructive emulation, positive competition, in the service of our Party and our people in all activities.

The Development
of the Struggle

*Extracts from a declaration made to the OSPAAAL General Secretariat in December
1968.*

1. SYNTHESIS OF THE SITUATION

The main characteristic of the present phase of our liberation struggle is
the progressive reversal of the relative positions of the two forces. While the
Portuguese colonialist forces are falling back more and more on the defensive,
our patriotic forces are developing the offensive both against the fortified enemy
camps still remaining in the liberated areas and against the colonial troops
in the other regions. While our action is increasingly assuming the character
of a mobile partisan war and we are reinforcing the capacity of co-ordination
of our activities on the different fronts, the enemy's actions are becoming
infrequent, being mainly restricted to acts of reprisal, terrorism and plunder,
with increasingly frequent aerial bombing and machine-gunning.

Meanwhile, having succeeded in consolidating the areas liberated and
controlled by our armed forces under the auspices of the Party's governing
bodies, we are making fruitful efforts there towards improving the production
of foodstuffs, education and health facilities – developing the new bases of our
political, economic, administrative, judicial, social and cultural life.

Apart from in the Cabo Verde and Bijagós Islands, and in the main urban
areas (Bissao, Bafatá and Gabo-Sara), where our action is still restricted to a
purely political level, the enemy is having to face the initiatives of our armed
forces on every side.

Also, having succeeded in constantly frustrating the political manoeuvres
of the Portuguese colonialists, aimed at creating divisions within the patriotic
forces and mystifying national and international opinion, our armed and political
actions have put a halt to the collaborationist activities of certain traditional
chiefs who were traitors to the nation, thus neutralising the harmful effects
of their attitude on certain sections of the population.

In the contested or partially liberated areas, we are constantly broadening
the fronts of our struggle and, in the flame of patriotism fanned by the fire of
our weapons, nursing the future of freedom, peace and progress for which
we are fighting.

The Portuguese information services themselves have had to admit, through the voice of Radio Bissao, that 'the bandits no longer want to stay in the bush; they are moving into the villages and drawing closer to the urban centres.' This reality is proudly expressed in one of our people's patriotic songs, which runs: 'Lala kêmà: kàu di sukundi kâ tê' ('The great humid plain has caught fire: they [the colonialists] have nowhere to hide').

2. SITUATION OF THE ARMED STRUGGLE

The colonialist forces now number about 25,000 men (army, navy and air force, police and special armed corps), with the reinforcements newly arrived from Lisbon, especially since last May, to counterbalance the intensification of our action and to replace the heavy losses suffered during the course of this year. For a small under-developed country such as ours (15,500 square miles, 800,000 inhabitants, of whom only about 100,000 are capable of usefully assisting our action against the enemy) an army of 25,000 well-equipped men, with the most modern material resources, assumes astronomic proportions, comparable only to those of the disaster which they are doomed to face in our country. And this in spite of huge expenditure on material of all sorts, and particularly American B26 bombers and German jet fighters (Fiat 91).

Portuguese actions, the frequency of which has dropped significantly in recent months, are characterised mainly by:

a) aerial bombing and intensive machine-gunning of the villages in the liberated areas and of places believed to conceal our bases;
b) a few vain attempts to land troops and set up camps in our liberated areas (particularly in the South of the country) with massive air support;
c) increasingly rare incursions into certain liberated areas close to the fortified camps, with the aim of terrorising the population, ruining the villages and destroying our crops and cattle;
d) desperate attempts to bring supplies into certain fortified camps by river and by air, rarely by land;
e) a few larger-scale operations in contested areas.

The bombing and machine-gunning of villages and of our positions by their planes is the main action at present carried out by the enemy, this being in certain areas, and for long periods, the only manifestation of their presence. Several villages have been destroyed in recent months, notably in the North and Central-South of the country. This is understandable if one bears in mind the weakness of our means of anti-aircraft defence and our forces' lack of experience in this field. The civil defence measures which we have nevertheless taken have successfully prevented extensive loss of life among our peoples, frustrating the genocidal intentions of the Portuguese colonialists.

Attempts to land troops in our liberated areas with the aim of creating bridgeheads there have ended in failure. Except in very rare cases (using helicopter-borne troops) when the enemy has been able to destroy crops and cattle, their terrorist operations have generally ended in considerable losses for them in lives and material. Getting supplies to the fortified camps which are completely cut off by us is one of the major problems facing the enemy. With the support of aircraft which bomb and strafe the riverbanks, the enemy does still manage to supply certain camps by river.

In the contested areas, joint operations (called 'mopping-up operations') are generally just a waste of energy, as our forces take advantage of these opportunities to wreak havoc on the men and equipment of the enemy forces in ambushes and surprise attacks. This is proved by the fact that in spite of the numerous operations of this type carried out in the regions of Canchungo, S. Domingos and Bafatá, we have made considerable progress there, liberating new areas and controlling certain roads.

The adoption of the technique of strategic hamlets has not produced the expected results. Created mainly in areas under the influence of certain traditional chiefs, particularly in Gabú, these hamlets have been subjected to violent attacks by our troops and several of them have been destroyed. The populations, more realistic than the chiefs, are now fleeing from the hamlets, preferring to take refuge in neighbouring countries, or moving into the liberated areas or the urban centres. In addition, information from colonialist sources indicates that the morale of the Portuguese troops is getting progressively lower. Conflicts inside the barracks and the fortified camps are becoming more frequent. After the attempted armed rebellion within the air force in April 1965, which led to the arrest of over 100 military, including a senior officer sentenced to 28 years in prison, several other conflicts, generally severely repressed, have taken place in the course of the past year.

More than 7,000 young men, drafted into the army and destined mainly for our country, have been able to desert and hide in the countryside, or get abroad, especially to France.

Our own actions have been characterised mainly by the following activities:

a) attacks on barracks and fortified camps, particularly on those remaining in our liberated areas. These attacks have been made with mortars, artillery and bazookas. In the case of the weaker camps they have been followed by assaults using light weapons;
b) increasing the isolation of enemy positions by using heavy weapons against river transports, and by installing anti-aircraft weapons; destruction of the strategic hamlets;

c) ambushes and surprise attacks against enemy forces moving in contested or partially liberated areas; control of the main roads in these areas;
d) raids against the barracks in the areas that have not yet been liberated, aimed at increasing the insecurity of the enemy forces and of the individuals supporting them;
e) active defence and reinforcement of vigilance in our liberated areas.

The increasing use of aircraft and helicopters reflects the difficulties experienced by the colonial authorities in supplying their troops. In fact, given the impossibility of using almost all passable roads, including those in contested areas, and faced with the intensification of our action against river transports, the enemy is forced to use air transport to keep the troops supplied. Although we have sunk or seriously damaged several boats on the Farim, Cumbidjà and Geba rivers, our action in this field, as in the field of anti-aircraft defence (3 planes shot down and several others damaged) still shows serious deficiencies, particularly in cases where the river transports are escorted by aircraft.

Increasing the isolation of the enemy forces, which also demands the urgent development of effective anti-aircraft measures, is proving to be an indispensable measure for accelerating the total defeat of these forces. This isolation leads to physical and moral degeneration among the troops, and facilitates our actions against the fortified camps.

It is in ambushes and surprise attacks carried out mainly in the contested areas that we are inflicting the heaviest loss of life and destruction of equipment on the enemy forces. In fact, as the colonialist troops venture only very rarely into our liberated areas, it is elsewhere that we are really able to fully develop our military action, in the field of guerilla warfare. We can now state firmly that any attempt by the enemy to reoccupy the liberated areas will end in defeat, or will cost them an even higher price, in lives and equipment, than they paid at the time of the invasion of the island of Como in 1964.

We have made progress in co-ordinating the actions of our armed forces within each sector, and we are trying to effectively co-ordinate our forces on the regional and national level.

In the Cabo Verde Islands our Party, which has consolidated its bases and made major progress in mobilising the popular masses, has decided to move on to armed action as soon as possible, in order to answer the criminal violence of the colonialist agents. Despite the difficulties inherent in this, we must develop the struggle by every possible means in this part of our territory, and we will do so.

The situation on the level of the armed struggle is therefore generally favourable. The enemy is on the defensive, and we hold the initiative on all fronts. We must not lose sight of the fact, however, that the enemy, economically much stronger than us, has considerable human resources and efficient material means available with which to continue the war against us. They are still firmly established in certain urban areas, particularly in the main towns, and can still count on the money, arms, aircraft and other equipment which their allies are supplying.

3. THE POLITICAL SITUATION

The political conditions in our country before the beginning of our struggle – nationwide oppression, absence of even the most elementary freedoms, police and military repression – determined our actions, forcing us to start the armed liberation struggle. Now it is the latter – as the expression of our determination to free ourselves from the colonial yoke, and thus of our fundamental political choice – which is determining the enemy's political behaviour.

Swept out for good from our liberated areas, which cover more than half our national territory (about 60 per cent) and in which 50 per cent of our people live, Portuguese 'sovereignty' is now limited to the urban areas. In fact, Portuguese political domination, which generally took the form of more or less forced collection of taxes of every sort, has ceased to be possible even in the contested or partially liberated areas. In general, the inhabitants of these areas refuse to pay taxes. The colonial authorities have to tolerate this refusal, fearing that the use of force would produce a mass exodus of the inhabitants towards the liberated areas or neighbouring countries. Even in the urban centres, including the main towns, effective political control has become practically impossible, in the face of the growing influx of refugees from the combat zones and of the pressure maintained on these centres by our armed forces.

Having counted on the treachery of certain traditional chiefs who had promised the loyalty of the populations under their control, the Portuguese authorities now have to recognise their failure on this level, and have even stripped of their rank or arrested some of these chiefs. Progressively abandoned by the populations which they had controlled, the traditional chiefs who have betrayed their nation are today the object of suspicion from the colonial authorities and cannot hide their fear and their doubts when faced with the progress of our struggle.

The political manoeuvres of the Portuguese colonialists aimed at demobilising patriots and deceiving African and world opinion by promulgating false administrative 'reforms' and hinting at so-called internal autonomy, distant and undefined, have also met with failure.

A large part of the sector of the African petty bourgeoisie which had placed itself at the service of the colonialists, now has to face an agonising situation, prey to a double fear – that of the colonialist-fascist repression, and that of the justice of the patriotic forces. Some of these petty-bourgeois elements have been moved, or have asked to be moved (to Angola, Mozambique or Portugal), others have been arrested, and the majority hope to be able to go on deceiving the colonial authorities and managing to convince us of their nationalist feelings.

The dominant factor in the political sphere is the backlash of police repression, which is now striking not only patriots but also people who were considered favourable to the colonial regime. The President of our Party, Rafael Barbosa (Zaim Lopez) who was living under house arrest, has again been secretly moved to Bissao prison. The patriots Fernando Fortes, Quintino Nosolini and others, who had already suffered three years imprisonment, have been imprisoned again. The concentration camp on the island of Galinhas is being filled with patriots suspected of being members or sympathisers of our Party. About 80 patriots, among them some Party cadres, are still being detained in inhuman conditions in the infamous concentration camp of Tarrafal (Cabo Verde Islands).

In addition, certain people in the service of Portuguese colonialism have been arrested, and others, including Duarte Vieira and Godofredo de Souza, have died under interrogation. The lawyer Augusto Silva and the important businessman Severino de Pina, General Secretary of the Municipality of Bissao, have been arrested and transferred to the prison of Caxias, near Lisbon. These recent events demonstrate the confusion of the colonial authorities, under the local direction of 'governor' Arnaldo Schultz, trained by the Nazis and formerly Salazar's Minister of the Interior.

The main characteristics of our political action are the work of consolidating our national organisation and adapting its structure and its leadership to the new demands of the struggle. In the liberated areas we have strengthened the leadership organisation of the Party (inter-regional committee) by permanently establishing two members of the Political Bureau in each inter-region. The sector committees are developing their action among the population and a large number of village committees (section committees) have been created or renewed. The Party is making efforts to guarantee the normal and effective functioning of the base organisations, in the framework of a wide democracy under centralised leadership. In the contested or partially liberated areas political work is carried out mainly by the armed forces.

In the urban centres, in spite of the police and military repression, our militants are continuing to develop their underground work and maintain contact with the leadership. Our organisation has been consolidated in Bissao, Bolama and Bafatá, the main towns.

The higher Party organs are functioning normally and are dedicating themselves to the improvement of political work at all levels and to solving the various problems posed by the rapid development of our struggle. There have been four conferences of cadres this year, two for each inter-region. The work of these conferences, which have concentrated on the problems of organisation of the struggle and development of the liberated areas (production, security, education and health), has constituted a basis for elaborating general and specific directives for leaders at all levels. These conferences of cadres also gave attention to the study of the deficiencies and mistakes committed in our political and armed actions. Measures have been taken to progressively eliminate deficiencies and rule out mistakes.

4. ECONOMIC SITUATION

For some time now we have been able to eliminate the system of colonialist exploitation of our people in most of the national territory. This year we struck a severe blow against the remains of the economy of exploitation in the Eastern (Gabú-Bafatá) and Western (Canchungo-S. Domingos) regions.

Most wholesale and retail businesses in the secondary urban centres have had to close down, as the merchants and employees have fled from these centres to the capital. To get some idea of the catastrophic situation of the colonial economy, it is enough to recall that the *Companhia União Fabril* (CUF), the main commercial enterprise in Guinea, has been in deficit for almost three years, and has had to draw on its reserves to survive. In addition the colonial authorities, in a country which produces more rice than is needed for local consumption, have had to import large quantities of this cereal (10,000 tons from Brazil alone) to feed the troops and the urban populations.

Other economic activities have been practically paralysed. Apart from works of a military nature, public works and building are non-existent.

In the liberated areas we are continuing to give every attention to economic development, particularly with regard to increasing the production of crops. New areas of land were planted with rice and other crops during the last rainy season. Other products (leather, rubber from the forests, crocodile and other animal skins, and coconuts) have been shipped and sold abroad, although only in small quantities.

We are also trying to develop artisan work and small local industries. Because of technical difficulties (lack of means of transport and spare parts) we have had to postpone the reopening of the sawmills previously belonging to settlers in the forest of Dio. We are currently examining the possibility of starting up in the North a small rudimentary factory to produce ordinary soap, using palm oil.

To supply the basic needs of the population, two new people's stores have been created in the North of the country and in the Boe region. However we are facing grave difficulties in this, through lack of merchandise, in spite of the help given by friendly countries. Supplying the basic necessities of the inhabitants of the liberated areas is proving to be a major factor in the consolidation of these areas, giving encouragement in the struggle and demoralising the enemy.

The colonialists are making efforts to compete with our people's stores by greatly reducing the prices of goods in the areas which have not yet been liberated. We must successfully counter this competition. Every effort and sacrifice made with this aim will have favourable repercussions on the evolution of the struggle.

5. SOCIAL AND CULTURAL SITUATION

In order to counter the success of our struggle, the enemy has made efforts to improve certain social conditions, particularly in the urban centres, and even has extensive propaganda, mainly on the radio, aimed at convincing the population that it should repudiate our Party, claiming that life will be a 'bed of roses' if the 'Portuguese presence' is maintained in our country.

The flooding of thousands of people towards the main towns has created serious problems of overpopulation there, with effects on food supplies and on common crime. Unemployment is constantly growing. The hospitals and even the schools are occupied by troops, because of the lack of military installations. In Bissao, where the population has trebled in the last two years, theft, prostitution and general moral degeneracy are rife. Even within the ranks of the colonial troops increased medical facilities have not succeeded in improving the situation, with a large proportion of the military suffering from malaria or intestinal illnesses.

In the field of education, the situation is also very bad, in spite of the measures hastily taken by the colonial authorities to increase the number of official schools (from 11 to 25) and to give grants for study in Portugal. Almost all the elementary schools of the Catholic missions ceased to function years ago, when the majority of the African teachers joined our ranks. The few schools established in the unliberated areas have not even started functioning for lack of teachers, and a large proportion of the pupils have preferred to come to the nearby liberated areas and attend our schools instead. Secondary education (1 high school and 1 technical school in Bissao) uses teachers without any professional qualifications, notably the wives of officers in the colonial army and other people without any university education.

It would be naive to pretend that the progress achieved in our liberated areas has brought about a radical change in the social situation of the inhabitants. Our people, who have to face a colonial war whose genocidal intentions spare nobody, still live under difficult conditions. Entire populations have seen their villages destroyed and have had to take refuge in the bush. But everybody has enough to eat, nobody is subject to exploitation, and the standard of living is progressively rising. Demonstrating a political consciousness which is heightened every day, the people live and work in harmony, united in standing up to the evils of the war imposed on us. Apart from a few rare cases of lack of discipline, generally motivated by personal interests or understandable misconceptions, the people proudly follow the Party's directives. Four hospitals are now functioning in the interior of the country (2 in the South, 1 in the North and 1 in Boe), with a total of about 200 beds, and the permanent attendance of doctors helped by sufficient nurses and having the equipment necessary for surgical operations. Also dozens of dispensaries established in the various sectors give daily assistance to the combatants and to the people. The hospital at Boe has now been improved and has departments of general medicine, surgery, orthopaedics, radiology, anaesthesia and analysis. In the past year 80 nurses have been trained (30 inside the country and 50 in Europe), and 30 more are being trained at the moment. We are soon going to set up a new rural hospital, exclusively for orthopaedics.

Bearing in mind that we started from nothing, and that the Portuguese colonialists had only three hospitals and a few dispensaries in the whole country, the importance of the results already obtained, with the help of certain friendly countries and organisations, is obvious.

Progress made in the field of education has far surpassed what we thought possible in our conditions. 127 primary schools are now functioning in the liberated areas, attended in 1965/1966 by 13,500 pupils aged 7 to 15. Considering that at the start of our struggle there were in the whole country only 56 primary and elementary schools (11 official and 45 mission schools) with a maximum total of 2,000 pupils, it is easy to understand the enthusiasm of our children and people for the Party's success in this field.

As in other fields, progress in the field of education has brought with it new demands, and here too we are facing difficulties at present. Particular difficulties are those of publishing books in Portuguese for the various classes, of providing educational materials and clothing for the pupils, and of maintaining the pilot school and a few others set up near the frontiers. But the several thousand adults who have already learned to read and write, as well as the young people from the primary schools, are now discovering a new world before them; they understand the reasons for our struggle and our Party's aims better, and make no secret of their enthusiasm and renewed confidence in the future.

7. OUR STRUGGLE IN THE INTERNATIONAL CONTEXT

Our enemy, the Portuguese colonial government, has suffered shameful defeats on an international level this year. It has been excluded from various international organisations, including certain specialised UN agencies, and has been severely criticised and condemned within other organisations.

Although we greatly appreciate the efforts made by the United Nations and the moral and political value of its resolutions, we have no illusions about their practical effects. In fact we are convinced that given the contradictions which dominate the internal life of that international organisation and its proven inability to resolve the conflicts between colonial peoples and the dominating powers, the United Nations has done everything it can against Portuguese colonialism.

The Portuguese government is isolated internationally (as is proved by the voting at the UN), but this isolation covers only the political and moral field. In the basic fields of economics, finance and arms, which determine and condition the real political and moral behaviour of states, the Portuguese government is able to count more than ever on the effective aid of the NATO allies and others. Anyone familiar with the relations between Portugal and its allies, namely the

USA, Federal Germany and other Western powers, can see that this assistance (economic, financial and in war material) is constantly increasing, in the most diverse forms, overt and convert. By skilfully playing on the contingencies of the cold war, in particular on the strategic importance of its own geographical position and that of the Azores islands, by granting military bases to the USA and Federal Germany, by flying high the false banner of the defence of Western and Christian civilisation in Africa, and by further subjecting the natural resources of the colonies and the Portuguese economy itself to the big financial monopolies, the Portuguese government has managed to guarantee for as long as necessary the assistance which it receives from the Western powers and from its racist allies in Southern Africa.

It is our duty to stress the international character of the Portuguese colonial war against Africa and the important, and even decisive role played by the USA and Federal Germany in pursuing this war. If the Portuguese government is still holding out on the three fronts of the war which it is fighting in Africa, it is because it can count on the overt or covert support of the USA, freely use NATO weapons, buy B26 aircraft for the genocide of our people (including from 'private parties'), and obtain whenever it wishes money, jet aircraft and weapons of every sort from Federal Germany where, furthermore, certain war-wounded from the Portuguese colonial army are hospitalised and treated.

It is our armed liberation struggle which will eliminate Portuguese colonialism in Africa, and at the same time put an end to the anti-African complicity of Portugal's allies. This struggle also offers us the advantage, among others, of getting to know in a real way who are the friends and who are the enemies of our people.

Various successes obtained by our delegations at international conferences, the showing of films made in our country, both in Africa (Conakry and Dakar) and in Europe, the growing support which our organisation is finding among the anti-colonialist forces – all these mark considerable progress in our action on an international level during the past year. We also presented to the UN, at the session of the Committee on Decolonialisation held in Algiers in June, some unusual evidence of our situation – that of journalists and film-makers who have visited our country, supported by ample film and photographic documentation. However, we must continue to use every possible means of improving our action on the international level.

8. PERSPECTIVES FOR THE STRUGGLE

a) The central perspective for our struggle is the development and intensification of our fight on its three fundamental levels: political action, armed action, and national reconstruction. In order to do this, we must above all:

b) constantly improve and develop political work among the popular masses and the armed forces, and preserve at all costs our national unity;

c) further strengthen organisation, discipline and democracy within our Party, continually adapt it to the evolution of the struggle, correct mistakes and demand from leaders and militants rigorous application of the principles guiding our actions;

d) improve the organisation of the armed forces, intensify our action on all fronts and develop the co-ordination of our military activities;

e) increase the isolation of the enemy forces, subject them to decisive blows and destroy the remnants of tranquility which they still enjoy in certain urban centres;

f) defend our liberated areas against the enemy's terrorist attacks, guarantee for our people the tranquility which is indispensable for productive work;

g) study and find the best solutions to the economic, administrative, social and cultural problems of the liberated areas, increase industrial production, however rudimentary, and continually improve health and education facilities;

h) accelerate the training of cadres;

i) fight and eliminate tendencies towards opportunism, parasitism, arrivism and deviation of our action from the general line laid down by our Party, at the service of our people;

j) strengthen and develop our relations with the peoples, states and organisations of Africa, and tighten the fraternal links which join us with the neighbouring countries and with the peoples of the other Portuguese colonies;

k) strengthen our relations of sincere collaboration with the anti-colonialist and anti-imperialist forces, for useful co-operation in the common struggle against colonialism, imperialism and racism.

Within the framework of an armed liberation struggle, whatever the stage of its evolution, no organisation would be so imprudent as to fix in advance a date for independence. We are however convinced that we have covered most of the long road to freedom and gone through the most difficult stages. This much depends essentially on us, on the efforts and sacrifices which we are prepared to make, in the framework of a multiform and necessarily rational action, which takes into account our own experience and that of others. The continuation, the definitive success and the length of our fight must however depend, to a certain extent, on the concrete solidarity which Africa and all the anti-colonialist forces will be able to give to our people.

Analysis of Different Types of Resistance

The following text was transcribed from recordings of talks given in creole by Amílcar Cabral at a PAIGC staff seminar held between 19–24 November 1969.

1. POLITICAL RESISTANCE

Our resistance, comrades, might be compared, for example, to the following: a family or village in our land that needs to grow rice. It has two helpings of rice. It knows that if it saves one helping to sow there won't be enough rice to go around and give everyone something to eat. But it saves that helping and sows it, and if the field is worked well, that one helping might yield 10, 20, even 30 helpings, depending on the terrain. This is similar to the resistance of a people, comrades.

We all had our lives, any one of you could be at home right now, with your family, living under colonialism, sure, but at home with your family. Some of you were maybe even lawyers working for the Portuguese, the Tugas, just as there are others who still are lawyers working for the Tugas, or maybe you were a doctor working for the Tugas, just as there are others still working as doctors for the Tugas, or engineers, just as there still are others, or farmers, mechanics, carpenters, tailors, *sepoys*, soldiers etc.[16] But we decided to make of our heads, seeds that are sown in the ground and produce new plants. Some disaster might occur, of course. It might not rain, for example, and all the seeds dry out. The seeds are then lost, we've achieved nothing, and on top of everything else we're all hungry. Or maybe we don't properly protect the field we've worked and pests, birds or monkeys get in and spoil our crops.

The resistance of a people requires courage if we are to turn ourselves into seeds and grow to become a new plantation that will bring joy to our people through freedom. That's the risk, the so-called risk of resistance. Some will get left behind, but more will grow each day, others will push on ahead. And a resistance will only ever triumph if it grows day by day.

---

16 *Translator's note*: Tuga or Tugas (plural) is a somewhat pejorative term for Portuguese people, first employed by Africans during the liberation struggle. Cabral occasionally refers to '*os portugueses*' (the Portuguese), but usually employs the term '*os tugas*', and we have chosen to distinguish between the two usages here. Generally, Cabral employs 'the Portuguese' to mean Portuguese people as a whole, and 'the Tugas' to mean Portuguese colonialists.

A people's struggle, a people's resistance, takes many forms. As I've said before, our resistance began a long time ago. Our resistance began in Guinea the day the Tugas got it into their heads that they would dominate us, exploit us. In Cape Verde, our resistance began the day it became clear, from the state of our society, utterly dependent on the Portuguese colonists, that our people were being exploited, humiliated and exported like animals, dying of hunger.

It was resistance at the individual level, people doing what they could. Resistance through emigration: our Manjaco people who left for France, for Senegal, our Balanta people who left the Mansôa area, who resisted there first, then moved to the Nalus area, resisted there and then moved to the Bofá area, to the Cóia area etc., in the Republic of Guinea. All of this is resistance, comrades. The resistance of one or two souls brave enough to give a *sepoy* a slap and then be beaten to death for it; the resistance of people who were summoned by the Chiefs of Post, but fled. Individual resistance of every shape and form. But others come together to resist, based on race, based on age group, based on family, based on other things. All it takes in a land is for a few sons and daughters to gain consciousness and see the path they must take for that resistance to become clearly defined.

Resistance is a natural thing. Any force exerted on a given object produces resistance, that's to say a counter force. And the counter force to colonialist and imperialist force is a national liberation movement. Such a tension can only be resolved through political work or, in certain situations, it might take the form of armed struggle, as in our case. And then, bit by bit, certain types of resistance become defined within the overall scheme of resistance. It is essential that every militant and supervisor is fully aware of these different types of resistance. But it's even more important that we understand why we are resisting, what we are resisting for. We must clearly understand the aims of our resistance.

Resistance is the following: destroying something to construct something else. That's what resistance is. What do we want to destroy in our country? Portuguese colonial domination. Just that? No. At the same time we want to destroy any other kind of colonial domination, any other kind of foreign domination of our land. We want our own people, our sons and daughters, to control our destiny in Guinea and Cape Verde. That's the number one thing we want.

Furthermore, and this has been a basic principle throughout the life of our party, we want to destroy any possibility that those who liberate us today, abuse us tomorrow. Our aim is not to destroy the Portuguese colonialists and colonialist domination only to then have some group of our own take their place. Our aim cannot be to take over the Palace of the Governor so that some new governor can do whatever he likes. The same goes for the Chief of Post's house, the Administrator's house. Our aim is to smash the colonial state in order to create a new state, a different state, one based on justice, work and equal opportunity for every child of our land, here in Guinea and in Cape Verde.

We want, therefore, to destroy everything that obstructs our people's progress, every relationship in our society, in Guinea and Cape Verde, that counters our people's progress, counters our people's freedom. Ultimately what we want is this: real and equal possibilities for every child of our land, for every man and woman to be able to advance as human beings, to fulfil their potential; to develop their physical and spiritual selves and reach the heights of their true potential. Anything that prevents this from happening in our country must be destroyed, comrades. Step by step, one step at a time if need be, we must destroy it and build a new life. That is the main aim of our resistance.

We cannot accept any kind of abuse, any kind of group or clique privileges, anywhere in our land, if we really want to liberate our people. Because we are not only going to liberate our people from the Tuga colonialists, but from everything that blocks our people's path to progress. We must destroy all ignorance, poor health and fears of every kind, bit by bit, step by step.

We understand that there is fear in our country today, fear within our struggle, and maybe there still will be tomorrow and for a good while after that. Fear of the *polon* tree, for example, or fear of horns. But one day, sooner or later, when all our people have learned to read and write well, when everyone has been to school and learned what fear really is, what life is, what nature is, when everyone understands what the *polon* tree is, what lightning flashes and bolts are, what the moon is, the stars, and everything else, then rest assured, comrades, no one in our country will fear horns anymore, or pop-eyed witchdoctors.

When we have achieved this, we will have truly liberated the people of our country. Because our people are under huge pressure, comrades, not from the colonialists and not from lack of work, but from fear. A fearful people is an enslaved people. Fearful of going hungry, fearful of not getting enough work, fearful of illness, fearful of beatings, fearful of being deported to São Tomé, fearful of being imprisoned unjustly. But even more than that, fearful of witchdoctors, fearful of fortune tellers, fearful of what *marabouts* say, fearful of the supposed spirit of the bush, the *iran*, fearful of the dark forest, fearful of lightning flashes and bolts. Only a wretched people has so much fear, comrades.

A people so full of fear, yet capable of taking up arms against the colonialists, of wrenching them from our land. See the contradiction there, comrades? This clearly shows we are capable of anything, and that's precisely our party's aim: to reach our full potential. This is what we seek through our resistance. To eradicate everything that's preventing us from fulfilling our true potential.

We do not want our sons and daughters to be fearful of their parents, not tomorrow, though we can perhaps tolerate a little bit of it today. No, they should be respectful, but not fearful. We no longer want to see our sons and daughters tied up to be beaten. This belittles our people, comrades, it blocks our people's path. We no longer want to see anyone in our country tied up and beaten. Crooks and good-for-nothings will be judged, and if necessary they will be shot, but they will not be treated like dogs. We no longer want to see any human beings in our country treated like dogs.

And it is our job to destroy, through our resistance, anything that makes puppies of our people – our men and our women – so that we may advance, grow, rise up like flowers from our soil. We must do everything we can to make our people feel like valued human beings. This is our task, comrades. If we can't understand this, we won't understand anything.

This is what we're sacrificing ourselves for, this is what we're fighting for. We must be aware of what we want to destroy in our country, and what we want to construct. This is the first set of circumstances we require for our resistance to truly advance. If this is to happen, it's imperative that we're all aware of certain issues. For example: Who are we and who is our enemy? We've been explaining this for a long time now. But we have to understand where we've come from, our struggle's point of departure, our resistance. I've already explained this to you, just a few days ago, right here, what we were before this struggle, before this organised struggle. The political, economic, cultural and social circumstances of our country. And we must clearly define the ways we have carried out and will carry out our resistance.

Our resistance evolves in a variety of forms, comrades. First comes political resistance, first and foremost: Political Resistance. That is why we began our resistance by creating our party, a political tool. But there are other types of resistance too: economic resistance, cultural resistance and armed resistance; each one is an essential component of our struggle, comrades, of our resistance. These four types of resistance represent the minimum of what can be done and we have to develop each one more by the day. This is what our struggle has been about all along, comrades, whether we were aware of it or not. This is what our struggle has consisted of so far.

For this very reason, our party's programme has, right from the start, clearly defined what we see as our political aims. It's easy to say fight, take up arms and go on strike, but it's not enough to just fight with a gun in your hand, you need to fight with political consciousness in your head too. We need to be aware that it is man's consciousness that guides the gun and not the gun that guides his consciousness. The gun's worth lies in the fact that there is a man behind it, holding it. And, of course, the more politically conscious the man is, the more the gun is worth, and if the man's consciousness serves a just and well-defined cause, then the gun is worth all the more.

We must ensure our political resistance is clearly defined because our enemy puts political pressure on our political resistance in order to try to destroy it. We must clearly define our political resistance, inside and outside our country, and know exactly what we must do. And it has been clearly defined for a long time now. If anyone doesn't know it, then they simply haven't wanted to know.

The first requirement of political resistance, comrades, is to unite the people. We have already discussed this in terms of party principles, what our political resistance is made up of has, by and large, already been defined. Unite: gradually create a national consciousness, because at our point of departure there was no national consciousness, we were, due to our own history and the work of the Tugas, divided into groups. The 'civilised' and the indigenous, city people and bush people, Balantas, Pepels, Manjacos and Mandingas etc. So our first job is to create a national consciousness in a certain number of our people, in Guinea and in Cape Verde. This is why our party programme states this so clearly: national unity in Guinea, national unity in Cape Verde.

We must seek, through our political resistance, in service of our overall resistance, to unite all our people, as many as we can. But as I've told you before, this means uniting without any opportunism, rejecting opportunism of every kind, because our resistance is not designed to serve a particular clique or to produce chiefs. It's not Cabral's resistance, I don't need others to serve me. If I'd wanted to, in 1960 I could have become the leader of all the Dakar 'movements', I could have united them all under me. Even our comrade Luiz Cabral, when he left here and went to Senegal, they met with him and made him the following proposition: Leave the PAIGC, come work for us and become our leader. He told them never to say such a thing again because he's PAIGC through and through. From that day forth, they became his enemies. Even people who had been guests in his house became enemies. Because we will not accept opportunism of any kind. We reject all opportunism, comrades.

National unity, yes, national consciousness, yes, but not with traitors, not with opportunists, not with people without morals. We cannot create national unity with thieves, liars and crooks. We're creating national unity with one true objective: to combat the enemy, to fight the enemy, but at the same time to fight against every negative element in our midst. This is a fundamental aspect of our political resistance, one that comrades must fully understand in order to orientate themselves in their work, whether it be as a militant or a supervisor.

We have to be vigilant and not allow anyone to divide our people. We have to clearly define, as I've already said, who our people are at this stage in our history. So let me repeat it: our people are all the sons and daughters of our land, in Guinea and Cape Verde, who want rid of the Portuguese colonialists, that's all. Anyone who wants to get rid of them is one of us, and we don't want anyone dividing our people. Be vigilant, because those who divide us are our enemies, worse even than the Tugas, who will undoubtedly soon be gone.

In our political resistance we must continually raise the consciousness of every militant engaged in the struggle or with the party. We must urge everyone to better themselves in terms of their work and knowledge. This is the only way of making our most valued resource, our men and our women, even more valuable.

We have to fight to ensure the principles we've established, and which we speak of here, are applied, so that everyone, every man and woman, has the opportunity to advance. Failure to do so is a betrayal, sabotage of our political resistance. And we must organise, organise. This is why our party started to organise itself, right from the beginning, clandestinely at first, in groups of three, in cells, in cities, and then in the bush, in small groups, out in the open where it was possible to do so and hidden wherever we had to hide. Then came organised villages and, step by step, we advanced: Party Committees, Area Committees, Regional Committees, Inter-regional Committees.

Step by step we transformed our party leadership, continually improving the way we organised ourselves, according to the reality of our struggle, in order to improve our political resistance. And every day, every day, we have endeavoured to clarify why we are fighting, what we want, so that everyone advances knowing exactly what they're doing and why they're doing it. This foundation is essential to being able to politically resist our enemy's manoeuvres, their propaganda, and being able to advance our political resistance, for our political resistance is the most essential form of resistance, comrades, within our overall scheme of resistance.

We have spoken often about the need to enlighten the masses of our land, to do so on a daily basis, to tell the truth above all else, to never lie to them, to never trick anyone, we have no need to trick people. If we start tricking and lying, we are ruining our political resistance. If there are difficulties, say so, clearly; if we triumph, say so, clearly; if we lose, say so, clearly. Because no struggle brings only victories. If there were only victories, it would be no struggle at all. There are victories and defeats, there are difficulties, there is sometimes despair too, but we always move forward. We must seek, by enlightening the masses of our land, by clearly demonstrating the enemy's intentions, to stop the enemy from misleading them. This is one of our essential tasks, comrades, and one that, unfortunately, some comrades seem to have forgotten about.

Given the particular circumstances of our struggle, given our need to build national unity in Guinea, we must make more of an effort to win over those brothers and sisters who certain chiefs have turned away from the struggle, especially among the Fula and the Manjaco. Our party established an entire policy because of this, and to deal with this, distinguishing between the population and their chiefs. Treat the population well, do your utmost to cause them no harm. This is precisely why, when we started the fight in Gabú in early 1965, we gave orders for our command not to fire a single shot for a whole month against anyone from our land who, having been tricked by the Tugas, took up arms against us. We talked about this, we discussed it, and a few of our comrades even died without firing a single shot. Comrade Lúcio can tell us all about this, he saw it. But we did this to win people over, to reinforce our political resistance, to increase our unity in terms of our engagement.

In Cape Verde, while we understand that our struggle is primarily being fought on behalf of those who are suffering, those who have no land to work, who have no jobs, who are contracted to go and die in Sao Tomé; those mothers who lug sacks around at the docks in São Vicente, who die of hunger alongside their sons and daughters in times of crisis; while we understand all this, our orders are to recruit as many people as possible to our cause. Even those on the Tugas' side. To those sons and daughters of Cape Verde who are in good employment, living well, we state our case clearly: the country is yours, join us so that we may advance. Because the first step in a political resistance is joining as many people as possible together for the fight.

In Guinea, it's the same thing. Our struggle in Guinea is not, as far as I'm concerned, being fought to improve my life in material terms. If I were ever to have in our country, in Guinea or in Cape Verde, the lifestyle I used to have ... Or if the leaders of our country tomorrow, in Guinea or in Cape Verde, were to live as well as I used to live in Portugal, then that would mean our country was very rich. But we must be vigilant and not let our leaders live like this, because it is too good a life for a poor country that still has so much work to do. Our struggle in Guinea is, to begin with, being fought on behalf of our people in the bush, people who have lived for centuries and centuries within the same village, never straying more than five kilometres from their homes; people who don't know what schools are or that medicines exist to treat the illnesses that swell their bodies.

Our resistance in Guinea sets out to end every kind of abuse, it is against anyone who's abusive, in the bush just as much as the cities. It is for the sons and daughters of our land to be able to gain a proper understanding of their professions and so that no foreigner gets to rule over our land. And knowing this, or in spite of this, we seek to join everyone together in our cause, people of every social class, even Jaime Pinto Bull, as I said to you only today. To Jaime Pinto Bull, I say, 'Leave the Tugas and come and join us.'[17] In Cape Verde, I say the same thing, loud and clear, to Júlio Monteiro, to Aguinaldo Veiga, to Antero Barros and so many others: 'Leave the Tugas, stick with us, for the country is yours too.' We are not the only ones who have the right and the duty to fight for our country, there's plenty of room for all of us. This is the path of political resistance for those of us who really want to fight and give it our all, for those who want to serve their own people and not just their own stomachs.

In terms of our political resistance within our land, we must do everything we can to channel all our forces into our political resistance. Our party has done a lot in this regard, maybe we should or could have done more, but we've done a lot. And the triumphs of our struggle, the successes of our struggle, the continuity of our struggle, the prospects of our struggle today, show that our party has won some great victories in this sense. Nevertheless, there are still traitors within our land, there are still Tugistas, Tuga puppy-dogs. There are still people in our midst who might pass over to the Tugas tomorrow because their ambitions, their obsessions, their vanities, their vices mean they cannot put up with the demands and rigours of our party's work.

---

17 *Editor's note*: Jaime Pinto Bull was leader of the FLNG in 1962. The FLNG was a political party that was opposed to Cabral's Marxist doctrine and the PAIGC but also fought for independence.

In terms of political resistance outside our land, we have to make a big effort there too. Our principal objective externally, given our circumstances, is to gain everyone's political support, in order to reinforce our political resistance.

Our party has worked hard to win, fought to win outside political support within Africa and in the wider world. Since 1960, we, the people of Guinea and Cape Verde, have been fortunate in that I was voted for, chosen from amongst all our comrades in the Portuguese colonies who are with us in this struggle, to go out and denounce Portuguese colonialism to the rest of the world. And in February 1960 we gave our first international press conference, in London, revealing Portuguese colonialism for what it is, and we wrote our first pamphlet, the first pamphlet against Portuguese colonialism written by a son or daughter of the Portuguese colonies. It was published in English in England, under the name of Abel Djassi. There and then our political resistance in the international realm, in the external realm, began to take shape, within the framework of the Portuguese colonies generally, but moving towards our own framework, that of Guinea and Cape Verde, and therefore the framework of our party.

Externally, the principal objective of our political resistance is to gain allies, to gain political support and thus isolate the enemy politically. To this end, from as early as 1960, while preparing our people for the armed struggle, we began to go to conferences and international meetings, raising our issue, fighting to be heard, multiplying our efforts, courting all necessary support and seeking to isolate the enemy internationally.

Seeking to isolate the enemy in regards to its own people is another issue. This is why, right from the beginning, within the framework of our political resistance, we have made it clear that we are not fighting against the Portuguese people. Everyone in our party knows this. We are not fighting against the Portuguese people, we are fighting against Portuguese colonialism, against Portuguese colonialists. We are fighting to get the Portuguese colonialists out of our land. But we've been even more clear about it than that: we, the people of Guinea and Cape Verde, the PAIGC, are not fighting against Salazarism or fascism in Portugal. That's the Portuguese people's job, not ours. This is an important point to make in order to isolate the Tugas from their own people.

Within Guinea we have managed to isolate them a little. We saw that, whereas in early 1959, as well as during the August 1959 strike, the Pidjiguiti massacre, some Portuguese civilians took up arms against us, civilians have not been willing to take up arms in the war. A number of civilians have even sided with us. This is a triumph for our party, for it shows that they fully understand we are not against them. This is what isolating the enemy from its own people is, isolating them from the masses.

And in Portugal today, an increasing number of people, more and more by the day, look favourably upon the PAIGC. There is great respect for our party in Portugal, more than you might imagine, comrades. Some of the Tugas in Portugal maybe have more respect for our party than some of you sitting here. Forgive me, but it's true. And public opinion against the colonial war being waged in our country grows by the day, because our party has managed to nurture this aspect of political resistance, isolating the enemy, distinguishing between the enemy and the masses, isolating the enemy in relation to its people.

It could be better, of course, but there's not enough time for everything to be brilliant. We have stated our case in relation to the Portuguese people and defined how prisoners are to be treated, how deserters are to be treated, in order to win over more and more of the Portuguese people, to isolate the people from our enemy, the Portuguese colonialists. And now we understand that the best form of propaganda our party has ever had, the best propaganda concerning our struggle, our resistance, has come from Portuguese deserters, from Portuguese prisoners even. This is one of the greatest triumphs of our struggle.

There have even been Portuguese deserters who, after we sent them away, wrote to us asking us to accept them as naturalised sons of the land, because they want to spend their lives working for the PAIGC. This shows how successful we've been in our work. Since the very start of the struggle, in documents some of you comrades will perhaps know, we have addressed settlers in our country, saying to them clearly: 'You are the wheels on the old colonialist car that wants to carry on exploiting our people.' But even settlers have a place in our country, if they want it. We want to make a country where anyone from anywhere in the world can come and live, provided that they respect our people's right to rule over ourselves; to come and live and work, for that's the way it should be. This was the first reason why many civilian Tuga settlers demobilised, rejecting the colonialist path.

We reached a point in around 1964 where, had the authorities allowed it, the Tuga settlers would have all left. But although our struggle is an armed one, we refuse, out of respect for our own form of political consciousness, to abuse Portuguese soldiers in any way. If any of our comrades have committed crimes like those the Tugas commit against us, then they have been disobeying party orders.

At the start of our struggle there were comrades who suggested that, within the scheme of our overall struggle, we should commit certain atrocities. But we refused to do so. Certain things that have happened in other African countries have no place in our struggle. No matter what justification an African might give for killing women, for killing the white children of our land, just because they are white, we reject such actions once and for all. Why? Because what we want is a political resistance that serves our people, we do not want our people to become bloodthirsty, we do not want our people to shed blood just for the sake of shedding blood. If blood is to be shed, it is to be shed politically, to serve the future of our country.

Every time we kill someone it is because that someone has a gun pointed at us, turned against the rights of our people. We have issued orders saying that anyone who took up arms against us but lays down their weapons will no longer be considered our enemy: they will be seen as a human being and must be treated well. Our comrades have, thankfully, understood this properly and respected it. And if someone does not respect it, they are sabotaging our party's work, our political resistance.

The work we do with the people of other Portuguese colonies is very important within the scheme of our own political resistance. We've said it before, but of all the resistance movements in the Portuguese colonies, our party has concerned itself most with this. Right from the start, we have always raised the issue: we are one, fighting together, because there is but one enemy. There have been ups and downs in terms of our forming an alliance with other movements, there have been betrayals from other movements, but the PAIGC, comrades, has always been loyal and shown unconditional solidarity to resistance movements in other Portuguese colonies. Certain comrades within our party have even raised this as an issue: How is it that we're the only ones who honour our CONCP commitments? Our answer is that we honour them because it's in our interest to do so, it's not just in the interest of others, but ours too. We had to sacrifice members of the party command to go and work for the CONCP, when other movements gave none. But in the same spirit, we will always defend, against anyone and anything, the need for all students of the Portuguese colonies to join together in a single organisation (the UGEAN).[18] Fortunately our more disciplined comrades understood this well.

There is only one thing we refuse to do and that is to join forces with false resistance movements in other Portuguese colonies. We will not join up with movements that don't advance themselves and that give themselves over to the imperialists, for we do not want to replace one kind of domination of our land with another. We join with those movements our analysis has shown are pure, those that intend to fight the proper way, and we have no regrets in this area so far. This, comrades, is a fundamental aspect of our political resistance: our unity, our comradeship, our collaboration, our close bonds to the liberation movements of Angola, Mozambique and São Tomé.

We ourselves, the PAIGC, are working hard to help unite different movements in Mozambique, towards the creation of FRELIMO. And we ourselves, the PAIGC, helped form the MPLA in Angola. This is not vanity speaking, it is common knowledge, the sons and daughters of Angola know this well. To serve the interests of our own people, comrades, we have taken risks in Angola, attending clandestine meetings at a time when several Angolans had been imprisoned by the PIDE. But we had to go to Angola and hold meetings.

---

18 *Editor's note*: The General Union of Students from Black Africa under Portuguese Colonial Domination (*União Geral dos Estudantes da Africa Negra sob Dominação Colonial Portuguesa*).

We set up an agronomy contract in Angola and used it to go there and gather comrades together to discuss the path we must all follow in the struggle to free our lands. All this under the PIDE's watchful eye, comrades. And after having done other work in Angola besides. What for? To serve the people of Guinea and Cape Verde, comrades.

We don't have some obsession with trying to serve the people of Angola, Angola's own sons and daughters are perfectly capable of serving their own people, although our consciousness as human beings means we would be happy to serve in Angola just as we would be happy to serve in Mozambique, the same as in Guinea or Cape Verde. And only members of the party who have attained true political consciousness are capable of serving in any country, fighting the common enemy.

We have always staunchly defended the need for unity among resistance movements in the Portuguese colonies. Thankfully, after all the difficulties, after all the problems, we are now all in agreement on this and this is very important. It is another great victory against Portuguese colonialism, comrades.

And together we are working to realise another of our party's dreams, which is to gather together all the students from the Portuguese colonies in a single organisation. This would be another great triumph within the overall scheme of our political resistance, because the enemies of our people, the enemies of today or tomorrow, are also active within the student realm, trying to win people over and hold back the lives of our people.

In terms of our political resistance outside our land, we are constantly seeking to develop and reinforce our relationships across Africa. To start with we fought with great courage in Conakry, for example, in order to win the friendship, esteem and solidarity of the Republic of Guinea. This was an essential aspect of our political resistance, comrades. Indeed, at that stage of our struggle, it was arguably our party's biggest triumph, the most far-reaching, by which I mean it had the biggest consequences, way beyond what most of you can imagine. We have also made a big effort and showed great patience, determination and persistence to win over the people of Senegal, despite Senegal's reluctance, despite Senegal's rejection, despite Senegal creating 'movements' against our party. But after several years' work, we reached an agreement with the government of Senegal, another great victory in the overall scheme of our political resistance and one we must work to reinforce every day, indeed take to another level because our circumstances are very different today.

In African terms, working within the limits of what's possible, of course, and according to our limited time and resources, we have endeavoured to reinforce friendships with other independent African states. Our party has developed a deep friendship with a number of African heads of states. Let us recall the deep bonds of friendship that link us to Algeria, the United Arab Republic, Tanzania, Congo-Brazzaville, to name but a few. We seek to develop friendships with the Ivory Coast and Tunisia. As a party we have decided to push further and reach out to all the independent states of Africa. This is important work in our political resistance.

Through our bravery and hard work, through our victories, through our resistance and our endeavour, we have managed to win over all the African people aligned under the OAU and establish our party, our people, as the leading liberation movement in Africa.

This is a great victory in political terms, comrades, in terms of our political resistance. And we are constantly working to strengthen our friendship and collaboration with other liberation movements in Africa. We have a great sense of unity and trust with the movements in South Africa, who are fighting against colonialist racism; with movements in Rhodesia, in Southeast Africa and, before they became independent, in Zambia and Kenya. Through our persistent work, we are developing friendships with them all, but always based on consciousness, never on opportunism, knowing how and who we choose to be friends with. Because if you don't know how to choose your friends properly, if you don't have some sort of criteria, if it's not based on principles of respect, then you end up choosing mischief-makers, not friends.

One of our party's greatest triumphs within the context of our political resistance, the result of intense work over a number of years, has been to demonstrate the value of our struggle to progressive forces around the world, especially within the socialist community. We have shown them the value of our work and demonstrated our responsibility as a party, while earning their trust, appreciation and indeed admiration, so much so that, thanks to our political consciousness and the triumphs of our political resistance, they've become firm friends who help us in our struggle.

Our party has even had some success in terms of political resistance relating to countries allied with Portugal. We've never gone around claiming that our struggle is against all the capitalist countries in the world. We've never done this, we say we're fighting Portuguese colonialism, that's our task.

We make the issue very clear, be it to the Americans or the Germans, the English, the French, we say we're not fighting you, we're fighting Portuguese colonialism. And if we haven't got more out of them yet, or haven't got anything at all, then the fault lies with them rather than our party, because they have commitments with the Portuguese colonialists, because they have imperial interests, and those interests are bigger than any kind of humanitarian interest they might have in our struggle.

Even so, we have achieved a number of victories. We have sometimes seen Western countries abstain and vote neither for nor against Portugal. This, in itself, is a huge victory for us, comrades. A huge victory. We have managed, for example, to visit certain countries and hold press conferences, raise our issues and, above all else, win the support of anti-colonialists in those countries. This is important, comrades. Be it in America, England, Italy, France etc. progressive forces have huge admiration for the PAIGC, comrades. Only those unacquainted with our relationships and all the correspondence we receive fail to appreciate this.

But we recently achieved an even bigger victory. A Western country that has dealt with Portugal in commercial terms has declared itself to be entirely on our side: Sweden. And now it is helping us, substantially. This year we will start to receive this help, not in the form of money but in goods, medicines and school materials, to help our people economically and culturally. Comrades, this is a real triumph for us and opens up a great breach in Portugal's international alliance. Colonialist Portugal is fully aware of this and furious.

The Soviet Union has helped us, but the Tugas didn't get furious about that; they complained, but not much, they knew this was only to be expected. It was the same thing with China, with Cuba. Portugal has diplomatic relations with Cuba, but didn't cut off those relations. The Tugas know we get arms from Cuba, and other things. They know there are Cuban doctors who assist us; they know all this very well, it's not like they've suddenly arrested a Cuban and found all this out. But they didn't make much fuss about it, they didn't get as furious as they did about Sweden.

Sweden said it would help us and the Tugas became immediately furious, they recalled their ambassador, cut off commercial ties, sent people out into the streets to protest and prevented dockers from unloading Swedish ships. Because they know the significance of this. They know this is a breach in terms of its Western alliance. They know it might be taken as a lead for other progressive forces to follow, in America, England and France, for example, where people might rise up and petition their governments to help freedom movements in Africa. The Tugas are afraid of this precedent, comrades. This should give you an idea of just how successful the party has been this year, a great victory achieved through our political resistance in the international sphere.

In summary, comrades, our political resistance must revolve around three fundamental points: to achieve national unity in our land and put that unity entirely at the service of our struggle, at the service of our people, under the flag of our party; to further isolate the enemy from its allies, from its partner countries, from anyone that might support it; and to win over more allies to our cause, gaining ever more support without ever compromising on our principles. This is how we must orientate our struggle, doing our work properly and never forgetting that our fight is fundamentally a political fight, which is why we must ensure our political resistance triumphs.

2. ECONOMIC RESISTANCE

In our afternoon session yesterday, we looked at how our resistance is a response to Portugal's colonial dominance of Guinea and Cape Verde. We showed comrades what this means, what the principal aspects of our resistance are and how, throughout our struggle, the party has followed a trajectory that responds to the needs of the resistance according to the specific situation in our land.

We spoke yesterday about political resistance and saw how, operating in conjunction with political resistance, there is also economic resistance, cultural resistance and armed resistance. All these types of resistance exist in our country and have done ever since we began our struggle, developing by the day, even when many comrades were not aware of it.

Today we will speak a bit about another important aspect of our resistance, economic resistance. As every comrade knows, our struggle is a political struggle because we are seeking to win our right to be a free and sovereign people, in other words to govern ourselves, by gaining national independence for our country. But at the root of this truth is another truth, which is the following: colonialism is, first and foremost, economic domination. Colonialism, or imperialist domination, seeks, in the first instance, to dominate others economically. To this end it adds a political domain and spreads its imperialist or colonial state forces throughout the land it wants to dominate economically. This being the case, we must recognise that the principal aim of our resistance and our struggle is, at root, to free ourselves economically, although to do this we must first achieve political freedom.

In other words, a country is only truly liberated if it manages to rid itself of every aspect of foreign dominance over its economy, if it truly manages to free itself from foreign exploitation. This is what freedom is for a country dominated by colonialists.

Every country has its natural resources and its population, which is its greatest resource. A population develops its work and productivity capacity, its natural resources, which might be actual or potential, and its means of production, but under colonialist or imperialist domination none of these things are free, nor developed freely, they're subjected to imperialist domination. Winning true independence is having the ability to freely develop a combination of factors known as the *productive forces* of a country. You can see, therefore, that, when it comes down to it, our resistance is aimed at resolving an economic issue, although it has to achieve political aims first, the political aspect always being very important. But in any case, this is why our economic resistance is so important.

As I've said before, every struggle, but specifically our liberation struggle, has two components that must come together: destruction and construction. We see this clearly in our political resistance, we have to destroy the Portuguese state, we have to destroy the political concepts the colonialist Tugas have put in our heads. We have to destroy, in the long term, and in the short term overcome, any erroneous political assumptions that might exist in people's heads, within our population, within our different classes and ethnic groups, assumptions that might hinder our people's march towards the path of progress.

We have to construct a new state for our country, one based on the freedom of our people, on democracy, on working towards progress. We have to construct a national consciousness among our people, we have to constantly develop our population's political consciousness, and we have to construct all the necessary political means, organisms and organisations required to defend the national liberty that we've won.

Economic resistance is likewise a matter of destruction and construction. The objective of our economic resistance is to destroy the Portuguese colonialists' exploitation of our people. This means that our struggle had to be aimed, right from the start, at putting a complete stop to the exploitation of our land by the Portuguese colonial regime. We know that exploitation in Guinea works principally through our people essentially being forced to buy agricultural products at prices determined by colonialist state businessmen, and through being obliged to grow groundnuts and sell them at prices likewise determined by the Tugas. The level of exploitation is such that, were anyone to properly do the sums, they would conclude that groundnut cultivation in Guinea is in fact forced labour, because the money a family farming groundnuts gets for however many groundnuts they harvest, regardless of their area of land, is not enough to pay a wage, even a tiny one, to all the people in the family who work at it all year round.

In other words, we must draw the conclusion that our people work for Gouvêa, Ultramina and all the other companies that buy groundnuts, for free, because the money they get for these groundnuts may be enough for them to pay the family tax, buy a cut of fabric for the mother and a few other bits and bobs. But if we make proper calculations, if we take wages into account and other expenses that should be factored in, we see that the price paid for the groundnuts doesn't cover it, that this is agricultural exploitation. And this is what we want to destroy, what we knew we had to destroy; we had to destroy the relationship of economic exploitation the colonialists had with our people. And we had to destroy other forms of economic exploitation besides, even if they were dressed up as legitimate administrative running costs, such as the various types of unfair tax our people had to pay to the colonial Portuguese state.

In Cape Verde, our principal aim is to destroy a system of exploitation based on large properties that afford no land to our people. Our people are forced into being tenants, whether they farm or not, they have to pay rent, live in poverty, suffer from hunger and even risk being sold or contracted as forced labour in other colonies. We must destroy this.

In Guinea, we have managed to destroy a lot already. Just a few days ago, for example, Radio Bissau announced that a Greek ship had docked bringing three tonnes of rice. We can see from this that we have managed to inflict a degree of destruction on the Portuguese regime because, as we know, our people were practically forced to sell the rice they grew to Ultramarina, to be milled and then sold back to us. But the Tugas now have to import rice. Last year they imported over 10,000 tonnes of rice from Brazil alone, this year they've already taken delivery of 3,000 tonnes. And anyone who's been following the official statistics will have seen that groundnut exports have fallen a lot. There are practically no exports from our land at present. Portuguese ships bring in war materials and provisions for the troops or goods for the cities, and leave almost empty. They mostly just take away scrap metal from trucks and other things our soldiers have destroyed.

We have, therefore, already destroyed much of the Portuguese economic system in our land, but we must destroy it all, completely. But then what do we construct? We must start constructing our own economy now. Indeed we have been constructing it for a few years now because it's all very well and good to say let's fight, in political terms, in military terms, but people cannot fight properly with an empty stomach and poor health. This is another form of resistance. It's impossible to resist without food, it's impossible to resist without good health. We therefore have to develop our economy, find the best way to move our economy forward, even during our struggle, because we have to guarantee the minimum conditions necessary for our people to make a living, for our soldiers to have the means to live. Furthermore, we have to make a real effort to gradually improve living conditions for our people, so that they feel the sacrifices they're making, for our country's independence, for our party's flag, are worthwhile.

As a party we've done what we can, but we – party militants, supervisors, soldiers, leaders – haven't been able to improve the living conditions of our people or show them that poverty can and will end. Above all else, we need to raise consciousness so everyone understands that, while there is poverty in our country today, it will end tomorrow, but it depends on us, our work, our advancing the struggle. Because anyone who has practically nothing today but trusts that they'll have plenty tomorrow if they work hard, is no longer poor; they're rich, because they trust in the path and see it's open to them. We have to do our utmost in this regard, because we know that anyone living in poverty is easy prey for the enemy, is easily captured to work against the interests of our people. For example, we only have to consider the following: Who in our land provide the most services to the Tugas? Are most servants drawn from people with or without means? It's plain to see that most of the people who become servants to the Tugas are people without means. In Bissau, the PIDE recruits most of its agents from among the unemployed and the idle.

Faced with our need to put up economic resistance, we must clarify the following: What is the enemy doing to destroy our economic resistance? Because they aren't just fighting us with arms, they're fighting us economically too. On the one hand, in the areas they still control, they're making a big push for economic development, saying life is going to improve, giving jobs to people to show that life really is improving, trying to establish paddy fields, provide goods etc ... For example, everyone knows that more goods and nice things are arriving in Cape Verde than ever before. This is in order to put a stop to the kind of shortages that foster revolts. Even in Guinea, numerous things the Tugas used to buy off us, like rice, they're now buying elsewhere for much higher prices. This is in order to exhaust our economic resistance. They are making a big show of creating large paddy fields in the Tite area, the island of Bissau has been almost entirely transformed into paddy fields, and so they are trying to find ways to provide an economic lift to the areas they still control in order to show people that life is improving, that people don't need to join our struggle.

On the other hand, the Tugas are going to great lengths to try to completely destroy the economic base of our struggle. Bombings, napalm, helicopter attacks that terrorise local populations so that people take flight and leave our country for Senegal or the Republic of Guinea. This is good for the Tugas because local populations are then not working the land in the liberated areas and providing us with the economic means needed to support our struggle. And if that doesn't suffice, if local populations hide or refuse to bow to Tuga demands, the Tugas burn our crops and our villages, destroying everything, killing our cows, killing any creature that moves. And criminals that they are, they kill our local populations too, children, women, the elderly, never mind adult men. This is not just because of the war, no, it's in order to destroy our economic resistance, to end it. They know as well as we do that if we don't have an economy, if our land does not have the economic means to support our struggle, if we don't have food, if we don't have the capacity to provide our people and soldiers with food, then there can be no war, comrades, there can be no struggle.

The enemy, therefore, is destroying everything it can, even things like medicines and fabrics, things we get for our people, for our 'people's stores', for our hospitals etc. Our enemy is making every effort to put a stop to these things. That we've managed to establish stores in certain areas, where our people can go and get fabrics, shoes and other things they need, is one of our enemy's biggest defeats in economic terms. The Tugas want to find our stores and burn them down as soon as possible, because they know these stores give us economic strength and that this translates into political strength in the context of our struggle.

To combat our economic resistance, the Tugas are prepared to torch the entire country if necessary, employ what's known as the 'scorched earth policy', in other words, to reduce everything to ashes rather than have us win our fight. We must therefore be vigilant and know exactly what we must do when faced with such criminal intent on the part of the Tugas, intent we've ample proof of having come to fruition in certain areas of our land. We have to be firm in our economic fight.

This is why, right from the start, our party has thought about and tried to implement a programme of economic resistance. We must adapt it, of course, tailor it to suit our conditions as best we can, and we must mobilise all our forces, channel our energies into our economic resistance, especially the energy of local populations, of our militants in the villages and the liberated areas. At the same time we must gradually increase our destruction of the enemy's colonial economy and make secure plans to boost our own production, agricultural products and artisanal products and other things besides. We must try to destroy the enemy's economic means, their cars, their factories, their reserves, their warehouses, their boats, their roads, to completely shut down their economic exploitation of our land.

You will have seen, comrades, that we started out by sabotaging roads, bridges and everything else. This was our first act of economic resistance, and an act of political and military resistance, carried out against the colonialist enemy. And we too, if the enemy has established itself in a particular area and in such a way that the only means to force them out is by setting fire to everything, then we will do so, we have the right to do so because it's our land. It's better to completely torch everything and force the Tugas out, and then rebuild the area, than leave the area untouched and let the Tugas remain there indefinitely, dominating our people. This is something we need to be conscious of, while pursuing a strategy that seeks to minimise the need to destroy things, things that may currently be under colonial control, but that were originally made by us.

This has, in fact, always been our party's policy. It's important to understand our great need to destroy the Tugas' supply chains. This is why our party has been so insistent on the need to attack boats on rivers and trucks on roads, because boats and trucks not only bring war supplies but serve the enemy's economy. When we attack boats and trucks we attack the enemy from a military perspective and, just as importantly, from an economic perspective too. We have to do everything in our power to boost the economy of our land, as part of our struggle, just as we've been trying to do, but more so, more and more every day, boost our economy even in a time of war, improve living conditions throughout the land. And we have to do our utmost so that we depend less, less and less every day, on things that come from outside our land, in other words we have to try and become self-sufficient.

The party issued important guidelines in regards to agricultural development, improving our production, increasing our agricultural output, making other things such as artisanal items, even to make more soap within our land, to try and develop our population's every cottage industry. This is all in our party guidelines. Why? To see if we can become self-sufficient. Our land has its own particular conditions, of course, some of which, unfortunately, severely limit the scope of what we can do in this field. We were already substantially behind the rest of the world, economically speaking, and being so far behind made successfully carrying out certain basic principles of economic resistance all but impossible, but that's no reason not to do the best we can. We cannot expect ourselves to be self-sufficient in terms of fabrics, for example, which our people are used to buying, as they are shoes, collars, needles, sewing machines etc., things that count among the basic needs of our people, albeit needs created under colonialism. We cannot expect this because there are no factories that make these things in our land.

Numerous agricultural crops have never been introduced and they cannot be quickly established in a time of war. But we ought to be able to get some of them going all the same. We cannot expect ourselves to be self-sufficient in medicines, even simple medicines, but there are other things we can in fact do. Increase rice production, increase manioc production, grow more potatoes and other types of produce, safeguard production in all the areas of land we control, for example. Vastly increase production. This we can do and, given the circumstances of our struggle, it needs to be the bedrock of our economic resistance.

We must also, and I've already spoken about this, seek to develop our artisanal industries: earthenware, mats, cloths, weaves, etc. Our party did some work in this area, but it didn't have the desired effect. Because in the midst of war, the situation in our land being what it is, certain supervisors forgot about our guidelines in this respect – to develop, multiply and diversify production, to vary our country's agricultural produce. We have achieved one or two successes, of course, there are areas where rice production has increased a lot, areas where more manioc is now being produced, where more potatoes are being grown, but we must nonetheless recognise that we are a long way off what we are capable of.

While it is true that in some areas, Quinara, for example, local populations that did not previously farm are now farming. It is also true that other areas, where the local population used to farm a lot, are now farming less, because of the war. And the departure of so many people to Senegal has been, and continues to be, a great setback to our economic resistance. It is a setback because all these people who leave our land are potential farmhands who might be working in our liberated areas, but they go and work in Senegal instead, boosting the Senegalese economy and diminishing our own economy and our economic resistance against the Portuguese colonialists.

We must be clear and say that certain party leaders and supervisors, at all levels, have not treated our economic resistance importantly enough. We have always said that it's not only the people who should work the land, it's not enough to simply ask local populations to produce more, soldiers should also work the land and produce too. In the rainy season, we have to mobilise all our available forces, make the entire population work harder, make soldiers plant, make the militias plant. In some areas this has been possible, but we have to recognise that in other areas, even where the soldiers have had little to do, because the area is liberated, they don't plant and they simply wait for the local population to provide them with food. And in some areas we have now reached a point where, because of a lack of rain the previous year, for example, the local population cannot provide them with food, the soldiers have grown nothing for themselves and they have to ask the party leadership to send them food.

We must be clear and say to comrades that if, in order to fight the Portuguese colonialists, we have to provide food to our soldiers deep in the bush, then the Portuguese colonialists will be in our land for the next hundred years. And this will primarily be the fault of party supervisors who have proved themselves incapable of getting soldiers to plant in planting season. Some soldiers won't even help the local population to plant when we've told them they must. Within the context of our economic resistance, we need to co-ordinate our work in order to safeguard our war economy and ensure we get supplies to the front, to our soldiers, and to our people, providing them with the necessary staples.

Unfortunately, we face great difficulties in getting hold of staple products because we haven't got enough money. The situation in our land being what it is, whereby we have destroyed bridges, roads etc. and when we haven't got any cars anyway, even if it were possible to use the roads, we cannot establish an overseas trade that would allow us to sell things to the outside world and buy things in return. Providing the necessary staples to our population is, therefore, essentially a matter of relying on offerings and donations sent by our friends and allies. In the meantime, we must, and I've said this before, campaign daily to raise people's respect for those who work, make sure working is highly valued, convince the sons and daughters of our land that working the land is not to be scorned. On the contrary, it's the noblest, healthiest and most invaluable work anyone in the land can do right now.

Unfortunately, in our African heads we still view work as an activity of little value, especially working the land – that anyone who works the land only does so to give themselves something to eat, it's the work of the desperate. But we have to, within the context of our economic resistance, do a better political job of persuading our people, our population, every one of us, that working the land, growing crops, is not just something you do in order to eat, but in order to provide the country with produce to export, to have plentiful things to sell and thus convert into other things – that growing things is the most important, most dignified, most invaluable work there is in our land, comrades, whether it be in Guinea or Cape Verde.

Within the context of our economic resistance, we must be capable, today, but above all else tomorrow, of getting every social class in our country to produce a little bit more, of getting every ethnic group in Guinea, or every race, as we tend to say, to expand the range of products it produces. We cannot allow one ethnic group to just produce rice; they have to produce rice, corn, beans, manioc etc., greens even, and other things like that, because we must improve our people's diet. The entire population of our land can and must produce everything, we have to develop a range of different crops everywhere in order to boost our productivity. And we must steadily urge, that's to say encourage, or coax, our most valued producers to produce even more. We have to develop friendships with our most enthusiastic and committed rice growers, show our appreciation for them, our commitment to them, turn these sons and daughters of our land into household names, hold them up as examples for others to follow.

We must gradually find a way to solve the problem of smallholder farming in our land, because at present our country, due to it being so far behind, it doesn't really even have smallholders, not in Guinea. In Cape Verde, the problem is different because there are a lot of smallholder farmers, albeit not as many as we'd like, because the majority are tenant or associate farmers. The fundamental problem is getting people to work together in these conditions. In Guinea, we'll have to set up co-operatives, bit by bit, at first fostering increased co-operation between families and later selecting our best militants to manage the co-operatives as a whole, to develop a co-operative system, for this is, as we see it, the fastest way of developing our agricultural sector and, therefore, the future economy of our land. And we should immediately start to experiment with properties previously controlled by the colonial state.

This is why our party issued orders for any farms or allotments abandoned by the enemy, or by those fleeing the war, to be taken over by the party and run by designated management committees. But we have to admit that, in the vast majority of cases, comrades, supervisors, have paid insufficient attention to these instructions, to our party's guidelines. Most of these farms and allotments have failed, thus far, to deliver the yields it ought to have been possible to get from them, nor have they been kept in the kind of conditions they should have been kept. Some of them lie abandoned, full of straw, with crops withering away or spoiled, while others have been targeted with bombings by the Tugas, their bombs destroying our fruit trees and whatever else was there.

As part of our overall struggle, we must all be clear-headed about what our main area of activity is in terms of our economic resistance. Given our specific situation, as you all well know, our main activity is agriculture, we haven't anything else in our land. It's agriculture today, it will be agriculture tomorrow and it may very well be agriculture long after that. We therefore have to make every effort to advance our agricultural sector, raising political consciousness among our comrade farmers, and among our countrymen farmhands, showing everyone that the agriculture route is the first and surest route to success and the advancement of our people. Furthermore, that taking the agricultural route today opens the way to our potentially developing industry tomorrow, to create a higher standard of living.

But we have to make our agriculture as productive as possible first, for we are still some way behind, conditioned by our African lives into thinking that agriculture is just subsistence farming, whereby everyone produces no more than what's needed to feed their own family. This is an agriculture with no surplus whatsoever, where nothing is saved for tomorrow, sometimes not even enough to plant for next season. And in economic terms, in the colonial context, agriculture was a means of exchange with the Tugas and no more, with them exploiting us, our people producing groundnuts, harvesting coconuts, beeswax and honey, to exchange with the Tugas, or to sell them a bit of rice, and that was it. What little money this generated soon consumed itself and every year the sons and daughters of our land, the farmers and planters, started the season in the exact same miserable position they started the previous one, advancing not one iota. That's the nature of our agricultural sector.

In some places people used to say agriculture was the art of being poor but happy and carefree. In our case, agriculture will likely remain the art of being poor forever, unless we change the type of agriculture we do, unless we truly revolutionise our agricultural sector. We actually have pretty good agricultural conditions, both here in Guinea and in Cape Verde, despite there being periods of drought in Cape Verde, for this need not be disastrous to agriculture nowadays, not with all the scientific advances mankind has made and that anyone can make use of.

Only by making genuine advances in agriculture will our land become properly productive. We are sure that certain areas of our land can produce two, three, four, even ten times more than they produce now, if techniques are improved, if the soil is properly looked after, if seeds are carefully selected, if crops are properly cared for, if we put in a lot of good, hard work. In many areas of our land, were we to have fertiliser and manure, were agriculture to be combined with raising livestock, as it ought to be, then we might increase production dramatically. In terms of agriculture, raising and rearing livestock on a large scale, pedigree cattle – we can do it; poultry, of every type – we can do it. If we truly have the will, we can do it, if we're truly committed, if everyone shows willing and commitment and puts in the work. Our country cannot advance if we just raise a few chickens, if we just let a few chickens loose in the bush and then catch them when they're ready to eat or sell. That's not raising chickens, it's picking them the way you might pick *dênde* or toll fruit out in the bush.

We have to truly improve all this before we can start thinking about how our country can advance in other areas. In industrial terms, for example. And we have to consider the specific issue of cattle-raising, that's to say livestock, for it could provide us with tremendous riches, comrades, both in Guinea and in Cape Verde. Guinea, within the overall African context, is among the countries with the highest density of livestock, but Cape Verde, despite the occasional droughts and lack of rain, is capable even now of exporting leather, of exporting hides to Portugal and other places. So as we can see, we must, starting from now, lead our lives down the agricultural route and, precisely so that our agriculture can properly advance, develop our cattle-raising.

Unfortunately, due to this war, in the midst of our struggle, we have not given due attention to this aspect of our work, we have not controlled our livestock riches. A lot of our livestock in the north went to Senegal with the refugees, to the great satisfaction of our Senegalese brothers. Other people moved to the

Kundara area. The Tugas then feasted on our cows in a frenzy, they've even exported our cows. But we ourselves, supervisors and leaders, have not paid this sufficient attention, have not worked properly with local populations and shown them how important it is that we preserve our livestock riches. Today, hardly any of our chickens and goats are eaten by the Chiefs of Post and *sepoys*, thankfully, but what have we done so far to preserve our animals, to look after them properly, to get our people to take better care of them, to handle the matter better?

Our political, security and health commissars and supervisors have not given a moment's thought to our livestock riches, with one or two exceptions, obviously. I could mention, for example, the case of one of our supervisors who, in an area where there are calving cows, where all the cows are calving cows, wrote to me asking me to send milk because two children had been born and they didn't have any milk to give them, when in actual fact anywhere there are calving cows, there is milk. He might have found milk for the children in any house where cows were calving, so I sent word back telling him to go out and find some cows to milk because I certainly wasn't sending any. And he managed it. Comrades often don't think for themselves, don't consider the context, as in this case and others, unfortunately. They want to have things easy, whereas if we work at it, we could have milk whenever we want it in our land. We might even make cheese in the liberated areas, we could make butter in the liberated areas, it's not that hard, anyone out there can be taught to make butter.

During the rainy season, for example, you cannot plant onions, but in the dry season, which is coming up in November, you can; any army unit, no matter where it is, can find a spot by their hut to set aside as a vegetable patch and plant onions, garlic. All you have to do is designate a couple of comrades to keep an eye on things, near a river so they can be watered properly. This could be in Corubal just as much as it could be in Candjabari or anywhere else, we can grow things throughout the land, near a spring in the south, in Cubisecco, or in Quinara, or in any other spot. But no one does this because they just wait for the party to send whatever they need. They forget that this is just wasting time, precious time that could be spent helping our people to advance, helping our struggle to advance, instead of on satisfying basic needs.

We must admit that our party has not achieved any major successes in this area, beyond the fact that there are more paddy fields in a few places, rice production has increased a bit, manioc and a few other things are being farmed more than they were. There has been moderate success in terms of the political work of persuading local populations to grow things they're not accustomed to growing, but no more than moderate success because our supervisors have not afforded due importance to the matter of developing our economy as much as we possibly can. We're not asking for miracles, just doing what's possible.

We are an agricultural country, we must get everyone to grow things, local populations, troops, even schoolchildren, they must grow things too. We issued orders, for example, for every school to have a field for growing produce. It's still very unusual to find a school that uses its field for growing produce, but supervisors go there, see this and say nothing, leaders go there, see this and say nothing. And the result is that we even have to send rice to our boarding schools for the children to eat. We might very well ask ourselves: What are these children doing there? What is the point of teaching them to read if they cannot work a patch of land? We cannot let our people fall into bad habits. We want to learn to read, to learn about everything, but we have to work to become self-sufficient first because no one else in the world is going to provide us with food and a people incapable of feeding itself cannot aspire to anything else in life.

We must, of course, avoid all luxuries, all fineries and fripperies, during our struggle, our war. And what little we have, in our people's stores, we have to manage to ration properly, to distribute fairly so that the greatest possible number of people can benefit from a resource the party has created.

And we should already be making plans for our country's economy under independence. We cannot just leave it until tomorrow, we have to start today, all of us. The party has to properly understand the specific possibilities of our land, in every branch of the economy, and make conscientious, science-based plans for the development of our country. If we aren't capable of doing this, of establishing what specific economic path we need to take for our country to advance, of establishing an economic policy specific to our land, then we are getting ourselves killed and running ourselves into the ground for nothing; our bodies will be wounded and our lives pointlessly ruined, because of our inability to generate the revenues required to advance, to move our people forward as we promised them we would after all the sacrifices we asked them to make for this war.

We must, therefore, today and tomorrow, in terms of our economic resistance, channel our efforts towards the following aim: to increase output of every kind of product throughout the land and to increase that output evermore by the day. We must be capable of getting the maximum out of our land, out of every patch of land the country has to give. We have to be economical, in other words increase our gains and reduce our expenses.

This is something comrades find hard to understand, even today, when our party has practically no income, aside from selling a few kola nuts, or selling a few lizard or crocodile skins. The party has practically no income, yet comrades are not in the least bit careful, they pay not the least attention to the fact that we have so little to spend. Whatever we give certain comrades flows through their hands like water in the Rio Corubal or Rio Geba. Come on, let's spend, it'll never run out. This happens even with things of great importance, like munitions. We've proved ourselves incapable of rationing our arms properly. A good many weapons spoil through lack of care, munitions are wasted for lack of care and excessive usage.

But we do understand, all of this is a new experience, a new war, in our land, we're able to accept that, given the context, difficulties and inefficiencies are inevitable. But there are other instances, like with petrol, like with medicine, even with rice in areas that do not produce rice, for example, where, as many comrades know, things like this happen: a group of soldiers have to take rice with them because in the area where they're going, like the border zones, it's not possible to get rice from the local population. We have rice available at the moment so we give them two months' worth of rice. And what happens then is that they eat this rice within twenty days, all of it. How is this possible when we have no income? We have to put a stop to this, comrades.

Another important matter in the context of our economy is, of course, transport. It's a difficult issue to tackle at present because we are at war, we're in the midst of war and trying to destroy the enemy's economy, we're destroying roads and if we can destroy every last possible means of the enemy moving around our country, by road or by river, then all the better, for we haven't destroyed everything yet. This is good for us on the one hand, but it's bad for us on the other, because our economy, if we wish to develop it in certain areas, we're going to find we cannot, because we have no roads. We don't have time to tarmac roads etc. But we should still start thinking about the issue today, as something to be tackled tomorrow. And we must think seriously about the benefits of ensuring a fluvial means of transport, that's to say river transport, because our land in Guinea is rich in channels, in waterways that we can move our produce along, and we should create new possibilities in this regard tomorrow. And at the same time we have to think about the possibility of ensuring there are water links between our continental land and our Bijagós islands, between our continental land and our Cape Verde islands. Because only when a land's communications network flows like blood around a human body can a country truly advance.

A transport system, its communications network, is as important to a country that wishes to advance as blood vessels, arteries etc. are to a human body. We must give due thought to this, starting today, and indeed we've been thinking about it all year. But that doesn't mean we shouldn't do everything we can to safeguard our transport now. The party has done its utmost to provide trucks to bring supplies to our people, to provide boats to bring supplies to our people. We're possibly the only liberation struggle in the world where supplies are delivered to certain areas by boat. Our party has managed to safeguard this, despite the difficulties, despite the total lack of care comrades pay to our equipment. But in our interior, especially in Guinea, where we are already at war, we have to be able to safeguard our means of transport too. It cannot be done via road. We have lots of rivers, let's make sure there are enough canoes, let's build more canoes.

The Tugas understand this so clearly that one of their main jobs is to go around smashing up our canoes. So we must be more resolute. For a start, we must not allow the Tugas to smash up our canoes, we must hide the canoes we use for transporting our materials, be it goods or people, we must use them and then hide them properly. Unfortunately, many comrades go down the river in their canoes and just leave them there, right where the Tugas can find them and smash them up. There are thousands of ways to hide a canoe. But if, through bad luck, the Tugas do manage to smash our canoes, then we must put more people to work building new ones, get people who know how to do woodwork to build some more. We never lack boats in Boé. Why? Because we gave Idrissa one job, to build canoes. But in other areas, the Tugas have smashed our canoes and, although some comrades thankfully do find ways of resolving this, of getting hold of more canoes, others send me telegrams – 'Cabral, the Tugas smashed our canoe' – and what am I supposed to do, when he's the supervisor, he's there, he's in charge of the local population, he's in charge of the soldiers? Why doesn't he get someone to build canoes?

Many comrades think we should get motorboats, and in fact we do have a few, but we cannot solve the problem this way because we can't just buy boats to put everywhere. We have made a big effort to get motorboats for some areas, boats with outboard motors, and we still have a few outboard motors. But the fact is that in some areas, like Quiláfine, for example, comrades completely wrecked the motor in a matter of days. I myself went to Ghana to buy new motors, but they were all wrecked within the month because comrades chose to play with them rather than use them only when required. And comrades pay no heed to the following simple rule: to use a motor you must mix gasoline and oil. But no, they haven't any oil so they just put gasoline in and off they go, wherever they want.

This, comrades, is disastrous from an economic point of view. Then they say they have no supplies because they have no means of transporting them. This isn't right.

Another form of transport we could make good use of in this war is the bicycle, like the Vietnamese did. Our country has certain characteristics that make it a little more difficult, perhaps, but our land generally resembles Vietnam a lot. We've experimented with this. We've got comrades to transport things by bike, but the bikes all broke after a few days. Some comrades even stopped riding them halfway through their journey and put the bikes on their heads, carried them like that. Why? They said they weren't used to them. Porterage can be very difficult by bike, but it has been proven, by the experience of people elsewhere, that one bicycle, well-worked, well-prepared, with poles to support the load, can carry 250 kilos. A man can't even carry 20 kilos. We can deliver supplies to areas of our land, many areas, just by using bikes. Of course, it's difficult, sometimes rivers have to be crossed, flooded areas etc. It's difficult, but we can use bikes for porterage.

If we give a bicycle to a comrade to go, for example, from the border to Cubacaré, it can be done by bike, but with a load it's difficult, that's the problem. The bicycle could be a brilliant means of porterage in our land, but we need our comrades in the vanguard to help, we need our more enlightened vanguard comrades to set the example, to stick at it, to show that it's possible. Then we can be like the Vietnamese people who were able to carry loads over long distances just by bicycle, until they defeated the enemy.

I remember, for example, a great thing our comrades did in the south of our land. We wanted to get some heavy artillery to Cubucaré and Tombali. It was very difficult to carry because these weapons weighed over 15 kilos. So our comrades built a raft and travelled up the Rio Balana to the border to collect the weapons and took them back that way. This just goes to show that when we want to be, when we really put our minds to it, we're capable of anything. We are capable of doing great things, things like this. How many times has the Rio Farim been blocked off, but comrades have managed to find a way through, to get past, because they had to, because a supervisor comrade said: come on, keep going, toughen up. Unfortunately, not all comrades are like this. We could do with more of them, given all our responsibilities, given all the things we need to do to advance our fight.

The issue of transport has been raised with comrades many times. No one can expect the party leadership to send supply trucks into the interior of our country. There are some parts where we have entered with trucks, but they were very particular circumstances. Party supervisors have to be capable of resolving transport issues themselves. It's incredible, for example, incredible that Sector Two on the East Front sometimes lacks munitions, but no other sector makes any effort to get munitions to them. There are munitions available, in vast quantities in some areas, and so the only reason there are munitions shortages in other places is that comrades can't be bothered to go and help others solve a problem. Even with rice, in some areas there's an abundance of rice, in other areas there's very little, but it's very unusual to see rice being taken from one place to the next because it doesn't even enter people's heads to try and find solutions to such issues. It is done sometimes, yes, but all that proves is that it could always be done if we so wanted. It's a matter of doggedness, of dedication, of paying attention, of turning our thoughts into actions in order to better serve our party.

To advance with our struggle we must, in terms of our economic resistance, avoid overburdening our people lest they start to think our party wants to exploit them too. We have always issued comrades with party guidelines that say do not take people's belongings, people's chickens, people's cows. If things are given to us, fine, we accept them, but we must never demand things, we must never take anything by force. This rule has not always been well respected, not always. We must be aware that anyone who seeks to exploit our people like this is a criminal, that they benefit the Tugas, that they are enemies of our people and our party.

When these things occur we need to know exactly who acted against our people so that they can be reprimanded and indeed shot, if necessary, even if they're a chief or a supervisor. Some comrades have made a big effort to prevent abuses being committed against our people. Some party leaders have tried hard to prevent abuses, but not all: some. And some supervisors have tried hard to prevent them too. But we have to put a stop to abusive behaviour of every kind in our country. We have to reduce the excessive burden on our people and show them that we do not mean, and never will mean, to cause them harm.

Furthermore, we need to encourage those in our land who produce the most, find ways to reward them with praise, with prizes, with awards. We want to see the following happen in our country tomorrow: for the names we celebrate to those people who produce the most. Whoever produces the most rice in the country, a person, a family, a cooperative, whoever it is, we must celebrate their name, give them prizes, proclaim them the best people in the land. Whoever produces the most groundnuts, whoever manages to produce the most palm oil etc, comrades. And we have to come down hard on those who don't work to help our country get what it needs to get out of the land, as part of our economic resistance.

Of course, we'll have other problems to deal with in the future, important ones, like developing and stabilising our internal market, the commerce within our country, or like developing as much trade as possible with other countries, establishing, in other words, an entire system of international trade, or like looking into pricing issues within our country. Sometimes we're so engaged in the struggle that we think it's just a matter of killing the Tugas, of fighting them and taking over the country. But the biggest issues lie ahead of us, comrades. We have to be clear in our understanding of who's going to control our country's commerce. Our commerce remains in the hands of the Tugas for now, it's our land but the Tugas still control our imports and exports. This is something we will have to establish for ourselves in the future. Our party will have to be clear in its planning of this, to avoid any confusion and to cut off, right from the start, any attempts at exploiting our people.

And we have to combat, starting now, any mistaken ideas about our economy. One major mistake we're still making today is the following: no one pays any taxes now that they've been liberated. This is a mistake. We have to be able, after we've liberated an area like Cubucaré, for example, to quickly establish what taxes people should pay. Taxes don't even have to be in money form, they might be *in kind*, as it's called, which means paying taxes in the form of produce, just so our people don't lose the habit of paying taxes, so that nobody thinks there will no longer be taxes to pay once we've taken control of the country. No country in the world can advance without taxes. This has been a mistake. But it has been a necessary mistake, in the context of a mentality that wasn't yet truly nationalistic.

We, as a people, were yet to acquire consciousness as a nation. And in terms of land, if we had, at the same time as liberating Cubucaré, started collecting taxes there, then maybe the people would have sided with the Tugas. That's why we made this mistake, but we have to explain this to people, to clearly say, as we in fact always have said, that they may not be paying taxes today, but they will have to pay them again tomorrow. Most of our people know this, they already understand this. But we must explain that the taxes they will pay tomorrow are not the same as the taxes they paid to the Tugas. Not in terms of the tax base, that's to say the criteria, the rules governing who pays what taxes, nor in terms of expense, that's to say what the taxes are used for. Tax revenues in our land must be used to raise our people's standard of living, in economic, social and cultural terms.

We must always have a plan if we want our economic resistance to triumph, a plan designed to triumph over the Tugas today and our underdevelopment tomorrow, to triumph over our country being so far behind. We must gain a full understanding of our land's particular conditions, here in Guinea and in Cape Verde, in order to make specific plans to advance our country's development. Otherwise, it's like entering a room in the dark and crashing into everything, knocking the furniture over, banging our heads against the wall, walking face-first into it, having no idea what we're doing. This is vitally important if we are to triumph tomorrow, comrades, vitally important in the context of our economic resistance. We must avoid, now and in the future, any obsession with making extravagant plans. We must do what is possible, at every stage of our evolution, this is something we really must understand.

We must avoid, or clamp down on, people standing around with their arms folded. Today and tomorrow in our country, everyone capable of working must work. People who don't work have no right to anything in our country, that's the way it must be. People of worth, work; people who don't work are worthless. And the best people are those who work the most. That's the way it must be in our country and it should be the same with our struggle too. At this stage of our life as a party, we have to move the hardest-working comrades to the front and let no one be in any doubt about the following: those who proved their worth by working hard yesterday move forward. But those who stop working today because they worked hard yesterday are of no worth to us, never were of any worth. I often say that in terms of our party's work, everyone is like a stalk on a banana tree, you have to produce bananas every year. You can't think that because you were a stalk last year you've done your bit, no. Everyone is capable of becoming another stalk. With the banana tree, every stalk that produces fruit has to be cut back to let a fresh stalk grow, to bear more fruit. It's the same with our lives and with the party.

Nobody should think they can sleep in the shadow of the work they did yesterday. There are a number of comrades in our party who think that because they put a lot of work in during mobilisation, because they put a lot of work in during the early stages of the guerrilla struggle, because they put a lot of work in at a particular moment securing supplies, because they were good leaders of the guerrilla forces or the army etc. they can shrug their shoulders today, skulk and skive off work, put their lives on hold, hide themselves away at some base or even beyond our borders. We cannot have this, comrades. In our party nobody wins unless we all give more every day; more work, more sacrifice, more willing and more determination.

Another serious issue in our party, in our struggle, is the following: some comrades have been wounded, but are now fit again, because thank God (we say thank God, but also thanks to our party) out of every 500 wounded comrades, say, 480 recover and can, therefore, go back and fight. But there's now a tendency, comrades, for the following to happen: 'I'm wounded, I'll turn my injury into something more serious so that I can stop fighting. I went to Ziguinchor, I was lucky enough to get as far as Conakry, I didn't die, I was slightly wounded, now I'll fight no more.'

No, comrades, this is demobilisation, it's deserting. In any country where people have gained political consciousness, in any struggle where soldiers fight with consciousness, taking a beating gives them more courage, yet more will to fight, because they are now not only defending a cause they believe in, they're now determined to make the enemy pay for what they did to them. In other countries there are soldiers who have lost legs begging for artificial legs so that they can go back and fight. In other countries there are political commissars who have been, for example, wounded in the arm, the doctor tells them to rest for six months so that the arm can heal and they tell the doctor to cut the arm off, for that way they can recover in two weeks and return to the fight. Because a political commissar needs a head but he can do without his arms.

But in our country, there are commissars who are lucky enough to hurt no more than a finger, yet that's enough of an excuse for them to stop, they can't go on.

Comrades, thankfully the majority of our people are not like that, I know it's not everyone. Thankfully we have many comrades with bullets lodged in their bodies who are so firmly committed to our work that sometimes we're the ones who have to persuade them to withdraw from the frontline. There are comrades who have been wounded three times, four times, who are firmly committed to our struggle, more enthusiastic by the day, more courageous. They are the custodians of our party, comrades, they are the true sons and daughters of our people, the future custodians of our land, no question. They are the new leaders and I, for one, say this to them: comrades, you give me strength. Some of them are sitting here now. You give us all strength and vindicate all the sacrifices we're making to move forward. There are other wounded comrades who are not here today such as, for example, comrade Kemo, who was wounded, he hadn't recovered yet but there was an attack and he went back to join it, isn't that right, comrades? We sent him to Europe for treatment and all he wanted was to get back as quickly as possible. And in fact, the day I went to visit him, in the country where he was being treated, I found him at the airport, ready to come straight back to the bush, no questions asked, no demands. Because there are others who get wounded or taken sick and use it as an opportunity to demand things of the party, like asking the party to pay them. But those comrades who ask for nothing, who give us their effort, their energy, their all, are not only serving the armed struggle, the political struggle, they're contributing to our economic resistance too, in the face of an enemy that we must destroy economically.

Indeed, we must avoid any squandering, by which I mean spending where we can economise. We must avoid this, especially with food, for example, even at our schools, our resthouses and other places there is sometimes a lot of food left over, a lot of rice, and people come and get these leftovers to use as pig-feed. Why don't we make more of an effort to measure out the right amount of rice, enough for every comrade while also rationing the party's rice supply? Comrades in Conakry, or Zinguinchor, who use cars, drive round and round as much as they like, when they could get all their things done in just a few trips. Besides, there are others driving around too, they could go in the same car at the same time with another person, but they refuse to do this, they even hide so that they can then go out on their own later. They don't understand that this is just wasting petrol and creating problems for the party.

In our economic resistance we have to clamp down on any sneakiness, robbery, bribery, corrupt people who make the most of any opportunity to steal, be it money the party has given to them to administer – for a resthouse or boarding school – or other things like cows, taking them and sending them to be sold beyond our borders, for example. This is a form of robbery too. We must clamp down hard on this, comrades. We must proclaim our respect and consideration for those party comrades who have never been tempted to do any of these things, quite the opposite in fact, those whose behaviour has always been exemplary and who have sought to help others stay clean.

We Africans have a reputation, because of our underdevelopment, whereby it's assumed that everyone in a position of responsibility, for resources, money and other such things, is on the take. And the kind of things we've seen happen in other independent African countries should make us nervous. So too should things that have happened here, with our own comrades even, at least some of them. This makes us nervous, comrades, very nervous. We must remind comrades, supervisors and soldiers for the most part, that taking things from the enemy at a time of war, though justified, is still stealing. I'm not talking about taking things from our people in the villages, for there's no justifying that, I'm talking about taking things from the enemy at a time of war and keeping them for yourself. That is stealing and the first step to becoming a crook.

Our soldiers are honest people, reliable, decent, dignified, the best sons and daughters of our land. Therefore, when one of our soldiers takes a watch, a bracelet, a gold chain or whatever, takes it from the enemy, he must show it to his chief, his leader, he mustn't just keep it, because if he does then he's no longer a soldier fighting to liberate his country, he's a highwayman. Some comrades don't understand this, they don't understand how much they come down in our estimation, those of us who are serious about our party's work, when they hang some great big gold medallion around their neck, taken from some village or some encounter with the enemy. Many comrades don't understand this, but they really come down in our estimation. Even wristwatches, of course, if someone takes a wristwatch in a war they can keep it, but they must show it to their chief first, get permission from their chief to keep it. And if he already has a wristwatch and wants to keep a new one, he must first give his old one to a comrade who hasn't got a watch. But no, some comrades take things and keep quiet, and in this way, they show that they're still not conscious of their own worth, of the work they're doing, the sacrifice they're making. They value a watch more than they value themselves, when tomorrow they'll be able to acquire, and honestly, as many watches as they want. We have to stop this, comrades.

And in economic terms, as in any other terms, we have to clamp down on extremist tendencies, such as comrades who say: 'Let's force our people to do a job.' No, comrades. Making our people grow things by force, no. It might even work, but we don't want it, we don't want any extremism, it shows a lack of understanding for the present and the future of our struggle. And especially within the context of our future, when planning for our life tomorrow, we must avoid all extremism, everything over-the-top, all ambitions to be excessively progressive. For example, there may be comrades who lay out the issue in the following way: we are somewhat behind in our country when it comes to agriculture, while everyone else wants to give up on agriculture; England became developed and now few people work in agriculture, as France advanced its number of farmers declined and its industry grew. We see that the way countries advance today is through heavy industry, so we, in Guinea and Cape Verde, post-independence, should give up on agriculture and focus on heavy industry too.

But we must likewise be vigilant so as not to make the very opposite mistake, for there are those who think the following: we should leave our country as it is, this is the way it's meant to be, we're Africans, we must have our *régulos*, people who work the land for them, people who sell things etc.[19] Then we'll be good Africans with our traditions, our customs, where the Balanta grow rice, the Fula grow groundnuts, the Felupe grow rice, the Manjaco grow groundnuts and rice and other things, the Bijagós pick coconuts, the Cape Verdeans produce corn, only to then die of hunger when there is no corn. No, this is the opposite of extremism and we don't want this either. To put it in the language of today, what I described first is to lurch to the left and what I described second is to lurch to the right. This doesn't mean the centre is necessarily best. A lot of

---

19 *Editor's note*: *Régulo* means 'village chief'.

people think the centre is best but that's not true, what's best is knowing how to combine one side and the other in order to move forward. Finding the right path through an area of land doesn't mean going straight down the middle, you combine one side with the other. You can't do anything in the centre, but this is a complicated discussion to save for another day.

We must, then, in terms of our economic resistance, as with our other forms of resistance, overcome our weaknesses and constantly improve on our strengths. Cut out our weaknesses and nurture our strengths. That concludes today's conversation about our resistance in the economic sense.

3. CULTURAL RESISTANCE

We must remember that it's not enough just to grow things, fill your belly, have good politics and wage war. If a man or woman does all this without advancing as an intelligent human being, the primary being in nature; without sensing their knowledge of the environment they live in and the world in general is growing by the day; without, in other words, advancing in a cultural sense, then everything that man or woman does – grow things, preach good politics, fight – amounts to nothing.

In our specific situation, we have to pay particular attention to our cultural resistance. Our party has paid considerable attention to this right from the start and launched a number of important initiatives, beginning with the Cassacá Congress, although we were advising people on the need to support our struggle through cultural resistance long before that. Indeed, it might be said that the very creation of our party, which has planned and advanced our national liberation struggle, was a cultural act in itself. Our very existence is a clear demonstration of cultural resistance, evidence that we want to be ourselves, Africans from Guinea and Cape Verde, and not Tugas. Our culture is not the Tugas' culture, although our culture nowadays has some influences from Tuga culture. Therefore, every politically conscious soldier, supervisor and militant should clearly understand that fighting the enemy is also a form of cultural resistance, indeed the armed struggle is possibly our primary act of cultural resistance.

We have to work hard to erase colonial culture from our heads, comrades. And whether we like it or not, in the city or in the bush, colonialism has filled our heads with a lot of things. Our work, therefore, should be to get rid of what's harmful and keep what's helpful. Because not everything colonialism gave us is harmful. We must be able, therefore, to erase colonial culture from our heads while keeping elements of human and scientific culture the Tugas brought to our land inadvertently that also ended up in our heads.

A specific example: I am African, maybe I think, like other Africans still do, that in order for certain things to happen in my life I need to satisfy the will of the *iran*. I go to talk to him and he tells me that whatever it is will only happen if I offer him a little girl, no more than three years old, three rainy seasons, for him to kill and use in a sacrifice, and then whatever it is I want will happen. This kind of thing still exists in Africa, indeed if we look properly maybe there are people in our land who still believe in this stuff. I remember a comrade called Alfucene who we sent to fight in Gabú – remember, Lúcio? One day he came to tell me that the *iran* in Gabú didn't want us fighting there unless his son was sacrificed first. I interpreted this in the following manner: Alfucene, who was originally from Gabú, was trying to find a way of becoming chief there. He wanted to be the chief of Gabú and so he wanted it to look like the *iran* was interested in his son, and therefore he should become chief. I said to him: 'Comrade, if this is how we're going to fight in Gabú then let's find this *iran* and kill him, because he's the Tugas' *iran*, they installed him, he's not from our land.'

But it could be that I, as an African, still have this kind of thing in my head. There are children being killed right now, as I speak, in certain parts of Africa in order to satisfy the will of the *iran*. I never had this stuff in my head. I grew up in Africa, but I learned the following: Children are the most wonderful and delicate things in the world. We must give our children the best of what we've got. We must educate them to grow up free-spirited, to understand things, to be good and kind, to avoid all wickedness. We must, therefore, never cause them harm, much less kill them. I am therefore obliged to defend my country from people who get this kind of cultural belief in their heads.

But I, though I am African, have also had a lot of contact with the Tugas, so maybe I've got it into my head that I'm a child of civilised people and I am civilised. I went to school, I never lived in the bush, the bush is dirty, I had a decent house even though my mother was poor. Maybe I think I've got nothing in common with people in the bush, that our brothers and sisters in the bush are backward and I'm superior to them. This is the colonial mentality, copying the mentality of the Tugas, the colonialists. We have to erase this, from my head and everyone else's.

I will, therefore, provide some concrete examples of what we should preserve from the contact we've had with other realities, and what we should erase from the contact we've had with our own reality. This will enable comrades to understand what our cultural resistance consists of. Because our cultural resistance consists of removing colonial culture and the negative aspects of our own culture from our spirit and environment, while at the same time creating a new culture, one that is based on our traditions but that respects everything the world has achieved for the good of humankind.

A lot of people think that for Africa to resist culturally it has to do the same things it did 500 years ago, or 1 000 years ago. Yes, Africa has its culture, we're firmly of that opinion ourselves. Some aspects of that culture are eternal, they never end, they might be endlessly transformed along the way, but they never end. Our types of dance, for example, our own African rhythms. But nobody should think that the drum is solely an African thing, that certain types of dress are only to be found in Africa, straw skirts, palm leaf skirts etc., nobody should think that eating with your hands is solely an African thing, that sitting on the ground only happens in Africa. People all over the world go through periods like this, there are still people elsewhere in the world, in Brazil, for example, who are worse than us for some of these things, as there are in Indonesia, Polynesia, the Far East.

A lot of people think that to defend African culture, for Africa to culturally resist, we have to defend the negative things about our culture. No, we're not of that opinion. Because culture is also a product of a people's level of economic development. Our opinion is that eating with your hands, and even singing certain types of songs or dancing a particular way, depends on the lives people lead, what crops people grow, what riches they produce, what things they make. This is why Balanta songs are different from Mandiga songs, for example. When analysed, Balanta songs, deep down, are songs about men on the plain. If we compare Balanta songs to European songs, we'll see how similar they are to Alentejo songs, slow and choral. Because there are certain types of economic lives and geographical environments that produce certain types of songs. People who live in the mountains have certain types of song, people who live with livestock have their own particular way of dancing, people who live in the woods, on their own, with no livestock, have a different kind of dance. People who live in the savannah, where there are giraffes and other things, have another kind of dance. That's the way it is, be it in Africa, Asia or the Americas.

And so too does the type of relationship we have with nature vary according to our economy, our economic development. People who believe cows are gods honour cows in their dances. The dance will represent God as a cow. But people who think God hides in the forest will perform a dance that shows their respect for the forest, their songs will have a certain kind of music and lyrics related to this. This scenario is repeated everywhere in the world, wherever there are particular economic conditions and a particular situation related to nature. People who are still afraid of lightning bolts, thunderclaps and flooding rivers will have the same kinds of songs and dances. There may be one or two differences, but they will be similar. Of course, if we compare our dances to European dances, to city dances etc., we'll find not the least resemblance, but these are ultra-modern dances. If we compare our dances to folkloric dances, let's say the arts and customs of people from eastern Europe, and even more so from Asia, we'll find dances that are very similar to our own, comrades.

Our point of view is, that we must show resistance to preserve what is genuinely helpful and constructive from our culture, but in the knowledge that, as we advance, our clothes, our eating habits, our ways of dancing and singing, everything about us will inevitably gradually change, especially inside our heads, our relationship to nature, even our relationship to one another.

For example, we Africans are in a situation whereby we need protection because we still haven't dominated nature. So we need what is known as *organic security*. Organic security means the more people we have around us, the more secure we feel. If I'm out in the bush on my own, I'm afraid, but if I'm with several other people, I feel better. But there's a contradictory side to this rule of organic security, and that's when you don't trust the people around you. Our security needs are such that we always need someone beside us, but because security cannot be guaranteed, and because our need for security is so great, we start to distrust those we are with. And so what happens in our environment, even with people we trust, is this: yesterday you trusted them, but when they come along today and offer you their hand, you don't trust it. You take their hand, but now you're suspicious of it. Some people might even wash their own hand afterwards, for fear of catching something. They might even be suspicious of eyes. And there are people who take advantage of this by popping out their eyes.

I remember our comrade Luciano, strong, brave, a little confrontational sometimes, who was chief of our resthouse when we were training comrades. There was this miserable creature in Conakry who was obsessed with Luciano being Muslim and who sided with the opportunists of the moment. He was a nasty piece of work, truth be told, and Luciano was very afraid of him, he didn't want anything to do with him, unless it was to beat him up. One day the man came by our resthouse, Luciano advanced on him, berating him etc. Then the man pulled out a horn, pointed it at Luciano and said to him, 'Ah!' Luciano backed away immediately, afraid of the horn.

Comrades, we laugh about this now, but several comrades seated here are still afraid of horns. Today we laugh even though we're afraid, but rest assured that tomorrow the sons and daughters of our land, in Guinea and in Cape Verde, where there is also a lot of fear (Don't let the lads from São Vicente or Praia who come here with their own obsessions give you the impression that there isn't also fear in the bush in Cape Verde, or fear of *marabouts*. Once, when I fell sick, my mother took me to see the *marabout* because she thought someone must have wished me ill. They have, fears of how the cards fall, fear of hair. They make charms out of hair to free themselves from evil), but rest assured that tomorrow in Cape Verde, just as much as in Guinea, the sons and daughters of our people will not be afraid of horns. A horn is just something that's rich in calcium and grows on the heads of certain animals, that's all it is, comrades. If we burn it, it has a particular smell, due to the proteins and other chemical properties it has. A horn does nothing. But today, it doesn't matter how loud I shout this, no one listens, you don't believe me. And I'd be a fool to try and argue with you over this, I know.

All I'll say is this: fight tough and work hard, because the sons and daughters of your sons and daughters are not going to believe in things like this, not if we fulfil our duty to our people, not if we do it properly. Because the Swedes, those two who you can see over there, the parents of the parents of their parents also believed in horns. And the way people were buried in ancient Sweden was the same as the way people are buried in our country today. They buried their ancient Swedish kings in ancient times, the same way we bury our kings. Their kings took to their graves with all their belongings, just like ours, that's when their wives weren't killed and put in the grave too. The Vikings, who are the ancestors of today's Swedes, never went to war without their charms. One day we were in Cuba, Osvaldo and I, sitting watching a Viking film on TV, I'd seen enough films about the Vikings by then, but Osvaldo was watching it. Suddenly the warriors appeared and Osvaldo said, 'But look, comrade, they've got loads of amulets!' Well of course they did, nobody should think that we Africans are so smart we thought of amulets, and because we've got amulets we can go to war. The Vikings loved their charms, the Franks, comrades, the people of ancient France, when they fought Caesar of Rome, they covered themselves in charms. The ancient English did, American Indians too.

In China, Mao Zedong had his work cut out trying to end the use of charms and even today it hasn't entirely stopped, witchcraft hasn't stopped in China. There are ethnic groups in China that use spells. If we read Vietnamese books, we'll see that witchcraft exists in Vietnam too. One of the great Vietnamese chiefs said that they had to let people carry charms in order to get them to fight. Some people shave their heads, we too shave ours before doing certain things, we make a ceremony of it, even when we know for certain that it's wrong, applying only the tiniest bit of rationality to avoid trouble.

No one should think that because these things exist here among us, because we are Africans, we are superior to other people, that we know about charms and no one else does. The lopé loincloth, for instance, people all over the world have used loincloths, some people still use them today, all over the place. The *bubu*, a cloth worn in the Ghanaian style, they had much the same thing in ancient Rome. Look at films about the Romans, they called their cloths 'togas', but it was a cloth like any other. Sandals and cloths, that's all they wore. But today people go about in cloths as if you only get them in Africa, as if we Africans are the only people who know what a cloth is.

This is a consequence of our state of economic development, no more than that. It's good, it's ours, but we can't go around thinking it's any more than that. The day will come when your descendants will forget about all this. It's just a shame we won't live long enough to see it. They'll be like us today when we look back at the way the Vikings lived, thinking them fools, failing to comprehend that the Vikings lived their own lives in their own era. They didn't do anything without checking with their warlock first. The king never went anywhere without his warlock by his side. Before the Romans went to war, they cut open the stomach of a chicken to see if it was an opportune moment to fight. There were even people who were called 'augurs' who the chiefs consulted to find out if they should go to war or not.

In ancient Greece, which was the centre of the civilised world, witches who lived in the mountains, called *pythia*, were consulted to learn of the destiny of wars, people's lives etc. and people took them offerings, because God was among them. It's like with our *iran* in Cobiana, comrades. But this was 3,000 years ago in Greece. Even longer ago in ancient Egypt, all the Pharaohs had their own witches and God was a bull, the Bull of Apis, so the cow was untouchable, because the cow was sacred, like it is today in India. In India they don't eat beef, there are people who die of hunger sitting beside their cow, because the cow cannot be killed, for the cow is God. They take their cows to the river to wash them, and everyone goes into the water with the cow, to wash in God's water.

We have to understand all this properly in order to base our cultural resistance on what our cultural resistance should really be about. We have to erase from our country all the harmful influences of colonial culture, comrades. And the first cultural act we must perform in our land is the following: unite our people, develop a new sense of *patriotism* in each and every one of us, and make this patriotism, this love for our country, inseparable from our need to fight. This is the first part of the culture we must establish in our country. And we must show the value in resisting the enemy, the foreigner in our land. Show that we are joining forces to stop our people, the sons and daughters of our land, from being trodden on and humiliated by another people. We must ensure it is clearly understood that we have the same rights in our own land as anyone else has in their own land. This will be a huge leap forward for our culture if we manage it, and we will manage it, very soon, because the war itself will do it for us.

Furthermore, comrades, we must foster a spirit of heroism in all of us, but especially in our soldiers, the courage to rigorously follow our party's guidelines. If the enemy needs to be killed in a certain place, then go there and kill him dead. This has to be our culture, comrades. Only when a man is capable of doing this is he truly cultured. And when a group of men and women like those gathered here today, faced with a given fact, are capable of uniting together and acting like a single being, then they have become cultured.

Take this for an example: there is a lot of quarrelling amongst our Mandinga population, arguing amongst themselves, some acting like they're better than others, set-tos, stealing. It's even said that when a Mandinga says one thing, he means quite the opposite. So they seem like a divided people. But when it comes to a cultural activity, such as praying, they become one. Pick any other ethnic group and the way they're hopelessly reverential before the *iran*. For example, you might say to a Balanta or a Manjaco the following: 'Look, Bobô is a good lad,' and they'll think you must be friends with Bobô to say a thing like that and they'll repeat this to others. Some will believe you, others won't. But if you say the *iran* of Cobiana said 'Bobô's a good lad,' it doesn't matter whether they're in the Soviet Union or wherever, they'll believe you. All you have to say is the *iran* said it and everyone will believe you, Mandingas, Mancanhas, Pepels,

Balantas, everyone. So you can see how, when it comes to cultural situations, people are capable of uniting, even a divided people like ours has been

That's why, when we say we're capable of uniting to resist our enemy, we are gaining in culture. It also proves that we do, in fact, have a culture and we must, as a party, as a political organisation, be able to nurture this spirit of culture in our people, in Guinea and in Cape Verde, nurture it more by the day, specifically the idea that you have to be a patriot to be a child of our people. Furthermore, at this stage in our struggle, that you have to love our party to be a child of our people. That's the culture in our land nowadays. What's most essential in our culture today is not teaching people to read and write, that's necessary too, we've spoken about this, but right now it's not essential that you reach second grade. What is essential is that you properly understand what our party wants, what we want, what we are seeking to do, what we are doing, what our struggle is, where we're going. That is what's important, comrades. Being prepared to give your life. Any man capable of giving his life for our party, no questions asked, is a cultured man in our country right now.

And in considering our struggle, we might compare, for example, Guinea's different races to see which ones are more or less cultured. Sometimes those who know more about certain things may come across as being less cultured. But any Mané or N'Bana out there in the bush toiling away and sticking to their task is more cultured than an Alvarenga man or anyone else who might be more educated but continues to follow the Tugas. This is because their work in the bush conforms to mankind's relationship with society and nature while serving the interests of their own people today in order to achieve a higher standard of living tomorrow. That's culture, comrades. Properly understanding your country's specific situation in order to transform it in progressive terms.

We must instil in each and every one of us a sense of how certain victory is, a spirit of trust in victory. This is a cultural act, comrades. It enables us to withstand hardship, to never give up, to not lose hope after a defeat, because every struggle has its defeats. There are defeats within our struggle too, this is part of the struggle, that is why it is a struggle. But we should be constantly building up people's confidence in victory, we should be doing everything we can for the enemy to lose hope, for our enemy's agents to lose hope, to show them that they have no chance, that they will definitely lose. That is culture, comrades.

And we must, based on our love of our country and our people, based on our love of our party, develop our dances, our songs, our music, put on plays, even acrobatic displays, do impressions of other people etc...Impressions of the colonialist settlers, for example, Senhor Fulano is very important. We should develop all of this, to serve our struggle, to serve our cause, but with updated content, that's to say, with new words and facts.

This is the great value of, for example, Balanta, Beafada and Mandinga songs, and others too, creole ones, Macanha, Pepel etc. or the *mornas* and *coladeiras*, music that has always been a basic part of our struggle, celebrating our party, hailing the names of our courageous soldiers, singing about our battles, our attacks on Tuga planes etc., showing how far our people have come in this war. This is what our culture is, this is what we should be developing now.

In parallel, of course, we should move towards opening up our people's minds, in terms of literature, science and more. Because we know illiterate people cannot form a good country. We need people who can read and write. Everyone who can read and write should teach those who can't. This has been in our party guidelines for a long time now and a long time ago our party started to open schools, to improve the training of our teachers, to establish a context in which we can advance down the path of scientific understanding in regards to life and the world.

Our new culture, whether inside or outside school, must serve our resistance, must serve to help fulfil our party's programme. This is the way it has to be, comrades. Our culture must develop in national terms, in relation to our land, but without dismissing or disregarding other cultures. It must be developed with intelligence, making the most of what other cultures have to offer, taking what's good for us, anything that can be adapted to suit our living conditions. Our culture should develop based on science, it should be scientific, that's to say it shouldn't believe in imaginary things.

Our culture should make sure that, come tomorrow, none of us think a lightning flash is a sign of God's anger, that thunder is the sky's voice expressing the *iran*'s fury. In our culture, come tomorrow, everyone must know that, although we dance when there is thunder, thunder is really just two clouds crashing into each other, one with a positive electrical charge and one with a negative electrical charge, and when they collide it causes a spark, which is the lightning, and a noise, which is the thunder. It's like when you put two electrical wires together, one positive and one negative, and it makes a spark. That's what lightning is, but in the sky, the electricity of the clouds. The noise is the collision of two clouds, which we call thunder.

Not only is this true, but bearing in mind the speed of sound through air, when you hear thunder you can even work out where the two clouds are colliding, because light moves faster than sound. You see the flash and then a bit later you hear the thunderclap. Let's say the difference between the moment when you see the lightning and the moment when you hear the noise is five seconds, you can work out where the two clouds met and how far away they are from us, because the speed of sound through air is 340 metres per second. So, if you count the seconds after the flash and get to five, and then multiply five by 340 you get 1,700. That means the two clouds collided 1,700 metres away from us, causing the lightning and thunder.

A lightning bolt is just an electrical spark that, due to particular conditions, falls to earth and sometimes does so with sufficient force to cause a bit of damage, just as an electric current can sometimes cause things to explode in a house. Or the bolt might hit the earth with minimal force, land somewhere and just disappear. It could even pass through a human body and disappear into the ground, because the earth is also charged with electricity and, because it's the opposite kind, it attracts the spark. That's why they put lightning rods on houses, so that the lightning bolt goes straight through the house and into the earth, harming no one.

Comrades, we must base our culture on science. We have to remove everything unscientific from our culture, if not necessarily today, then tomorrow. If we work hard today, we can rest assured that this will be possible tomorrow.

Our culture has to be popular, that's to say a culture of the masses, everyone has the right to culture. It likewise has to respect the cultural values of our people, those that deserve to be respected. Our culture cannot be a culture of the elite, aimed at a group of people who know a lot, who understand things. No. Every son and daughter of our land, in Guinea and in Cape Verde, has the right to advance culturally, to participate in our country's cultural acts and to express and create culture.

We need to foster a spirit of understanding in terms of distinguishing between the city and the countryside. We should note that, while our cities develop foreign customs day by day, some good, others bad, although we're generally quicker to adopt the bad ones: alcoholism, prostitution, banditry, con-artistry, muggings, certain types of theft etc. In the bush life is more pure, which isn't to say there aren't people who steal there. But there's a big difference between a thief in Bissau and a Balanta thief. The Balanta thief, generally speaking – and things have perhaps changed since the colonialists came, due to the colonialist influence – steals things here, there and everywhere, but with no particular interest in keeping what he steals, what interests him is the stealing itself.

That's why he'll often steal something and pass it on to someone else, never to see the stolen item again, because theft is a sport in Balanta custom, it's to show skill, intelligence. I wear glasses and I look after them carefully, but a person like that might think, I'll have to keep playing until I can grab them when he's not looking. The person is showing that they're more skilful than me, that they can get one over on me. This is what stealing means to the Balanta. It's stealing as an intellectual exercise, as an exercise in physical and intellectual skill, without any interest in owning what's stolen.

That's why a young Balanta man, when the time comes to celebrate him reaching adulthood, might list all the things he's stolen over the years, in order to demonstrate his worth, his skill, and the elders praise him and are proud of him if he's their son, because he's shown himself to be a person of high calibre. Stealing in the city is not like that, no. The thief in the city steals to feed his people, or else to get rich. Not to mention another kind of stealing that's deemed legal in the business world, for example, legal theft.

We must be able to distinguish between our bush and our cities, to make sure that all our city impurities don't spread to the bush. Let me repeat, this doesn't mean there aren't bad things in the bush. There are many bad things there, even examples of human sacrifice, of children being beaten etc. It's dreadful the way children are beaten in our country. We must clamp down on this. And we must dispel any notion that the bush is pure, that there's nothing bad there, that it's only the city that's bad. No, there are good things and bad things in the city and in the bush, it's just that, in comparative terms, the city is less pure than the bush. And we must work hard to make sure our rural areas progress more by the day, in the cultural sphere as much as in every other sphere.

We have to make all our people conscious, comrades, starting today, all our soldiers, our militants, our local populations, make them conscious of the following: when a human being is doing a job, they must do it well, as perfectly and as quickly as possible, and in the most straightforward of fashions. We must develop in our spirit, in the spirit of all our people, the idea of perfection. We still don't have much of a sense of perfection. Look at that curtain, for example, not a single comrade managed to see it, get up and straighten it. A nail we're knocking into a wall, an item of clothing we're making; if it's wonky, that's no problem for us. We don't have much of a sense of perfection. If we're doing an ambush, we'll do it as best we can.

Any comrade who trained abroad, or already had the knowledge, knows how to do an ambush properly: such a weapon needs to be put in such a place, another weapon in such a place, so many men here, so many men there, so many men as back up, attack the enemy at a particular point. But how many comrades actually do this, how many? When done well, the results are extraordinary. But comrades generally overlook these things.

As with ambushes, the same goes for meetings where people are to go and speak. Comrades must go and speak at a meeting, but they don't bother to make notes, they do nothing and just improvise. They might end up saying all kinds of things, when all they have to do is a little bit of preparation, to refresh their memory. Today there is a meeting in such and such a village; sit down and think about what the issues are in that village, make notes. You're a political commissar, the party trusts you, you *are* the party at that moment, are you just going to go and talk for the sake of talking? A bit of research is required, that doesn't mean preparing a whole speech, there's no point in giving a big speech to our people in the bush. Or sometimes there is, but either way, you need to make notes on the various issues, think about what's going to be discussed. This is very important. There are supervisor meetings everyone wants to go to, without anyone having any idea what they're going to say when they get there.

Or meetings are held like this: several supervisors meet in the north or the south of the country and what do they decide? To do things that are already in the party guidelines. Comrades send me reports of meetings and when you look at what decisions were made, it's things that are already in our guidelines, which they've not read. Not only that, they come up with a slightly lesser or worse version of what we already have. When there's a supervisor meeting, it's to discuss, how are we progressing in fulfilling the party's guidelines? Make notes and then discuss. Or maybe a problem arises concerning the Inter-Regional Committee; make notes beforehand and go and discuss.

Perfection in our work, this is very important, but so too is perfection in the way we dress. How many times have I told comrades to straighten their collar, to tuck in their shirt. A people that is fighting for its independence, for its dignity, has to, starting today, walk around with clean feet. When we're walking in the mud, we show patience, but when we get out of the mud, we wash our feet. Clean clothes. If you've only got one set, take them off, tie a cloth around you, wash them, then put them back on clean. Comb your hair. If you don't have a comb, if you can't buy one, then make one out of a bit of wood if necessary. It seems like some comrades are maybe quite proud of their untidy hair. Perhaps it seems like an unimportant thing, but it is important. The way we behave is very important in terms of dignity and opening up new paths in life.

The Tugas used to say we were very dirty, but then when we dressed well they called us 'negroes who think they're professionals'. That was the Tugas' stance. But we have no such complex, we are simply against any kind of dirtiness, we are against filth. It amazes me, for example, that some comrades are just as capable of sleeping on the floor as in a bed. It's all the same to some comrades, though fortunately not all of them, and it doesn't matter to them whether the room is clean or full of rubbish. Some comrades, supervisors even, are incapable of cleaning, even in the midst of utter filth. They're prepared to give their life for their country, but they're not prepared to pick up a brush, to sweep the floor, the backyard, they're not prepared to tend a little garden, even when, despite their work duties, there is still time for this.

There are some comrades who make their bases nice and tidy, and I would never, even if I'm not particularly in favour of a certain base, say a word against them because I see effort there, the will to be tidy. But others don't want to know. Anyone, man or woman, willing to give their life to the cause should be clean, they should live in a clean environment and make sure everyone around them is clean. Because only then can they be clean of spirit, cleaner by the day.

We need to introduce the notion of timekeeping into our culture, comrades, into our actions. We didn't invent the clock, but we can still embrace timekeeping. We are in fact going against the culture of our people in this, comrades, for they know perfectly well what timekeeping is. They understand it very well, they know, for example, that if they don't plough by a certain moment, things will turn out bad, that seeds must be sown so many days after the first rains, otherwise things will turn out bad. So many days after the plant sprouts in the rice nursery by the house it must be transferred to the field, otherwise it won't take. After turning the rice field, after cutting the mangrove, a certain amount of time has to pass before you can start to plant, because otherwise it will be too salty, etc.

But we, comrades, many of us have no concept of time whatsoever. There are people who have to get up at five in the morning, and they get up at nine. An ambush needs to be performed from four in the afternoon, but they don't get there then, they show up the next day and find the Tugas have already been and gone. A garrison must be attacked at six in the afternoon, but they arrive in the dead of night, or maybe it was arranged for midday but they get there late and leave it for the next day, but the same thing happens the next day. How many times have our commanders failed in attacks or ambushes due to lateness? Some delays are justifiable, because of our difficult conditions, but others are simply due to a lack of care, a lack of awareness, a lack of order, a lack of decisiveness.

Sometimes a comrade is given a mission to take a letter somewhere quickly. They stop off on the way for whatever reason, their own amusement, and so it takes three or four days when it should have gotten there in a day. This is not good enough. You cannot win a war like this, much less build a country. We must have a better concept of timekeeping. Our comrades, political commissars, security commissars etc have to be on time wherever they go. I don't want anyone coming to me and saying they couldn't make it on time because they haven't got a watch. We do not need clocks to be on time. We can decide to meet when the sun is at its highest. There is sun in our country. When the cockerel calls for the first time, it's time to get up. When the sun is at noon, it's time to go. You don't need a clock to respect the time, comrades. A clock is just to provide a little extra help.

Our people lived without clocks for centuries, but those who lived under the right economic conditions to invent clocks, invented them. But it wasn't the clock that made the people of Europe advance, no. It was working for long hours and advancing so much that they could invent the clock, the modern clock, because everyone has the old clock, you just have to put a stick in the ground and depending on where the shadow is, that's the time. It's a sun clock. A person's shadow can be a clock, because in the morning a shadow is on one side and in the afternoon it's on the other. At midday many people say shadows disappear, because it's right under their feet, the sun is right above us, it's noon.

We have a lot of work to do, comrades, we have to make the most of our time. We have to try and be practical in our work, we have to instil in our comrades the spirit of being practical. We need to stop overcomplicating things. Or dispel from our spirit our magical interpretation of reality. We still often have a way of thinking whereby when we sit down and talk a thing through thoroughly, until we're all in agreement, we tend to think that the thing is already done, and we're happy as if we have in fact done the thing and maybe we even ought to celebrate, because the discussion went so well. But the discussion ends, everyone goes away happy with life and satisfied because they're going to do such a great job, but they don't then get down to actually doing the job, because it's already done in their heads.

But if we look at this closely, we can see how this corresponds to our own way of life, to how we're convinced that *marabouts* or witchdoctors are capable of pointing a finger at us and making us fall over. Sooner or later we'll have to realise that this is a lie, that they're not capable of doing anything. But it's in our heads, we think it or believe in it. And there are many other things like this besides. We think like this before an ambush, for example, we end up very satisfied with our plan, but then take no practical measures to ensure its success, to make sure everything runs smoothly with no mishaps, because everything's fine in our heads, because in our magical interpretation of reality, we think the job's already been done.

We must eradicate this from our midst, we all have to do it, as some comrades already have been doing. Discuss things, but then put them into practice, correctly, properly, without any mishaps, because our trouble is starting things but not finishing them. When we start on a job, we go at it full of enthusiasm, for example, we're going to build an underground warehouse to keep materials in. We make an enthusiastic start, but after a while we stop and everyone forgets about it. Look at independent Africa, so many things are started and never finished. Because it's enough for us to create the thing in our heads and that's it, never think about it again. How many things have we planned during our struggle, in political terms, in military terms, in education, in health, and never done? We start, but all it takes is for one small difficulty to emerge and that's it, it advances no further. We have to clamp down on this hard, very hard.

I could give many examples of things we've started but never finished. People who've started things and never finished them, organisations that started things and never finished it, and always for one of two reasons: they either realised it wasn't worth doing or they were unable to finish it. If they realised it wasn't worth doing, they were doing something they shouldn't have been doing in the first place, the matter wasn't properly thought through. Before starting on something we must study it to work out whether it's worth doing or not, not just start and then stop. This is a waste of energy, it's squandering. Or else they were unable to finish it, but if you can't finish something you've started then that's just pathetic, you'll never achieve anything in life. We must put a stop to this, comrades.

Perfection, making the most of our time and being practical in what we do, having the capacity to see a task through to the end, every task that needs doing. This is very important, comrades, it's fundamental to our culture, comrades, it's a new dynamic, for our culture and our land. Because even if an entire week is required for an ambush to be done well, at a particular point on a road, then we should do it, take the whole week, the whole month even. We should organise our troops in such a way so that a group is always on that road, circling, moving etc. but they must always be there. If we know the enemy has to pass there, we mustn't leave, we have to see the job through until the end. What we can't do, as I've already said, is come along to perform a great ambush, wait for an hour or two, three or four, the enemy hasn't come, some people say they're coming others say they're not, and so we end up leaving. The enemy passes by a little later on and delivers its supplies to the garrison.

With rivers it's the same thing. The attack has to take place at the scheduled time, otherwise why set a time? An attack is scheduled for five o'clock, but five o'clock passes, six o'clock, and it's left for another day, and the attack never gets done. Why do comrades mess with their own heads like this? Why? We schedule something for five, having confirmed that five is the right time to do it, or we schedule something for ten having confirmed that ten is the best time to pull it off. Knowing the enemy as well as we do, we must know when the best time to attack them is. We have to exploit this knowledge to the maximum.

We must learn to use our resistance as propaganda, this too is a cultural act. Through all the means we have available. One of the greatest triumphs of our party is our Radio Libertação station, our newspapers, *Jornal, Imprensa, Informação*, both inside and outside our land. We all know the value of, the power of our Party Broadcaster, which transmits messages to our people and which we ought to steadily try and improve, because it's a vital propaganda tool for us, a means of promoting our resistance.

And, within the framework of our other activities, we should fly the flag for literacy throughout the land. We are pleased because so many comrades have already improved their knowledge during the struggle. Many of our country's elders have learned to read and write, our youngsters even more so. These days it's rare to find a bi-group that doesn't have at least someone who can't read or write, but it used to be that there would be many people who couldn't read or write, there were a lot of bi-groups in which practically nobody knew how to read or write. So we have to keep increasing this level of learning.

But there are a lot of comrades who reached second grade, or first grade, or second year. University graduates sometimes spend several days with their fellow comrades, doing nothing, spending their spare time relaxing, sprawled out or telling tales, without thinking to say, 'Comrades, those of you who've had no learning, come here and I'll teach you.' Or those of you who've had some, come and I'll teach you a bit more. But most comrades don't think like this, they prefer telling tales or wandering around in the bush or in Conakry or Zinguinchor or Dakar.

We've a lot of work to do if we're going to build a new life for our country, comrades. We must, for example, and the party has already started doing this, instil the idea of cleanliness, or hygiene, as it's called, in our people. Our people are clean, they love washing, they like brushing their teeth, they do it all the time, but not everyone. There are those who don't like it much and those who might wash and then throw themselves in the mud again afterwards, for whatever reason. We have to work to show people that their lives, the length of their lives, depends a good deal on them having a clean home. If people live amidst dirt and other things, it's bad for them because such an environment is good for bugs that can cause humans harm. Flies and other bugs that bring all kinds of illnesses thrive in dirt. We must explain the principles of hygiene to our people. This is a fundamental aspect of our cultural resistance.

We started to set up health brigades, but where did we get with them? Not very far given what we needed to do. But the political commissar should be a hygiene advocate, the security commissar should be a hygiene advocate, the commander of the armed forces should be a hygiene advocate. Wherever we go, we must insist on cleanliness. Even in Boké, for example, inside a resthouse, or outside, supervisors visit them, find everything dirty and say nothing. Only one or two people worry about cleanliness. We cannot have things so dirty, we must clean, we must sweep. We have to develop a spirit of cleanliness, comrades, of hygiene.

Every supervisor and militant in the land must be a hygiene advocate. Wherever they go, they must demand cleanliness, and they, as good supervisors, must be the first to pick up a sweeping brush if necessary. Be the first to clean up, to show others there's no shame in it, that they're fighting for their country, that they're prepared to give their life to our struggle but they're not prepared to live amongst filth, just because nobody bothers cleaning up, because they think cleaning is beneath their status. How can this kind of attitude put people on the right path, how can it rid us of dirtiness?

Because if we ask ourselves what are we fighting for, we might very well answer that our struggle is to ensure that not one poor soul in Guinea or Cape Verde has to live in squalor, that it's to eradicate filth and mess from our midst. When we achieve this, we'll have advanced a long way in our struggle. We have asked comrades to persuade our people to build latrines, for example. This does not mean that latrines are a sign of progress; no, latrines themselves are not progress, people that do their business in the bush may well be more advanced than people with latrines. But making latrines is a sign of us advancing in other areas, because putting distance between ourselves and where we do our business is a way of us avoiding diseases. Because we all know there are certain places where you have to hold your nose when you pass by or else... But it's the same in other African countries, even in cities you sometimes have to hold your nose when you pass by certain places. There's dirtiness everywhere. Those of us who are prepared to die for a cause, for our people's happiness and progress, must be prepared to clean, because it's easier to clean than die.

Of course, we have to remove everything from our schools that was put there by the colonialists, everything that shows a colonialist mentality. We've already started, we're publishing new books that speak of our party, our struggle, our country, our people's present and future, our people's rights. There are some comrades who think that to educate our sons and daughters properly we should not speak of our party. What nonsense! Any teacher who thinks like this is no teacher at all. The way we see it, a teacher is someone who educates our sons and daughters on our struggle, the rights of our people, our party, our party's anthem, our party's worth, as well as the A, B, Cs, the Cat and the Fox, the Wolf and the Little Goat etc. The party should also be present, the leader of the party, the leadership of the party, the strength of our struggle, the strength of our people, the strength of our party, the duty of our people.

When I went to school they taught us about the birth of Jesus Christ, that the Virgin Mary had a child as a virgin, and I even repeated this stuff back, it apparently made sense to me at the time. The miracle of the ascension, there were lots of miracles in the approved books of the time, the miracle of the roses and all the rest. Why then, if back then they taught children about miracles, can we not teach our people about the even greater miracle that is taking place in our country: men and women joining together and mobilising the population to fight to end their suffering, to end poverty, to end misery, to end the beatings and kickings, to end forced labour, etc.? Is that so hard to understand? Any child can understand that.

And we should make of every knowledgeable party supervisor and party militant a teacher. School teachers are not the only ones who have a duty to teach, every commander, every member of the party leadership, our political commissars, security commissars, nurses; everyone has a duty to teach, to be always instructing, explaining, telling, clarifying, helping. Only by doing this can we move forward, comrades. We cannot leave the mission of educating to teachers alone.

We have to make the most of every opportunity – and comrades who know me well, who deal with me a lot, know this is how I myself behave – we have to turn every conversation we have, of no matter what nature, into a class, into a mini lesson. Someone or other will learn from it. Every conversation we have should be a lesson, that way we save time, we advance. But if we just sit around telling tales about back in Pelon, Mansôa and other places, without giving a thought to learning, we're wasting time, comrades, we're not advancing.

We must avoid any kind of superiority complex on the part of those who know things and any kind of inferiority complex on the part of those who do not. A person with the capacity to teach must not distance themselves from anyone, especially not now, and especially not from our people. On the contrary, they should go deeper, immerse themselves in our people. I have explained this to comrades, for example, to comrades who go away to study. So far there have been two tendencies when people come back: one is for them to mix with our people, but to blend in so well that they make the same mistakes our people make; others, however, come back as trained engineers and want to immediately become party leaders. Isn't Bôbô Keita in charge? Bôbô doesn't have my level of studies, I'm an engineer and he barely went to school, he should be out, he gets so many things wrong etc. etc. he's holding back the work of our party, he's ruining everything.

These are two extremes that we don't want. What we want is for those who go away and study and acquire more knowledge to come back and show respect for our leaders, because they are our leaders whether they went to school or not. But when they notice some flaw in our operations, we want them to get among their comrades and help improve things, help make sure we raise our standards by the day. This advice comes from someone who knows more than we do, who's had the opportunity to learn things others haven't and who's here to help us. Mix, blend in, but don't forget you have to help improve things, raise standards day by day.

We must clamp down on opportunism of every kind, even in culture. For example, some comrades think that when it comes to education in our land it is imperative that we start teaching in creole right away. Then there are others who think it would be better to teach in Fula, in Mandiga, in Balanta. This is a nice thing to hear, any Balanta person would be happy hearing it, but it just isn't possible right now. How are we going to write in Balanta? Who knows the phonetics of Balanta? People don't understand that these things have to be studied first, even creole. For example, I might write *n'ca na bai*. Someone else might write *n'ka na bai*. It's the same thing. You can't teach like this. To teach a written language you need to have a certain way of writing, so that everyone writes in the same way, otherwise we'll be bedevilled in confusion.

But many comrades, with a sense of opportunism, want to forge ahead with creole. We will teach in creole, but only after studying it properly. Right now the language we use for writing is Portuguese. That's why anything goes here, Portuguese is as valid as creole. We are not somehow more sons and daughters of our land if we speak creole, that's just not true. We are more sons and daughters of our land if we follow our party's rules, our party's guidelines, and serve our people well.

Nobody should have a complex because they don't speak Balanta, Mandiga, Pepel, Fula or Mancanha. If they speak them, all the better, but if they don't, they can still make themselves understood, even if it's through hand gestures. If you're doing good work for the party, you move forward. Because who speaks better Manjaco than Joaquim Batican, the traitor? Do any comrades know more Fula than the traitor Sene Sané, more of the Fula 'doctrine' than the traitor Tcherno Rachid? Be patient, comrades. Who speaks better Balanta than the traitor Fuab? We need to have the courage to put things to comrades straight. Our values, yes sir, but with no opportunism.

We need to have a real sense of our culture. The Portuguese language is one of the best things the Tugas gave us because a language doesn't prove anything. It's just a tool humans use to relate to one another, a tool, a means of speaking so that we can express the facts of life and the world. Just as mankind invented the radio so that we can talk over great distances, without speaking a particular language, using signals, so too did mankind, at a particular time in our development, invent speech, we felt the need to communicate and did so through talking. We developed our vocal chords etc. until finally we spoke. And because language depends on the environment we live in, different people created their own languages.

We might notice, for example, that people who live close to the sea have lots of words related to the sea in their languages, people who live in the bush have lots of words related to the forest. People who live in the bush don't know how to say motorboat, for example, they don't know what a motorboat is because they don't live near water. There are lots of things to do with the sea and navigation in the languages of certain European people, like the Portuguese, for example, because the Portuguese live by the sea. Such things are the way they are for a reason.

Language is a tool that mankind created, through hard work and struggle, to communicate with others. And this gave humans a tremendous new power, because then nobody was stuck on their own, they started to communicate with others, men with other men, societies with other societies, one people to another, one country to another, one continent to another. How wonderful! It was the first natural means of communication, through language. But the world has advanced a lot since then.

We haven't advanced that much, not as much as the rest of the world, so our language only got so far, as far as we reached as a society, the world we lived in, whereas the Tugas, despite them being colonialists, lived in Europe, so their language advanced a lot more than ours, allowing them to express certain truths, for example in relation to science. They might say this, the moon is a natural satellite of the Earth. 'Natural satellite'; say that in Balanta; say it in Macanha. You have to do quite a lot of talking to say it; it's possible to say, but you have to talk a lot to explain that a satellite is something that rotates around something else. Whereas in Portuguese one word is enough, and said in such a way that people anywhere in the world can understand. And mathematics, we want to learn mathematics, don't we? Let us say, for example, the square root of 36. How do you say 'square root' in Balanta? We have to speak the truth if we want to understand ourselves properly. I might say, 'An object's weight is a product of mass times gravitational acceleration.' How are we going to say that? How do say 'gravitational acceleration' in our language? You can't say it in creole, you have to say it in Portuguese.

But if our country is to advance, in a few years' time every child of this land will need to know what gravitational acceleration is. I'm not going to explain it now, because there isn't time, we've got a lot of work to do. But comrades, to really advance, tomorrow not only our leaders but every child of nine must know what gravitational acceleration is. In Germany, for example, every kid knows. There are so many things we cannot say in our language, yet some people want us to ditch the Portuguese language because we are Africans and we must reject the foreigners' tongue. What these people really want is to advance themselves, not advance their people. We, as a party, if we want to lead our people for a long time yet, if we want to advance as a people in science and in writing, we have to use the Portuguese tongue. And it's an honour to do so. It's the one thing we have to thank the Tugas for, the fact that they left us their language after robbing us of so many other things.

When the day comes that we've completed an in-depth study of creole, found out all the appropriate phonetic rules for creole, then we can switch and start writing in Crioulo. But we're not forbidding anyone from writing in creole, if someone wants to write a letter to Tchutchu in creole, they can go ahead write it. When he replies, he'll write in a different way, but it'll be understood, that's fine. But Crioulo is no good for science. Even in Balanta, I remember a comrade of ours, Ongo, who unfortunately died. Ongo and I wrote to each other in Portuguese, changing into creole now and then, and he wrote in Balanta too. Because it is possible to write in Balanta, anyone who knows enough Portuguese will be able to write in Balanta. You might say for example *Watna* or else *n'calossa*. I know how to write these things, but in my own way. Another person will write them their way. Even *djarama* in Fula can be written with a d and a j or it can be written just with a j, but it reads as *djarama* because a j at the start of a word is the same as dj. But we have to establish rules, like in Mandiga and other languages, we need to establish rules first.

This is the way it has to be, comrades, because we need to take as much as we possibly can from other peoples' experiences, not just rely on our own experience. But if we want to use other peoples' experiences and apply them to our own land, then we have to use expressions from other peoples' languages. Now, if we already have a language with which we can do this, let's use it, there's no harm in that whatsoever.

It's all the same to us if we use Portuguese or Russian or French or English, so long as it serves our purpose, the same way that it doesn't make any difference if the tractors we use are Russian, English, American so long as they lead us towards our independence, so long as they enable us to work the land. Because language is a tool, and it just so happens we already have a language that serves our purpose and that everyone understands. So we're not going to make everyone learn Russian, that would be pointless, especially not when we have our own language, creole, that is so similar to Portuguese. If our schools teach students how creole was derived from Portuguese and African languages, people will be able to learn Portuguese much quicker. Creole hinders people learning Portuguese because they don't know what the link between Portuguese and creole is, but if they understand that link then it can help them learn Portuguese.

We must end our people's general indifference towards matters of culture by making conscious decisions and showing determination in what we do. We have already made inroads in this regard, and we must do away with the idea that if something comes from abroad it must be good and we should accept it, or else that because it's foreign it's worthless and we should reject it. This isn't culture, it's an obsession, it's a complex, either of inferiority or stupidity. We must be able to look at things from abroad, accept what's acceptable and reject what's useless. We must be capable of making a critical evaluation. And if we look carefully at our struggle, we'll see that part of what we've been doing has involved the constant application of the principle of critical assimilation, that's to say, making the most of what others have already done by determining, through our own critique, what serves our country's needs and what does not. Creating based on accumulated experience.

These are some of the aspects of our resistance in cultural terms, comrades, which is what I wanted to speak to you about today.

4. ARMED RESISTANCE

Comrades, over yesterday and today we've sought to clarify the nature of our resistance in general terms, as a response to Portuguese colonial oppression, and to define, albeit briefly, the various forms of resistance our struggle takes. Each form is a response to a form of Portuguese repression: political oppression met with political resistance; economic oppression met with economic resistance; cultural oppression met with cultural resistance. It remains for us to talk about our armed resistance, which is how we meet armed oppression, colonialist aggression. This is a form of resistance that comrades, of course, already know a fair bit about, because it is more visible than the other forms of resistance.

We have already spoken about the beginning of our armed resistance. Comrades have heard about how our armed resistance is a political act on the one hand, because we are engaged in a war in our land in response to the Tugas engaging in war. But above all else, because we could find no other way for us to claim our political right to rule over ourselves, for our people to determine their own destiny and for us to advance, like other people of the world, down the path of progress. Earlier today, I reminded you that our armed resistance is also an expression of our cultural resistance, because by risking our lives every day, we are rejecting the condition of second-class Portuguese, or in fact third-class Portuguese, or even puppy-dog status, that the foreign Portuguese colonialists wish to impose on us.

We have, through our party's work, become conscious that we are part of the African people, that we belong to the continent known as Africa, that is our destiny. We are human beings like any other human beings, deeply connected to the rest of humanity, in the first instance, to Africa and, as Africans and as humans, we have just as much right to lead free and dignified lives as do the people of Portugal or any other place in the world. Without disrespecting the Tugas, our personality is not the same as theirs, though some of us may be the sons and daughters of Tugas or the descendants of Tugas mixed with Africans. We want our dignity back, our own personality, in order to stand up for our rights and for everything that forms the legitimate basis of our people's culture.

We have also shown comrades that our armed resistance can, ultimately, be seen as the continuation of the resistance our people showed – in Guinea in particular, because Guinea was conquered by the Tugas – during the war of colonial conquest waged in our land for almost 50 years. Today we take up arms again, continuing our ancestors' fight, those who refused to give up the right to determine their own lives. In regards to Cape Verde, our struggle, which remains political today but may become armed tomorrow. It can be seen as the continuation of the resistance shown by those Africans, sons and daughters of Guinea and the surrounding areas, who were taken to Cape Verde as slaves, who resisted as slaves, who suffered, rejected and fought the Tuga slavers who dominated them and sold them to America, Brazil and other parts of the world, as if they were beasts.

We must, therefore, conclude that our armed resistance is, in the first instance, the continuation of a longer struggle in defence of our dignity as Africans. We have a tradition of fighting, of defending our liberty and our right, as a society, to our own history and to taking our own path towards progress, just like any other people anywhere in the world.

We know who we are, we've already spoken about this a lot. We have clearly defined our position geographically, economically, culturally and socially, both before and after the Tugas came to our land. Before the colonial situation and after the colonial situation.

We are part of a multitude of different peoples on the African continent who came into contact with Europeans after the European route to Asia, to the Far East, via the Mediterranean was shut off by the Turkish empire, which had conquered Southern Europe, Eastern Europe and Asia Minor. Hemmed in by the Turkish, the Europeans needed to find new routes to access the riches of Asia, which they'd become accustomed to buying, trading and exploiting. From that moment on, the Europeans, and the Portuguese in particular, because they were located on the tip of Europe, by the sea, began a series of navigations, which have come to be known as 'the discoveries'. The Tugas are obsessed with thinking that God revealed the sea route to them so that they could discover new countries, discover new worlds. This is a lie.

The Tugas took to the seas firstly because they lived at the sea's edge and secondly because Portugal was very poor and had lots of people it could employ as sailors, unlike other countries in Europe that had fewer people prepared to spend a life at sea. But thirdly, and most importantly, because Europe had no choice but to take to the sea to find a new route to the Indies. No God revealed the sea route to the Tugas. This is quite obvious when you consider that the Tugas soon went back to being poor and wretched, to boasting the smallest navy of any country in the world with a navy. This needs to be made very clear, the events that led to us coming into contact with the Tugas.

The Tugas initially established relationships with different African peoples based on equality and, in a few cases, inferiority on Portugal's part, because some countries in Africa were much more developed than Portugal was at the time. I can tell you that the king of Ghana, for example, and the king of Mombasa and Melinde, on the East African coast, and the king of Congo, were all a bit shocked by the Tugas' poverty and the gifts the king of Portugal sent them, compared to what they might have sent to the king of Portugal. Portuguese kings wrote lovely letters to African kings requesting good relations, praising them, inviting them to trade, with due respect. But it's been proven that the Portuguese kings were always giving secret orders, instructing their people to find ways to trick, to steal etc ...

So the Tugas established relationships with us, we Africans, trade relations along the coasts of our African lands, initially based on equality and respect. Even after a long time had passed there were still signed trade accords, in Guinea, for example, between the Pepel and Portuguese kings. And the Tugas, in order to trade with our land and with other parts of Africa, paid taxes, as did other European countries besides, countries that later turned into colonialist and imperialist countries.

Europe gradually transformed, becoming advanced in commercial terms and industrially developed, England especially. As capitalism developed at great pace, new needs arose in Europe. The accumulation of capital brought the need for new raw materials, to develop Europe further, as a response to European poverty, but so too the need for new markets to sell European products to. Before this, because of warring in Africa, wars fought among Africans themselves (the area our country lies in now saw lots of wars, for example, especially inwards from Futa-Djalon, where various African military aristocracies fought with each other to conquer land for pasture, for farming etc.), there were a lot of prisoners of war in Africa who were used as slaves. In Africa itself, economic and social systems were built around slavery, albeit a slavery with its own characteristics, different to slavery on other continents.

Systems of slavery still exist in Africa today. Indeed, when you stop and think about it, a *régulo*'s errand boys are really no more than slaves, comrades. Some of our 'elders' have boys, here in our land, in the bush, who are like slaves. They're given food, they have children, but all those children are raised to serve the same 'elder'. Their children's children's children remain servants. This is called slavery. We Africans, with our own concept of slavery, were open to the idea of arranging slaves for others.

America was discovered around this time and began to be colonised shortly thereafter. Brazil, in South America, islands like Cuba, Jamaica, the so-called West Indies, some Latin American countries, especially in Central America, and what's known as North America, colonised by the English. In Brazil and the southern part of North America, where the climate was harsher, in areas that were a bit behind, agriculture went down the hard labour route and the Europeans who'd left Europe to colonise it were somewhat well-to-do. They'd been expelled from Europe, persecuted because of their religion, because of their politics, because of the class struggle in Europe. These kinds of people weren't about to pick up a hoe and start working the land, so they went out into the world to find people to do this work for them. Africa made for easy pickings in this sense, because there was slavery in Africa, Africans were used to buying and selling slaves. And so the Tugas, who regularly navigated the Atlantic ocean, and others like the French, the Dutch who knew the crossing from piracy, stopped being pirates. Instead of robbing at ports and at sea, they bought or hunted slaves in Africa to sell in America or the New World. A new type of trade began, slave trading.

The slave trade went on for a long time, long enough for more than a 100 million Africans to be sold around the world, many of them, according to researchers, dying at sea, through debility or shipwrecks. African men and women were taken to various parts of the world, but especially to America.

Time passed and disputes started between the English on one side, along with a few other European countries, and America on the other, disputes over economic competition. Because America's rise had basically been facilitated by slave work, whereas in England, for example, there were no slaves and wages had to be paid. So there emerged in England, not out of humanitarian feeling, but out of economic necessity, out of the need to halt the march of American development, the idea of ending slavery.

Great theories were advanced about how slavery was a crime against humanity. Which is true, it is a crime, but it had been a crime for a very long time. Slavery must end, great propaganda, international summits etc. until there came a point when slavery was eventually outlawed. But the Tugas, already quite stubborn back then, went on slave trading for a good while yet, with their fine slaving warehouse on the Cape Verde islands, out in the Atlantic Ocean. Other slaves were taken to Portugal. In Portugal there are still places that have 'negro' in their name, because there were so many slaves there. Poço dos Negros, for example, because there were lots of black people there who were kept as slaves and then, after the end of slavery, when they became free, they remained in Portugal. Even in the Alentejo there is a village where there are a lot of mixed-race people, descendants of Africans who the Marquês de Pombal sent to populate the Alentejo.

With slavery ending in Europe, the idea of giving slaves their freedom spread through America too and slavery was outlawed throughout the world. The north of North America was industrialised while the south produced raw materials, based on slave labour. The idea emerged, in order to protect the industrial and economic interests of the north, to end slavery in North America. The idea was to take away the advantage the great proprietors of the south, the owners of vast swathes of land and slaves, had over the industrialists in the north. Lincoln, the American president based in the northern states, decided to end slavery. There was a war because of this. The south immediately declared that it was no longer part of the United States, that it wanted no part in any kind of federation, that it would be an independent state, and keep its slaves. War broke out, a harsh war, between Americans and Americans, supposedly about the slaves, because the north wanted to free the slaves. A lie. The north wanted to end the advantage the south had because it had slaves and the north did not.

And if we study this further, we'll see that the Europeans who settled in North America were of a different origin in the north and south. Place names in the north have certain roots, while those in the south have others. There are a lot of French names in the south, for example, and names from other countries. Because Americans, as you all know, are not from America. The real Americans are the Indians, almost all of whom were killed by Europeans. But the so-called Indians of North America are not Indians at all, of course, they're redskins who were called Indians because when Christopher Columbus discovered America he thought he'd reached India. When he saw people he called them Indians and they got stuck with that name, though they're not Indian at all.

A new era began, comrades, a world in which slavery had ended. The world was transformed by this. But in the meantime, capitalism in Europe had developed a lot, vast accumulations of capital, industrial development, the need for raw materials, the need, as I said, for new markets. The most developed European states decided to actually take control of Africa, to end the historical tradition of small-scale trading, small-scale contracts and respect for Africans. The European states, England, Germany, France and Belgium, started to argue over who would take control of Africa. They determined to share Africa out, first through the companies they created, then through the states themselves, through colonial wars of occupation. It's a long chapter in history and I'm not going to recount it all now, but that's basically how our lands became colonies, occupied by colonialists.

And from that moment on, regardless of whether we were developed or not, or whether we were as advanced as the Europeans, our own history stopped. We were dragged into the history of the Europeans. Our history, our freedom and the freedom of our productive forces were taken away from us, seized by the colonialists. Of course, they were facilitated in this by the fact that we ourselves were forever divided. You'll know that in Guinea, for example, the Tugas fought against us one by one, defeating us one by one, race by race, and by using some races against others. It might be said that had certain Manjacos had not helped the Tugas fight other Manjacos, it's hard to see how the Tugas could have ever defeated the Manjacos. It might also be said that had the Fula not helped the Tugas fight the Pepels, and especially had Honório Barreto not tricked the Pepels of Bissau into serving the Tugas, then the Tugas may well never have established themselves in our country.

A lot of people are not aware of the role Honório Barreto played in the Tugas' conquest of Guinea. Honório Barreto, son of Rosa de Cacheu, from the island of Santiago in Cape Verde, and João Barreto, who was a sergeant in the Portuguese army. He was a black man, born in Guinea and a descendant of Cape Verdeans, a mixture of Cape Verdeans and Manjacos, as Rosa was also said to be. She was the daughter of a Cape Verdean man and Manjaca woman who was taken to Cape Verde. Dona Rosa de Cacheu, was related to indigenous Africans from the region of Teixeira Pinto, Cacheu as far as the river, which was called the Rio São Domingos back then and is known as the Casamansa river today. She was so liked amongst Africans that they agreed to whatever she said. She practically ran the economy.

Honório Barreto, her son, was educated first in Cape Verde and later in Portugal. He was a student of mathematics in Portugal, though he never finished his studies. He was a good guitar player and a bit of a reveller, and he returned to Guinea to take over his parents' business affairs. João Barreto had earlier been taken prisoner for rebelling against the ruling government, because he was a democrat, not one in favour of independence, but in favour of other Portuguese people who were democrats.

After his father died, Honório Barreto took over the family's business affairs and became the richest man in Guinea. When faced with the Pepel revolt – there was only one governor on the ground among the Pepel people in Guinea and Cape Verde at the time, and he reported to Praia – the governor general of Cape Verde and Guinea sent a proposal to the Portuguese crown, Queen Dona Maria at the time. He said that if she wanted Guinea to remain at peace, to end the wars there and for Portugal to genuinely take control of Guinea, then she should install Honório Barreto as governor. I read the letter the governor wrote to Dona Maria in the colonial archives in Lisbon. It said,

> I have the honour of proposing to the queen that she choose as Governor of Guinea, albeit acting under my command, an illustrious and intelligent young man by the name of Honório Barreto, who attended such and such a school etc etc. and who is as Portuguese as any of us. And I advise her to do this because, as the richest man in Guinea, no one has a greater interest in maintaining the Portuguese presence in Guinea than he does.

The queen understood this and Honório Barreto was named governor of Guinea. Barreto established a plan of action for the Tugas to conquer Guinea: if he took proper control of Cacheu, Geba and Bissau for the Tugas, no one else would be capable of taking Guinea and they could put down any indigenous revolts. His plan was very well thought out, very intelligent.

But when, for example, the Tugas became angry with him later, because he was black and in charge, he pulled off a great trick, giving everything up, returning to Cacheu and shutting himself away in his property there. When the Portuguese subsequently had difficulties with indigenous populations, they called for him, to avoid having the Pepels rise up against them. He returned. At one point, for example, the king of Intim, N'Dongo, one of the strongest of the Pepel kings, surrounded Amura, the fort of São Jose in Bissau, with his men. He did it so well that the Portuguese died of starvation, unable to get out. Their ships never reached Bissau.

Barreto was in Cacheu and the Portuguese sent for him. People came from Cape Verde, Tugas who were in Cape Verde, and called for him. He agreed and went to talk to the Pepel king and promised him that Pepel rights would be respected, that Portugal would not take their land in any way whatsoever, and that they would be paid taxes etc. He even made out a written contract. Meanwhile, the Tugas arranged for a large force to be sent from Portugal, departing Lisbon for Guinea, and when they arrived they massacred the Pepels.

Another time Barreto made a contract with the *régulo* of Djeu de rei, the island across from Bissau, in which the *régulo* and the Tugas agreed to the following: the *régulo* would leave the Tugas alone, he would not make war with them, and the Tugas would give him a certain amount of firearms, iron bars and litres of sugar cane every year. This is written on a signed contract, archived in Lisbon, which I've also read. I'm trying to give you an idea of how Barreto knew exactly what to do to serve Portugal's interests.

His plan did, in fact, allow him to take control of Guinea and hand it over to the Tugas, as intended. Because he took control of Guinea at a time when the English and the French came along, wanting Guinea for themselves. The English wanted Bolama, the French wanted everything from Casamansa down. Barreto was a great Portuguese 'patriot'. He put up a strong resistance, accepting none of the promises or offers the French and English made him and keeping Guinea exclusively for the Tugas. The Tugas are right to build a statue of Honório Barreto in our land. The Tugas wouldn't have Guinea if it weren't for Barreto. That's the truth of it. But we, too, should have some respect for Barreto.

We can be critical of his attitude, but he was a brave man. At that time, with the prevailing mentality, as an individual who emerged from amongst our people but who was educated by the Portuguese, amongst the Portuguese, speaking good Portuguese, playing the guitar, singing *fados* etc. There wasn't anything else he could really do, comrades. He was given a job and he did it well, for he was a brave man. Today we might not understand how the descendants of Honório Barreto, for example the Alvarengas (because nha Rosa was called Rosa Alvarenga, João Barreto and Rosa Alvarenga became the Carvalhos Alvarengas etc. The Barretos, were also an entire family. These two families joined together in our land and produced fine people, such as comrade Barreto, who's seated over there), how these descendants of Barreto can still side with the Tugas, given the new phenomenon, given our people's struggle and independence in Africa, given the liberation struggles taking place everywhere. That Honório Barreto might serve the Tugas, sure, any one of us might have chosen to do that, if we'd had his education and lived in the same moment of history as he did. But that the descendants of Barreto, whether they went to school or not, still choose the Tugas today is not only difficult to understand, it's unforgivable. So, comrades can now see where we emerged from, how we fell into the hands of the Tugas in the first place.

As for Cape Verde, as comrades will know, there was no conquest of Cape Verde. Cape Verde is a group of islands that the Tugas 'found' around that time.

They came upon the western tip of Africa, where Dakar is today, and because of its green-ness, for at the time they discovered it the place was very green, and because it was a cape, that's to say a bit of land that sticks out into the ocean, they called it Cape Verde (Green Cape). A few days later, advancing out into the ocean, they came across some islands and because they were near the green cape, they called them the Cape Verde islands. Then each island got a name. The one they discovered in the month of May became Maio island, the one they discovered on St Tiago's Day became Santiago island, the one covered in salt became Sal island, the one that looked pretty in the distance became Boa Vista island, all names based on the Tugas' Christianity and their particular way of seeing things. But as you'll know, the area where Dakar is located today is called Région du Cap Vert. In Dakar you see a lot of things with Cap Vert written on and people think that's where Cape Verde is, which is why I've given you this explanation.

There was no one living on the Cape Verde islands at the time they were discovered. But there are theories that people had been there before, particularly people from the African coast, Manjacos as well as Lebus. Lebu fishermen from the Senegalese coast could have got as far as the Cape Verde islands in their canoes, for it has recently been proven that some of their canoes, *nhomincas* canoes, for example, were capable of covering those kinds of distances. Besides this, there is the historical theory that the Phoenicians, who were an ancient people who inhabited what is now Lebanon, in Asia Minor, people we tend to call Syrians, navigated around Africa back in ancient times. It's said they completed what's known as the circumnavigation of Africa over a thousand years ago, and that they passed through the Cape Verde islands and lived there.

Nevertheless, when the Tugas came across the Cape Verde islands, out in the middle of the ocean, they found no one living there. And when the slave trade started to develop they decided to take slaves there and turn the Cape Verde islands into a slaving warehouse. When the slave trade started to come to an end, each island passed into the hands of an important white man, a Dom whatever, 'dom' coming from domain, meaning ownership. These men put the slaves to work but exploited them like slaves or as servants in the landowner's house. This is our point of departure, the situation the Tugas created in Africa.

Now that we fully understand our point of departure, we need to understand where we're going to with our armed struggle. Our armed struggle, as we've said, is a form of political struggle that seeks to liberate our country from colonial and imperial economic exploitation. This is what our fundamental aim is. Liberate the productive forces of our country, from oppression, from colonial imperialist domination.

But here's a question: Are we doing all this just to go back to where we were, back to a Cape Verde of slaves, of serfs, of people raised to be servants? Are we doing all this to go back to a time when Manjacos and Pepels were always fighting and when Mandingas and Balanta could never get along? This is the hard part. No, we are liberating our country in order to advance, like other people in the world; to progress, to lead lives of dignity, for there to be unity in our country, nationwide; to help raise a new and better Africa. This is what the objective of our struggle is, within the context of the wider world and the whole of humanity, a humanity we belong to as human beings.

When it comes to our struggle, every shot we fire at the Buba garrison or at a Tuga on the road or in an ambush is, therefore, a political act of the highest order. We are serving humanity, comrades, we are serving our people, our country, Africa, humanity. This is the sense of responsibility we bear when we fire our guns, when we wage war in our land to free our people.

That is why we must coordinate our armed struggle in the best way possible according to our reality on the ground, and according to other peoples' experience of struggle, when that experience is relevant to ours. We must avoid doing anything in our struggle, and we have been avoiding it, anything that in any way denigrates human dignity. Our party forbids any criminal act, anything done in the name of our struggle that is hateful in spirit or bloodthirsty. We do feel hatred and we shed the blood of the colonialists who dominate us, but we do so knowing exactly what we are doing and why, comrades, there can be no room for confusion. That's why we're having trouble getting our Felupe brothers to join us, because they think that when you kill someone in war you have to chop their heads off and cut off their ears. We have difficulty accepting this. But it comes easy to the Tugas.

That's why our war is quite different to many other wars in Africa, comrades. And our enemy, who are criminals of the worst kind, barbaric, the very worst kind of people, among the worst people to ever walk the earth, are ashamed in the face of our purity of purpose, the high-mindedness of our struggle for national liberation.

We have to fight against any mistaken ideas, any opportunistic ideas in our struggle, and we have to defend the party line to the maximum, as you already know.

Our party understood the need to mobilise the masses to fight, to organise the masses to fight, and so we mobilised the masses, we knew this had to be the first stage of our struggle, comrades, and we did a good job of it. And if we want to continue with the job, and we must continue, then we need to be continuously mobilising and organising the masses. We created armed groups almost naturally, rooted in our people's environment, supported by our people. Groups that developed bit by bit. We carried out actions against the enemy, developed our struggle step by step, created new types of fighting groups, improved our weapons, always with the support of our people. We've done our utmost to extend the war into every area of our land and today all that remains, more or less, is to take the armed struggle to the islands: Bissau island, Bolama island, the Bijagós archipelago, the Cape Verde archipelago. We've engaged in armed struggle in every other part of our country. We've even carried out attacks in

Bissau, and on Bolama too. We attacked Bolama just a few days ago, the Tugas announced it on their radio.

We have to be able, through our armed struggle, our armed resistance, to maintain our strength, to preserve our strength but also build up our strength by the day. A people that takes up arms but isn't able to preserve its strength and build it up by the day ends up losing, because an armed uprising either gains in strength and advances or else it disappears. And the best way of building up our strength is to remain constantly active.

Carrying out an armed struggle, our armed resistance, is like being a gymnast in a way, for the more actions you perform, the more movements you make, the more gymnastic you become. Many of our comrades unfortunately do not understand this and are capable of spending hours on end doing nothing, or in fact destroying our strength, because the less active a soldier is, the harder it is for them to perform the next action.

We managed to lead our people into taking up arms, step by step, in three stages: first stage, the sons and daughters of our land, people of the bush and the city, became guerrillas. Not many people, but we gradually increased the number of guerrillas, and we transformed our guerrilla forces into a regular army. But right after that, we gave people in the villages arms, creating militias. And now, bit by bit, we are providing arms to everyone, our entire population, in the liberated areas at least. An armed people. For this is the defining feature of an armed resistance, a people fighting for its liberty.

What is our objective? To destroy enemy forces; to destroy, by any means necessary, every sign of life in the enemy. War is hard, it's not nice, it's difficult, but nobody goes to war for fun, only criminals kill for the fun of killing. Nevertheless, war is killing, comrades. Whoever kills the most, and commits the fewest mistakes, wins the war. That's why our objective, in terms of our armed resistance, is to eliminate every last sign of life in the enemy. We are obliged to eliminate the colonialist Tugas; any Tuga who wields a weapon against us, against the freedom of our people, must be eliminated.

And within our struggle, we must co-ordinate our work in such a way so that we lose as few of our own armed forces as possible. Indeed, as a party we have sought to co-ordinate our fighting tactics, as well as our overall strategy, in such a way so as to minimise the number of comrades who die in the war. We must fight our war, do everything possible at every stage, but prepare today to fight tomorrow's stage better. This has been our party's guiding principle. We have recommended that our comrades act with the utmost caution, that we carry out actions against the enemy only when it's the right moment to act, but that we do act, for the land is ours. We must remain constantly active because it's constantly possible to act, given the right circumstances, circumstances we ourselves can create.

We have sought to preserve life, to protect the lives of our comrades to the maximum. And it's fair to say that many of the comrades we've lost in the fight have been lost due to mistakes they themselves made. Mistakes in terms of vigilance, mistakes in terms of security, mistakes of calculation, even mistakes in disobeying party guidelines. A lack of care taken on paths that might be mined, a lack of care taken crossing rivers that might be patrolled by enemy boats. How many times have comrades reached rivers to cross and, instead of establishing communications with the other side, where comrades are well placed to monitor the enemy's movements, they just jump in their canoes and set off? They get halfway across and encounter the Tugas.

It happened to me crossing the Rio Farim on my way back from the north of our country. Before we'd reached the other side an enemy boat appeared at the bend in the river. It was coming up right behind us when we made land, in the middle of a mangrove. And we all know that comrade Luiz Cabral, for example, had to throw himself into the water with other comrades, they very nearly died, because an enemy boat was right on top of them. How many comrades have died like this? It's just a lack of care, a lack of attention to detail, a lack of appreciation that doing a thing well means thinking it through properly. Too much trust in luck!

Comrades have died, for example, in bombings through lack of attention, not taking proper care with planes, not following the party rules – make shelters, leave the base. People die at war, it's normal to die at war, anyone who goes to war knows that they may live or they may die. But whether they die or not is to a large degree dependent on the mistakes they make, whether they do or do not follow instructions issued by the party, by whoever's leading you, on how best to preserve their life. And preserving your life doesn't mean cowardice, it doesn't mean refusing to fight the war. So many comrades have died outside of the war in this struggle, so many comrades have died outside our territory when, had they been inside our territory, they might not have died. Sometimes comrades are on the frontline for years, then one day they leave and go back to their village, and the Tugas kill them as soon as they get there. So we shouldn't be afraid to die at war, but to die for a reason, to die usefully not pointlessly (at random), just because you trusted your luck.

We are proud that, compared to other wars, be they in Africa or outside Africa, few people have died in our war relative to how many might have died, given our particular circumstances. Our party has understood how to co-ordinate the struggle to keep loss of life among comrades to a minimum. And for comrades who are wounded, we've done our utmost to aid their recovery. This is one of the strengths of our struggle. Therefore, not only must we defend ourselves, with constant action, because the best form of defence in an armed struggle like ours is action, the best form of defence is attack, but also defend the conquests we've made. That said, this shouldn't be confused with tying ourselves down just to defend a liberated area, rather than going to the front to attack the Tugas in their garrisons. We have to find ways of defending the liberated areas, but defending the liberated areas must not stop us from advancing on the enemy and hitting them with ever more strikes.

As the war has advanced, our party has managed to adapt our combat structures. Comrades will remember well what the struggle was like at the start. Bit by bit we modified our guerrilla groups, we created our army corps and our army units, we created commands, we started to co-ordinate our fight in terms of zones, different regions. Before, for example, our army command was our party's central committee, but as our armed forces grew and the war advanced, we had to separate local leadership of the party from leadership of the armed forces, although the leaders of the armed forces were also party leaders. We created war fronts, army corps, different sectors of the struggle etc. all of which shows comrades how dynamic our struggle has been.

And one of the great strengths of our struggle is the following: we have never let our struggle crystallise or become frozen in a given state of evolution. On the contrary, we have made sure it has constantly evolved, forever adapting to changing circumstances. We were able to transition from pistol to mortar, but through a process of modification, adjusting our entire structure until we arrived at the mortar. We have been able to change the nature of our fight, open up new fronts in the struggle, open up new fronts at the right moment. Sometimes, of course, given our circumstances, there's been a bit of a delay. And sometimes we have made mistakes, such as, when we created units called sections that had too many people in, we had to reduce them in size afterwards. You'll remember the Pidjiguiti section, the Vitorino section etc., which we later had to divide up because there were too many people for the command to coordinate at the time. It was too much, so we ended up with bi-groups.

For it should be said that in a war like ours, in a terrain like ours, the best way to fight is in reduced numbers, with people divided into small groups. Look at the attack a few days ago in Pitche, after the meeting we held with comrades in Gabú. We were happy with comrade Baro Seidi in the end, with the attack he led, but we told him he could still do better. He basically acted on a whim, him and Buonte Na Sansa, his political commissar. After that meeting, he went back with his soldiers and attacked Pitche with two groups of 18, entering the Tugas' garrison, catching the Tugas unawares in their shelters, demolishing a number of houses etc. In other words, we remain convinced that the best way to fight this war is with small groups and lots of courage, making the most of our weapons, our light weapons especially, comrades.

Unfortunately, ever since we've had mortars, and I've said this before, our comrades in the infantry have gotten a bit lax and left 'Patchanga' bullets rusting in their chambers. But we're fighting this, the leadership of the party is fighting this, I'm fighting this, you'll be aware, for example, that I'm taking people out of the infantry and placing them in other army corps and sending them to other places. And our comrade commanders, our leaders, thankfully have a clear understanding of this and are helping us a lot in this sense. There's no point in having five bi-groups to get the Tugas out of the Buba area or the Cubucaré area when if you join two bi-groups from one side and three from the other, to make five, we might take them north to reinforce our offensive in Chão dos Manjacos or in Nhaera, for example. Both of them are extremely important to us.

We must, therefore, with every step we take, yesterday, today and for as long as our struggle lasts, co-ordinate our struggle, have total control of our struggle, know exactly what's happening where. And we must do everything we can to ensure that relations between our armed forces and our people are as good as they possibly can be. We must convince our people, through our gestures, actions, and words, that our troops are their own sons and daughters, that they're fighting to defend them, that our soldiers come from their bosoms, their bellies, and are here to defend them, not to harm them.

Several comrades in the armed forces, even some supervisors, have hindered our party's efforts, seriously hindered our struggle, by spoiling the relationship between the armed forces and our local population. As I've already said, this is a crime of betrayal, it serves the Tugas. We have to clamp down very hard on this, really clamp down on it. And I can say to comrades: no matter how strong the party is, if we do not maintain a good relationship with our people, day in day out, if we do not reinforce and grow this relationship every single day, through political work and the concrete actions of our armed forces, our struggle will be condemned to failure.

In order to recruit new people to the armed forces, to ensure that we have the local population's support, even to justify the sacrifices we're asking everyone to make, it is essential, comrades, that we develop, on a daily basis, good relations between the armed forces and the population of our country. Does this mean that we must avoid causing any harm in places where we must cause harm to advance? Patience, comrades, we will do what we have to. But we will not cause harm out of individual interest, because someone is obsessed with beating people up, kicking out or whatever. We do it only in the interest of our own people.

As I've already said, it's good for us to be clear, at every moment of our armed struggle, about where we're heading, about how our struggle is progressing at every given moment. Our objective is to get the Portuguese colonialists out of our country, out of Guinea and Cape Verde. The idea, the aim isn't to just lash out at the Tugas, to throw them to the ground like we would in one of our country's wrestling bouts. Our objective is to get the colonialist Tugas out of our land.

Look at the case of the Vietnam War, which led to the independence of the Republic of North Vietnam. When the war ended, with triumph for the Vietnamese at Dien Bien Phu, where they surrounded and defeated around 30 000 French, the French had 500,000 soldiers in Vietnam, well-positioned, in all areas. But because of the defeat at Dien Bien Phu, which was an enemy camp, and because of the political pressure in the international sphere, France was obliged to concede. Some army officials were furious at the time, such as General Salan and others. Why? Because the French were still strong, stronger than ever.

Take the specific case of Algeria. When Algeria gained independence through negotiations at Evian, the French presence had never been stronger in Algeria, with French troops everywhere, all ganged together, hundreds of thousands of French troops as well as a million French civilians, many of them armed. But it was because of political work, political pressure exerted within the country, and because of the courage of the Algerian people, tremendous courage, comrades, the great sacrifices made by people in the cities. When, for example, the French outlawed protests in Algiers (saying that anyone who took to the streets would be killed), the Algerians, men, women and children, went out into the streets one Sunday waving their flag. The French killed over 600 Algerians in a single day, on the streets of Algiers. But the next Sunday the Algerians took to the streets again. Courage is required, comrades. We should appreciate that in our war, compared to the wars for independence in Vietnam or Algeria, we've had it okay, hardly anyone has died.

And while we wage war, our people in Bissau delight in our victories. My goodness, people are being invited to all kinds of places they never used to go, permits to go to Portugal, Mr Mamadú Djassi has appeared in the newspaper, esteemed Mrs Dona Mariama Camará in Bissau, reaping the rewards of our struggle already. In Algeria, while soldiers were fighting in the crags, the bush and the mountains, people in the city rose up in force, in protest and unarmed, to show the French that they simply had to leave. And because this prompted assassinations and massacres, world opinion, public opinion even in France, turned against the French government.

It can be said that one of the major forces that helped win the war in Algeria was public opinion in France itself, and those sons and daughters of Algeria who lived in France, numbering more than 500,000, who committed acts of sabotage in France itself. But as you know, many others sided with the French, so there were Algerians killing other Algerians, in Algeria and in France. But the force of global public opinion won out, along with the courage of the Algerian people and the sacrifices they agreed to make, because more than one and a half million people died in Algeria, comrades, died for their independence. Twice the entire population of Guinea died in the war in Algeria during seven and a half years of struggle.

But the objective of a war of liberation is not just to get the enemy to ask for mercy, to admit that they've lost. That's not it. It's for them to sit down and admit that we're right, that we should take control of our own country. That's why we must understand where we're going with this war. And the more we beat the enemy the better, in every little battle and confrontation, because then the sooner the day will come when they decide to leave because things have gotten so bad.

Thankfully, the Tugas already know they've lost here, but they haven't left yet, don't forget, so we haven't defeated them yet. They know they have to hold on because Angola and Mozambique are holding on and so they have to be strong and hold on a bit longer, provided we don't advance on Cape Verde. The day the struggle starts for real in Cape Verde, further down the line, the day we take up arms there, the war will end here for certain. That doesn't mean it can't end without war breaking out in Cape Verde, because it can. But it's true that when we launch the war in Cape Verde, the Tugas will be afflicted on all fronts.

Comrades, it forever bears repeating that the essential objective of our armed resistance is to achieve something we've been unable to achieve through politics alone. It is to open up new prospects for our people, prospects of independence, peace, work and justice, the prospect of progress. We are convinced that our party can achieve this.

In accordance with our people's destiny, a destiny we ourselves are now shaping, and in accordance with the historical demands of our time, our party's mission is to, through our political, economic and cultural resistance, and through the hard but necessary actions of our armed resistance, open up a new path to our people, give them the security they require and assure them that tomorrow their lives will progress. This is our mission, comrades. Especially those new comrades who are gaining ever more responsibility within our party.

New Year's Message, January 1969

Extracts from message recorded in the studios of Radio Libertação and broadcast on 1 January 1969.

To the people of Guinea and Cabo Verde
To the cadres, militants and combatants of our Party
Compatriots and comrades

At the beginning of this new year of 1969, in which our armed struggle for national liberation ends its sixth year, I have great pleasure in addressing to you this message of greetings, of felicitations and of certainty of final victory for our glorious fight against the criminal Portuguese colonialists.

Our people, the cadres, militants and combatants of our great Party have good reason to celebrate the new year and the anniversary of our struggle with strengthened hope and with greater certainty of the final victory of our struggle for the independence, freedom, peace and progress of our people in Guinea and Cabo Verde.

As you all know, we started virtually from nothing. In the face of the repression and the crimes of the Portuguese colonialists we managed to organise and consolidate our Party and, step by step, to develop the armed struggle in Guinea, and we have now freed from colonial domination more than two thirds of our country and more than half our population. We are preparing for a new phase of the struggle in Cabo Verde. We are developing production, education, health facilities and trade in our liberated areas. We have made the name of our people well known in Africa and in the world. We have created and are creating hundreds of political, military, technical and scientific cadres. We guarantee, with complete certainty, the continuation of our struggle until final victory.

For six years the criminal Portuguese colonialists, with the help of their allies, have used every available means of destruction against us and have increased the strength of their troops sevenfold; they have changed their governor and commanders as we would change shirts; they have tried every sort of propaganda, lies and political intrigues to demobilise our people and our combatants; they have committed acts of aggression against neighbouring countries and have done everything possible to halt our struggle – but they have not succeeded.

On the contrary, our people are becoming more aware of their strength and our Party is growing stronger each day, our armed forces are more powerful than ever, with more combatants and cadres, with greater experience and more powerful weapons. This, compatriots and comrades, is the greatest victory of our people and our great Party in these six years: the successful continuation of our struggle, the constant improvement of our political and military organisation, the ever-growing certainty that no power on earth can halt the advance of our people towards national independence. This is also the greatest defeat for the Portuguese colonialists who have done everything to stop our struggle but today are forced to recognise that this is impossible.

Compatriots and comrades: those of you who have heard or read the speech of the new head of the Portuguese government to the National Assembly of his country will be proud of the outstanding place given to our struggle in that speech. In fact, the new head of the criminal Portuguese colonialists could not conceal the desperate situation of the colonial war in our country and in his speech he had to make propaganda for the successes and importance of our struggle.

You will also have heard the speech made in Bissao a few days ago by the military governor of the criminal Portuguese colonialists. This speech too was good propaganda for our struggle because it clearly showed the desperate situation of the Portuguese military governor here in our country and because it once again showed to our people and our combatants that our struggle is a just one and that we have a right to the progress for which we are fighting. Money to buy more traditional chiefs, salary increases for officials, wage increases for workers, schools, hospitals, surfaced roads, various agricultural improvements, electricity and water for all houses, ventilator fans and refrigerators for families, etc, etc – all this was promised by the military governor of Bissao.

Our people, whether they be in the towns or in the countryside, know what the promises of the criminal Portuguese colonialists are worth, but they know above all that our dignity as an African people, our struggle, the independence we have already won in the greater part of Guinea, cannot be bought. They know too that without our struggle, without the great victories won by our Party, the Portuguese military governor would not have needed to make all these promises in order to try to deceive us and remain in our country. This is why on hearing promises of so many good things our people in town and country will certainly have said as usual: 'Djarama PAIGC – thanks to the Party!'

At the beginning of this new year of struggle we must tell the criminal Portuguese colonialists, loudly and clearly, that if this is the way they want things they are going to pay dearly, very dearly, not to *remain* here but to be *driven out* of our country! Whatever works they hastily carry out on Bissao island or in some urban centres, whatever last-minute efforts they may make, they are surely going to be run out of our country, because our people are going to free ourselves completely from the odious Portuguese colonial domination and build for ourself, through work in dignity and independence, a life of liberty, justice and progress for all, the main objective in the programme of our great Party.

We are going to make the year 1969 – which marks the 10th anniversary of the Pijiguiti massacre – a year of decisive enlargement of the struggle, a year of even greater victories than those won previously, a year in which we will prove to the criminal Portuguese colonialists that our people does not need their consent to be a free and independent nation with its own personality in the international field.

We must mete out just punishment to the traitors among our people, those who continue to serve the criminal Portuguese colonialists against the interests of our people. We are going to show these traitors clearly that it is now time to decide: either they must cease being the servants of the Portuguese colonialists or they must be totally destroyed.

We must intensify our struggle, our political work and our military action, and bring armed struggle to every corner of our country in which there are still colonialist troops. In our political work, we are going to create more *comités de base* for the Party, increase production, improve education, health services and all the other services of our developing state. In the armed struggle we are going to use more weapons, and more powerful weapons, reinforcing the initiative and ease of movement and fire for our Popular Army, to inflict new and more crushing defeats on the criminal Portuguese colonialists.

Until the total liberation of our people in Guinea and Cabo Verde.
Forward, compatriots and comrades, in our glorious struggle for national liberation!
Long live the courageous combatants, cadres and militants of our Party!
Long live the PAIGC, strength, guide and light of our heroic people!
Death to the criminal Portuguese colonialists!

The Tactic of Division

Excerpt from a message in September 1970, on the occasion of the 14th anniversary of the founding of the PAIGC.

Lately the Portuguese colonialist criminals have resorted to another tactic in order to attempt to end our struggle: divide our people and get Africans to fight Africans. This is an old and widely used tactic, both by colonialists and in colonial imperialist wars, but we must denounce it and combat it vigourously, so that this new and criminal initiative taken by the enemy shall suffer a great defeat. The colonialists have now invented what they call the 'ethnic congresses' in our country. Their aim is to co-opt some of our brothers with high positions and honours, and even more to destroy the awareness and the national unity which both our party and the struggle have already achieved. By holding these so-called congresses and promising each ethnic group its own leader, the colonialists hope to revive the tribal tendencies which we have already extinguished, and to sabotage from the beginning the possibilities of a harmonious national existence for our people in the independence which – they know it well enough – we will certainly conquer.

By pretending to want to create a political authority for those populations in the form of chiefs that they can still control, they really wish to prepare the field for new conflicts among the ethnic groups, so that the Balanta may not be able to relate to the Manjacos nor the Fulas with the Pepels, in order that confusion be established among us, thus rendering impossible the life of the African nation which we are building. The colonialists, with all their congresses, their activities bring obvious harm to our people. But they will not succeed, because our party exists, because our people is increasingly more aware of its rights and duties as an African people, because no manoeuvre will be able to block the victorious march of our armed struggle for liberation. And those who, either by ambition or opportunism, allow themselves to be deceived by the lies of congresses will waste their time and will be marked as deliberate traitors to the interests of our people and of those of Africa.

Always seeking to divide our people, the Portuguese colonialist criminals have been developing a great campaign against the Cape Verdeans on their radio, especially in the vernacular languages of Guinea. In this campaign, as well as in a certain number of letters sent to leaders of our party, with promises of honours and riches, they claim that they will expel all Cape Verdeans who serve colonialism in Guinea, and that they will offer the positions which the latter now occupy to what they name 'the real children of Guinea'.

The colonialists know that the political, moral and fighting unity of our people in Guinea and the Cape Verde Islands is the main strength of our party and of our struggle. They also wish to destroy it, by attempting to create hate where it has never existed, to diffuse lies, to stir up lust and to awaken a sense of ambition and opportunism among those who, even if they are not participating in our struggle, are nevertheless nationalists who wish the independence of our country. But even there they have completely failed. Firstly, since the real nationalists from Guinea are neither racist nor opportunist, and they know who their leaders are and the value of a unity of the people of Guinea and the Cape Verde Islands.

Secondly, because the colonialists are lying when they say that they are going to expel the Cape Verdeans. They will not be able to do so, because they need the Cape Verdeans and the Guineans who are in their service. And the colonialists are well aware of the service which they would render our Party if they really did expel the Cape Verdeans from Guinea. But they have already rendered us this service, because they have clearly shown to all the children of Cape Verde who serve the colonialists in Guinea that we are right: the colonialists use them while at the same time having no consideration whatsoever for them.

They must thus, together with the best children of our country – of Guinea and Cape Verde – become aware of their situation and support our Party and our struggle, with a view to the total liberation of our African nation. The colonialists have already failed, since their propaganda has not until now found an echo other than from those individuals who are socially *déclassé*, drunkards, robbers, even criminals, integrated in a so-called 'Committee for a Better Guinea'. But these traitors, who have not the least respect for our people, are aware of one thing: they must enjoy the privileges of colonialism while it lasts, because it will be the real children of Guinea and Cape Verde, who are militants and fighters from our party, who will condemn them and punish them for being in the service of the enemy of both our country and of Africa.

Portugal is not an
Imperialist Country

Extract of a speech given at a solidarity rally in Helsinki, Finland on 20 October 1971.

You know that in our fight we do not try to explain to our militants, our people, our populations, how deep and complex is the fight against imperialism. Our people's situation was such, prior to the beginning of the fight, our political experience so slight, that it would have been difficult for us to pose the question of this fight on the basis of one directly aimed against colonialism and imperialism. We were forced to conduct our people's mobilisation and organisation for the struggle, at first, on the basis of concrete everyday problems of their life, moving later to larger concepts, to generalised views of colonialism and imperialism. Today people understand very well what is meant by colonialism, and Portuguese colonialism in particular, and are beginning to develop in their minds a clear notion of the phenomenon of imperialism. But last year, during a meeting with the members of our party's local units, I was discussing with them problems concerning Portuguese colonialism, and I said that Portugal is not an imperialist country; it is a colonialist country in the imperialist chain, but that its own nature is not that of an imperialist country.

Anyone familiar with Portugal's economy throughout its history quickly realises that the Portuguese economic substructure has never attained a level which we may term imperialist. After the Treaty of Methuen of 1701, Portugal became a semi-colony of England, and at the level of Africa's exploitation it has been and still is nothing but an intermediate agent of our people's imperialist exploitation. It is the policeman of this exploitation, but it is not the real imperialist power which exploits our people. We have but to be reminded that most Portuguese industries, including that of the famous Porto wine, railways, telephones, etc. belong, just as do Portuguese mines, to foreign enterprises. We have but to be reminded that more than 60 per cent of its exports from Angola and Mozambique go to the U.S., England, Belgium, France, West Germany, but not to Portugal.

But my peasant comrade, from a village party unit, who knew nothing of such things, when he heard me say that Portugal is not imperialist, told me; 'Cabral, everyone tells us that we fight against imperialism, that we fight against the Portuguese, but now you're telling us that they are not imperialists; so, tell me: who is Mr. Imperialism that everyone speaks about but no one sees?' We see thus posed, in the language of a peasant, the main question of the fight against imperialism, that is, the distinction between imperialism and imperialist domination. Sometimes we hear people cry out 'Down with imperialism' in their own country, but in reality they are fighting against imperialist domination. It appears to be of vital importance to distinguish imperialism from imperialist domination, to situate both in their historical perspective and to define their geographical locations.

As you well know, a new system of production and its distribution, called capitalism, emerged historically out of the Middle Ages. In certain countries capitalism developed with all the contradictions inherent in the development known as imperialism. Imperialism – as you know better than myself – is the result of the gigantic concentration of financial capital in capitalist countries through the creation of monopolies, and firstly of the monopolies of capitalist enterprises. This monopoly domination is essentially and characteristically an economic phenomenon. Then there follow implications of a political, social, cultural, moral character. We must thus distinguish the economic fact of these implications on the one hand, and characterise the relationship of capitalism with the rest of the world, on the other. It is not an over-statement to assert that, from the moment that the economic and financial (thus monopolistic) domination attained a certain level and thus was consolidated, a relentless struggle began between free enterprise capital and financial capital, the latter represented by monopolies and banks. Even a superficial analysis of contemporary and present-day economic history shows that, in general, financial capital i.e. imperialism, is the victorious element in this fight. This is to say that capitalism has given birth to imperialism, and has created the conditions necessary for the destruction of the former.

You know that this new situation is characterised by complex contradictions that lead to a permanent confrontation, be it an open and peaceful one or not, between the imperialist countries themselves, in search of a new equilibrium in the relationship of forces, and in function of the need to obtain raw materials and markets. Imperialism appears, when analysed in this fashion, with its real face, situated where it really belongs, that is, in the capitalist countries which have become imperialist ones. Thus, imperialism exists in capitalist countries and not in our countries.

It was the steadily increasing need for new markets and raw materials, the insatiable thirst for surplus value, which determined the imperialist domination of the world. By the time imperialism had attained a very high level, it had already made a first division of the world; it is at the beginning of this century that it proceeded, as you know, to make a new partition, particularly of Africa, by means of the Berlin Conference. That is to say that the internal concentration of financial capital in capitalist countries goes hand in hand with the monopolisation of colonies, their conquest by imperialist countries.

It is in the framework of this colonial monopoly that the sharpest contradictions among capitalist countries themselves have been revealed, leading to two world wars. It is also in this framework that it is interesting to consider how Portugal, a non-imperialist country, an underdeveloped country, succeeded in preserving its colonies, despite the fierce jealousy of the imperialist countries. We can say clearly that England is responsible for this success. At the time of the Berlin Conference, Portugal was really a semi-colony of England. England pursued the tactic of defending Portuguese interests vigourously because it knew that, if Portugal could preserve its colonies, England would be able to exploit them as if they were its own. England prevented Angola and Mozambique in particular, but also Guinea, the Cape Verde Islands, etc., from becoming prey for the other imperialist countries. In the course of the partition, they were preserved by Portugal but exploited by England as well.

Thus, imperialist domination is the economic and political domination of non-capitalist countries or peoples by imperialism or imperialist powers. This is to say that we consider imperialist countries as a core in the general framework of the world economy. They have created on their periphery countries dominated by imperialism. If a country was still at a non-capitalist stage of development, the domination was purely colonialist. If such a country had already certain beginnings of capitalism, the domination was neo-colonialist, or semi-colonial. Thus imperialism, or rather the domination of people by financial capital, operates in colonialist, neo-colonialist, or semi-colonialist forms. It is this domination which is found in our countries, from Vietnam or China, to Cuba, or Tierra del Fuego, or Chile, as well as for a time in certain European countries, such as Portugal and others. It is this imperialist-dominated area which is generally called today the poor South in contrast with the rich North.

But it is important to distinguish the various situations found in both the poor South and the rich North. It is not all homogeneous. We lack the time necessary to analyse this distinction. We would simply like to emphasise its existence. Countries such as Sweden, Finland and others, even though they belong to the rich North, have never been imperialist countries.

What is important is to conclude by saying that the fight against imperialism must be fought within the imperialist countries, and the struggle against imperialist domination must be fought in our own countries. In this fight against imperialist domination in our countries, we consider that the most important struggle today is the one directed against neo-colonialism. In its classical form colonialism exists no longer, even if we are fighting an archaic Portuguese colonialism, whereas neo-colonialism continues to establish its roots everywhere in the world by means of puppets in order to deceive the people in their struggle for real liberation. Cuba fought against a neo-colonialism practically as old as its fictitious independence, and was able to win. Vietnam presently fights courageously against an also quite neo-neo-colonialism, and will undoubtedly win in South Vietnam just as it has won in North Vietnam.

What is important is to recognise the obvious character of the intimate link between the fight against imperialism in imperialist countries, and that against the imperialist domination in our countries. The eventual destruction of financial capital within the capitalist world necessarily implies the destruction of imperialist domination. If, by some miracle, monopoly financial capital in the United States were to be destroyed, and if this country were to become a progressive one the Vietnamese people's fight would cease to make sense.

What is important is to realise that the progressive destruction of imperialist domination of our countries is a decisive factor in the destruction of financial capital in imperialist countries. In this intimate and dynamic connection between these struggles, is located the decisive importance of the unity and solidarity of all anti-imperialist forces in the world. Unity and solidarity are decisive factors for the overall success of the fight against imperialism.

The Danger of
Destruction from Within

*From a message sent in March 1972 to all those holding posts of responsibility in
the PAIGC.*

Driven to despair in face of the victorious advance of our struggle and the defeats
which they suffer every day in our country as well as on the African and international fronts; convinced of the difficulty if not of the impossibility of buying or of
bribing the leaders by means of work *outside of the party*; frightened by the name
and prestige which our party is increasingly acquiring in Africa and the rest of
the world; realizing that their policy in Guinea will not bring success, since the
population of the urban centres is more and more interested in the struggle and in
the party – the Portuguese colonial criminals and their representatives in Guinea
have decided to establish a new plan in order to attempt to stop our struggle and
in order to ensure the continuation of our people's exploitation: *they now wish to
destroy our party from within*. They are determined to do everything – to pay whatever
price so that they may sow confusion and division within the leadership of the
party, in order to weaken the unity of the party, to destroy the party from within.

What is the plan of the Portuguese colonial criminals and of their representatives in our country?

According to the information which I have received from various reliable
sources, this is their plan:

First stage: Profit from the fact that a large number of our compatriots are
presently leaving Bissau and other urban centres in order to join the party, by
introducing within us some of their reliable African agents, to whom Spínola
promises honours and money, were they to succeed in their mission.[20] These
agents, who may be either new or old party members, are trained by the PIDE in
the techniques of political sabotage, provocation and the instigation of confusion
within an organisation. *In the first stage these agents must:*

a) pretend that they are good militants, and be devoted to the struggle of our
    people against the Portuguese colonialists.
b) make a detailed reconnaissance of the life of the party, its problems, and
    mainly of the weaknesses of our organisation, so that they may be fully

---

20 *Editor's note*: General António Sebastião Ribeiro de Spínola was chief of the
    Portuguese armed forces at the time of the struggle for independence.

exploited; inform the colonialists of the situation within the party.

c) detect who are the 'dissatisfied' militants, and principally who are the 'dissatisfied' leaders; establish bonds of friendship and comradeship with such 'dissatisfied' ones, and always support their point of view in what concerns the leadership of the party, particularly the Secretary-General.

d) take advantage of every occasion to sow confusion in the minds of the militants and leaders, to provoke, and remove authority from and disrespect the leadership of the party, in particular the Secretary-General. In order to do so, these agents must always uphold a position as 'defenders' of the militants' rights, incite them into disrespecting the leadership, and create the spirit of indiscipline and division within the Party.

e) sow misunderstanding within the Party, on the basis of racism and, if possible, on the basis of tribalism, even on religious differences, in an attempt to pit the Guineans against the Cape Verdeans, the latter against the former, the tribes one against the other, the illiterate against the intellectuals, the Muslims against the non-Muslims and vice-versa – all this in order to destroy the unity of our party and the unity of our people, which are the main strength of our struggle.

Second stage: After having created confusion and division within the Party and obtaining the support of the 'malcontents', after being certain that a certain number of militants and leaders would be willing to betray the leadership of the Party, the Secretary-General in particular, these agents would:

a) create an underground network of militants and leaders in every sector of our life and struggle, notably among the armed forces. To do this they would have to contact the leaders the militants, and the fighters who, for whatever reason may be 'dissatisfied' with the leadership of the Party. These contacts would have as their aim sabotaging the action of the real leaders who are loyal to the Party, and subsequently creating confusion and division all over.

b) create a 'leadership' parallel to the real leadership of the Party, composed of one or more agents and several 'dissatisfied' leaders. The agents would do everything in their power in order to make some of the present leaders of the Party participate in this underground sabotage group, in particular those who, on the basis of the errors which they have committed and the criticisms of which they were the object, are not 'happy' with the leadership of the Party, in particular that of the Secretary-General.

c) This underground 'leadership' of sabotage and destruction of the Party would then contact the parties and the governments of the neighbouring countries, notably that of the Republic of Guinea, in order to obtain their support against the real leadership of the Party, particularly against the Secretary-General. They would also, as far as possible, contact some ambassadors of friendly countries, in an attempt to create confusion, to show that there is 'division' within the party and to obtain the support of such countries.

d) At the same time as they are engaged in this work of internal destruction of the party and of its external support, the agents and their accomplices would do everything in their power to provoke and bring into discredit the Secretary-General of the Party, to sabotage his authority and prestige, to prepare the way for the elimination of the Secretary-General from the executive of the party, or even if necessary, his physical destruction. On the other hand, the agents and their colleagues would conduct a major propaganda campaign to popularize among the militants and fighters the names of other leaders (former and current), which they would present as being the sole and true leaders of the party, against the leadership of the Secretary-General.

e) In this second stage, in agreement with prepared plans, the colonialists and their allies will engage in a large campaign at the African and international levels about the 'divisions' within the party in order to discredit the present executive and in particular the Secretary-General. Within the country, the colonial troops, would launch major offensives in order to terrorise and discourage the populations and the combatants.

Third stage: If the colonialists' agents who penetrated our ranks were not to be discovered and exposed in time, and if they would succeed in accomplishing their mission, above all if they were to obtain the cooperation of some of our most important party leaders as well as the support of the neighbouring countries, particularly the Republic of Guinea, then there would begin the third stage during which they would:

a) strike a blow against the present party executive, in order to eliminate the Secretary-General and all the leaders loyal to the line of our party, to the unity and struggle of our people in Guinea and in the Cape Verde Islands against the Portuguese colonialists, for the total independence of our African country. If they are not able to accomplish this, they will try to assassinate the Secretary-General as well as some other leaders.

b) form a new party executive based on racism and on tribalism and religious beliefs if necessary, in order to ensure the division of our people and its demobilisation and capitulation to the colonialists. They would change the name of our Party.

c) stop all the activities of the struggle both inside our country and abroad, notably in the Republic of Guinea; take possession of all the goods of the party, with the support of the traitors, in order to paralyse all the activities of the struggle and to prevent resupplying the armed forces; arrest and destroy all members loyal to the party.

d) contact the Portuguese Government, with Spínola as the intermediary, for the purpose of false 'negotiations', with the aim of obtaining the 'internal autonomy' of Guinea (Bissau), for a so-called 'self-determination under the Portuguese flag'. The creation of a puppet 'government' of Guinea, which would from then on be called 'State of Guinea' and which would belong to the 'Portuguese Community'.

e) In line with the promises and plans of Spínola and the Portuguese colonialists, important posts in the political scene and within the armed forces would be assigned to all those agents who would accomplish this mission, as well as to all the leaders of the party who would be their accomplices and who would help carry out the plans. Moreover, they would all be well remunerated for their betrayal of our great party.

On the African Revolution: Homage to Kwame Nkrumah

This speech was given at the symposium organised by the Democratic Party of Guinea, at the People's Palace in Conakry, on the occasion of the day dedicated to Kwame Nkrumah, 13 May 1972.

After the speeches we have heard today and, most of all, after the statement, as militant as it was moving, by our elder brother and companion in struggle, President Ahmed Sékou Touré, what more is there to say? But we must speak, for at this moment if we did not speak, our heart might break.

Here, beside the mortal remains of President Kwame Nkrumah – one of the greatest men mankind has seen this century – we are living an epoch-making moment in the history of the struggle for liberation and progress in Africa; we might say simply, in history.

We must, therefore, meditate deeply on this moment, and draw all the lessons from events: as President Kwame Nkrumah would say, the positive lessons and the negative lessons.

Before saying a very little of what I have in my heart and my head, I should like to greet all the delegates here and on behalf of the African liberation movements, to recall that the fact that we should all be here together, beside the mortal remains of President Kwame Nkrumah, is not only evidence of respect and consideration for this person and his achievement, but likewise a pledge to the total liberation of Africa and the progress of African peoples.

On behalf of the combatants of our Party, who are the legitimate representatives of our people in Guiné and Cape Verde, we should like to offer our fraternal condolences to his widow, Madame Nkrumah, to the whole Nkrumah family, to the President and our companion in struggle Ahmed Sékou Touré, who was always a faithful comrade of President Nkrumah to the Ghanaian people and to the whole of Africa!

However, our tears should not drown the truth. We, as freedom fighters, are not weeping for the death of a man, even of a man who was a companion in struggle and exemplary revolutionary. For, as President Ahmed Sékou Touré often says: 'What is man before the infinite and transcendent becoming of peoples and mankind? Nor are we weeping for the Ghanaian people, whose finest accomplishments, whose most legitimate aspirations are smothered. Nor are we weeping for Africa's betrayal. But we are weeping with hatred for those who were capable of betraying Nkrumah in the ignoble service of imperialism!

But treason, like fidelity, is characteristic of man. Treason to Ghana, as to the Congo and elsewhere in Africa, has a positive aspect: it shows the true human dimension of African man. And, in this specific case, it allows one better to grasp the true stature of Nkrumah as a political giant, and contributes to immortalising him further.

We have heard talk of rehabilitation for Nkrumah. We understand this expression only in the sphere of the language of diplomacy, or of tactics, because for us, as freedom fighters, those who must truly be rehabilitated are those who in betraying the Ghanaian people and Africa betrayed Nkrumah. Africa, by demanding through the voice of the people of the Republic of Guinea, interpreted faithfully, as always, by President Ahmed Sékou Touré, that Nkrumah be restored to his rightful place – on the highest peak of the Kilimanjaro of the African revolution – Africa is rehabilitated before itself and before history.

We have heard much said today about the action and gigantic achievement accomplished by Nkrumah in a relatively short time.

President Nkrumah, to whom we pay homage, is primarily the strategist of genius in the struggle against classic colonialism. He is the man who created what we might call 'African positivism', to which he himself gave the name *positive action*. Positive action has been the best, the most appropriate solution found for the struggle, in the context of British colonial domination.

We pay homage to the pioneer of Pan-Africanism, to the tireless, constantly inspired combatant for African unity. We pay homage to the avowed enemy of neo-colonialism in Africa and elsewhere, to the strategist of the economic development of his country.

As far as neo-colonialism is concerned, everyone now knows that Nkrumah's book *Neocolonialism: The Last Stage of Imperialism* is a profound, materialist analysis of reality, the terrible reality which neo-colonialism is in Africa. As far as his country's development is concerned, we reject the slanderous criticisms by Africa's enemies – and some of the Western press, even some cesspits which pass themselves off as being the African press – criticisms which purport to show Nkrumah's economic bankruptcy. Everyone knows very well that from 1970, on the basis of all the economic measures taken by Nkrumah and his government, Ghana was to become a fully developing country which would show the world that Africa was not only able to win political independence but also to build its economic independence.

We hail in Nkrumah the freedom fighter for the African peoples, who was always able to grant unconditional support to the national liberation movements. And we wish to say to you here that for us in Guiné and Cape Verde, while it is true that the primordial external factor in the development of our struggle was the independence of the Republic of Guinea – the heroic '*No*' of the Guinean people on 28 September 1958 – it is also true that we embarked on the struggle with the strong encouragement of the practical support of Ghana, and particularly of President Nkrumah.

We hail finally Nkrumah, the philosopher and thinker. As President Sékou Touré said, philosopher and thinker because he could apply himself to the consequent practice.

We hail likewise and pay homage to the personal friend, to the comrade who could always encourage us in the difficult but exciting struggle we are waging against the most retrograde of all colonialisms. Portuguese colonialism.

We must remember at this moment that every coin has two sides. All of life's realities have two aspects: positive and negative. Positive action always opposes and is opposed by a negative action and vice versa. If President Nkrumah lives on in the history of Africa and the world, it is because the balance of his *positive action* is not only positive, but also shows an epoch-making achievement, fruitful creative activity in the service of the African people and of mankind.

We must however draw the lesson from all events. Even at this moment of grief, we must ask ourselves some questions the better to understand the past, live the present and prepare for the future.

For example, what economic and political factors made the success of the betrayal of Ghana possible, despite Nkrumah's personality, courage and positive action?

True, imperialism is cruel and unscrupulous, but we must not lay all the blame on its broad back. For, as African people say: 'Rice only cooks inside the pot'.

Just how far would the success of the betrayal of Ghana have been linked or not to the questions of class struggle, contradictions in the social structure, the role of the Party and other institutions, including the armed forces, in the framework of a newly independent state. Just how far, we wonder, would the success of the betrayal of Ghana have been linked or not linked to the question of a correct definition of that historical entity, that craftsman of history, the people, and to their daily action in defence of their own conquests in independence. Or then, just how far might not the success of the betrayal be linked to the key question of choice of men in the revolution?

Pondering on these questions might perhaps enable us to understand better the greatness of Nkrumah's achievement, likewise the complexity of the problems that he had to face, so often alone. Such problems will surely bring us to the conclusion that, so long as imperialism is in existence, an independent African state must be a liberation movement in power, or it will not be independent.

President Nkrumah understood this truth very well and never tired of pointing it out to us during the long, friendly conversations that we had whether in Accra or here in Conakry. It is enough to read his works again to see that they are studded with preoccupations over these questions.

There are truths that we must utter to each other at this moment, but we must above all tell those who would like to shed crocodile tears over the mortal remains of Kwame Nkrumah.

The African peoples and particularly the freedom fighters cannot be fooled. Let no one come and tell us that Nkrumah died from cancer of the throat or any other sickness. No, Nkrumah was killed by the cancer of betrayal, which we must tear out by the roots in Africa, if we really want to liquidate imperialist domination definitively on this continent.

But we, Africans, strongly believe that the dead remain living at our side. We are societies of the living and the dead. Nkrumah will rise again each dawn in the heart and determination of freedom fighters, in the action of all true African patriots. Nkrumah's immortal spirit presides and will preside at the judgment of history on this decisive phase in our peoples' lives, in lifelong struggle against imperialist domination and for the genuine progress of our continent.

We, the liberation movements, will not forgive those who betrayed Nkrumah. The Ghanaian people will not forgive. Progressive mankind will not forgive. Let those who are due for rehabilitation make haste to rehabilitate themselves. It is not yet too late.

As an African proverb says: 'Those who spit at the sky will soil their face'. Those who have tried to soil the brilliant personality of Kwame Nkrumah should now understand very well that the African people are right. Another African proverb says: 'A hand, however big, can never cover the sky'. There it is; those who have tried to disparage the magnificent achievement of Kwame Nkrumah must today admit that this African proverb is right as well.

Before closing – although we know that we should not do this – allow me, on behalf of all the African freedom fighters, to offer fraternal and militant thanks to the people of the Republic of Guinea, to the Democratic Party of Guinea, and to their beloved leader. President Ahmed Sékou Touré, for this further evidence of unlimited courage they have shown us. First, in welcoming Kwame Nkrumah, and giving him his due position as co-president of this Republic. Then, in insisting and by fighting for the national funeral to be held here in Guinea. African soil and symbol of African liberation and dignity.

If at this moment of grief in our life, a new understanding could be born between Guinea and Ghana, we should all be deeply content and it would be another significant achievement of Kwame Nkrumah.

For us, as Africans, the best homage we can pay to Kwame Nkrumah and his immortal memory, is reinforced vigilance in all fields of the struggle, more strongly developed and intensified struggle, the total liberation of Africa, success in development and economic, social and cultural progress for our peoples, and in the building of African unity. That was the fundamental aim of Kwame Nkrumah's action and thought. This is the oath we should all take before history in respect of the African continent.

For us, freedom fighters, the finest flowers with which we can garland Kwame Nkrumah's memory, are the bullets, the shells, the missiles of every kind that we fire against the colonialist and racist forces in Africa.

We are certain, absolutely certain that framed by the eternal green of the African forests, flowers of crimson like the blood of martyrs and of gold like the harvests of plenty will bloom over the grave of Kwame Nkrumah; for Africa will triumph.

The Role of Culture in the Struggle for Independence

A paper prepared for the UNESCO Meeting of Experts on the Concept of Race, Identity and Dignity, held in Paris in July 1972.

The struggle of peoples for national liberation and independence has become a tremendous force for human progress and is beyond doubt an essential feature of the history of our time.

Objective analysis of imperialism as a fact or historical phenomenon that is 'natural', even 'necessary', to the economic and political evolution of a great part of mankind, reveals that imperialist rule, with its train of misery, pillage, crimes and its destruction of human and cultural values, was not a purely negative reality.

The huge accumulation of capital in a half dozen countries of the northern hemisphere as the result of piracy, sack of other people's property and unbridled exploitation of their labour, did more than engender colonial monopoly, the sharing-out of the world and imperialist dominion. In the rich countries, imperialist capital, ever looking for higher profits, heightened man's creative capacity. Aided by the accelerated progress of science and technology, it profoundly transformed the means of production, stepped-up the social organisation of work and raised the standard of living of vast sections of the population.

In the colonised countries, colonisation usually arrested the historical development of the people – when it did not lead to their total or gradual elimination. Here imperialist capital imposed new types of relationships within the indigenous society whose structure became more complex. It aroused, fomented, inflamed or resolved social contradictions and conflicts.

With the circulation of money and the development of the domestic and foreign markets, it introduced new elements into the economy. It led to the birth of new nations out of ethnic groups or peoples at varying stages of historical development.

It is no defence of imperialist domination to recognise that it opened up new worlds to a world whose dimensions it reduced, that it revealed new phases in the development of human societies and, in spite of or because of the prejudices, discriminations and crimes it occasioned, helped to impart a deeper knowledge of mankind, moving as one, as a unified whole amid the complex diversity of its various forms of development.

Imperialist rule fostered a multilateral, gradual (sometimes abrupt) confrontation on the different continents not only between different men but between different societies.

The practice of imperialist rule – its affirmation or its negation – demanded and still demands a more or less accurate knowledge of the people dominated and their historical background (economic, social and cultural). This knowledge is necessarily expressed in terms of comparison with the dominating power's own historical background.

Such knowledge is an imperative necessity for imperialist rule which results from the usually violent confrontation of two different identities, distinct in their historical backgrounds and antagonistic in their functions. Despite its unilateral, subjective and often unjust character, the search for such knowledge contributed to the general enrichment of the human and social sciences.

Indeed, man has never shown such interest in learning about other men and other societies as during this century of imperialist domination. An unprecedented amount of information, hypotheses and theories were thus accumulated concerning subjugated peoples or ethnic groups, especially in the fields of history, ethnology, ethnography, sociology and culture.

Concepts of race, caste, clanship, tribe, nation, culture, identity, dignity and many more besides have received increasing attention from those who study man and the so-called 'primitive' or 'evolving' societies.

More recently, with the upsurge of liberation movements, it has been found necessary to analyse the characteristics of these societies in terms of the struggle that is being fought, so as to determine which factors spark off or restrain this struggle. Researchers generally agree that, in this context, culture takes on special importance. Any attempt to throw light on the true role of culture in the development of a liberation (pre-independence) movement can be seen as making a helpful contribution to the general struggle of peoples against imperialist rule.

Because independence movements are as a rule marked even in their beginnings by increased cultural activity, it is taken for granted that such movements are preceded by a cultural 'renaissance' of the dominated people. Going a step further, culture is regarded as a method of mobilising the group, even as a weapon in the fight for independence.

From experience of the struggle of my own people and it might be said of all Africa, I feel that this is a too limited, if not erroneous, conception of the vital role of culture in the development of liberation movements. I think it comes of generalising incorrectly from a real but restricted phenomenon that appears at the level of colonial elites or diasporas. Such a generalisation is unaware of or disregards an essential factor – the indestructibility of cultural resistance by the mass of the people to foreign rule.

With a few exceptions, the era of colonisation was too short, in Africa at least, to destroy or significantly depreciate the essential elements in the culture and traditions of the colonised peoples. Experience in Africa shows that (leaving aside genocide, racial segregation and apartheid) the one so-called 'positive' way the colonial power has found for opposing cultural resistance is 'assimilation'. But the total failure of the policy of 'gradual assimilation' of colonised populations is obvious proof of the fallacy of the theory and of the peoples' capacity for resistance.

On the other hand, even in settlement colonies, where the overwhelming majority of the population is still indigenous, the area of colonial and particularly cultural occupation is usually reduced to coastal strips and a few small zones in the interior.

The influence of the colonial power's culture is almost nil outside the capital and other urban centres. It is only significantly felt within the social pyramid created by colonialism itself and affects more particularly what may be called the indigenous petty bourgeoisie and a very limited number of workers in urban centres.

We find then that the great rural masses and a large fraction of the urban population, totalling over 99 per cent of the indigenous population, are virtually isolated from any cultural influence by the colonial power. This implies that not only for the mass of the people in the dominated country but also for the dominant classes among the indigenous peoples (traditional chiefs, noble families, religious leaders) there is usually no destruction or significant depreciation of culture and traditions.

Repressed, persecuted, humiliated, betrayed by certain social groups which have come to terms with the foreigner, culture takes refuge in villages, in forests and in the minds of the victims of domination, weathering all storms to recover all its power of expansion and enrichment through the struggle for liberation.

That is why the problem of a 'return to the source' or a 'cultural renaissance' does not arise for the mass of the people; it could not, for the masses are the torch-bearers of culture; they are the source of culture and, at the same time, the one entity truly capable of creating and preserving it, of making history.

For an accurate appreciation of the true role of culture in the development of the liberation movement, a distinction must therefore be made, at least in Africa, between the situation of the masses who preserve their culture and of the social groups that are more or less assimilated, uprooted and culturally alienated.

Even though marked by certain cultural features of their own indigenous community, native elites created by the colonising process live materially and spiritually the culture of the colonialist foreigner with whom they seek gradually to identify themselves in social behaviour and even in their views of indigenous cultural values.

Over two or three generations at least under colonisation, a social class has been formed of government officials, employees in various branches of the economy (especially trade), members of the liberal professions and a few urban and agricultural landowners. This indigenous lower middle class, created by foreign rule and indispensable to the colonial system of exploitation, finds itself placed between the mass of workers in the country and in the towns and the minority of local representatives of the foreign ruling class.

Although its members may have more or less developed relations with the mass of the people or the traditional chiefs, they usually aspire to a way of life similar to, if not identical with, that of the foreign minority. Limiting their relations with the masses, they try to become integrated with that minority, often to the detriment of family or ethnic bonds and always at personal cost.

But despite apparent exceptions, they never succeed in crossing the barriers imposed by the system. They are prisoners of the contradictions of the social and cultural reality in which they live, for they cannot escape their condition as a 'marginal' class. This marginality is the real social and cultural drama of the colonial elites or indigenous petty bourgeoisie. While living conditions and level of acculturation determine its intensity, this drama is always lived at the individual, not the community, level.

Within the framework of this daily drama, against the background of the usually violent confrontation between the mass of the people and the ruling colonial class, a feeling of bitterness, a frustration complex, develops and grows among the indigenous lower middle class. At the same time, they gradually become aware of an urgent need to contest their marginal status and to find an identity. So they turn towards the other pole of the social and cultural conflict in which they are living – the mass of the people.

Hence the 'return to the source', which seems all the more imperative as the sense of isolation and frustration of this lower middle class grows. The same holds true for Africans dispersed in colonialist and racist capitals.

It is not by chance, then, that theories or movements such as Pan-Africanism and Negritude (two pertinent expressions based mainly on the notion that all Black Africans are culturally identical) were conceived outside Black Africa. More recently, the Black Americans' claim to an African identity is another, perhaps desperate, expression of this need to 'return to the source', though it is clearly influenced by a new factor – the winning of independence by the great majority of African peoples.

But the 'return to the source' neither is nor can be in itself an act of struggle against foreign (colonialist and racist) rule. Nor does it necessarily mean a return to traditions. It is the denial by the indigenous petty bourgeoisie of the superiority claimed for the culture of the ruling power over the culture of the dominated people with which this petty bourgeoisie feels the need to identify.

This 'return to the source', then, is not a voluntary step; it is the only possible response to the irreconcilable contradiction between the colonised society and the colonial power, between the exploited masses and the foreign exploiters.

When the 'return to the source' goes beyond the individual to find expression in 'groups' or 'movements', this opposition turns into conflict (under cover or open), the prelude to the pre-independence movement or struggle for liberation from foreign yoke.

This 'return to the source' is thus historically important only if it involves both a genuine commitment to the fight for independence and also a total, irrevocable identification with the aspirations of the masses, who reject not only the foreigner's culture but foreign rule altogether. Otherwise, it is nothing but a means of obtaining temporary advantages, a conscious or unconscious form of political opportunism.

It should be noted that this 'return to the source', whether real or apparent, is not something that happens simultaneously and uniformly within the lower middle class. It is a slow, discontinuous, uneven process, and its development depends on each person's degree of acculturation, material conditions of life, ideological thinking and individual history as a social being.

This unevenness explains the splitting of the indigenous petty bourgeoisie into three groups in relation to the liberation movement: a minority which, even though it may want the end of foreign rule, hangs on to the ruling colonial class and openly opposes the liberation movement in order to defend and secure its own social position; a hesitant or undecided majority; another minority which helps to create and to direct the liberation movement.

But this last group, which plays a decisive role in developing the pre-independence movement, does not really succeed in identifying itself with the mass of the people (with their culture and their aspirations) except through the struggle, the degree of identification depending on the form or forms of the struggle, the ideological content of the movement and the extent of each person's moral and political awareness.

Culture has proved to be the very foundation of the liberation movement. Only societies which preserve their culture are able to mobilise and organise themselves and fight against foreign domination. Whatever ideological or idealistic forms it takes, culture is essential to the historical process. It has the power to prepare and make fertile those factors that ensure historical continuity and determine a society's chances of progressing (or regressing).

Since imperialist rule is the negation of the historical process of the dominated society, it will readily be understood that it is also the negation of the cultural process. And since a society that really succeeds in throwing off the foreign yoke reverts to the upward paths of its own culture, the struggle for liberation is above all an act of culture.

The fight for liberation is an essentially political fact. Consequently, as it develops, it can only use political methods. Culture then is not, and cannot be, a weapon or a means of mobilising the group against foreign domination. It is much more than that. Indeed, it is on firm knowledge of the local reality, particularly the cultural reality, that the choice, organisation and development of the best methods of fighting are based.

This is why the liberation movement must recognise the vital importance not only of the cultural characteristics of the dominated society as a whole but also of those of each social class. For though it has a mass aspect, culture is not uniform and does not develop evenly in all sectors, horizontal or vertical, of society.

The attitude and behaviour of each class or each individual towards the struggle and its development are, it is true, dictated by economic interests, but they are also profoundly influenced by culture. It may even be said that differences in cultural level explain differences in behaviour towards the liberation movement of individuals of the same social class.

It is at this level, then, that culture attains its full significance for each individual – comprehension of and integration within his social milieu, identification with the fundamental problems and aspirations of his society and acceptance or rejection of the possibility of change for the better.

Whatever its form, the struggle requires the mobilisation and organisation of a large majority of the population, the political and moral unity of the different social classes, the gradual elimination of vestiges of tribal or feudal mentality, the rejection of social and religious taboos that are incompatible with the rational and national character of the liberating movement. And the struggle brings about many other profound modifications in the life of the people.

This is all the more true because the dynamics of the struggle also require the exercise of democracy, criticism and self-criticism, growing participation of the people in running their lives, the achievement of literacy, the creation of schools and health services, leadership training for rural and city workers, and many other achievements that are involved in the society's 'forced march' along the road of cultural progress. This shows that the liberation struggle is more than a cultural fact, it is also a cultural factor.

Among the representatives of the colonial power as well as in their home countries, the first reaction to the liberation struggle is a general feeling of surprise and incredulity. Once this feeling, the fruit of prejudice or of the planned distortions typical of colonialist news, is surmounted, reactions vary with the interests, the political opinions and the degree to which colonialist and racist attitudes have crystallised among the different social classes and individuals.

The progress of the struggle and the sacrifices imposed by the need to take colonialist repressive measures (police or military) cause a split in metropolitan opinion. Differing, if not divergent, positions are adopted and new political and social contradictions emerge.

From the moment the struggle is recognised as an irreversible fact, however great the resources employed to quash it, a qualitative change takes place in metropolitan opinion. The possibility, if not the inevitability, of the colony's independence is on the whole gradually accepted.

Such a change is a conscious or unconscious admission that the colonised people now engaged in the struggle have an identity and a culture of their own. And this holds true even though throughout the conflict an active minority, clinging to its interests and prejudices, persists in refusing the colonised their right to independence and in denying the equivalence of cultures that right implies.

At a decisive stage in the conflict, this equivalence is implicitly recognised or accepted even by the colonial power. To divert the fighters from their objectives, it applies a demagogic policy of 'economic and social improvement', of 'cultural development', cloaking its domination with new forms. Neo-colonialism is, above all, the continuation of imperialist economic rule in disguise, but nevertheless it is also the tacit recognition by the colonial power that the people it rules and exploits have an identity of their own demanding their own political control, for the satisfaction of a cultural necessity.

Moreover, by accepting that the colonised people have an identity and a culture, and therefore an inalienable right to self-determination and independence, metropolitan opinion (or at least an important part of it) itself makes significant cultural progress and sheds a negative element in its own culture – the prejudice that the colonising nation is superior to the colonised one. This advance can have all-important consequences for the political evolution of the imperialist or colonialist power, as certain facts of current or recent history prove.

If culture is to play its proper role, the liberation movement must lay down the precise objectives to be achieved on the road to the reconquest of the rights of the people it represents – the right to make its own history and the right to dispose freely of its own productive resources. This will pave the way to the final objective of developing a richer, popular, national, scientific and universal culture.

It is not the task of the liberation movement to determine whether a culture is specific to the people or not. The important thing is for the movement to undertake a critical analysis of that culture in the light of the requirements of the struggle and of progress; to give it its place within the universal civilisation without consideration as to its superiority or inferiority, with a view to its harmonious integration into the world of today as part of the common heritage of mankind.

The Relevance of Marxism-Leninism

Amílcar Cabral's response to a question after a speech in Central Hall, London on 26 October 1971.

Question: Besides nationalism, is your struggle founded on any ideological basis? To what extent has the ideology of Marxism and Leninism been relevant to the prosecution of the war in Guinea-Bissau? What practical peculiarities, if any, have necessitated the modification of Marxism-Leninism?

Cabral: We believe that a struggle like ours is impossible without ideology. But what kind of ideology? I will perhaps disappoint many people here when I say that we do not think ideology is a religion. A religion tells one, for example, that Christ was born in Nazareth and performed this miracle and that and so on and so on, and one believes it or one doesn't believe it, and one practises the religion or one doesn't. Moving from the realities of one's own country towards the creation of an ideology for one's struggle doesn't imply that one has pretensions to be a Marx or a Lenin or any other great ideologue, but is simply a necessary part of the struggle. I confess that we didn't know these great theorists terribly well when we began. We didn't know them half as well as we do now! We needed to know them, as I've said, in order to judge in what measure we could borrow from their experience to help our situation – but not necessarily to apply the ideology blindly just because it's a very good ideology. That is where we stand on this.

But ideology is important in Guinea. As I've said, never again do we want our people to be exploited. Our desire to develop our country with social justice and power in the hands of the people is our ideological basis. Never again do we want to see a group or a class of people exploiting or dominating the work of our people. That's our basis. If you want to call it Marxism, you may call it Marxism. That's your responsibility. A journalist once asked me: 'Mr. Cabral, are you a Marxist?' Is Marxism a religion? I am a freedom fighter in my country. You must judge from what I do in practice. If you decide that it's Marxism, tell everyone that it is Marxism. If you decide it's not Marxism, tell them it's not Marxism. But the labels are your affair; we don't like those kind of labels. People here are very preoccupied with the questions: are you Marxist or not Marxist? Are you Marxist-Leninist? Just ask me, please, whether we are doing well in the field. Are we really liberating our people, the human beings in our country from all forms of oppression? Ask me simply this, and draw your own conclusions.

We cannot, from our experience, claim that Marxism-Leninism must be modified – that would be presumptuous. What we must do is to modify, to radically transform, the political, economic, social and cultural conditions of our people. This doesn't mean that we have no respect for all that Marxism and Leninism have contributed to the transformation of struggles throughout the world and over the years. But we are absolutely sure that we have to create and develop in our particular situation the solution for our country. We believe that the laws governing the evolution of all human societies are the same. Our society is developing in the same way as other societies in the world, according to the historical process; but we must understand clearly what stage our society has reached. Marx, when he created Marxism, was not a member of a tribal society; I think there's no necessity for us to be more Marxist than Marx or more Leninist than Lenin in the application of their theories.

Culture, Colonisation, and National Liberation

A speech given upon the award of an honorary doctorate by Lincoln University, USA in 1972.

The people's struggle for national liberation and independence from imperialist rule has become a driving force of progress for humanity and undoubtedly constitutes one of the essential characteristics of contemporary history.

An objective analysis of imperialism in so far as it is a fact or a 'natural' historical phenomenon, indeed 'necessary' in the context of the type of economic-political evolution of an important part of humanity, reveals that imperialist rule with all its train of wretchedness, of pillage, of crime and of destruction of human and cultural values, was not just a negative reality. The vast accumulation of capital in half a dozen countries of the northern hemisphere, which was the result of piracy, of the confiscation of the property of other races, and of the ruthless exploitation of the work of these peoples, will not only lead to the monopolisation of colonies, the division of the world, and imperialist rule.

In the rich countries, imperialist capital, constantly seeking to enlarge itself, increased the creative capacity of man and brought about a total transformation of the means of production thanks to the rapid progress of science, of techniques and of technology. This accentuated the pooling of labour and brought about the ascension of huge segments of population. In the colonial countries where colonisation on the whole blocked the historical process of the development of the subjected peoples, or else changed them radically in the name of progress, imperialist capital imposed new types of relationships on indigenous society, the structure of which became more complex, and it stirred up, fomented, poisoned or resolved contradictions and social conflicts; it introduced, together with money and the development of internal and external markets, new elements in the economy; it brought about the birth of new nations from human groups or from peoples who were at different stages of historical development.

It is not to defend imperialist domination to recognise that it gave new nations to the world, the dimensions of which it reduced and that it revealed new stages of development of human societies and in spite of or because of the prejudices, the discrimination and the crimes which it occasioned, it contributed to a deeper knowledge of humanity as a whole, as a unity in the complex diversity of the characteristics of its development.

Imperialist rule on many continents favoured a multilateral and progressive (sometimes abrupt) confrontation not only between different men but also between different societies. The practice of imperialist rule – its affirmation or its negation – demanded (and still demands) a more or less accurate knowledge of the society it rules and of the historical reality (both economic, social, and cultural) in the middle of which it exists.

This knowledge is necessarily expressed in terms of comparison with the dominating subject and with its own historical reality. Such a knowledge is a vital necessity in the practice of imperialist rule which results in the confrontation, mostly violent, between; two identities which are totally dissimilar in their historical past and antagonistic in their different functions. The search for such a knowledge contributed to a general enrichment of human and social knowledge in spite of the fact that it was one-sided, subjective, and very often unjust.

In fact man has never shown as much interest in knowing other men and other societies as during this century of imperialist domination. An unprecedented mass of information, of hypotheses and theories has been built up, notably in the fields of history, ethnology, ethnography, sociology, and culture concerning people or groups brought under imperialist domination. The concepts of race, caste, ethnicity, tribe, nation, culture, identity, dignity, and many other factors have become the object of increasing attention from those who study men and the societies described as 'primitive' or 'evolving'.

More recently, with the rise of liberation movements, the need has arisen to analyse the character of these societies in the light of the struggle they are waging, and to decide the factors which launch or hold back this struggle. The researchers are generally agreed that in this context culture shows special significance. So one can argue that any attempt to clarify the true role of culture in the development of the (pre-independence) liberation movement can make a useful contribution to the broad struggle of the people against imperialist domination.

In this short lecture, we consider particularly the problems of the 'return to the source,' and of identity and dignity in the context of the national liberation movement.

The fact that independence movements are generally marked, even in their early stages, by an upsurge of cultural activity has led to the view that such movements are preceded by a 'cultural renaissance' of the subject people. Some might go as far as to suggest that culture is one means of collecting together a group, indeed one *weapon* in the struggle for independence.

From the experience of our own struggle and one might say that of the whole of Africa, we consider that there is too limited, even a mistaken idea of the vital role of culture in the development of the liberation movement. In our view this arises from a fake generalisation of a phenomenon which is real but limited, which is at a particular level in the vertical structure of colonised societies – at the level of the *elite* or the colonial diasporas. This generalisation is unaware of or ignores the vital element of the problem; the indestructible character of the cultural resistance of the masses of the people when confronted with foreign domination.

Certainly, imperialist domination calls for cultural oppression and attempts either directly or indirectly to do away with the most important elements of the culture of the subject people. But the people are only able to create and develop the liberation movement because they keep their culture alive despite continual and organised repression of their cultural life and because they continue to resist culturally even when their politico-military resistance is destroyed. And it is cultural resistance which, at a given moment, can take on new forms (political, economic, military) to fight foreign domination.

With certain exceptions, *the period of colonisation* was not long enough, at least in Africa, for there to be a significant degree of destruction or damage of the most important facets of the culture and traditions of the subject people. Colonial experience of imperialist domination in Africa (genocide, racial segregation and apartheid excepted) shows that the only so-called positive solution which the colonial power put forward to repudiate the subject people's cultural resistance was '*assimilation*'. But the complete failure of the policy of 'progressive assimilation' of native population is the living proof of the falsehood of this theory and of the capacity of subject people to resist. As far as the Portuguese colonies are concerned, the maximum number of people assimilated was 0.03 per cent of the total population (in Guinea) and this was after 500 years of 'civilising mission' and half a century of 'colonial peace'.

On the other hand, even in the settlements where the overwhelming majority of the population are indigenous peoples, the area occupied by the colonial power and especially the area of *cultural influence* is usually restricted to coastal strips and to a few limited parts in the interior. Outside the boundaries of the capital and other urban centres, the influence is almost out. It only leaves its mark at the very top of the colonisers' social pyramid – which created colonialism itself – and particularly it influences what one might call the 'indigenous petit bourgeoisie' and a very small number of workers in urban areas. The influence of the colonial power's culture is almost nil.

It can thus be seen that the masses in the rural areas, like a large section of the urban population, say, in all, over 99 per cent of the indigenous population are untouched or almost untouched by the culture of the colonial power. This situation is partly the result of the necessarily obscurantist character of the imperialist domination, which, while it despises and suppresses indigenous culture, takes no interest in promoting culture for the masses who are their pool of manpower for forced labour and the main object of exploitation. It is also the result of the effectiveness of cultural resistance of the people who, when they are subjected to political domination and economic exploitation, find that their own culture acts as a bulwark in preserving their *identity* where the indigenous society has a vertical structure; this defence of their cultural heritage is further strengthened by the colonial power's interest, in protecting and backing the cultural influence of the ruling classes, their allies.

The above argument implies that, generally speaking, there is not any marked destruction or damage to culture or tradition either for the masses in the subject country or for the indigenous ruling classes (traditional chiefs, noble families, religious authorities). Repression, persecution, humiliation, betrayal by certain social groups who have compromised with the foreign power, have forced culture to take refuge in the villages, in the forests, and in the spirit of the victims of domination. Culture survives all these challenges and, through the struggle for liberation, blossoms forth again. Thus the question of a 'return to the source' or of a 'cultural renaissance' does not arise and could not arise for the mass of these people, for it is they who are the repository of the culture and at the same time the only socio-structure who can preserve and build it up and *make history*.

Thus, in Africa at least, for a true idea of the real role which culture plays in the development of the liberation movement a distinction must be made between the situation of the masses, who preserve their culture, and that of the social groups who are assimilated or partially so, who are cut off and culturally alienated. Even though the indigenous colonial elite who emerged during the process of colonisation still continue to pass on some element of indigenous culture, yet they live both materially and spiritually according to the foreign colonial culture. They seek to identify themselves increasingly with this culture both in their social behaviour and even in their appreciation of its values.

In the course of two or three generations of colonisation, a social class arises made up of civil servants, people who are employed in various branches of the economy, especially commerce, professional people, and a few urban and agricultural landowners. This indigenous petit bourgeoisie, which emerged out of foreign domination and is indispensable to the system of colonial exploitation, stands midway between the masses of the working class in town and country and the small number of local representatives of the foreign ruling class. Although they may have quite strong links with the masses and with the traditional chiefs, generally speaking they aspire to a way of life which is similar if not identical with that of the foreign minority. At the same time, while they restrict their dealings with the masses they try to become integrated into this minority, often at the cost of family or ethnic ties and always at great personal cost. Yet, despite the apparent exceptions, they do not succeed in getting past the barriers thrown up by the system. They are prisoners of the cultural and social contradictions of their lives. They cannot escape from their role as a marginal class, a 'marginalised' class.

The marginal character of their role both in their own country and in that of the colonial power is responsible for the socio-cultural conflicts of the colonial elite or the indigenous petit bourgeoisie, played out very much according to their material circumstances and level of culture but always resolved on the individual level, never collectively.

It is within the framework of this daily drama, against the backcloth of the usually violent confrontation between the mass of the people and the ruling colonial class that a feeling of bitterness or a *frustration complex* is bred and develops among the indigenous lower middle class. At the same time they are becoming more and more conscious of a compelling need to question their marginal status, and to rediscover an identity.

Thus they turn to the people around them, the people at the other extreme of the socio-cultural conflict – the masses.

For this reason arises the problem of the 'return to the source' which seems to be even more urgent than the serious isolation of the petit bourgeoisie (or native elites) and their acute feelings of frustration, as is the case when African diasporas are sent to countries with colonial or racist traditions. It comes as no surprise that the theories or 'movements' such as Pan-Africanism or Negritude (two pertinent expressions arising mainly from the assumption that all black Africans have a cultural identity) were propounded outside Black Africa. More recently, the Black Americans' claim to an African identity is another proof, possibly rather a desperate one, of the need for a 'return to the source' although clearly it is influenced by a new situation: the fact that the great majority of African people are now independent.

But the 'return to the source' is not and cannot in itself be an *act of struggle* against foreign domination (colonialist and racist) and it no longer necessarily means a return to traditions. It is the denial, by the petit bourgeoisie of the country, of the usurped supremacy of the culture of the dominant power over that of the dominated people with which it must identify itself. The 'return to the source' is therefore not a voluntary step, but the only possible reply to the demand of concrete need, historically denied, and enforced by the inescapable contradiction between the colonised society and the colonial power, between the mass of the people exploited and the foreign exploitive class, a contradiction in the light of which each level of social stratum or indigenous class must define its role.

When the 'return to the source' goes beyond the individual and is expressed through 'groups' or 'movements', the contradiction is transformed into struggle (secret or overt), and is a prelude to the pre-independence movement or of the struggle for liberation from the foreign yoke. So, the 'return to the source' is of no historical importance unless it brings not only real involvement in the struggle for independence, but also complete and absolute identification with the hopes of the mass of the people, who are struggling not only against the foreign culture but also foreign domination. Otherwise, the 'return to the source' is nothing more than an attempt to find short-term benefits, knowingly or unknowingly a kind of political opportunism.

One must point out that the 'return to the source', apparent or real, does not develop at one time and in the same way in the heart of the indigenous petit bourgeoisie. It is a slow process, broken up and uneven, whose development depends on the degree of acculturation of each individual, of the material circumstances of his life, on the forming of his ideas and on his experience as a social being. This unevenness is the basis of the split of the indigenous petit bourgeoisie into three groups when confronted with the liberation movement: (a) a minority, which, even if it wants to see an end to foreign domination clings to the dominant colonialist class and openly oppose the movement to protect its social position; (b) a majority of people who are hesitant and indecisive; (c) another minority of people who share in the building and leadership of the liberation movement.

But the latter group, which plays a decisive role in the development of the pre-independent movement, does not truly identify with the mass of the people (with their culture and hopes) except through struggle, the scale of this identification depending on the kind or methods of struggle, on the ideological basis of the movement and on the level of moral and political awareness of each individual.

Identification of a section of the indigenous petit bourgeoisie with the mass of the people has an essential pre-requisite: *that, in the face of destructive action by imperialist domination, the masses retain their identity*, separate and distinct from that of the colonial power. It is worthwhile therefore to decide in what circumstances this retention is possible; why, when and at what levels of the dominated society is raised the problem of the loss or absence of identity, and in consequence it becomes necessary to assert or to re-assert in the framework of the pre-independence movement a separate and distinct identity from that of the colonial power.

The identity of an individual or of a particular group of people is a bio-sociological factor outside the will of that individual or group, but which is meaningful only when it is expressed in relation with other individuals or other groups. The dialectical character of identity lies in the fact that it identifies and *distinguishes* that an individual (or a group) is only similar to certain individuals (or groups) if it is also different to other individuals (or groups). The definition of an identity, individual or collective, is at the same time the affirmation and denial of a certain number of characteristics which define the individuals or groups, through *historical* (biological and sociological) factors at a moment of their development. In fact, identity is not a constant, precisely because the biological and sociological factors which define it are in constant change. Biologically and sociologically, there are no two beings (individual or collective) completely the same or completely different, for it is always possible to find in them common or distinguishing characteristics. Again the identity of a being is always relative, even circumstantial, because defining it means picking out more or less strictly and cautiously the biological and sociological characteristics of the being in question.

One must point out that in the fundamental duality given in the definition of identity, sociology is a more determining factor than biology. In fact, if it is correct that the biological element (inherited genetic structure) is the inescapable physical basis of the existence and continuing growth of identity, it is no less correct the case that the sociological element is the factor which gives it objective substance, by giving content and form, and allowing confrontation and comparison between individuals or between groups. To make a total definition of identity the inclusion of the biological element is indispensable, but does not imply a sociological similarity, whereas two beings who are sociologically exactly the same must necessarily have similar biological identities.

This shows on the one hand the supremacy of the social over the individual condition, for society (human for example) is a higher form of life; it shows on the other hand the need not to confuse, in arriving at identity, the *original identity*, of which the biological element is the main determinant, and the *actual identity*, of which the main determinant is the sociological element. Clearly the identity of which one must take account at a given moment of the growth of a being (individual or collective) is the actual identity, and awareness of that being reached only on the basis that his original identity is incomplete, partial and fake, for it leaves out or does not comprehend the decisive influence of social conditions on the content and form of identity.

In the formation and development of individual or collective identity, the social condition is an objective agent arising from economic, political, social and cultural aspects which are characteristic of the growth and history of the society in question. If one argues that the economic aspect is fundamental, one can assert that identity is in a certain sense an expression of the economic reality. This reality, whatever the geographical context and the path of development of the society is defined by the level of productive forces (the relationship between man and nature) and by the means of production (the relationship between men and classes within a single society). But if one accepts that culture is a dynamic synthesis of the material and spiritual condition of the society and expresses the close relationship both between man and nature and between the different classes within a single society we can assert that identity is at the individual and collective level and beyond the economic condition, the expression of a culture. This is why to attribute, recognise or declare the identity of an individual or group is above all to place that individual or group in the framework of a culture. Now as we all know, the main prop of culture in any society is the social structure. One can therefore draw conclusion that the possibility of a given group keeping (or losing) its identity in the face of foreign domination depends on the extent of the destruction of its social structure under the stresses of that domination.

As for the effects of imperialist domination on the social structure of the dominated people, one must look here at the case of classic colonialism against which the pre-independence movement is contending. In that case, whatever the stage of historical development of the dominated society, the social structure can be subjected to the following experiences: (a) *total destruction*, mixed with immediate or gradual liquidation of the indigenous people and replacement by a foreign people; (b) *partial destruction*, with the additional settling of a more or less numerous foreign population; (c) *supposed preservation*, brought about by the restriction of the indigenous people in geographical areas of special reserves usually without means of living, and the massive influx of a foreign population.

The fundamentally horizontal character of the social structure of African people, due to the profusion of ethnic groups, means that the cultural resistance and degree of retention of identity are not uniform. So, even where ethnic groups have broadly succeeded in keeping their identity, we observe that the most *resistant* groups are those which have had the most violent battles with the colonial power during the period of effective occupation (the Manjacos, Pepels, Oincas, Balanta, Beafadas). Or those who because of their geographical location have had least contact with the foreign presence (the Pajadincas and other minorities in the interior).

One must point out that the attitude of the colonial power towards the ethnic groups creates an insoluble contradiction: on the one hand it must divide or keep divisions in order to rule and for that reason favours separation if not conflict between ethnic groups: on the other hand to try and keep the permanency of its domination it needs to destroy the social structure, culture, and by implication identity, of these groups. Moreover, it must protect the ruling class of those groups which (like, for example, the Peul tribe or nation in our country) have given decisive support during the colonial conquest a policy which favours the preservation of the identity of these groups.

As has already been said, there are not usually important changes in respect of culture in the upright shape of the indigenous pyramid or of the indigenous social pyramids (groups or societies with a State). Each level or class keeps its identity, linked with that of the group but separate from that of other social classes. Conversely, in the urban centres, as in some of the interior regions of the country where the cultural influence of the colonial power is felt, the problem of identity is more complicated. While the bottom and the top of the social pyramid (that is the mass of the working class drawn from different ethnic groups and the foreign dominant class) keep their identities, the middle level of this pyramid (the indigenous petit bourgeoisie), culturally uprooted, alienated or more or less assimilated, engages in a sociological battle in search of its identity. One must also point out that though united by a new identity – granted by the colonial power – the foreign dominant class cannot free itself from the contradictions of its own society, which it brings to the colonised country.

When, at the initiative of a minority of the indigenous petit bourgeoisie, allied with the indigenous masses, the pre-independence movement is launched, the masses have no need to assert or reassert their identity, which they have never confused nor would have known how to confuse with that of the colonial power. This need is felt only by the indigenous petit bourgeoisie which finds itself obliged to take up a position in the struggle which opposes the masses to the colonial power. However, the reassertion of identity distinct from that of the colonial power is not always achieved by the lower middle class. It is only a minority who do this, while another minority asserts, often in a noisy manner, the identity of the foreign dominant class, while the silent majority is trapped in indecision.

Moreover, even when there is a reassertion of an identity distinct from that of the colonial power, and the same as that of the masses, it does not show itself in the same way everywhere. One part of the middle-class minority, engaged in the pre-independence movement, uses the foreign cultural norms, calling on literature and art, to express rather the discovery of its identity than to draw on the theme of the hopes and sufferings of the masses. And precisely because it uses the language and speech of the colonial power, the minority only occasionally manages to influence the masses, generally illiterate, and familiar with other forms of artistic expression. This does not however remove the value of the contribution to the development of the struggle made by this petit bourgeoisie minority, for it can at the same time influence a sector of the uprooted or those who are latecomers to its own class and an important sector of public opinion in the colonial metropolis, notably the class of intellectuals.

The other part of the lower middle class which from the start joins in the pre-independence movement finds in its prompt share in the liberation struggle and in integration with the masses the best means of expression of identity distinct from that of the colonial power.

That is why identification with the masses and reassertion of identity can be temporary or definitive, apparent or real, in the light of the daily efforts and sacrifices demanded by the struggle itself – a struggle which, while being the organised political expression of a culture, is also and necessarily a proof not only of *identity* but also of *dignity*.

In the course of the process of colonialist domination, the masses, whatever the characteristic of the social structure of the group to which they belong, do not stop resisting the colonial power. In a first phase – that of conquest, cynically called 'pacification' – they resist gun in hand foreign occupation. In a second phase – that of the golden age of triumphant colonialism – they offer the foreign domination passive resistance, almost silent, but blazoned with many revolts, usually individual and once in a while collective. The revolt is particularly in the field of work and taxes, even in social contacts with the representatives, foreign or indigenous, of the colonial power. In a third phase – that of the liberation struggle – it is the masses who provide the main strength which employs political or armed resistance, to challenge and to destroy foreign domination. Such a prolonged and varied resistance is possible only because while keeping their culture and identity, the masses keep intact the sense of their individual and collective dignity, despite the worries, humiliations and brutalities to which they are often subjected.

The assertion or reassertion by the indigenous petit bourgeoisie of identity distinct from that of the colonial power does not and could not bring about restoration of a sense of dignity to that class alone. In this context we see that the sense of dignity of the petit bourgeoisie depends on the objective moral and social feeling of each individual, on his subjective attitude towards the two poles of the colonial conflict, between which he is forced to live out the daily drama of colonisation. This drama is the more shattering to the extent to which the petit bourgeoisie in fulfilling its role is made to live alongside both the foreign dominating class and the masses. On one side the lower middle class is the victim of frequent if not daily humiliation by the foreigner, and on the other side it is aware of the injustice to which the masses are subjected and of their resistance and spirit of rebellion. Hence arises the apparent paradox of continuing colonial domination; it is from within the indigenous lower middle class, a social class which grows from colonialism itself, that arise the first important steps towards mobilising and organising the masses for the struggle against the colonial power.

The struggle, in the face of all kinds of obstacles and in a variety of forms, reflects the awareness or grasp of a complete identity, generalises and consolidates the sense of dignity, strengthened by the development of political consciousness, and derives from the culture or cultures of the masses in revolt one of its principal strengths.

In conclusion, we would like only to tell you that we are very glad to be here with you and that we are very honoured by the degree conferred on our people through myself by the University. We have a great task to do yet. We haven't finished the liberation of our country, but we have liberated more than two-thirds of the country. We are now creating a new life in the country and we are stronger than ever in this fight. But we have to finish totally with the Portuguese colonial presence in Guinea-Bissau and the Cape Verde Islands. We have the pleasure to announce that last week we finished the elections in all liberated regions of our country for the creation of our first national popular assembly. Maybe it is a coincidence but a very good coincidence that at this very moment you, our brothers and sisters of Lincoln University, decided to concede to our people this great honour which we received here on behalf of our people. Thank you very much.

Fruits of a Struggle

Despite certain appearances and a feeble propaganda which, however, continues with a favourable echo in certain segments of the western press, Portugal's worsening political and economic situation is something the Portuguese authorities themselves, at all levels, are no longer able to hide. This fact, reflected in various areas of Portuguese society, is chiefly the result of the crime of human perversion committed by the government over the last ten years since it unleashed the colonial war in Angola which it then extended to Guinea and Mozambique. This fact – dramatic today but no doubt tragic tomorrow for Portugal – is the result of the policy of absurdity, of irrationality and lies, practiced by the Portuguese ruling class which not only obstinately scorns the rights of the African people and of international legality, but even acts conscientiously against the very interests of the Portuguese people.

It is this reality, most evident over the course of the last two years and particularly during 1971, that explains the bankruptcy of Marcelo Caetano's demagogic policy, the increasing gulf between the ruling class and popular sectors (workers in the city and, in the countryside, anti-fascist students and intellectuals), the increasingly frequent and intense convulsions in Portuguese society and, as an extreme expression of opposition, the revolutionary armed actions that these recent times have produced in Portugal.[21] The limited and irregular character of these actions should fool no one. For a fraction of Portuguese society, however small, despite the inveterate nationalism which is the common characteristic of all Portuguese, to have taken the decision to resort to violent measures of resistance – and this without any reproval by the popular masses – indicates that the Portuguese state of mind in the face of the aggravation of the socio-economic and political situation has reached limits of desperation.

Pursuing the Salazar policy of a colonial war of genocide against the African peoples, Marcelo Caetano not only deceived those who believed in his 'political intelligence.' He also lost or is on the way to losing the only opportunity a Portuguese has had since the time of the maritime discoveries, to have his name written down favourably in history. But he cannot understand or refuses to understand the meaning of history, or even the interests of his people, which should surprise no one who knows the process of his ideological formation. Today, after three years in power, the present head of the Portuguese government cannot hide his perplexity and even his confusion in his speeches and public positions, in the

---

21 *Editor's note*: Marcelo Caetano was the Prime Minister of Portugal from 1968–1974.

face of the socio-economic and political reality of the complexity of diversities, if not of divergencies, that he insists on calling the 'Portuguese world.'

The timid reforms, principally those of an administrative nature, which he has begun and has dared to have included in the new Portuguese Constitution, have convinced no one except those already convinced. These have also disappointed the most important segment – because they are activists – of his so-called 'liberals' or less reactionary supporters. This is how the conflict occurred within the so-called Portuguese National Assembly during the recent discussion of the Constitutional revision, a conflict which, if parliamentarianism weren't just a caricature in Portugal, would have ended with the fall of the government.

The unquestionable truth about present-day Portuguese life is the following: while Portugal maintains and accentuates day by day the dubious privilege of being the most backward country in Europe, the Portuguese government deliberately sustains three colonial wars of genocide in Africa and stubbornly keeps the Portuguese people in ignorance and misery, exiled from Europe and the world, isolated from all scientific and technical advances that people everywhere are achieving today. As always, the Portuguese exist without the most elemental rights of man.

The truth, which the Portuguese masses are becoming more aware of all the time, is that galloping inflation as well as population decrease due to emigration and war, the high cost of living and public and international debts, lack of manpower and a stagnant Portuguese economy are the concrete result of the absurd colonial policy of the Portuguese ruling class that Marcelo Caetano is accustomed to serve.

Prisoner of the unfortunate Salazar heritage fiercely defended by the 'ultras' of the regime, confused by his own measures, Marcelo Caetano has plenty of reason to shift from perplexity to desperation. Much more so when the resistance of the African peoples and of the Portuguese people themselves to colonial wars is more vigourous and effective every day.

Thus, the victimised attitude that the head of the Portuguese government now evidences is quite understandable. And so in his speech of July 23, 1971, explaining the incidents that occurred in the Portuguese National Assembly, after having deplored the fact that 'unfortunately' we are not in the position of people who can 'demand greater liberty in the name of our immortal forebears,' he stated:

On my shoulders weigh the responsibilities of national defence, with military operations in three overseas provinces and a vulnerable rear guard. Not a day passes on the international scene without our adversaries striking a new blow against us, which forces us to give constant attention and permanent efforts to the diplomatic struggle and to clarifying the poisoned opinion of foreign countries.

If by this statement the head of the Portuguese government recognises publicly for the first time the real existence of colonial wars – which he calls 'military operations' – it is no less certain that he also seeks to enlighten 'the poisoned opinion of foreign countries,' that is to say, he persists in flouting respect for international law.

In the same speech, after having recognised that 'in the interior of the country [that is, in Portugal] the enemy finds support [...] and increasingly seeks to infiltrate the schools, the armed forces and the corporate organisation,' he says:

> And while we must face all this, we must first of all consider the real needs of the people, then the struggle against inflation which, like a cancer, eats away the economy of every country today, destroying price stability and facilitating everything from salary demands up to the problems of economic development of a nation that cannot or must not become stagnant nor lose its blood because of the demands of social improvement formulated by a population that wants precisely the broadest perspectives for education and welfare. All this takes money, and God knows how hard it is to find it!

With this Jobian lament, which needs no comment, Marcelo Caetano seeks to justify the fact of not moving 'as rapidly' as his 'young friends' would like. But if it is true, as he says in his speech in an allusion to the French Revolution, that when a Jacobin was made minister he didn't then become a Jacobin minister, the policy and the arguments of Marcelo Caetano prove to the hilt that when a Salazarist is made President of the Council, he becomes a Salazarist President of the Council.

In effect, despite shades of originality and liberality, it is precisely the profoundly Salazarist nature of Marcelo Caetano's policy – the obstinacy in perpetuating fascism in Portugal and colonialism in Africa – that explains the very slight, almost non-existent, results of his three years of government whose balance he explained in his speech of September 27, 1971. In this speech, in which he called upon the 'Portuguese worthy of this name' to unite around the 'governors elected by them' (sic), he stated:

> We try valiantly to face up to national problems. We succeed in maintaining the defense of the overseas provinces against the subversion supported more and more each day by instigation of that incredible organisation called the United Nations [sic] [...] and if we are not disheartened in the overseas struggle, neither have we given quarter to those who seek to bring terrorism to the metropolis.

The same terms, the same obstinacy.

But Marcelo Caetano does not deny that facing up to problems does not mean solving them. This is why, after having flashed before the traditionally poor Portuguese people the vision of the 'models of development of the traditionally rich part of Europe,' he recalls, so that there will be no dreams, that in Portugal 'a dangerous mentality is being created of demanding rights and facilities absolutely incompatible with the country's realities and possibilities.'

And then comes the traditional lament:

I would be failing in my responsibility to tell the truth to the Portuguese if I did not remind them that we live in very critical hours, hours in which national problems are aggravated by uncertain conditions in economic and in international policy. Let no one think that we are rich in human and material resources.

Clearly, the people of Portugal who live in misery and see their sons faced with the dilemma of clandestine emigration or death without glory in colonial wars, will doubtless be the judges.

These quotations, perhaps too long, nevertheless have the purpose of demonstrating in the words of the head of the Portuguese government himself, that if it is true that the myths, the tactics, the lies, arguments and objectives of the fascist colonial regime have not changed in the slightest with the disappearance of Salazar, the socio-economic and political degradation of Portuguese society as a result of the colonial wars is a fact that the laments of Marcelo Caetano cannot hide. To be aware of this is of capital importance within the framework of the perspectives for the development of our struggle.

Still more realistic than Marcelo Caetano is the confidential report of the Portuguese high command drawn up in 1970 under the title, 'Report from Psychological Section No. 15'. In this document, which analyses in detail the action of the liberation movements and of Portuguese means against the colonial war, as well as the methods, action and results of psycho-social warfare the authors reveal:

The proliferation of anti-governmental organisations and the attempt at general agitation lead to the creation of a climate of psychological instability that affects the activity of the students and, therefore, affects the country, which appears upset and does not know what to do to lead its children along the correct path.

After having made a long allusion to the increasingly difficult situation that is wreaking havoc among the colonial troops, with desertions and demands increasing, the report concludes:

The enemy [that is, the liberation movements and the forces against the colonial war] have perfected and increased their efforts on all fronts, internal as well as external.

In the metropolis, in general, the population continues to show little interest in the overseas war and is unaware of the effort expended by the armed forces. The student masses show themselves to be strongly susceptible to the propaganda of peace. The working masses, with no knowledge of great national problems, easily allow themselves to be dragged along by propaganda oriented toward demands for better pay and better social conditions. The most developed groups continue to be the focal points of subversion and the organizations that arise are proof of great efficacy. Overseas, generally, the indigenous populations continue to lean toward subversion, notably when it demonstrates that it has force, or when geographic conditions make the action of our troops difficult or impossible. The aboriginal populations on the periphery of the major urban centers, generally lacking tribalization, continue to evidence great susceptibility to enemy propaganda. The European population continues to demonstrate openly its adherence to the war but does not cooperate against subversion except when its material interests are directly threatened.

The psychological situation is precarious, both in the metropolis and overseas.

Thus, the situation becomes increasingly aggravated in every way and one might ask why the Portuguese government, which is conscious of the difficulties it now has and will have to face later, obstinately continues its absurd and criminal policy of perpetuating colonial war and domination over the African peoples. It is not difficult to recognise that the principal reasons for the unaltered continuation of Portuguese colonial policy lie in the following facts:

1. Portugal's chronic and characteristic underdevelopment, its lack of valid economic infrastructures, make it incapable of considering a process of decolonisation in which the interests of the Portuguese ruling class would be safeguarded within the framework of a neo-colonial situation or of effective competition with other capitalist powers.
2. The inhibiting effects of almost half a century of fascism on a society which, throughout its history, has never really (or to any extent) known the rights of man, liberty and the practice of democracy.
3. The imperial mentality of the Portuguese ruling class and the ignorance, the myths, beliefs, prejudices and narrow nationalism that characterise the culture of major sectors of the Portuguese population which, for centuries, has been subjected to the doctrine of *European superiority and African inferiority*, and to the myth of the 'civilising mission' of the Portuguese with respect to the African peoples who are considered to be 'savages.'

Despite the whims of the Portuguese colonialists as far as the 'creation of multiracial societies,' this doctrine, to which the fear of 'communist subversion' has recently been added, crowns the crystallisation of a *primitive racism* often without any evident economic motivation.

The racist character of the Portuguese intervention is amply evidenced in the disregard for Africa's cultural values as well as in the most abject crimes committed by the administration and the Portuguese colonists during the golden era of colonialism. Today it is evident in the cruelty that characterises the actions of the colonial troops. But there is a tendency at present, in the face of African resistance, for it to manifest itself in the paternalism and false preoccupation with 'achieving the social advancement of the African within the framework of the Portuguese nation.'

Portuguese racism, which is one of the subjective causes of the continuation of colonial wars, reaches its maximum in the top levels of the ruling class. Thus General Kaúlza de Arriaga, one of the most outstanding personalities in Portuguese colonial leadership, commander-in-chief of the colonial troops in Mozambique and aspi*rant* to the job of President of the Republic, touching on the Portuguese strategic problem (Volume XII of the *Lessons in Strategy from the Courses of the High Command 1966/67*), states: 'Subversion is above all a war of intelligence. One must be highly intelligent to engage in subversion; not everyone is capable. Very well, the black peoples are not highly intelligent, on the contrary, of all the peoples of the world they are the least intelligent.' (sic)

In these same lessons, the author, who believes that the 'exportation of African slaves to Brazil was a good thing' and that the 'tribal state of the black population is favourable to Portuguese strategy,' reveals in all its cruelty the principal objective of the present Portuguese colonial policy: *to maintain white domination over black populations*.

After having, pointed out that the danger lies in the increase in 'evolutionised blacks,' Kaúlza de Arriaga affirms:

> We are not capable of maintaining white domination, a national objective, unless the white population achieves a rhythm that matches and outnumbers, however slightly, the production of evolutionized blacks [sic]. On the contrary, if the whites are outnumbered by the production of evolutionized blacks, then one of two things is bound to occur: either we install apartheid, which would be terrible and in which we would be unsuccessful, or we will have black governments with all the consequences that this implies (destruction of the overseas provinces, etc.).

The racist boss then explains the tactic required to avoid such a situation:

> The white population does not contemplate the equilibrium of the black demographic potential, it contemplates the equilibrium of evolutionized blacks [...] and thank God, since it is impossible to see that all blacks are evolutionized, it is possible, almost certain, that we will be able to situate

there in Africa enough whites to balance the blacks who will become evolutionized.

On this basis, after having stressed that 'we will not be too effective in the production of evolutionized blacks; we must promote them, yes, but it's not necessary to exaggerate,' the general and presidential asp*irant* reveals the master line of present Portuguese strategy in Africa: 'First an increase in the white population, then a limitation of the black population.' In the face of the difficulties of the problem and convinced of the myth of the great fertility of the African, he suggests, although in a negative form, the practice of scientific birth control: 'Clearly, it is an extraordinarily difficult problem since we cannot distribute a birth control pill to each black family [...] but what we can do is not overstimulate the increase of the black population.'

One of the principal objectives of Portuguese colonial wars in Africa thus becomes most evident: given the immediate impossibility of limiting birth control by ensuring the supremacy of the white population, they resort to the physical liquidation of populations by the increasingly intense use of aerial bombardment by napalm and other means of massive destruction of the African man under the deliberate practice of genocide.

This objective, whose realisation clashes with the effective armed resistance of the peoples of the Portuguese colonies supported by African and international solidarity, nevertheless reveals the full extent of the criminal character of the moral, political and material support that Portugal receives from its allies through NATO and on a bilateral basis. In reality it is no secret to anyone today that without the aid of its Western and racist allies, the Portuguese government would in no way be able to continue the colonial wars in Africa and repress the legitimate aspirations of the people of Portugal for peace and progress.

It is with full consciousness of the situation of the enemy of our people and of the internal and external factors and circumstances that made possible and condition its criminal attitude, that we must analyse the situation of our struggle and the perspectives for its evolution at each moment.

The political-military action of the Portuguese colonialists in our country continues to have as its fundamental objectives:

a) to defend and consolidate the positions they still occupy in the urban centres and in some zones that are still not liberated;
b) to demobilise the populations in the liberated regions;
c) to perpetrate the violent destruction of the human and material means that serve as the base of the victorious development of our struggle;
d) to maintain war for the sake of war, to make Africans fight against Africans;
e) to maintain at all price, the presence of colonial troops in the principal strategic points with the hope that our political-military organisation, in the long run, will enter into crisis and wind up in disintegration;

f) to withdraw from our people the fraternal solidarity and logistic support we have in neighbouring countries, by means of open aggression or armed provocation against these neighbouring countries.

In its efforts to apply these objectives, the enemy continues to practice the policy of attack and deceit, making a certain number of concessions of a social nature to the population it still controls and fiercely repressing all those who, individually and collectively, are suspected of nationalism or of concrete support to our party. The enemy, who acts with the conviction that the African peoples are 'the least intelligent in the world,' has not, however, attained the hoped-for results and his desperation in the face of failure is becoming more evident each day.

In urban centres and other zones still occupied (some coastal areas, the islands of Guinea and the Archipelago of Cape Verde), the enemy's position is less secure all the time. This is the result, on the one hand, of the most vigourous daily attitude of our armed forces and, on the other hand, of the development of clandestine work by our party in the urban centres of the continent and in the islands.

In Guinea, the enemy continues his policy of lies, demagogic concessions, promises of promotion of Africans, even of a 'social revolution' (sic) which, if it were the case, would not only carry out the socio-economic program of our party, but would also give our people a much more advanced standard of living than that of the people of Portugal. To complete the farce, the present head of the Portuguese colonialists – the sinister General Spínola – now promises to 'give the people self-determination under the Portuguese banner.' Fervently clinging to the theories of General Kaúlza de Arriaga, who considers the black to be an unintelligent person, the military government of Guinea seeks to live the fable of the wise man who had promised the king he would be able to teach an ass to read. Like the man in the fable, he is doubtless convinced that in the long run either the ass or the king will die; or perhaps he will die.

Having almost reached the end of the four-year mandate during which our struggle, that he had sworn to liquidate, has developed, intensified and consolidated itself on all fronts and levels, General Spínola is beginning to demonstrate his confusion, ever greater because of the growing support that the populations of the urban centres themselves give to our party.

Thus, after the attacks against Bissau and Bafatá, and faced with a broad and favourable reaction by the populations of these cities, the military governor issued a menacing declaration on July 25 over Radio Bissau, and dropped his paternalistic and reformist mask, revealing his true nature.

It is worth quoting certain passages from this declaration which, like the attacks against Bissau and Bafatá, marks the beginning of a new stage in the conflict that opposes us to the government of Portugal. It affirmed:

With all the circumstances this province has gone through, it should surprise no one that rumours – sometimes fantastic – should circulate, since this is a constant matter everywhere at all times, which we cannot pretend to avoid totally [...]. Nevertheless, the volume and nature of the rumours that have recently circulated have unfortunately found a certain receptivity among the most timorous. This has caused a climate of unjustified apprehension in the capital of the province. But it is necessary to demand that an unequivocal position be taken that returns the situation to normal so that no one can harm anyone whose serene capacity to judge is upset by fear.

After having noted that 'adequate measures have been taken to ensure peace and security at all times,' it threatens the most severe repression:

It is also important that there be no illusions concerning the firmness that the government will use to guarantee the peace, order and security of citizens. Any attempt against individual or collective security will consequently be considered an act of betrayal against the people of Guinea. Proceedings against the authors will be inexorably applied in the name of respect for the principles of the liberty and equality we defend and to which all good Guineans so correctly aspire. And any breach of civil discipline that, can disturb the normal complicity, an act of betrayal of the people will, as such, be repressed without the slightest contemplation and with all the severity merited by the enemy, as well as all those who support his interests, which have nothing in common with Portuguese Guinea.

It is true that no one should have any doubt as to the fact that the normal rhythm of life in the city will be preserved at all costs and under all circumstances. Whatever measures are necessary will be used, and their effectiveness will be doubted only by those who do not yet know the firmness and determination of the governor of the province.

If it is true that this declaration confirms the fact that the populations in the urban centres, in particular in Bissau, support the struggle (as the secret report of the Portuguese high command notes), there is no doubt that this is also the confession of the failure of the so-called policy of 'better Guinea,' as well as of all the attempts made by the colonialists to consolidate their present positions.

Faced with the patriotic resistance of the people in the liberated regions who are increasingly aware of the realities and objectives of the struggle and are better off because of party organisation, the Portuguese colonialists have intensified bombings and acts of terrorism during 1971. They could do this because they have received new airplanes and helicopters from their allies, but nevertheless, they have not achieved their objectives. The organisation of self-defence among the population is very efficient, both with respect to bombardments and to terroristic attacks and attempts to burn our crops in order to conquer us by hunger. What they succeeded in destroying during the first months of 1971 is not sufficiently significant to upset the victorious advance of our struggle. On the other hand, in the absence of an effective anti-aerial defence, the measures of civil defence generally adopted by the people have contributed to a significant drop in the number of victims of barbarous actions by the Portuguese airmen.

The attempt to maintain war for the sake of war, and involve Africans – most of them recruited by force – in fighting against Africans, is a pressing need for the colonialists because of the heightened resistance and conflicts within the colonial troops. But it is doomed to failure, especially after the shameful defeat suffered by the colonialists during the imperialist aggression against the Republic of Guinea. In Conakry as in Koundara and in Gaoual, the Portuguese, along with the European militarists and the mercenaries from the Republic of Guinea, were responsible for a certain number of the so-called 'African units' the overwhelming majority of whom did not return to Bissau because they were dead or imprisoned. This fact, which caused protests by the victims' relatives in Bissau and in other urban centres, is a tragic lesson for the Africans who still allow themselves to be enrolled in the Portuguese colonial army. On the other hand, the liquidation, in the course of this year, of certain of their leaders such as 'Captains' João Bacar Djaló and Guela Baldé, and 'Lieutenant' Loro Bamba, has upset the sinister plans of the colonialists. And so they face growing difficulties even in the recruitment of mercenaries and right-wing common prisoners, and desertion mounts within their supposed 'African companies.'

As for the enemy's positions, we attacked all of them during the first months of 1971, including the capital, Bissau. Today, the colonial troops know they are not safe in any part of our country. Meanwhile, civilians in the urban centres, particularly the Portuguese, currently live in a permanent state of alert and scarcely conceal their fear. The majority of the officers are sending their families back to Portugal. Not only has the enemy seen the security of his troops diminished but he has also had to recognise that our party's solidity has increased and that our armed forces are stronger than ever. Taking into account the disparity of material and human resources between the enemy and our forces, this fact represents a great defeat for the Portuguese colonialists.

In desperation, the enemy has multiplied armed provocations and criminal acts against neighbouring countries despite the condemnation of the United Nations and world opinion. There have been various aggressions against the population of Casamance (Senegal) and the frontier zone with the Republic of Guinea. In their dream of freeing themselves from the weight of our struggle, the Portuguese colonialists, with the support of their allies, are preparing a new imperialist aggression against this latter country. As with the preceding one, such aggression will have as its objective the overthrow of the regime of President Sékou Touré and replacing him with a government favourable to Portuguese domination of our country.

The Portuguese colonialists are also doomed to failure on this level: our relations with the governments and peoples of the neighbouring countries are better all the time and no aggression against the Republic of Guinea could deter the advance of our struggle. An eventual aggression in any form will contribute to strengthening still further the ties that join our people to those of the Republic of Guinea and will reinforce African and international solidarity with our struggle.

The modifications, introduced in the structure and functioning of the directive organ of the party by the meeting of the broadened Political Bureau held in April 1970, have permitted a great improvement in the work of militants and those responsible for various levels of our activity. The political work of the local commissaries and Political Action Brigades (PAB) has shown itself to be much more effective in the organisation and leadership of people in the liberated zones as well as in the realization of new initiatives determined by the top leadership of the party. Despite certain difficulties in starting the work of the National Committees of the Liberated Regions (NCLR), the regional committees (RC), the zonal committees (ZC) and the village committees (VC) have worked at a normal rhythm and have been highly productive.

After the work was begun toward the end of 1970, the party secretary-general held many reunions with delegates from the base committees (close to 200 delegates, a third of whom were women). These meetings, really seminars, were enthusiastically welcomed by the village committees and by the people, and have had visible results in the militant spirit and actions at the base. This is an initiative that we must continue to develop with great attention.

The results of the school year have been encouraging, both with respect to the schools in the liberated regions (despite the terroristic action of the enemy) and in the Friendship Institute. Close to a hundred boys and girls have been selected this year to continue their studies in friendly countries, and have already left.

In health, where there is still a certain amount of confusion and a certain inefficiency in the work of the intermediary cadres, particularly the nurses, there has been an overall improvement in administering medicine and in assistance to the population. The vaccination campaigns, particularly against cholera, have allowed us to avoid serious problems. However, despite the return to the country of a number of doctors trained during the course of the struggle, we have run into certain difficulties in this area. A large number of the foreign doctors who came to give us their assistance became ill and had to interrupt their activities.

Despite insufficient rain during the agricultural year 1970–71, general production covered the needs of the population and there was enough for the basic nourishment of the fighters. The return to the country of various technical cadres in agriculture (agronomists, technical agents and other specialists) trained abroad will permit a considerable improvement in assistance to the peasants, but above all will permit certain limited projects to be carried out and certain experiments to be made that will serve as the basis for agricultural development, which is the principal factor in our economy.

The people's stores have been greatly improved with respect to the articles placed at the disposal of the people, principally cloth, thanks to international solidarity.

On the Cape Verde Islands, conscious of the progress our party has made over the course of recent years, which is reflected in the strengthening of our clandestine organisation and the growth of a nationalist spirit within the population, the Portuguese colonialists are reinforcing their vigilance and repression everywhere. Fourteen fellow countrymen were arrested and accused of belonging to PAIGC and of an attempt to detour a trading ship toward Dakar. Nevertheless, under pressure of public opinion, the Portuguese colonialists found themselves forced to absolve another four fellow countrymen on trial in San Vicente who were part of a previously arrested group.

As a result of a criminal policy of abandoning the people of the archipelago to natural contingencies, the people are still suffering hunger after three years of drought. The colonialists have tried to take advantage of this circumstance to destroy the bases of our struggle's advancement in the islands, and have resorted to the exportation of workers to São Tomé and Portugal where some 10,000 Cape Verde natives have been sent.

Our party's denunciation in April 1971 of the starvation situation, forced the colonialists – who refused to accept the humanitarian aid of international solidarity – to take certain measures to 'combat the crisis.' But these measures did not succeed in deceiving our people who, aware of the necessity to free themselves from colonial domination in order to get rid of misery and hunger, increasingly support our party's activities. The reality of the increase in party activity .in the islands and of the support it has there is recognised by the enemy himself. For example, in the secret report by the Portuguese High Command the enemy states:

Over this period there have been two subversive appeals directed to military officers, sergeants and soldiers of Cape Verde. On the night of 31 December, pamphlets were distributed on three islands; in May, packages with PAIGC pamphlets destined for the islands were intercepted in Lisbon.

Actually, on 31 December, pamphlets were distributed simultaneously on all the populated islands.

During the first months of 1971, conflicts between segments of the population and the colonialist troops increased significantly on the main islands. The colonial, civil and military administration is more isolated every day. An abyss between the colonial class and the people, between the servants of colonialism and the patriots, is progressively widening.

During the meeting of the Higher Council for Struggle (CSL) held in August 1971, which made a deep study of the principal problems of our life and our struggle, important decisions were taken with the aim of strengthening and improving political works, consolidating the structures for our development, and intensifying and broadening of our armed action. Among the decisions, it is important to single out the creation of the first National Assembly of the people of Guinea, which will be selected at the appropriate time and will give our people an essential organ of sovereignty that will open new perspectives for our political action, in our own country and abroad. It is equally appropriate to mention in particular the decisions related to strengthening the armed struggle, the development of the struggle on the Cape Verde Islands and, on the human level, the creation of the Red Cross of Guinea and Cape Verde. With the permission of Radio Senegal (three times a week) and Radio Mauritania (once a week) – which have joined the programs already being broadcast over the Voice of the Revolution (in the Republic of Guinea, four times a week) – we have greatly amplified the possibilities of reaching our people and those of Africa.

On the African level, our relations with independent countries have been broadened and consolidated over the course of the first months of 1971. In addition to the consolidation of our relations with neighbouring countries – among them the Republic of Senegal, which evidences increasing interest in giving us all possible help – countries such as Nigeria, Somalia, Sudan, Tunisia, Libya, and other states have expressed a desire to extend bilateral aid such as others are now doing.

The Conference of Chiefs of State held in June of 1971 in Addis-Ababa was an important victory for the African liberation movement, in particular for our party. Once more, we were designated unanimously as the voice of the liberation movements at the conference. The decision to increase aid to the liberty fighters and the creation of a Special Commission of the OAU for western Africa whose subdirector, is a member of the leadership of our party permits us to anticipate a considerable increase in African solidarity with our struggle. The Liberation Committee unsparingly continues to give us all possible aid. In fulfilment of the decisions of the Special Conference of Lagos (December 1970), the committee gave our party special financial aid which was extremely useful.

We must stress that during the course of the conversations we have held with various African chiefs of state in Addis-Ababa, Conakry or in their own countries, as well as with the Secretary-General of the OAU and the members of the Executive Secretariat of the Liberation Committee, we have always encountered the greatest concern for our struggle and an enthusiastic desire to aid our party. It is a great stimulus for our people and for all the fighters of our organisation.

On the international plane, where the enemy himself recognises that he is more strongly accused, condemned and morally isolated despite the political and material support of NATO and other allies we have achieved considerable progress in the first months of 1971.

Relations of solidarity with the Soviet Union and other socialist countries are increasingly useful to our struggle. They are translated concretely into important aid in articles of primary necessity and in other materials we have already received this year. In the Western countries, the Support Committees in general have intensified their information activities and their collections of gifts of solidarity. Sweden has decided to double the aid it gave us last year; Norway and other Scandinavian countries also seem disposed to aid us. It is important here to mention especially the valiant attitude of the Norwegian Minister of Foreign Relations during the last meeting of the NATO Council in Lisbon where he denounced Portuguese policy and colonial wars as contrary to the interests of humanity and incompatible with the principles enumerated in the Charter of the organisation.

In Portugal the people are evidencing increasing awareness of the fact that the colonial war is a crime, against their own interests. Each day there are more demonstrations against colonial policy and the actions carried out by the brave Portuguese patriots of Armed Revolutionary Action (ARA) represent important victories in the common struggle against the colonial war and a guarantee of friendship and solidarity on the part of the Portuguese people that our people wish to maintain, develop, consolidate.

On the military level, the action of the Portuguese colonialists continues to be dominated by this truth, frequently recognised publicly by the colonial authorities themselves: *they cannot win the war they are waging against our African people*. This results not only from the growing combativity of our armed forces and the victories achieved on the battlefields, but also from the constant elevation of the level of our people's political consciousness. Aware of this fact, the colonialists try by every means possible to commit the most barbarous crimes against our people, to kill our cattle, burn our crops, in a word, to develop and intensify their criminal and terroristic activity, which gives the lie to their pretensions of socio-economic and political promotion of our people.

For this reason, the action of the enemy during the first months of 1971 was characterised by intense and continuous aerial bombardments, mainly with napalm, and by airborne troop assaults aimed at the destruction of villages, crop burning and cattle killing. As we said, having been provided by their allies with new and better planes and helicopters, the colonists have augmented their bombardments and terrorist actions. Nevertheless, in the face of the valiant resistance of the people and fighters, they have seldom achieved their objectives. The regions most affected by these criminal acts are precisely the most populous and those in which the party organisation is most developed: Cubisseco, Cubucare, Balana frontier zone (in the south), Oio and Saara (in the north).

Dozens of villages were destroyed, an appreciable amount of rice was burned in the regions of Unal, Tombali and Como and some 200 head of cattle were killed. Fortunately, the loss in human lives is far below the criminal intentions of the enemy who attacks hospitals and schools by preference and takes his principal victims from among the elderly and the children.

The action of our armed forces during the first semester of 1971, in the dry season, achieved a breadth and vigour never before equalled. It is a fact known to the Portuguese colonialists themselves that in order to sustain the impression created by its war communiqués – although these are never quite true – they have tried to make believe that the intensification and development of our armed struggle was due to the presence of foreign specialists, chiefly Cubans, within our armed forces. This lie, like so many other, has convinced no one who isn't already convinced, and has only served to improve once again the capacity and high level of initiative of our fighters who unsparingly sacrifice to put into practice the slogans of our party's War Council.

Restructured into various army corps and drawn in part from the defense forces of the liberated regions, thanks to the creation and strengthening of the Local Armed Forces, our National Armed Forces have developed and intensified their action on all fronts; by doubling the initiative, we have completely disoriented the enemy who sees his plans condemned to failure. We have carried out 86 attacks against Portuguese positions (at the rate of three attacks a day); we have laid eight fatal ambushes and put out of combat more than 250 soldiers and officers of the colonial army, among them 158 established dead. Among the operations we have carried out, we should note particularly the campaign successfully led by the army corps on the Kinara front (from April to June), where all enemy positions were attacked on various occasions and suffered great human and material losses; the actions that took place on the Catió front, where the city of the same name was attacked twice by our combatants causing great destruction; the actions on the eastern front where, on three occasions, the city of Gabú was the object of assault by our forces, which, in addition, laid the most damaging ambushes suffered by the enemy during the course of the struggle. In one of these ambushes, the garrison commander of Pitche was killed; ten trucks, a tank and various cannons were destroyed; finally, the no less important, intensive and continuous operations directed against Portuguese positions all along the Senegal border.

But the first semester of 1971 will go down in the history of our struggle as the period in which, for the first time, we have been capable of attacking all the urban centres still occupied by the enemy, including the capital Bissau, and Bafatá, the country's second most important city. The attacks against the colonial positions of Bissau and Bafatá mark a new stage in the political-military evolution of our struggle. If such were necessary, they are a new and clear refutation of the allegation that serves as a pretext for the criminal aggressions against our country, namely that we are acting from neighbouring countries.

It is a fact that the attack against Bissau was more of a warning to the population of the capital, and that to carry it out we had to attack seven enemy garrisons of logistic support. Thus the human and material losses to the enemy were not great, but the psychological and political effect of the action surpasses all others so far undertaken. In Bafatá, where our infantry entered and remained for some time without enemy response, our fighters destroyed four garrisons, the meteorological station, the airport control tower and various buildings of the military and administrative infrastructure, and several sections of the colonial troops were put out of combat. Our fighters also carried out 75 arrests of suspicious individuals in order to interrogate them, following which 58 were released.

During the period January–August 1971, we carried out 508 important actions:

- 369 attacks against garrisons in urban centres;
- 102 ambushes and other operations on the highways;
- 15 very important mining actions;
- 14 actions against river transportation; and
- 8 operations by commandos in urban centres.

Our forces put out of combat 480 dead, 735 soldiers and enemy agents, confirmed. The confirmed number of wounded (255) is far from corresponding to the real total. In effect, information from Lisbon and Bissau indicates that the military hospitals in these cities have never had as many wounded, as they have this year. On the material level, we have destroyed or damaged 90 military vehicles, sunk 28 ships and coast guard craft in the rivers, shot down two planes and three helicopters. Our forces, which have expelled the enemy from three battlefields and have demolished several encampments such as that in Umaru Cosse on the eastern front, seized an important supply of war materials, principally G-3 machine guns, Mausers, American bazookas and telecommunication apparatuses.

While it is true that this does not represent the victorious end of our armed liberation struggle, nevertheless there is no doubt that, for eight months of action, it is the best in our eight and a half years of struggle and represents a decisive contribution to the certain victory of our liberation battle. It is this result and all the victories achieved that explain the growing desperation of the Portuguese colonialists, the increasingly ferocity and savagery of their colonial war.

In order to try to justify their criminal obstinacy against our progress in the struggle, the Portuguese colonialists resort to every type of argument, such as that presented by General Kaúlza de Arriaga, for instance, who stated in the *Strategic Lessons of the Course of the High Command*:

Naturally, when our troops die in Guinea and we are spending a great deal of money there, we do not take these losses into consideration nor think that this money is spent only for the defense of Guinea. If this were the case, it would not really be reasonable; but a man who dies in Guinea indirectly defends Angola and Mozambique.

If this affirmation reveals to the fullest the miserable nature, the cynicism and the scorn of the Portuguese colonial leaders for human beings – for the Portuguese man himself – it has the merit of recording the community of the struggle and the interests that unite our people with the brother peoples of Angola and Mozambique. It clearly shows the degree of our responsibilities in the united struggle for the total liquidation of the Portuguese colonial presence in Africa.

To draw the best out of victories our people have achieved, and the successes already won this year, to meet the level of our responsibilities, we must make 1971 one of the most decisive periods in our long and rich struggle. We must constantly strengthen our awareness of realities and not forget that we face a desperate and unscrupulous enemy, be ready to make greater efforts and sacrifices, to overcome all difficulties, progressively correct our errors and deficiencies, continuously improve our individual and collective behaviour and our action in political and military areas, as in all other branches of the new life we have begun to build.

At the same time that we intensify our armed action and blunt the enemy's claws, we must pay greater attention to political work in our own country, in Africa and internationally. One of the principal forces, if not the main one, of the Portuguese colonies is the political and material aid of their allies. We must draw all the lessons from this reality, both for the present and for the future, develop and consolidate friendship and solidarity with all anti-imperialist and anti-colonial forces, tighten our links with the Africans and non-Africans who are aiding us in this difficult struggle and are giving us true proof of their friendship.

No manoeuvre, no crime of the Portuguese colonialists, no force in the world will be able to prevent the inevitable victory of our African people on the road of national liberation and the construction of peace and progress to which they are entitled.

The Struggle
Has Taken Root

Tricontinental published the press conference which Amílcar Cabral, martyr of the African Independence, held in Conakry in September of 1972, after the conclusion of a Week of Information to divulge the life and the struggle in Guinea-Bissau.

Everyone was aware of the famous call of the Portuguese government to the liberation movements of the Portuguese colonies. The Portuguese government offers 'the peace of the generous' to fighters of the Portuguese colonies. This is nothing new at all since throughout the course of liberation wars, governments have offered fighters the peace of the generous.

Whoever has carefully followed the position of the Portuguese government will certainly have observed that a very short time ago the fighters of the Portuguese colonies and particularly those in our country were considered big bandits, criminal people whom it was necessary to punish as severely as possible. The Portuguese government has moved from this only because it finds itself cut off.

Today is not yesterday. Our situation is different since the UN, through the Committee on Decolonisation, and after a special mission to our country, proclaimed that PAIGC is the only and legitimate representative of our people, and oriented all States, all organisations, all persons who wish to handle any problem relating to our people to go to PAIGC as their only representative. From that moment on Señor Caetano or any other spokesman of the Portuguese government no longer had the right to speak in the name of our people.

Unfortunately international information and press are dominated by forces that are not favourable to the people's liberation struggle. Even in Africa information comes solely from imperialist sources. We have asked for greater publicity within the UN and we consider that the results are small compared to our desires. We know that the members of the mission have made a lot of noise in the UN about this but, with certain exceptions, the international press and radio have not given the necessary publicity to this event; what they have noted are the lying declaration of the Portuguese colonialists who pretend that PAIGC confused the members of the mission by taking them through cities of the Republic of Guinea under Portuguese bombs. The Portuguese have said repeatedly that the mission did not visit the south of my country, but the mission described in a very detailed manner its visit to a school in the south of my country. A few days ago, the Portuguese bombed that school;

they assaulted it with 12 helicopters and they weren't satisfied until they had attacked that precise boarding school because it had been visited by the mission. We denounced this fact before the United Nations and have received a cable from the President of the Committee of investigations which says that our communiqué was considered an official document and that they are going to take all measures to denounce this crime by the Portuguese colonialists. This will not prevent us from continuing; we will make another boarding school and keep on educating the children.

As for the resolution, if depends on the activity of men whether resolutions have value, whether they are good or bad. Everywhere we have gone, and in different areas, we have confirmed that it has been taken very seriously, first of all by the Portuguese themselves, it opens new perspectives for our own action and we are determined to act, for to a certain extent it will depend on us to maintain its character. It will also depend on our African friends and on all our friends in the rest of the world.

The International Labour Organisation took a firm position against Portuguese colonialism and in favour of our struggle and in its last meeting, agreed that we it. This is also a political victory of great importance. We will try to develop our relations with the FAO and WHO and we can move forward since there is good will toward our demands on the part of these organisations.

The voice of Portugal inside the United Nations is actually very weak. It is enough to follow the voting to see how Portugal was beaten in a most shameful way and how only the racists vote for Portugal. Portugal's allies abstain when the moment comes to take important decisions, as for example, was the case during the Security Council meetings in Addis Ababa.

As far as the OAU is concerned, we have always said that we consider the aid it provides us through the Council of African Liberation to be very useful, but we consider that it is far from matching the needs of our present struggle. We hope that after the Rabat Conference, with the 50% increase in the budget for the African liberation fund, and above all with other contributions that can increase those funds substantially, the OAU will be in a position to provide us with more effective aid. We also hope that OAU aid will not exclude bilateral aid from African countries directly to our party, as occurred with some international progressive organisations.

We also feel very elated by the aid that Sweden has decided to give us. In three years, its aid to our party and our people – not military but humanitarian – has multiplied in accelerated form, with articles of primary necessity for supply to the liberated region. This is very important for us, as is the position of other Scandinavian countries. We have just received a letter from the Norwegian Foreign Relations Minister who announced aid of a million crowns in articles of prime necessity, and Denmark is going to help us in public health and other fields. The Finnish friends have just sent a memorandum to their government in which they urge that it agree to aid our party and other liberation movements.

Last year we visited Finland where our liberation movement was received by the President of the Republic.

Other organisations help us, including support committees created in countries allied with Portugal, such as England, France, Holland, Belgium, which issue a great deal of propaganda in favour of our struggle. Despite the fact that we are prohibited from going to France, there are French who send us fresh blood every two weeks. There are organisations such as the World Council of Churches; the Ranken Trust Social Service of England; the Conference of African Churches and other organisations that provide aid to us. Naturally, we have the support of the mass international organisations but it is political above all and we appreciate it very much.

We have always affirmed that aid from the socialist states is an important factor in our struggle.

We have issued an appeal in Rabat to all the governments of the NATO countries, and Portugal's allies in general, begging them to halt their aid to Portugal in all fields, since all serve the war when one is at war. We have said frankly that we cannot confuse Portuguese colonialism and Portugal's allies. But it is also necessary that these governments should be capable of understanding that the African peoples are not obliged to believe that they can be friends of Africa when they provide aid in arms, money and all means to the worst enemy of Africa, Portuguese colonialism. We consequently want to see these countries separate themselves from the government of Portugal and stop providing it with aid which serves to carry out the war against the African countries.

THE WALKING CADAVER

The whole world is aware that the Portuguese government is not able to carry out three colonial wars on the African continent and engage in repeated aggressions against the African countries. This very serious aspect was demonstrated on November 22, 1970, against the Republic of Guinea. It would not be able to engage in its criminal policy against the African peoples if it did not have the strongest, most effective and constantly more developed aid of its NATO allies. The aid provided by NATO is no secret to anyone, nor that Portugal uses and abuses it. Sr Caetano has repeated on various occasions in his speeches that he didn't know how to find the money to meet the increasing expenses of the war. Only the disingenuous can believe that with a loan of $500,000,000 – even if given under the guise of a loan for economic-social-cultural purposes – this bellicose government is not going to use it to unfold the war. If Portugal continues the war it is because its allies, especially those in NATO, provide it with substantial and increasingly developed aid.

Youth who represent the people of Portugal have carried out armed actions against the colonial government. Portuguese youth are increasingly opposed to the colonial war, there are mass desertions in the ranks of the colonial army. France now has the largest Portuguese colony because there are 600,000 Portuguese there, more than all the Portuguese colonists in the colonies. What is the reason? Lack of work in Portugal, the misery that Portugal has always suffered but suffers more today, especially the colonial war that forces families to mortgage their goods to send their children out of the country and avoid a useless and inglorious death on African soil.

We consider that an important reason for the Portuguese government's peace offer to the fighters for African freedom is the fact that they are deeply interested in becoming a part of the European Common Market (ECM). There have been very great obstacles to their attempt. One is that the countries of the ECM recognise that with three colonial wars on the African continent, and a population that is decreasing rather than increasing, it is not possible for Portugal to be a valid element in the ECM, much less when the whole world knows that it is an underdeveloped country and the most backward one in Europe. Meanwhile, Caetano believes in the magic of words and pretends that there is no war in our countries, in order to confuse the partisans of the ECM. Now he announces he is going to release 15,000 prisoners from the liberation movement in the Portuguese colonies. As a Portuguese refrain says: 'It's easier to discover a liar than a cripple'.

OUR INTERNAL ADVANCES AND FRONTIER AID

We ardently hope that the members of the ECM respect the principles that serve as the basis of their organisation and do not admit Portugal, aggressive country in Africa. We raise this problem on a basis of material interest, because it offers no value to the ECM as an associate.

While Sr. Caetano was making his speech trying to confuse his allies once more, our people in the liberated regions were holding elections for the regional councils and our first People's National Assembly. In the majority of sectors of the liberated zones these elections have been held and we even have the results from the majority of them and we will make them public at the opportune time, when we have completed elections for the People's National Assembly.

The creation of our People's National Assembly represents the culmination of the development of an essential stage of our people's sovereignty, of which the special mission of the United Nations had proof during the visit made last April. It is called upon to make very important decisions concerning our struggle and we hope to be able to hold a meeting of this Assembly before the end of this year.

We have the total support of all the independent African states, which have understood the significance of these initiatives, especially the creation of the regional councils and the People's National Assembly. Because of this, we have emerged from Rabat stronger because of the position concerning our party and our struggle adopted by heads of state and of government who offer proof of their desire to strengthen aid to the liberation movements and to do everything possible so that Africa may free itself as quickly as possible from the remains of colonial and racist domination that still exist.

In the present phase of the struggle we must act throughout the country. We are developing the clandestine organisation of our party in the urban centres, we are preparing our military for new actions. We are carrying out an action in the very interior of those centres against Portuguese military society, against the agents of the Portuguese colonial class, the military, the police.

The population of the urban centres, especially in Bissau, is increasingly favourable to the liberation struggle and to our party. The youth are abandoning these centres to join the ranks of the struggle. The military governor of Bissau has threatened the populations of the urban centres in a radio address, telling them that he will ferociously repress all those who disturb the peace. He was the hangman of the Portuguese, of the Portuguese workers, when he was the adjutant director of the republican national guard; he was the assassin of thousands of Angolans when he was the commander of the Portuguese cavalry in Angola. In the Republic of Guinea and Senegal he has already provided proof of killing, but his threats have not held back events, and the guerrilla organisation is stronger in the urban centres, and conditions for carrying out action in them are more favourable.

Our party has always operated so that the neighbouring countries would be logistics bases, but not bases for stationing troops. We have always said this in relation to Guinea and, having overcome certain difficulties which we also understand completely, we now have this arrangement with Senegal also. Naturally the base is much deeper in Guinea than in Senegal but we believe that our duty is to rely on what each of our African brothers can provide and not on all that we would like them to give us. We are very satisfied to be able to use Guinea and Senegal as transit points for certain materials that are essential to our struggle. Naturally each African country can also carry out the function of logistics base. We would once more like to pay homage to the determined action by the PDG in favour of our liberation struggle, the unconditional support of the entire Guinean people for our liberation fight against the fascist, colonialist, Portuguese hordes, and especially to the leader of the PDG, our brother and comrade, President Ahmed Sekou Touré. We also thank Senegal very much.

OUR STRUGGLE WITHIN THE ANTI-IMPERIALIST FRAMEWORK

Imperialism is one, therefore the struggle against it is one, and our people are aware of this, even the children.

We do not speak only of the common struggle of the peoples of Guinea, Angola, Cape Verde, Mozambique, but of all Africa in general against imperialism, that of the Latin American patriots, of the people of Viet Nam, of the other peoples of Indochina, of all African peoples against colonialism and neo-colonialism, of the exploited classes and foremost, those of Portugal, all are part of our own struggle.

We want all the world to be aware of this, so that all fronts of the struggle become stronger every day and so we all work together for the active unity of the anti-imperialist forces, since the imperialist enemy knows how to maintain his unity in confronting all those who want to free themselves.

New Year's Message, 1973

This message was released in January 1974.

Comrades, compatriots,

At this moment when we are beginning a new year of life and struggle and our fight for the independence of our African people is ten years old, I must remind everyone – militants, combatants, responsible workers and leaders in our great Party – that it is time for action and not words. Time for action in Guiné that is each day more vigourous and more effective, in order to inflict greater defeats on the Portuguese colonialists and remove from them all their criminal and vain pretensions of reconquering our land. Action that is constantly more developed and better organised in Cape Verde to carry the struggle into a new phase, in accordance with the aspirations of our people and the imperatives of the total liberation of our African country.

I must, however, respect tradition by addressing a few words to you at a time when all sane human beings – those who want peace, freedom and happiness for all men – renew their hopes and the belief in a better life for mankind, in dignity, independence and genuine progress for all peoples.

As you all know, in the past year we held general elections in the liberated areas, with universal suffrage and a secret vote, for the creation of Regional Councils and the first National Assembly in our people's history. In all sectors of all regions, the elections were conducted in an atmosphere of great enthusiasm on the part of the population. The electorate voted massively for the lists that had been drawn up after eight months of public and democratic discussions, in which the representatives of each sector were selected. When the elected Regional Councils met, they elected in their turn representatives to the People's National Assembly from among their members. This will have 120 members, of whom 80 were elected from among the mass of the people and 40 from among the political cadres, soldiers, technicians and others of the Party. As you know, the representatives for the sectors temporarily occupied by the colonialists have been chosen provisionally.

Today our African people of Guiné possess another organ of sovereignty, their People's National Assembly. In accordance with the Constitution we are drawing up, this will be the supreme organ of sovereignty of our people in Guiné. Tomorrow, with the certain development of the struggle, we shall also create the first People's National Assembly in Cape Verde. The joint meeting of the members of these two bodies will constitute the Supreme Assembly of the People of Cuba and Cape Verde.

The creation of the first People's National Assembly in Guiné is an epoch-making victory for the difficult but glorious struggle of our people for independence. It opens up new prospects for the advance of our political and military action, is the result of the efforts and sacrifices offered by our people in these ten years of armed struggle, and it is practical proof of the sovereignty of our people and their high degree of national and patriotic consciousness. I wish, therefore, at this moment to address my warmest congratulations to our people, to all the electorate, who as conscientious men and women have been able so worthily to accomplish their duties as free citizens of our African nation, to all the militants, responsible workers and leaders who, in the electoral committees or in other sectors of activity, have contributed their utmost for the success of this venture which will live in the history of our land. With equal enthusiasm, I congratulate the valourous combatants of our armed forces, who by their courageous action have created in all sectors the security needed for holding the elections in spite of all the criminal attempts of the colonialist enemy to prevent their taking place.

But a national assembly, like any organ in any living body, must be able to function in order to justify its existence. For this reason, we have a greater task to fulfil in the framework of our struggle in this new year of 1973: we must put our People's National Assembly into operation. And this we shall do, to implement completely the decisions taken by our great Party, at the meeting of the Supreme Council of the Struggle in August 1971, decisions which were enthusiastically supported by the people.

In the course of this coming year and as soon as it is conveniently possible we shall call a meeting of our People's National Assembly in Guiné, so that it can fulfil the first historic mission incumbent on it: the proclamation of the existence of our state, the creation of an executive for this state and the promulgation of a fundamental law – that of the first constitution in our history – which will be the basis of the active existence of our African nation. That is to say: legitimate representatives of our people, chosen by the populations and freely elected by conscientious and patriotic citizens of our land, will proceed to the most important act of their life and of the life of our people, that of declaring before the world that our African nation, forged in the struggle, is irrevocably determined to march forward to independence without waiting for the consent of the Portuguese colonialists and that from then on the executive of our state under the leadership of our Party, the PAIGC, will be the sole, true and legitimate representative of our people in all the national and international questions that concern them.

We are moving from the situation of a colony which has a liberation movement, and whose people have already liberated in ten years of armed struggle the greater part of their national territory, to the situation of a country which runs its own state and which has a part of its national territory occupied by foreign armed forces.

The radical change in the situation in our land corresponds to the specific reality of the life and struggle of our people in Guiné, is based on specific results of our struggle, and has the firm support of all African countries and governments and of all the anti-colonialist and anti-racist forces in the world. It also corresponds to the principles of the United Nations Charter and to the resolutions adopted by that international organisation, notably in its 27th session.

Nothing, no criminal action or conjuring trick by the Portuguese colonialists can prevent our African people, masters of their own destiny and aware of their rights and duties, from taking this transcendent and decisive step towards the achievement of the fundamental aim of our struggle: the winning of national independence and the building, in restored peace and dignity, of their genuine progress under the exclusive leadership of their own sons and daughters, under the glorious banner of our Party.

The epoch-making importance of the formation of the People's National Assembly, of the proclamation of the state in Guiné and of the creation of the corresponding executive bodies, who will be neither provisional nor living in exile, necessarily implies much greater responsibilities for our people and, particularly, for the militants, combatants, responsible workers and leaders of our Party. These historic initiatives demand from us all more efforts and daily sacrifices, more thought to act better, more activity to think better. They demand that we study every specific question that we have to resolve in such a way as to find the most appropriate solution for it in the specific circumstances of our land and our struggle. The initiatives demand that we intensify and develop our political and military action in Guiné, without neglecting the important activities we have developed on the economic, social and cultural levels. They demand that we successfully deploy the necessary efforts for the advance of the political struggle in Cape Verde and in order that our people in the islands should as soon as possible move into systematic, direct action against the criminal Portuguese colonialists.

In this perspective, we cannot for one moment forget that we are at war and that the principal enemy of our people and of Africa – the Portuguese Fascist colonialists – still nurture, with the sacrifice and misery of their people and by means of the most treacherous manoeuvres and most savage acts, the criminal intention and vain hope of destroying our Party, of eliminating our struggle and recolonising our people. For this reason, the greater part of our attention, our energies and our efforts must be devoted to the armed struggle, to war and to practical action by our national and local armed forces. For this reason, we must, in the course of 1973, set in motion all our human and material capacity and potential in order to intensify still further the struggle on all fronts to derive a greater return from the men, weapons and experience at our disposal, thereby to strike harder blows against the colonialist enemy by destroying a greater number of their living forces. For the history of colonial wars and our experience over ten years of struggle have taught us that the colonialist aggressors – and most particularly the Portuguese colonialist aggressors – understand only one language, that of force, and measure only one reality, the number of corpses.

It is true that in 1972 we inflicted heavy defeats and very significant losses on the criminal Portuguese colonialist aggressors. Within a few days our Information Services will publish the balance sheet of our action over the past year, which will be widely publicised by our broadcasting station Radio Libertação and by other information media. But we must recognise that the enemy, possessing more aircraft and helicopters supplied by their NATO allies, have significantly increased the shelling and terrorist raids against our liberated areas, have tried and are trying to create difficulties for us with their plans for reoccupying some localities within those areas. But above all we must recognise that, with the men, weapons and experience at our disposal, we could and should have done more and better. This is what we must do and certainly will do in 1973, the more so because we are going to use still heavier weapons and other instruments of war on all fronts.

On the basis of a greater number of better trained cadres and combatants with greater experience, we are going to make more effective use of all the means at our disposal and of those that we shall have, to strike decisive and mortal blows on the criminal Portuguese colonialist aggressors.

At the same time as we intensify armed action on all fronts, we must be capable of developing our action in the enemy rearguard and in the enemy heartland where they feel most secure. I congratulate here the brave militants who, by their determined action, struck important blows on the enemy over the past year, particularly in Bissau, Bafatá and Bula. But I draw everyone's attention to the need to develop and intensify this type of action. In fact the time has come when, on the basis of effective and strong clandestine organisation, we must destroy the greatest possible number of human and material assets of the criminal Portuguese colonialist aggressors in the urban centres of our land. In reality, we face a savage enemy who do not have the slightest scruple in their criminal actions, who use every possible means of trying to destroy us wherever we are. For this reason, and since we are struggling in our land for the sacred rights of our people to independence, peace and genuine progress, we must at this decisive moment strike against the colonialist and racist enemy – against them, their agents and their assets – telling blows wherever they are. This is an urgent task to which all the responsible workers and militants of this sector of the struggle must dedicate themselves with the greatest attention and most especially those comrades who with courage and determination are active in the urban centres and areas still occupied by the enemy.

I want to mention here an important question of the colonial war we face: the huge attempts the enemy have made to occupy or reoccupy some localities of our liberated areas. I remind comrades of the Party and our people that these attempts, successful or not, such as shelling and terrorist assaults, are characteristic of colonial war and necessarily form part of the action of the colonialist aggressor, especially when the patriotic forces have already liberated the greater part of the national territory, as in our case. We must therefore face this problem realistically and give it its correct evaluation within the general framework of our struggle, without exaggerating or minimising its importance.

As the comrades and above all the leaders and responsible workers of the Party know, in the context of its colonial war the colonialist aggressor faces a principal and insoluble contradiction, with which it has been taxed throughout the war. It is the following contradiction: so as to feel that it dominates the territory, it is obliged to disperse its troops, placing them so as to occupy the greatest possible number of localities. But by dispersing its troops, it becomes weaker and thus the concentrated patriotic forces can strike harder and mortal blows against it. Then it is obliged to withdraw to concentrate its troops and to try to avoid heavy losses in human lives, so as better to resist the advance of nationalist forces against whom it seeks to gain time. But by concentrating its troops, it abandons its military and political presence in vast areas of the country which are organised and administered by the patriotic forces.

In the current phase of our struggle and of the Portuguese colonial war, the enemy, blinded by despair at the defeats they have suffered and are suffering both in our land and at the international level, are trying, certainly in vain, to make the River Corubal return to the Futa Djalon instead of flowing towards the Geba and the sea. In this attempt, as in that of deceiving our people with the mirage of a 'better Guiné' Portuguese style, as with that of making Africans fight against Africans, they are doomed to failure: they will not be able to free themselves from the principal contradiction of their filthy colonial war.

What is important for us, on the basis of understanding the strategy to which the enemy are forced by the objective laws of colonial war, is not to worry too much because the enemy want to install themselves in Gampara, in Cabochanque, in Cadique or in other localities. The important thing is on the one hand for us to carry on with our plans for struggle and on the other to do our best to eliminate the greatest possible number of living forces of the enemy, when they install themselves or move to install themselves in any locality of our liberated areas. What counts is to strike hard blows at them, to allow them no rest, to turn an occupied position into a graveyard for their troops until they are forced to withdraw, as we have done in Balana, Gandembel and more recently in Cubisseco New Village. This is what we must do and will certainly do in any part of our liberated areas that the enemy occupy. We must also do this in their barracks and fortified camps still existing in our country.

Naturally in 1973 we must continue to intensify our political work among the mass of the people, both in the liberated areas and in the occupied zones of Guiné and in Cape Verde. Without in any way minimising the value of the work already done in this domain, which led to the failure of the spurious and notorious 'policy of a better Guiné', we must recognise that there are some sectors, if not regions, where political action is still deficient. In the course of this coming year, we have to make all the efforts needed to improve our action in these sectors, since, as we know, however important our armed action, our struggle is fundamentally a political struggle which has a specific political objective: the independence and progress of our land.

While I congratulate the comrades who in Guiné and in Cape Verde have greatly improved political work in the past year, I urge everyone to redouble efforts to consolidate and develop the political conquests of the Party and the struggle, constantly to raise the political awareness and patriotism of the mass of the people, of militants and of combatants, to strengthen the indestructible unity of our people, the essential basis of the successes of our struggle. In the sphere of security and control, to strengthen vigilance against the enemy and their agents, against all those who because of opportunism, ambition, moral weakness or servility towards the enemy might try to destroy our Party and hence the just struggle of our people for independence.

In Cape Verde, the events of September 1972, which constituted the first clash between the population of the archipelago and the forces of colonial repression, have once again shown the level of tension the political situation there has reached. In congratulating the patriots of Praia and S. Santiago, who acted with courage and determination in the face of provocation by the colonialists and their agents, I urge them constantly to improve their clandestine organisation, to operate with security and without enabling the enemy to eliminate the nationalist cadres, and to prepare themselves by every means within their reach for the new phase of our struggle in the archipelago, which is forced by the criminal obstinacy of the Portuguese colonialists. I reaffirm that the leadership of the Party is more determined than ever to do everything possible for the advance of the struggle in Cape Verde.

In view of the progress already made in the islands and the complexity of the particular problems to be solved, it has become necessary and urgent, in my opinion, to make a realistic modification in the structure of the leadership of the Party to give some comrades the possibility of devoting themselves entirely to development of the struggle in Cape Verde. Such a modification will be proposed to the next meeting of the Party leadership.

Still on the political level, I draw the attention of comrades to the diversity of new questions we have to study and solve in the appropriate way, which follow from the new prospects for development of the struggle which will be opened up by the proclamation of the state in Guiné: in the interior, improvement and development of the administrative services, creation of controlling bodies for our activities, a new population census, identification of all its component elements, etc; and in the exterior, organisation, control and protection of emigrant citizens, their identification with corresponding distribution of passports, mobilisation for the struggle of youth resident abroad, etc., not to mention the type of relations to be established at the international level. They are certainly new but very important questions that we must study thoroughly and solve in due course.

Concern with the war and with political work should not, however, make us forget or even underestimate the importance of our activities at the economic, social and cultural level, as the foundation of the new life we are creating in our liberated areas. We must all, but mainly the cadres who specialise in these matter, give the closest attention to questions of the economy, health, social welfare, education and culture, so as to improve our work significantly and to be ready to solve the great problems we have to face with the new situation the struggle is bringing. In this perspective, we must already face with determination and tenacity the key questions of improvement of supply and the living standards of our populations, taxes and exchequer, the new financial life we hope to establish, the currency we shall use, etc., as well as the type of social welfare we shall develop on the basis of our past experience, school systems and training of more cadres for national reconstruction and the building of our people's progress. So many new problems, but the more complex the more exciting, which we must be capable of solving at the same time as we intensify and develop our vigourous action at the politico-military level to expel the colonial troops from the positions they still occupy in our land of Guiné and Cape Verde. The specialist cadres of the Party must devote themselves attentively to the study and solution of these questions, in order to accomplish their duty towards our people.

On behalf of the Party leadership, I congratulate our agricultural producers in Guiné for the harvests collected last year, in spite of the scarcity of rains. I urge all to do more and better this year, to ensure a good crop for, as we know, this is the principal base of our life and our struggle, which the criminal Portuguese colonialist aggressors try to destroy by every means when they cannot steal from us the fruit of our people's labour.

But it is with sorrow that I recall here that at this very moment the populations of Cape Verde are menaced by famine. This is the fault of the Portuguese colonialists who never managed nor wanted to create the minimum of economic and social conditions in the archipelago to ensure subsistence and a decent life for the populations in years of prolonged drought Forced by the onward rush of the struggle and by the denunciation made by our Party before world opinion, the colonial Government of Portugal has granted loans and subsidies to Cape Verde in order, as the colonialists say, 'to relieve the crisis', meaning to avoid many folk dying of hunger at one time, but without preventing the weakest, above all children, from dying slowly from specific hunger or even total starvation. I raise my voice once again on behalf of the leadership of our Party to protest against this situation and to denounce the crime perpetrated by the colonial Fascist Government of Lisbon in transferring to Portugal about fifteen to twenty thousand young Cape Verdeans, to work in the mines, to sweep the streets in the main cities, for jobs as unskilled labourers, thus causing a great haemorrhage in the vital strength of Cape Verde, with the intention of barring the way to the advance of our liberating struggle. I appeal to Cape Verdean and Guinean patriots resident in Portugal to keep close contact and organise themselves, so that in conjunction with all the forced labourers transferred from Cape Verde they may develop their patriotic action in the service of the Party, our people and Africa, and at the right moment strike the blows the enemy deserves, thus making the fetish turn against the fetishist.

I draw the attention of those responsible for supply to the populations and principally of workers in the People's Stores, to the fact that this year the Party will have available greater than ever quantities of essential items which we must be able to put at the disposal of the populations of all the liberated areas, whatever difficulties we have to face. In fact both from the socialist countries, notably the Soviet Union, and from Sweden, Norway and other countries or humanitarian organisations, we are receiving aid which will enable us greatly to improve the functioning of the People's Stores as well as of health and education institutions. I hope that everyone will make the necessary efforts to make 1973 a year of greater efficiency still in supply to our populations of essential items.

As you all know, 1972 was a year of great and decisive victories on the international level for our great Party and our people. Among the main successes scored I want here to recall only the following: the now historic visit of the United Nations Special Mission to the liberated areas of our land, which brought important consequences for the prestige not only of our Party and our struggle but for all the liberation movements in Africa. In recalling this event, which the Portuguese colonialist aggressors wanted to oppose with their most savage crimes, I hail at the start of a new year the peoples of Ecuador, Sweden, Tunisia, Senegal and Japan, whose brave sons visited our land, as members of the Special Mission. I thank their respective governments for having agreed that their representatives should make such a visit and the United Nations Secretary-General for the determined way in which he applied a historic and transcendent resolution of the General Assembly of that international organisation.

The resolution of the United Nations Decolonisation Committee, in its April 1972 session, by which our Party was recognised by acclamation as the sole, true and legitimate representative of the people of Guiné and Cape Verde.

The resolutions of the United Nations General Assembly which, among other important decisions, confirmed the recognition of our Party as the sole and legitimate representative of our African people and called on all states, governments and national and international organisations and on the United Nations specialised agencies to reinforce their aid to our Party and always and only with the Party to treat all questions concerning the people of Guiné and Cape Verde.

The historic resolution of the Security Council which, under its first woman president, our Guinean sister and comrade Jeanne Martin Cissé, unanimously adopted a resolution condemning Portuguese colonialism and demanding that the government of Portugal cease the colonial war in Africa, withdraw its occupation troops and enter into negotiations without delay with the respective patriotic forces, which in our land are represented by our Party. For the first time in the political and diplomatic struggle against Portuguese colonialism, our Party spoke in the UN with observer status, and even the allies of the colonial Fascist Government of Portugal voted as a bloc against it in the United Nations Security Council. This resolution has and will now have prime importance in the future development of our politico-military action to expel the criminal Portuguese colonialist aggressors from our land.

Last but not least, I recall the resolutions of solidarity and unconditional total support adopted by the Conference of African Heads of State and Government in Rabat, at which our Party was once again chosen as spokesman for all the liberation movements in Africa.

The past year was in fact a year of great international victories, the more so as we are sure of moral, political and in some cases material support from independent African states, in the first place from the neighbouring and brother countries, the Republics of Guinea and Senegal, as well as that from all the genuinely anti-colonialist and anti-racist countries and forces. We are receiving or are going to receive in this coming year more material aid from the Soviet Union and all the other socialist countries, as well as from Sweden, Norway, Denmark, Finland, from various parties and political organisations in Europe and from humanitarian institutions like the World Council of Churches, Rowntree in Britain, the World Church Service, French People's Aid, the International Red Cross and from various support committees around the world. United Nations specialised or autonomous agencies, like the Economic Commission for Africa, UNESCO, UNICEF, the World Health Organisation, the High Commission for Refugees and the International Labour Organisation are developing, and will increasingly develop, co-operation with our Party, and tomorrow certainly with our state.

You all thus understand why the colonial Fascist Government of Marcello Caetano and its representatives in our land have good reason for being desperate. Unscrupulous as they are, with contempt for the interests and rights of peoples, including their own, they will lay their hands on any means, any crimes, to try to halt our struggle. You understand thus why the criminal Portuguese colonialist aggressors and their chief in our land are more enraged than ever, intensify the shelling and step up the assaults against our liberated areas, and make every effort to try to reoccupy some localities in these areas, with the purpose of consoling themselves for the military, political and diplomatic defeats we have inflicted on them, and with the aim of seeing if they can succeed with the new crimes they are committing in demoralising our forces and demobilising our populations. The defeats they suffered in 1972, both in our land and on the African and international level, explain the intensified aggression against our liberated areas, in particular against the region of Cubucare, which was visited in April by the United Nations Special Mission.

The desperation of the colonial Fascist Government of Portugal is the more understandable now that it is certain that the so-called 'policy for a better Guiné' has failed completely, and the Government senses that the lie about a policy for a 'better Cape Verde' will also fail. In regard to Guiné it is the colonial Fascist Government of Lisbon itself which, through the voice of the chief of the criminal colonialist aggressors, confesses this failure, when it declares that what the African man wants is to have – and we quote – 'his own political and social voice'. It is exactly what the African man of Guiné and Cape Verde wants. But we call that *independence*, that is to say the total sovereignty of our people on the national and international level, for them to construct for themselves, in peace and dignity, by the expenditure of their own efforts and sacrifices, marching on their own feet and guided by their own head, the progress to which they have a right like all the peoples in the world. And this in co-operation with other peoples, including the people of Portugal, who in three liberation wars against Castile in Spain struggled to win their own political and social voice, their independence – and won. We, like other people who have struggled and won, will continue the struggle in all its forms as long as it is necessary. Because we are in our land and because we have the certainty of winning.

As you know, while the populations of the urban centres occupied by the colonialists show increasing interest in the Party and the struggle, as is proved by the great number of youth who have abandoned Bissau and other trading centres to join the battle fronts, the situation in Portugal is speedily growing worse and the Portuguese people assert their opposition to the criminal colonial war with increasing clamour. For this reason, the colonial Fascist Lisbon Government and its agents in our land are racing to see if they can succeed in changing the situation before they are completely lost in their own land as well.

But they are wasting their time and in vain and ingloriously are wasting the lives of the Portuguese youth they send to war. They will commit still more crimes against our populations, will make many more attempts and manoeuvres to try to destroy our Party and the struggle. They will certainly carry on various acts of shameless aggression against the neighbouring countries. But all in vain. For no crime, no power, no manoeuvre or demagogy of the criminal Portuguese colonialist aggressors can halt the march of history, the irreversible march of our African people of Guiné and Cape Verde towards the independence, peace and genuine progress to which they have a right.

Forward comrades and compatriots in our heroic struggle for national liberation!
Health, long life and greater successes to our African people, to our brave
combatants, to all militants, responsible workers and leaders of our great Party!

Let us proclaim the existence of our state in Guiné and advance with the victorious struggle of our people in Cape Verde!

Let us expel the Portuguese colonialists from Cubucare as from all the regions of our land!

Long live PAIGC, strength, light and guide of our people in Guiné and Cape Verde!

Death to the criminal Portuguese colonialist aggressors!

MAP OF AFRICA, 1973

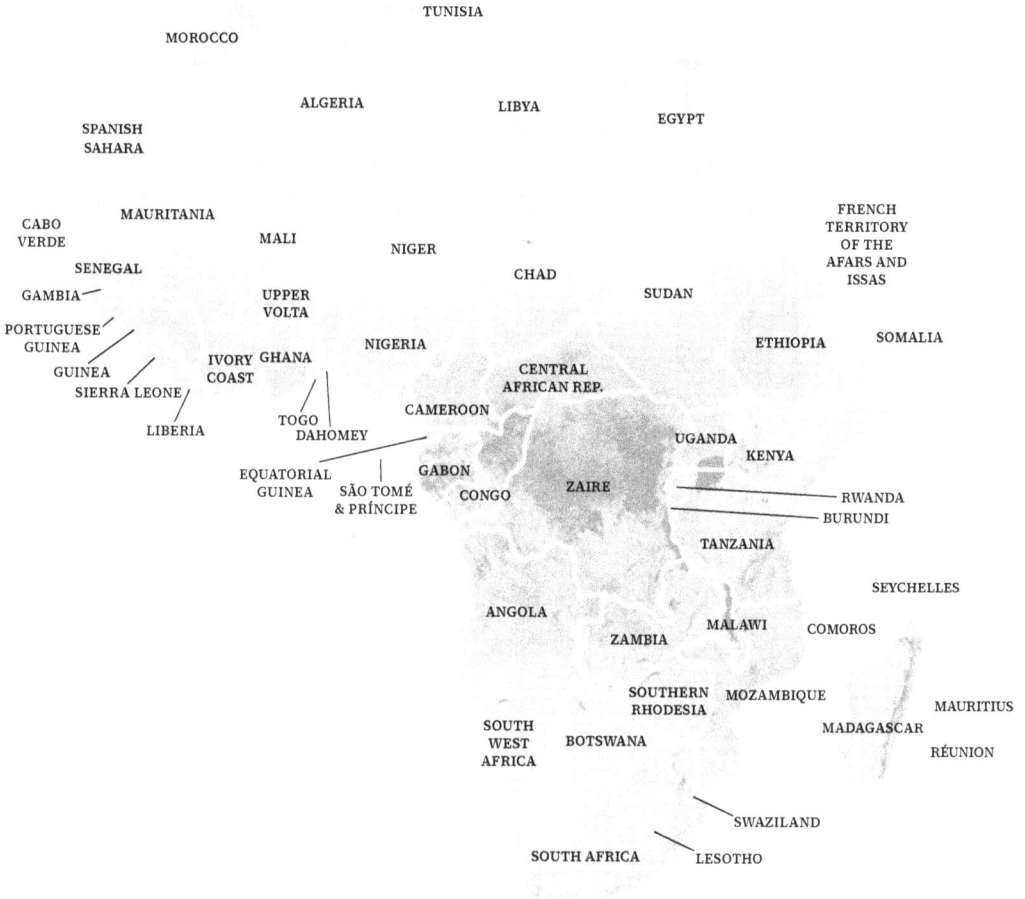

TUNISIA

MOROCCO

ALGERIA LIBYA EGYPT

SPANISH
SAHARA

CABO
VERDE MAURITANIA

FRENCH
TERRITORY
OF THE
AFARS AND
ISSAS

MALI NIGER

SENEGAL

GAMBIA

PORTUGUESE
GUINEA CHAD SUDAN

UPPER
VOLTA

GUINEA IVORY GHANA
COAST

SIERRA LEONE

NIGERIA

ETHIOPIA SOMALIA

CENTRAL
AFRICAN REP.

LIBERIA

TOGO
DAHOMEY CAMEROON

UGANDA KENYA

EQUATORIAL
GUINEA SÃO TOMÉ
& PRÍNCIPE GABON
CONGO ZAIRE

RWANDA
BURUNDI

TANZANIA

SEYCHELLES

ANGOLA MALAWI COMOROS

ZAMBIA

SOUTHERN
RHODESIA MOZAMBIQUE MAURITIUS

SOUTH
WEST
AFRICA BOTSWANA MADAGASCAR RÉUNION

SWAZILAND

SOUTH AFRICA LESOTHO

Capital Cities

ALGERIA - Algiers	EQUATORIAL GUINEA - Malabo	LIBYA - Tripoli	SOUTHERN RHODESIA - Salisbury	SWAZILAND - Mbabane
ANGOLA - Luanda	ETHIOPIA - Addis Ababa	MADAGASCAR - Tananarive	RÉUNION - Saint-Denis	TANZANIA - Dar es Salaam
BOTSWANA - Gaborone	F.T.A.I. - Djibouti	MALI - Bamako	RWANDA - Kigali	TOGO - Lomé
BURUNDI - Bujumbura	GABON - Libreville	MAURITANIA - Nouakchott	SÃO TOMÉ & PRÍNCIPE - São Tomé	TUNISIA - Tunis
CAMEROON - Yaoundé	GAMBIA - Banjul	MAURITIUS - Port Louis	SENEGAL - Dakar	UGANDA - Kampala
CAPE VERDE - Praia	GHANA - Accra	MOROCCO - Rabat	SEYCHELLES - Victoria	EGYPT - Cairo
CENTRL AFRICAN REP. - Bangui	GUINEA - Conakry	MOZAMBIQUE - Lourenço Marques	SIERRA LEONE - Freetown	ZAIRE - Kinshasa
CHAD - N'Djamena	IVORY COAST - Abidjan	NIGER - Niamey	SOMALIA - Mogadishu	ZAMBIA - Lusaka
COMOROS - Moroni	KENYA - Nairobi	NIGERIA - Lagos	SOUTH AFRICA - Pretoria	
CONGO - Brazzaville	LESOTHO - Maseru	PORTUGUESE GUINEA - Bissau	SOUTH WEST AFRICA - Windhoek	
DAHOMEY - Porto-Novo	LIBERIA - Monrovia	SPANISH SAHARA - El Aaiún	SUDAN - Khartoum